高等学校工程管理专业系列教材

MEM Engineering English
工程管理硕士专业英语

张静晓　徐　琳　主编
张　伟　主审

中国建筑工业出版社

图书在版编目（CIP）数据

工程管理硕士专业英语 = MEM Engineering English/
张静晓，徐琳主编. -- 北京：中国建筑工业出版社，
2024.5
高等学校工程管理专业系列教材
ISBN 978-7-112-29731-3

Ⅰ.①工…　Ⅱ.①张…②徐…　Ⅲ.①工程管理-英
语-研究生-教材　Ⅳ.①F40

中国国家版本馆 CIP 数据核字（2024）第 073044 号

责任编辑：李笑然　牛　松
责任校对：王　烨

高等学校工程管理专业系列教材
MEM Engineering English
工程管理硕士专业英语

张静晓　徐　琳　主编

张　伟　主审

*

中国建筑工业出版社出版、发行（北京海淀三里河路 9 号）
各地新华书店、建筑书店经销
北京科地亚盟排版公司制版
北京同文印刷有限责任公司印刷

*

开本：787 毫米×1092 毫米　1/16　印张：26½　字数：661 千字
2024 年 8 月第一版　　2024 年 8 月第一次印刷
定价：**68.00** 元（赠教师课件）
ISBN 978-7-112-29731-3
（42790）

序　言

近年来，全球范围内工程领域的迅猛发展使得工程管理这一专业领域备受瞩目。特别是在全球化的浪潮下，工程项目的复杂性和多样性呈现出前所未有的增长趋势。我国企业参与国际工程合作的数量逐年攀升，这要求工程管理专业人才不仅具备扎实的技术功底，更要具备过硬的英语沟通能力。如何更好地培养高水平工程管理专业人才，使其在跨国合作中游刃有余，成为了当前工程管理专业学位（MEM）教育亟待解决的重要问题。工程专业英语的学习，已经不再是提高综合素质的辅助手段，而是成为一个凸显 MEM 竞争力的关键因素。高校肩负着培养新时代人才的使命，因此 MEM 专业英语教育的迫切性凸显无疑。

MEM 专业英语教育的目标不仅是传授英语知识，更是要让学生深刻理解专业英语术语、了解最新的工程科技成果以及把握国际发展动态。我们期望，通过学习本教材，能够提升专业英语水平和跨文化沟通能力，成为新一代的国际化工程管理专业人才。本教材旨在为工程管理专业的学生和从业人员提供全面的工程专业英语培训和专业理论知识，使其能够轻松应对国际工程管理的各类挑战。本书弥补了工程管理专业英语教育领域的空白，为工程管理专业研究生以及从业者提供一本系统、全面、专业的高水平教材和学习手册。

本教材以英语为基础，涵盖了 MEM 学科所有知识领域，为 MEM 提供了一个全面的知识体系，真实反映了 MEM 知识领域的多层次性。从生产与制造系统工程到项目建设管理、现代项目管理，再到信息技术、物流系统设计和人因工程，每一章既进行了详细的理论解读，也配备了详细的案例应用，丰富了 MEM 的学习体验。可以说，确保 MEM 学生既精通工程管理专业学位知识体系又同步提升专业英语能力，是本教材设计的初衷所在。

本教材在"英语+"MEM 建设方面具有开拓性，教材建设的四大特色具体如下：

（1）内容广泛而专业。与传统英语教材不同，本书以广泛而专业的内容脱颖而出。通过深入研究和与国际专家的合作，作者精心策划了涵盖 MEM 领域最新趋势和学术前沿的教材。

（2）生动易懂的学习方式。本书采用独特的内容展示方式，将文本信息与图形插图相结合，使每一章节都富有吸引力且易于理解。将专业词汇与一般词汇分开，再加上句子解释，有助于 MEM 更高效地学习。

（3）融入前沿科技。为了应对新兴技术的变革，本书介绍了前沿的建筑工程技术，包括大数据、人工智能和数据库管理系统等。这种前瞻性的做法确保读者不仅精通传统实践，更能应对未来技术挑战。

（4）拓展视野的辅助材料。本书不仅限于传统教材的范畴，每章末尾都附有额外的阅读材料。这些材料经过精心挑选，与 MEM 实践相关，为那些希望深入了解特定主题的读者提供了额外的资源，从而拓展了他们的知识视野。

这本书是一支由长安大学和西北大学等知名学府的作者组成的专业团队的集体智慧结晶。通过专家之间的合作，使本书不仅学术严谨，也贴近工程管理专业从业人员的实际需求。愿本书成为语言和技术卓越的催化剂，赋能 MEM 和从业人员有力地参与到工程管理学科的国际化进程中。

张伟

清华大学 教授 博士生导师

全国工程管理专业学位研究生教育指导委员会秘书长

前　言

随着"一带一路"倡议的深入推进，全球区域经济合作不断加强，跨国工程项目合作日益增多，中国对外承包工程总数呈现高速增长趋势，企业对国际化应用型工程人才的需求更加迫切，对工程管理从业人员的英语水平和国际视野也提出了更高的要求。然而，当前国际工程项目具有复杂性、不确定性等典型特征，项目管理难度巨大，能够高质量服务于"一带一路"国际工程项目的国际工程管理人才严重短缺。高等教育肩负着新时代国际化人才培养、服务区域经济发展的使命。因此，亟须为高等院校工程专业学生和工程管理从业人员提供一本深入讲解工程专业英语术语、最新工程成果和国际发展动态的教材，从而为我国工程领域培养出更加具备跨文化交流能力的国际工程管理高质量人才。

工程英语内容涉及工程管理各领域的研究状况和最新进展，旨在帮助读者提升工程管理专业英语表达的专业性与准确性，通过英文文献的阅读和翻译能力训练，增强工程专业学生及从业人员的专业知识储备，在英文语境下拓展工程管理知识结构，从而为更好地从事相关理论研究和涉外实践奠定坚实基础。

本书内容新颖、覆盖面广、系统性强、可读性好，不仅适用于工程管理专业的研究生，同时对工程管理的从业者也具有一定的参考价值。主要内容包括：生产与制造系统工程与管理，工程或工业系统分析方法与优化技术，工程建设管理，现代项目管理与评价技术，信息技术与管理信息系统，服务系统运作与管理，物流系统设计、优化与供应链管理，人因工程、安全工程分析设计与管理，可靠性与质量工程，软件工程与互联网应用，标准化工程领域的研究与实践，创新与研发管理，投资决策与经济评价，公共事业及政府部门的工程决策与管理。

与以往的专业英语教材相比，本书的主要特色体现在以下四个方面：

（1）本书编写素材广泛、博采众长，突出系统性和专业性。通过对国外高校工程管理专业的深入调研，系统地确定了工程管理专业的知识范畴，选取能反映本领域最新动态和学术前沿的教材和专著，内容适量，难度适中，阅读性强，较多章节还参考和涉猎了国际权威学术期刊中的文献，体现了较强的学术性和专业性。

（2）本书编写图文并茂，对每个章节的知识点通过定义、理论、研究算法或计算工具、模型等进行生动和具象化阐释，提高了阅读性和可理解性。此外，将专业词汇（Professional Terms）和一般词汇（Words and Phrases）分开，以便使学生更为有效地进行学习和查阅。同时，专门设立"Sentence Illustration"板块，对疑难句子进行释义并对其中重点的语法难点进行举例讲解，有助于读者对句子结构和表达的活学活用。

（3）本书除了对工程系统、工程管理、工程技术进行分类介绍，还专门用一章（Information Technology and Management Information System）引入最新的施工技术，包括大数据、人工智能、数据库管理系统、数据挖掘、管理信息系统等，保障了本书的前沿性和前瞻性。

（4）为拓展学生的专业视野，对课堂内容进行补充和辅助，本书在每章最后编排"Reading Material"，补充了与工程管理实践切合度比较高的阅读材料。此外，还在本书的附录部分阐释了学术论文的选题技巧，以提升学生论文写作的能力和水平。

本书作者主要来自于长安大学经济管理学院和西北大学外国语学院。具体编写分工为：张静晓（长安大学）编写第 1、3、8 章，徐琳（西北大学）编写第 2、4、5、9、10、11 章，吴莹（西北大学）编写第 13、14 章，张渊（西北大学）编写第 6、7 章，赵丹晨（西北大学）编写第 12、15 章。全书由张静晓、徐琳担任主编并进行统稿。

本书正文参考的主要书刊、论文均标注于书后的参考文献列表中，在此向各参考文献的作者致以最诚挚的敬意！有问题或获取课件可发送邮件到具体邮箱：zhangjingxiao964@126.com。

限于编者水平，书中不妥之处在所难免，敬请广大读者批评指正。

Preface

With the in-depth promotion of the Belt and Road Initiative and global regional economic co-operation, the number of transnational engineering projects is increasing, as are China's foreign contracted projects. There is a trend towards rapid growth. Enterprises are demanding more international applied engineering talents, and setting higher requirements for the English level and international vision of those in project management. However, current international engineering projects are typically characterised by their complexity and uncertainty, among other things. This makes project management extremely difficult, and there is an acute shortage of international engineering management talents who can provide high-quality service for "Belt and Road" international engineering projects. Higher education shoulders the mission of training international talents and serving regional economic development in the new era. Therefore, it must be a priority to provide engineering students and those who work in engineering management with a textbook that comprehensively explains English engineering terms, together with the latest achievements and international developments in engineering. By this means we may cultivate high-quality international engineering management talents in China who are skilled at intercultural communication in the engineering field.

MEM Engineering English outlines the research status and most recent progress in various fields of engineering management, aiming to help readers to become more technically proficient and accurate in their use of English terminology for engineering, thereby enhancing the professional knowledge of engineering majors and practitioners through reading English texts and translation training. It further aims to expand the knowledge structure of engineering management in an English context, so as to lay a solid foundation for better engaging in relevant theoretical research and intercultural practice.

This book is original in content, broad in scope, and systematic and readable in style. These features not only make it suitable for graduate students majoring in engineering management, but also has a degree of reference value for those employed in engineering management. The main contents include: Process Engineering Management, Engineering or Industrial Optimization Methods, Construction Project Management, Modern Evaluation Technology of Project management, Information Technology and Management Information Systems, Service System Operations and Management, Logistics System Design, Optimization and Supply Chain Management, Safety Engineering and Management, Reliability and Quality Engineering, Software Engineering and Application, Standardized Engineering, Business Process Management, Innovation and R&D Management, Investment Decision and Economic Evaluation, Management of Public Utilities and Government Departments, and Government Departments.

Compared with previous professional English textbooks, the principal features of this book are reflected in the following four aspects:

(1) This book draws on a diverse array of materials, which highlights its systematic and specialized nature. Through drawing upon in-depth research into engineering management programs at foreign universities, this book systematically establishes the scope of knowledge covered by engineering management courses, and by selected textbooks and monographs that reflect the latest trends and academic frontiers in the field. The content of this book is measured in quantity and complexity, ensuring its readability. In addition, many chapters also reference literature from internationally renowned academic journals, further demonstrating the academic and professional nature of this book.

(2) This book is richly illustrated, and the knowledge points contained in each chapter are explained vividly and concretely through definitions, theories, research algorithms, calculation tools, and models. These two contribute to the readability and comprehensibility. Furthermore, the book draws a distinction between professional vocabulary (professional terms in construction management) from general vocabulary (words and phrases), allowing students to study and refer to them more efficiently. Moreover, a dedicated section entitled Sentence Illustration is included to explain difficult sentences and provide examples to illustrate key grammatical difficulties, thus helping readers to master sentence structure and expression.

(3) In addition to introducing engineering systems, engineering management, and engineering technology respectively, this book dedicates an entire chapter (Information Technology and Management Information Systems) to introducing the latest construction technologies, including big data, artificial intelligence, database management systems, data mining, and management information systems. This ensures the book is cutting-edge and forward-looking.

(4) In order to broaden students' professional horizons and supplement the classroom content, this book includes a section entitled Reading Material at the end of each chapter, which provides additional reading materials that are closely related to the practice of engineering management and the latest research trends. Furthermore, the appendix of the book explains the skills required in selecting a topic for academic papers, in the hope of enhancing students' abilities in writing papers.

The editors of this book come from School of Economics and Management, Chang'an University and School of Foreign Languages, Northwest University. The specific writing responsibilities are as follows: Chapters 1, 3, and 8 (by Zhang Jingxiao from Chang'an University); Chapters 2, 4, 5, 9, 10, and 11 (by Xu Lin from Northwest University); Chapters 13 and 14 (by Wu Ying from Northwest University); Chapters 6 and 7 (by Zhang Yuan from Northwest University); Chapters 12 and 15 (by Zhao Danchen from Northwest University). Zhang Jingxiao and Xu Lin served as the co-editors and responsible for the overall revision.

The main books, journals, and papers referenced in this book are labeled in the reference list at the end of the volume. The editors should here like to extend our utmost respect to the compilers of these references! The courseware of this book is also available via emailing to: zhangjingxiao 964@ 126. com.

The editors shoulder the responsibility for any remaining errors or shortcomings in the book and invite constructive criticism and correction.

Contents

Chapter 1
Process Engineering Management

1.1　Process Oriented Analysis

1. Introduction

1.1 Professional Terms, Words and Phrases, Sentence Illustration

Process Oriented Analysis (POA), which has been developed and refined over the last ten years for the analysis of complex production systems. Modern manufacturing machinery and plant automation are becoming more and more complex. As a result, human skills are even more important for the conception, planning, and setup of these systems. In addition, the comprehension required for the interaction of complex manufacturing systems and the behavior of single machines is now a key scientific issue. The goal of POA is to help engineers with conception, optimization, modernization, and maintenance. Existing instruments for the analysis of such systems with advanced technology that include all the technical and operational aspects are few in number and limited in performance.

Process Oriented Analysis can be used for the design of a new production system, for an engineering update, or for the reengineering of manufacturing systems. The main application fields of POA are in:

- System engineering and design for automated production plants.
- System analysis of business workflows with regard to profitability.
- System evaluation and improvement in safety and sustainability.
- Development, modeling and structuring of business processes.
- Optimization of static and dynamic behavior in partially and completely integrated systems.
- Support and documentation for operation and maintenance of complex production lines.
- Improvement of software design and maintenance for machine and process control.

POA assists the concurrent engineering of products, manufacturing processes, and production equipment, and helps to improve efficiency for modeling and development. It supports the lifecycle design of products by including technical, financial, and environmental evaluation parameters.

POA contains different graphical tools for the static (time-independent) and the dynamic (time-dependent) analysis of companies, plants, processes, and resources. Financially and environmentally relevant flows are modeled in static diagrams and are applied for the investigation and improvement of industrial systems. In turn, the dynamic system view allows a time-dependent analysis of a production system that enables straightforward programming and documentation. This leads to optimization by simulation as well as to programming of controls for production machinery and processes.

The POA method is very strict in rules and in relationships. The static and dynamic diagrams are absolutely consistent. A step-by-step procedure facilitates the transition from static analysis to dynamic programming.

Static Analysis：

（1）System Specification

The first step of an analysis is carried out using a static model, the Flow Diagram, which shows a production system or a service enterprise, depicting it by flows and processes. Processes describe the activities of people and machinery and the transformation of material, resources, and data within the system. Flows connect processes, acting as interfaces between them. The purpose of the functional analysis with the Flow Diagram is to get to know the system to be investigated：to specify processes, organize the workflow, find gaps in the information transfer, and streamline the operation. A first optimization takes place by rearranging processes, diverting flows, reducing interfaces, and eliminating redundant processes and flows. The Flow Diagram allows to do all this while keeping the purpose of the system in mind. At the same time, it provides as many details as necessary to fully describe the system while still presenting an overview of it.

Figure 1-1 shows an appendix surgery in a hospital, depicted with four processes and several flows. In process 1, the patient is examined, while in process 2, the appendix is removed. In process 3, the patient recovers, and process 4 provides various services that the patient is not aware of, but that enable the function of the hospital.

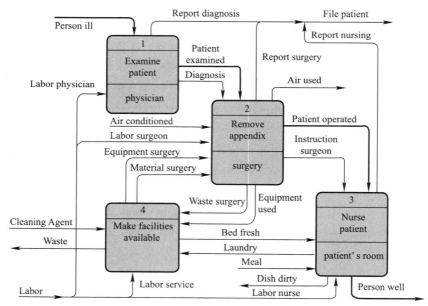

Figure 1-1　Flow Diagram of surgery in a hospital

（2）Economical Analysis

The economical analysis of a system starts by drawing a Flow Diagram. By adding quantities, numbers, and monetary values, the Flow Diagram becomes a Value Flow Diagram. Values expressed in Currency Units (CU) are allocated within the processes and assigned to flows in order to calculate the value of the product. Financial values and costs are connected graphically with the corresponding flows or processes in the diagram. Along the path of the production process chain, the value added is calculated. The value calculation is carried out in order to set the sales price for a product, to evaluate an investment in new production machinery, or to calculate the impact of a change in production parameters. Non-value-adding activities can be identified and eliminated. The value of the product at each step in the production is known. This is helpful for make-or-buy decisions.

Figure 1-2 shows the Value Flow Diagram for the preparation of "Spaghetti Bolognese" for a dinner with 40 guests. The diagram displays directly the costs that are associated with the production of the "Spaghetti al dente" and the "Sauce Bolognese". For the investigation using the Value Flow Diagram, the host's "labor", who cooks himself or herself, is introduced with a value in the diagram. The "Electricity" needed for the cooking is depicted. "Pot", "Saucepan" and "Bowl" carry values that are incurred by the cleaning and maintenance processes and are charged to the cooking processes. After being used, "Pot" and "Pan" leave process "Serve Spaghetti Bolognese" with the value of 0. 00 CU as soon as the spaghetti are transferred onto "Bowl. clean" for serving.

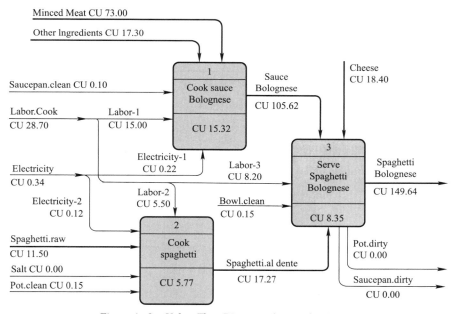

Figure 1-2　Value Flow Diagram of a spaghetti party

(3) Ecological Analysis

Ecological Analysis using the Resource Flow Diagram is based on the Flow Diagram, which is completed by resource flows and their values. The environmentally relevant values are calculated for the resource flows including mass, energy, and embodied energy calculation. Possibilities for recycling and reuse of waste heat and waste material are assessed by in-depth technical energy analysis. The energy consumption necessary for a product during its production and its lifetime is summed up as embodied energy. Calculation and optimization steps result in recommendations for improving the processing system.

The calculation and balancing of the resource flows and their values lead to a complete description of a production system concerning the consumption of resources and the production of waste and heat. At the same time, critical points in the production become visible, such as where resource loops should be closed and where potential for environmental optimization lies.

Figure 1−3 shows a process with attached flows from a Resource Flow Diagram of a dishwasher. The dishwashing process is organized into the prewashing and the main washing course. Both processes need energy and water. The product flow "Dish with food remnants" changes in the course of the processes. The mass of the product flow decreases because food remnants are washed from the dishes. The food remnants together with the "Cleaning agent" end up in the "Waste water." The consumed "Electricity" leaves the system as "Waste energy" in form of heat.

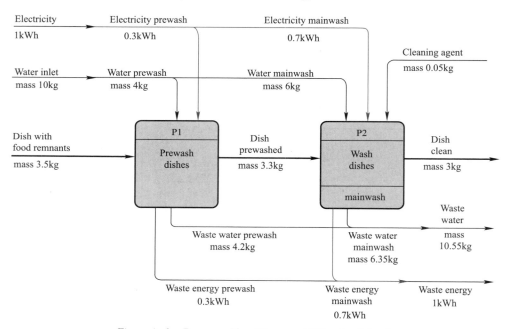

Figure 1−3　Resource Flow Diagram of "Do the dishes"

2. Case Tools

Several commercial software programs, so-called CASE tools, support the drawing of the diagrams as used for the method of Process Oriented Analysis. Besides the drawing of the diagrams itself, they help with the build-up of the model, hierarchical structuring including the numbering, set up and update of the data dictionary, and the consistency check of the model. CASE tools facilitate building and changing of models, creation of alternatives and variants within a model, and adding of subsystems and elements. The update of project documentation can be performed very efficiently.

The drawing of diagrams and the organization of the model with the database may also be done by hand or with a common software program for text editing and drawing if a CASE tool is not available. Table 1-1 shows the elaboration of a POA model with different tools.

Tools for the setup of a POA model   Table 1-1

Model components \ Computer support	Without computer support	Common software for text, tables and drawings	CASE tool
Diagram	Drawing by hand	Craphical software	Special software with pre-configured elements
Hierarchical structure	Process number by hand	Process number by hand	Automatic assignment of process number, automatic link within the hierarchy
Element specification	Written by hand	Tables with text-editing software	Specification window
Database, data dictionary	List by hand	Tables with text-editing, spread-sheet	Automatically built and updated
Rule and consistency check	By hand	By hand	Integral check
Report	Written by hand	Text-editing software	Selection of automatically generated reports

Several CASE tools for various purposes are commercially available providing a range of different diagram types. Table 1-2 lists criteria in form of a checklist that may help to select the CASE tool suited best for the project or company. The diagrams in this book are mainly drawn with System Architect. While this book is in preparation, POA designer is in development to support specifically the POA method.

Criteria and checklist for CASE tool   Table 1-2

Criterion	Requirement
Diagram types	Flow Diagram (equals Data Flow Diagam) State Chart (equals State Transition Diagram)
Notation of diagram symbols	There are different notations for the symbols: Rectangle with rounded comers for process (Gane & Sarson)
	Circle for process and state (Yourdon/DeMarco)
	Rectangle for state (Ward & Mellor)

continued

Criterion	Requirement
Additional features for diagram and symbols	Split and merge
	Optional third field for additional information in the process symbol
	Highlighting of loose ends of flows and transitions
	Formatting of line style and text
	Handling of changing of flow and transition paths
	Flow classification
	Automatic numbering of processes and states
	Automatic numbering of the elements in the hierarchy of the model
	Separate fields for condition and action for transitions
	Detailing of a process into a State Chart
Automated rule check for balance and consistency	Balancing rule for check in the hierarchy
	Dangling flows
	Duplicate flow names
	Processes and states without input or output
Element specification	Fields available
	User-defined changes of element specification
Report generation	Automated report generation available
	User-defined adaptations
	Choice of integrated parts
	Export into text-editing software
Program useful for networks	Possibilities for co-workers to work on one project at the same time

3. Simulation Model

Simulations were originally used to test machine controllers before exposing them to the challenge of real-world operation. Now, simulation is applied in a wide range of tasks in conception, design, and specification of manufacturing systems including order handling and management of supply chains. Ultimately, simulation is used for concurrent engineering and design of future manufacturing processes and equipments, to reduce the risk of development before full scale implementation.

（1）Purpose

Check manufacturing processes: The purpose of using a simulation model for a manufacturing plant is two-fold. First, a simulation model is a powerful method to check new manufacturing processes in their conceptual phase and to optimize and debug existing manufacturing systems. Second, a simulation model serves to establish the performance of investments in upgrading manufacturing plants. Typical targets are cutting back manpower or waste, streamlining and debottlenecking production, or evaluating new processes and machinery.

Consistency with environment: By programming a simulation model with POA, based on the Flow Diagram and the State Chart, the consistency of the program with the simulated environment is enforced. The structured drawing of the Flow Diagrams of the process or system and the setting-up of a State Chart allows programming the code in a fast and comprehensive way. Because Flow Diagram and State Chart serve at the same time as the documentation of the model, which makes it easier for other persons than the programmer to overview, maintain, adjust and update the code.

Optimization simulation and test simulation: There are two types of simulations treated in this book: the optimization simulation and the test simulation as a development tool of the real-time program. The procedure from State Chart to code is both applicable for simulation models (optimization simulation) as well as for real time programs.

In the case of a real-time program for a machine or production plant controller, the real-time program itself is made along by a test simulation. This model serves to check the code based on a simulated environment. After testing, the simulated environment is replaced by sensors and actuators, and the core of the simulation model develops into a real-time control program.

(2) Application

① Machine or Process Simulation

A POA simulation model is used for different purposes. For example, a simulation model of a machine or a production plant may be used to check the behavior and interfaces of a new machine, or the consequences of the replacement of old machines with new machines. In order to decide on options to include in the concept of the new machine, especially if some functions should be automated or not, the simulation is set up.

② Optimization of A Plant

The POA simulation model is used to optimize production plants, e. g. improve the behavior of a system with a big number of independent elements. The logistics and setup of such a system are typically simulated first, before designing and building the warehouse. Computer simulation helps in specifying the tracks and switches, deciding on the type of conveyor, conceiving the software for the operation of the warehouse, and purchasing the whole equipment.

The parameters, such as lot size, cost, stock level, and conveyor speed, of the warehouse, are optimized. The user interface in Figure 1-4 shows the simulation result, focused on costs and efficiency. In this case, the State Chart prepares and supports programming of the simulation model so that it corresponds best to the real-world processes and therefore allows an accurate logistical setup.

The simulation model will determine the optimal way to store the maximum amount of clothes in the minimum amount of space, the fastest way to recollect these clothes again in order to compile the shipment to retailers, the number of inlet and outlet stations, the length of the tracks of the automatic conveyors, and the number of operators necessary to run the warehouse.

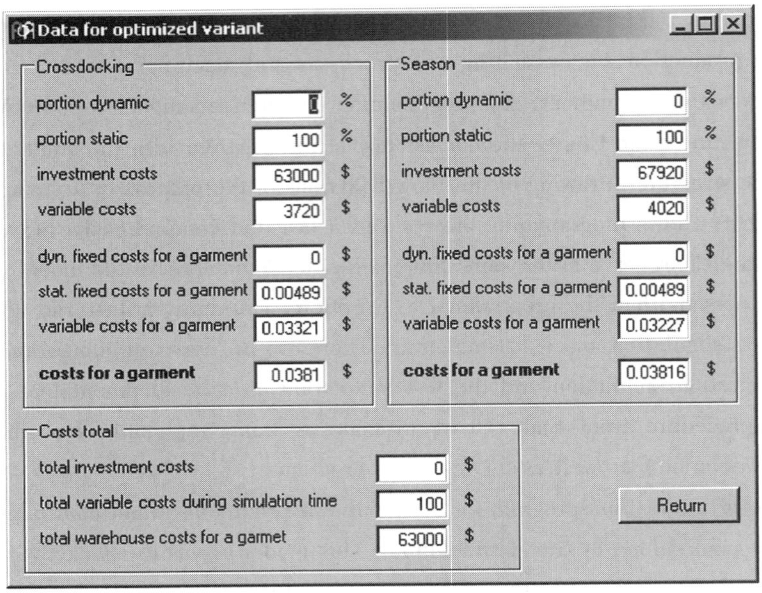

Figure 1-4　User interface of apparel warehouse

③ Type of Simulation：

Continuous, discrete, and static system behavior are treated by different methods. Figure 1-5 shows several analysis methods, whereas the dark shaded sections are covered by POA. These are mainly discrete and static system descriptions. The Flow Diagram is applied for static system behavior, the State Chart is applied for the dynamic system behavior.

POA is mainly used for the elaboration of discrete simulations as shown in Figure 1-5. The application on continuous systems is also possible if the concerning functions are suitably discretized. This issue is not treated in this book. The diagrams, which constitute the POA simulation model, pertain only to static and dynamic discrete systems.

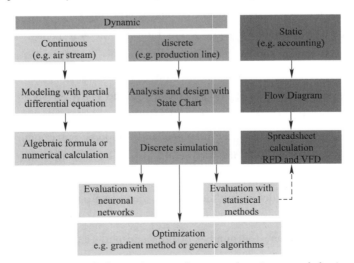

Figure 1-5　Tools for continuous, discrete and static system behavior

④ Programming with Support of POA Versus Simulation Package:

POA is a method for analysis and design. The resulting simulation model may be coded by any common programming language, the code is derived from the POA diagrams. POA provides the structure and the variables, as well as the flow of statements of the code. Alternatively, a current simulation package may be used to set up the simulation. In this case, POA is used first to check the feasibility of the proposed simulation package for the job, second to provide the system conception by defining the basis of structure, terms and specifications needed for setting up the simulation model with such a package, and third to document the whole project.

Various of such simulation tools are available that offer predefined modules for convenience of programming simulations. These modules are represented by icons as shown in Figure 1−6. The icons are assembled to build up the simulation model. Examples of simulation packages commercially available are SimFactory, ProModel, Arena, eM-Plant. These programs are useful for systems with few parameters and a limited number of independent processes. They are typically applied for problems in logistics, as e. g. waiting queues. On larger and more complex systems, these programs hit their limits regarding the number of manageable processes and functions. Real-world manufacturing systems often consist of hundreds of processes and flow, so that programming by setting and connecting icons is simply no longer feasible.

Figure 1−6　Icons for buffer, assembly station, and conveyor belt from eM-Plant

POA offers a method to simulate the behavior of manufacturing lines, machinery, and machine components with a large number of interacting elements. The size of the system to treat is limited only by the storage capacity and calculating performance of the computer.

Following to the simulation job, parts of the program may be further used to control a machine or plant in real time. In this way, analysis, design, and parts of the code are again useful for the real-world system. This is a distinct advantage in cost of system development and design.

1.2　Lean Production

1. Introduction

From their five-year worldwide study of the motor industry in the 1980s, the authors of *The Machine that Changed the World* assert that the lean production system is the superior way of producing manufactured goods. In making their assertion, they draw mainly on the evidence of Japanese automobile companies which, they argue, have developed the means for designing and building cars in less time with fewer people and lower inventories than Western manufacturers.

1.2 Professional Terms, Words and Phrases, Sentence Illustration

But what is lean production? This notion can best be characterized as a system of measures and methods which when taken all together have the potential to bring about a lean and therefore particularly competitive state, not only in the manufacturing division, but throughout the entire company. Four individual aspects can be identified:

— product development.

— chain of supply.

— shop floor management.

— after-sales service.

Here it becomes clear that production itself is only one field of activity in this new structural approach. Against this background the term itself must be seen as something of a misnomer. "lean management" or "lean industry" would be a much more appropriate description.

"Lean production", or rather "lean management", is an intellectual approach consisting of a system of measures and methods which when taken all together have the potential to bring about a lean and therefore particularly competitive state in a company. The main fields of activity concerned are product development, the chain of supply, shop floor management and to a lesser extent after-sales service. The portability of the concept in the light of changing circumstances can be called into question, but it nevertheless provides food for thought for the restructuring of industries whose production processes are out of date.

Occasionally, the essence of lean production is reduced to the notion that when compared with conventional systems only the half of all resources (time, costs, staff, etc.) are needed. The mere stipulation to restrict these factors in such a dramatic way is of course of little help when it comes to putting the idea into practice. Methods of rationalization have been systematically sought after for quite some time.

The essential elements of lean production are shown in Figure 1-7. A key feature is that fewer resource inputs are required by the manufacturing system (less material, fewer parts, shorter production operations, less unproductive time needed for setups, etc.). At the same time there is pressure for higher output performance to be achieved (better quality, higher technical specifications, greater product variety, etc.). This should result in greater customer satisfaction which in turn provides the opportunity for the lean company to gain a market share larger than those of its competitors.

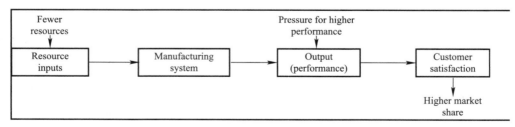

Figure 1-7 The essential elements of lean production

2. The Lean Product Process

This process guides you through each layer of the pyramid from the bottom up. It helps you articulate and test your key hypotheses for each of the five key components of product-market fit.

The Lean Product Process consists of six steps:

    (1) Determine your target customers.

    (2) Identify underserved customer needs.

    (3) Define your value proposition.

    (4) Specify your minimum viable product (MVP) feature set.

    (5) Create your MVP prototype.

    (6) Test your MVP with customers.

The last three steps reference the important lean concept of a minimum viable product (MVP). It's basically the minimum amount of functionality that your target customer considers viable, that is, providing enough value. When you are building a new product, you want to avoid building more than is required to test your hypotheses with customers. The term MVP clearly applies when you are building a completely new version 1 product (v1 for short). In addition, the idea of an MVP makes sense if you are redesigning an existing product or building v2.

The Lean Product Process also applies when you are not building a whole product, such as when you add functionality to or improve an existing product. In those situations, you can think of the process steps applying to a "minimum viable feature" instead, if that's clearer. Step 5 also refers to your MVP prototype. I intentionally use this broad term to capture the wide range of product-related artifacts you can test with customers. While the first "prototype" you test could be your live product, you can gain faster learning with fewer resources by testing your hypotheses before you build your product.

Not all six steps are required for every product or feature. Certain steps are required only when you are building a completely new product. Take for example, determining your target customers, identifying underserved needs, and defining your value proposition. Once you've successfully completed those steps for your product, you may not need to revisit those areas for a while. But after launching your v1 product, you would continue to improve and add functionality by looping through the three remaining steps: specifying which features to pursue, creating the features, and testing the features with customers.

To increase your chances of achieving product-market fit, the process is designed to encourage a certain amount of rigor in product thinking. In a sense, the process is a checklist to help make sure you've thought about the key assumptions and decisions to be made when creating a product. If you are not making these assumptions or decisions explicitly, then you are making them implicitly. The Lean Product Process helps you articulate the assumptions and hypotheses in your head (which you can revise later as you iterate). If you skip these critical thinking steps, you leave important elements—such as target customer and product strategy—to chance. A key concept in lean manufacturing, which inspiref Lean Startup, is the concept of rework: having to spend time fixing something that you did not build correctly the first time. Minimizing rework is a key tactic for eliminating waste. In addition to helping you achieve product-market fit, the Lean Product Process also enables you to do so more quickly by reducing rework.

To be clear, you will have some rework with the Lean Product Process. It is an iterative process that requires you to revise your hypotheses, designs, and product as you make progress— all of which could be considered rework. The goal of the process is to achieve product-market fit as quickly as possible. Quick but rigorous thinking that avoids or reduces rework helps achieve that goal.

3. The Kano Model

Another excellent framework for understanding customer needs and satisfaction is the Kano model developed by quality management expert Noriaki Kano. I first studied this model in my industrial engineering graduate program. As shown in Figure 1-8, the Kano model also plots a set of two parameters on horizontal and vertical axes: (1) how fully a given customer need is met (horizontal axis), and (2) the resulting level of customer satisfaction (vertical axis). The horizontal axis ranges from the need not being met at all on the left to the need being fully met on the right. The vertical axis ranges from complete customer dissatisfaction at the bottom to complete satisfaction at the top—consistent with the bipolar scale discussed earlier.

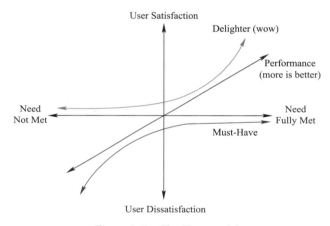

Figure 1-8   The Kano model

The utility of the model is that it breaks customer needs into three relevant categories that you can use: performance needs, must-have needs, and delighters. With performance needs, more is better. As the need is more fully met, the resulting customer satisfaction increases. Say you were shopping for a car and considering two different models. If they were identical in all aspects but Car A had twice the fuel efficiency (e. g. miles per gallon) of Car B, you would have a preference for Car A. Fuel efficiency is a performance benefit for cars.

Must-have needs don't create satisfaction by being met. Instead, the need not being met causes customer dissatisfaction. Must-have features are "table stakes" or "cost of entry"—boxes that must be checked for customers to be satisfied with your product. Sticking with the car example, seat belts would be a must-have feature. If you were interested in a car but realized it had no seat belts, you wouldn't buy it for fear of getting hurt if you were in an accident. Your must-have need for a reasonable level of safety is not being met. That being said, if Car A had five seat belts and Car B had 100 seat belts, you wouldn't say that Car B is 20 times better than Car A.

Once you have one seat belt per passenger, your must-have need has been met. Delighters provide unexpected benefits that exceed customer expectations, resulting in very high customer satisfaction. The absence of a delighter doesn't cause any dissatisfaction because customers aren't expecting it. Returning again to cars, GPS navigation systems were a delighter when the first car models came out with that new technology in the mid-1990s. They meant no longer having to print out directions from your computer and no more getting lost. This feature fundamentally changed how people drove from point A to point B, resulting in customer delight.

Going further back in time, cars did not always have built-in cup holders. Chrysler changed that when it introduced the minivan in the early 1980s, which had two functional cup holders sunk into the plastic of the dashboard. They were delighters because drivers no longer had to worry about spilling their beverages as they drove.

Of course, cup holders are now ubiquitous in cars—and an increasing percentage of cars come with GPS navigation as a standard feature. That illustrates an important aspect of the Kano model: Needs migrate over time. Yesterday's delighters become today's performance features and tomorrow's must-haves. Growing customer expectations and competition continuously raise the bar over time. This is another way of describing how, in the importance versus satisfaction framework, the upper value on the right side of the satisfaction scale gets redefined over time, moving yesterday's solutions to the left.

The Kano model also exhibits hierarchy, which I discussed earlier. For example, the fact that your product has a delighter doesn't matter if it's missing a must-have. A navigation system would be pointless in a car with no seat belts. You have to meet basic needs before you can get credit for performance features. And your product must be competitive on performance features before delighters matter. You can think of this as a three-tier pyramid with must-haves on the bottom, performance features just above that, and delighters at the top.

You can apply the Kano model to gain clarity about the problem space. Think about the customer benefits that are relevant in your product category and classify them into the three categories of must-haves, performance benefits, and delighters. Evaluating competitive products and reading product reviews can help inform you as you create this framework.

1.3   Smart Manufacturing

1. Introduction

1.3 Professional Terms, Words and Phrases, Sentence Illustration

The 2018 Gartner CIO Survey identified "Digital Initiatives" as the top priority for organizations in 2018 and 2019, tied with Revenue/Business Growth and ahead of other items, including Operational Excellence, Customer Experience, Cost Optimization/Reduction, Business or Financial Goals, Industry Specific, Business Model Change, Data and Analytics, and New Products and Services (Figure 1-9). Of course, "digital" can support all these aspirations, but we believe the pressure is there to be a more digital business, even for those companies in the manufacturing space not considered digital natives. "Smart Manufacturing" or "Industry 4.0" are now common buzzwords and many organizations have built strategies around these aspirations.

But what does Smart Manufacturing (SM) look like? A simple definition is an operation that maximizes data and connectedness to optimize its safety, reliability, and efficiency. While the underlying technologies have changed over the years, it can be said that the process industry has been pursuing Smart Manufacturing for more than 40 years.

At Linde, the journey started back in the late 1970s with the advent of industrial control computers. It continued through the next 20 years through both hardware and software. For example, the introduction of Programmable Logic Controllers (PLCs) in the late 1980s and the introduction of model predictive control in the mid 1990s are two foundational elements that have enabled further innovations over the past 20 years.

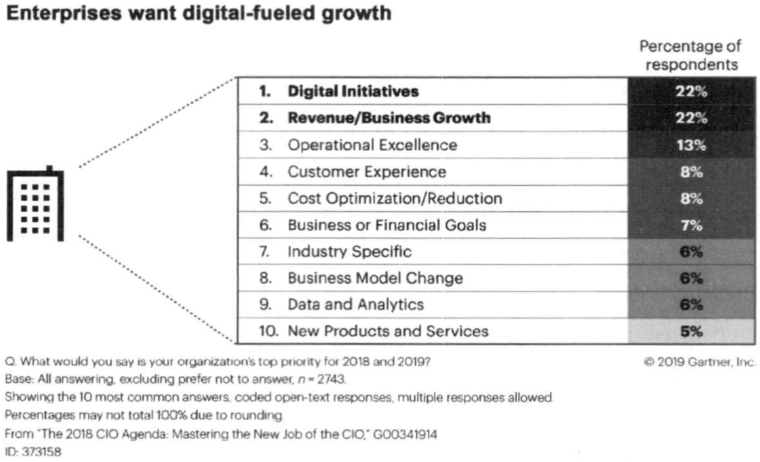

Enterprises want digital-fueled growth

		Percentage of respondents
1.	**Digital Initiatives**	22%
2.	**Revenue/Business Growth**	22%
3.	Operational Excellence	13%
4.	Customer Experience	8%
5.	Cost Optimization/Reduction	8%
6.	Business or Financial Goals	7%
7.	Industry Specific	6%
8.	Business Model Change	6%
9.	Data and Analytics	6%
10.	New Products and Services	5%

Q. What would you say is your organization's top priority for 2018 and 2019?
Base: All answering, excluding prefer not to answer, n = 2743.
Showing the 10 most common answers, coded open-text responses, multiple responses allowed.
Percentages may not total 100% due to rounding.
From "The 2018 CIO Agenda: Mastering the New Job of the CIO," G00341914
ID: 373158

© 2019 Gartner, Inc.

Figure 1-9　Gartner "Digital Strategy Execution: Navigate the Route to Success",
Jamie Popkin, Remi Gulzar, 30 January 2019

Manufacturing in recent decades has made amazing progress. At present, manufacturing has adopted and leveraged more and more the latest achievements in materials, mechanics, physics, chemistry, computer simulation technology, network technology, control technology, nanotechnology, biotechnology, and sensor technology. New manufacturing mechanism, manufacturing tools, processes and equipment continue to emerge. Manufacturing as a technology has developed into a new engineering science subject—Manufacturing Science. Cross-regional distribution of manufacturing resources in the era of economic globalization, has forced manufacturing collaboration a daily necessary means. The networked collaborative tools and systems are also increasingly rich. Intelligent Manufacturing has been recognized as the direction of manufacturing technology innovation, the maturity of the related theories and technologies will be one of the signs of the advent of knowledge economy.

Advanced manufacturing's role as the backbone of a country has been re-recognized and has aroused wide attention of major developed and developing countries. These countries have already started a series of advanced manufacturing technology research programs. Europe and the United States proposed "re-industrialization" in recent years to seize the commanding control of global industrial technology, and to further capitalize on the high-end manufacturing. In the U. S. , President Barack Obama has announced infrastructure and technology policy and steps to restore the center of manufacturing in the U. S. economy. In the face of fierce international competition in the 21st century, Chinese Government has planned accordingly and launched a series of major and key projects, carrying out special studies in the frontier of advanced manufacturing technology and equipment.

2. Methods or Tools

Smart Manufacturing Strategy—Understanding your business/operations customers.

As you start to build your "Smart Manufacturing" strategy, it is important to recognize the business/operations customers that will help you shape and organize your efforts. Again, organizations vary significantly, but in general there is some common structure that seem to be prevalent across many companies. Please see following content for your further consideration.

(1) Common Company Approach for Performance Rollup and Management

Company management system—within many integrated operating companies, a company management system has been adopted to help manage performance and drive ongoing continuous improvement. This is usually based on some form of measurement, and allows for monitoring of current performance against a baseline and/or benchmark. These KPIs (key performance indicators) are considered drivers to deliver against established financial, quality, customer, safety, and sustainability objectives. Some of these measures may be corporate common, while others are likely defined uniquely based on established "like operating technologies". Smart Manufacturing is a key enabler in helping to deliver common, automated calculations and rollup of KPIs across the company. It should be noted that the delivery of this measurement system is much more complicated than most people expect.

It is about much more than just creating a month end dashboard. It is about taking measurement closer to real-time and driver proactive action to impact results. The data trees used to calculate and summarize KPIs are usually very complex and require data from a multitude of sources. Development of the measurement system takes significant time and investment, and is generally always subject to continuous improvement. It is critical that performance calculations utilize trusted data that represents the single source of the truth and, whenever possible, not created in a manual process that is subject to individual bias. The future represents a journey toward autonomous calculation and rollup. This process is gradually developing the "language of your company".

(2) Common Processes Supporting Business and Operation Functions

Operations/manufacturing excellence—this is often perceived as an extension of the business operating system, but is generally much more focused on the production process. The objectives are usually to stabilize the production process (consistent performance), drive continuous improvement, and manage ongoing asset health. Although details likely vary across different "operating technologies", there are common processes that are used to monitor and manage operations performance. The intent here is not to expand on Operational Excellence or Lean

Manufacturing, there is significant documentation already available related to these programs. The key takeaway is that Smart Manufacturing can help support these efforts through the adoption of key digital technologies that can deliver common approaches and toolsets across the entire company. It is also critical that there is a strong data linkage between Operation Excellence/Lean Manufacturing and the Corporate Business Operating System. This is another key deliverable for Smart Manufacturing.

Common corporate function excellence—similar to the common concepts of Operations/ Manufacturing Excellence, many companies have dedicated corporate departments that define common processes and procedures within their particular function. Some common examples include EHS (environmental, heath, and safety), Finance, Customer Sales, Quality, Sourcing, Sustainability, etc. Also note that even technology functions have an internal operations concept of excellence which drives common processes and procedures. As a result, we can also add IT, Engineering, and R&D to this list of corporate functions.

(3) Common Processes Supporting "Like Operating Units"

"Like Operating Units"—many of today's large, global companies are leveraging a team of SMEs to support and drive continuous improvement across common operating units. Smart Manufacturing is being recognized as a key enabler for success through the adoption of new digital capabilities in support of these common processes.

New digital capabilities could include instrumentation/measurement devices, next generation automation, advanced process control (analytics/machine learning, etc.), mobility, and even MES/MOM applications for improved operations control.

Although the rate of change is accelerating due to the availability of new information technology (IT), the concept is really just the continuation of a journey that has been progressing over the last several decades in industry and manufacturing.

It should be recognized that the Smart Manufacturing strategy is only an enabler to achieve the broader vision highlighted here. As such, it should support the defined business and operations drivers and not be considered a standalone focus or set of deliverables.

Smart Manufacturing is really a means to drive continuous improvement through the ongoing adoption of new digital capabilities and related technologies. The related strategy needs to align with and support these common operating principles. As you prepare for the journey, it is essential to know your customer.

3. Models

ECM modeling:

In Linde, among the many potential algorithms and methods that can be used to develop an ECM system, a combination of PLS and PCA was selected because of the easiness in implementation and interpretation, robust and consistent abnormality detection results, and the indication of potential abnormal process variables. Some of the details, methods, and results are as follows.

PCA and PLS are designed to handle multivariate data by projecting the information contained in a set of highly correlated process variables onto low-dimensional spaces defined by a few variables, known as principal components or latent variables. PLS fundamentals were described in the Power Forecasting case study section. For completeness, a brief description of PCA fundamentals is given here.

The mathematical representation of PCA is

$$X = \boldsymbol{\varGamma}\boldsymbol{V}^T + \boldsymbol{G} = \sum_{a=1}^{A} \tau_a \boldsymbol{V}_a^T + \boldsymbol{G} \tag{1-1}$$

Where X is the input matrix $(K \times M)$; $\boldsymbol{\varGamma}$ is the score matrix $(K \times A)$, which is the new coordinates in the lower dimensional space; V is the loading matrix $(M \times A)$, which is orthonormal and the basis to span the low dimensional space; and G is the residual matrix $(K \times M)$. K is the number of observations; M is the number of variables of the X space and A is the number of principal components. τ_a and V_a, the ath column vectors of $\boldsymbol{\varGamma}$ and V, are the score vector and loading vector of the ath principal component, respectively. The score matrix $\boldsymbol{\varGamma}$ can be computed from $\boldsymbol{\varGamma} = XV$. Each score vector τ_a is a linear combination of the original variables and V_a is the corresponding combination weights. The principal components are ordered in a way such that the amount of variance described by each principal coinponent decreases as the number of principal components increases. The squared prediction error (SPE) for the kth row of X is given by $SPE_k = \sum_{m=1}^{M} \delta^2_{km}$.

As is common in the development of machine learning systems, the following steps are recommended: Preprocessing, modeling, and on-line model deployment.

For Preprocessing, the following operations are performed:

(1) Scaling: mean center and unit variance scaling.

(2) Detrending: depending on the data set, detrending may be needed as to focus on variable deviations.

(3) Outlier removal: this includes bad data and plant shutdowns among others.

For modeling:

(1) Apply PLS to make predictions for the independent variables $(\boldsymbol{Y})$.

(2) Apply PCA to those X variables of the PLS matrix whose residuals are not well explained by the PLS model alone.

(3) Obtain an estimate of X: $\widehat{X} = \widehat{X}_{PLS} + \widehat{X}_{PCA}$.

The second step is critical as to obtain an accurate model representation of the X variables. For the purpose of this study, an accurate model estimation of the X space is indispensable since once of the ECM primary tasks is to monitor the variable deviations and assess whether or not such deviations are significant when compared with historical variations among all process and machine variables according to the PLS and PCA model.

ECM models addressed here are typically built from hourly averages with 1 year of data as to capture process seasonality. If the model quality is deemed to be significantly deteriorated, on-line adaption may be performed.

For on-line model deployment, a missed data algorithm is applied when sensor data are missing, or historical data are faulty.

1. 4　Reading Material

1. Manufacturing for China

（1）Cornerstone of China's National Economy

The manufacturing industry is one of the pillar industries of China's national economy, the carrier for science and technology development and a bridge to productivity conversion. In 2010, China's share of global manufacturing output rose to 19. 8 percent. Comparing with 19. 4 percent of the U. S. , China has become the world's manufacturing superpower. With over 200 kinds of industrial products output as well as export ranking top one in the world, China has become a truly big manufacturing center of the world. However, there exists a considerable gap in China's manufacturing technology and equipment manufacturing capacity, compared with other manufacturing powers in the world. Many of research and development activities are visible in the area of advanced manufacturing theory and technology. Research institutes and universities are sought for providing the source of innovation for the production of China's manufacturing equipment to break through the blockade of high-end manufacturing technologies by developed countries. This is of great significance in helping ensure national security and sustain healthy and stable development for China. Furthermore, efforts are needed to carry out cutting edging research and development in Smart Manufacturing with aims to further expand and deepen the manufacturing technology innovation, help China develop into a high-end manufacturing power, accelerate the transform from "Made in China" towards "Created in China".

（2）Significance of Advanced Manufacturing Innovation

Smart Manufacturing research starts from a perspective of industrial chains, fostering a deep synergy among Internet of things, intelligent manufacturing and services science. Through mechanism innovation, Smart Manufacturing research often emphasizes collaborative research and innovation, leveraging resources worldwide, to advance manufacturing technology. It is a natural strategy for China to seek and incubate domestic and international R&D cooperation, make good use of available resources to establish Smart Manufacturing innovation platform, and aim to form a good research science and technology innovation system, improve scientific and technological innovation chains.

Evidently China is establishing national innovation platforms in smart manufacturing, an integrated area of the internet of things, intelligent manufacturing and service science for the development of theory and common technology research and application. Objective is to provide a solid theoretical basis and common technologies and innovative applications for the domestic manufacturing industries to upgrade, with original results achieved to help China's manufacturing sector to move to the high-end in the industrial chain with high value add.

China also needs to foster a talent based and academic exchange center with world acclaim in the field of smart manufacturing. Through attracting outstanding academic leaders and innovative teams, China provides facilities for undertaking major national basic and applied research projects, and evolves into an international well-known academic exchange center.

China is also developing nation-wide strategic leading-edge technology incubation bases for smart manufacturing. Through deep integration and synergy among Internet of things, intelligent manufacture and service science, smart manufacturing research could achieve major breakthroughs in key areas for the integration of advanced manufacturing, strategic emerging industries and modern service industry development with strategic cutting-edge technology incubation.

(3) Smart Manufacturing Research

In the face of fierce worldwide competition in the 21st century, Chinese government has planned accordingly and launched a series of major and key projects, carrying out special studies in the frontier of advanced manufacturing technology and equipment. In April of this year, the Ministry of Science and Technology, in combination with other ministries, has issued a "12/5" Manufacturing Information Technology Project Planning, outlining manufacturing information technology projects over the next five years for the development of manufacturing services, intelligent manufacturing. In recent years, the National Hi-Tech Research and Development Program (863 Program) in 2008 and 2006, has called for "advanced manufacturing technology major projects in the field of radio frequency identification (RFID) technology and applications", by the development and application of RFID technology to promote transformation and upgrading of China's advanced manufacturing. 863 Program in advanced manufacturing technology in 2010 set research themes of "WIA-based wireless monitoring and control technologies, devices and systems R&D" and "Cloud manufacturing service platform key technologies" and so on. 863 Program in advanced manufacturing technology in 2009 set a "service robots" key project theme. In 2007, 863 Program in advanced manufacturing technology had four topics including intelligent robot technology, extreme manufacturing technology and major products and facilities life forecasting techniques. China National focused basic research and development plan (973 Program) projects, such as 2005 digital manufacturing basic research and 2003 high-performance electronic product design manufacturing microscopic technology, digital new principle and new method. National Natural Science Foundation Major Focused Project, in 2003, had called for the key technologies in advanced electronics manufacturing and important scientific and technical issues in digital manufacturing theory in the network environment in 2003.

Development of the manufacturing industry so far has involved with multi-disciplinary applications, manufacturing technologies have more and more adopted the latest achievement in materials, mechanics, physics, chemistry, and computer simulation technology, network technology, control technology, nanotechnology, biotechnology, sensor technology. Currently, with booming economy, China has respected more a science and technology led economic development. Internet/Internet of Things, and next generation of information technology will lead to industry change, promoting the manufacturing industry to shift from the traditional manufacturing towards industrial chain-based manufacturing. The trend and requirements of digital manufacturing, service manufacturing, and intelligent manufacturing will become more apparent and prominent. Digital manufacturing will deepen the manufacture of hard power, and service manufacturing is to enhance the manufacturing soft power.

2. Projects Using POA Models

（1）Types of Projects

In this chapter, different kinds of projects are shortly outlined. To illustrate typical applications of POA and approaches to typical problems, case studies are given in this book. In the following, a short description of these case studies is presented to demonstrate the different kinds of projects carried out.

（2）New System Conception

In system design, a top-down approach is recommended according to the aspects of the system. In the case of a new system, processes should be grouped in order to minimize the number of flows. In manufacturing chains, processes should be defined and organized along the path of the product flow. Keeping in mind that flows specify interfaces between processes, a reasonable structure, typical for the specific production plant, should be used. Other flows, such as resources, material, and information, are directed so that the processes along the product flow are supplied optimally.

In the system structure, processes are specified and arranged so that the number of flows on the respective level is minimized. In reality, this is equivalent to avoiding unnecessary interfaces.

In Case Studies C4 and C5, new system concepts are created based on POA. Case Study C4 shows the conception of a new demagnetizing line for TV display tube masks. This process line was planned and realized based on the diagrams and calculations of POA. Also, the machine controls were programmed based on POA State Charts.

Case Study C5 introduces a completely new concept of a texturizing plant with a newly developed type of machine that doubles the speed of production. To obtain the best possible design for the new machine, a simulation model was programmed to determine the workflow and handling of the machine by the operators. Alternatives of automatic or manual operation on different jobs were investigated in order to establish priorities for the subsequent development of automation.

（3）Engineering Update

If the objective is to create an engineering update of an existing manufacturing line or plant, a different approach is employed. In this case, the existing structure of processes is broken down from the existing plant and examined in detail (As-Is Analysis). The primary task is to establish the degree of freedom available for alternative solutions. This is not a strictly top-down approach, since the constraints can occur on any level of detail and within any process. Working within a maze of constraints calls for a systematic method with a balanced assessment and comparison of the different solutions. The system model starts with the shop floor processes and is assembled in a bottom-up approach. Finally, the gaps are filled with a topdown approach.

The model of the present system state is changed in the course of the analysis and optimization. By combining processes, changes in the structure and possibilities to reduce interfaces are investigated. This way, a model of the desired system state (To-Be Model) emerges and is implemented step-by-step.

Case Study C6 demonstrates an engineering update based on POA. It introduces the concept for updating an over 50 years old underground cable car system in order to make it useful for the future. The technology controlling the cable car has become obsolete and did no longer comply with regulations. The new machine control allowing automatic, state-of-the-art remote operation was programmed based on POA State Charts, and tested for usability by persons involved in operation before deciding on the final implementation.

The parameters, such as lot size, cost, stock level, and conveyor speed, of the warehouse, are optimized. The user interface in Figure 1-10 shows the simulation result, focused on costs and efficiency. In this case, the State Chart prepares and supports programming of the simulation model so that it corresponds best to the real-world processes and therefore allows an accurate logistical setup.

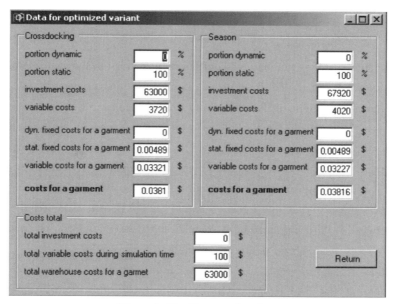

Figure 1-10　The user interface

The simulation model will determine the optimal way to store the maximum amount of clothes in the minimum amount of space, the fastest way to recollect these clothes again in order to compile the shipment to retailers, the number of inlet and outlet stations, the length of the tracks of the automatic conveyors, and the number of operators necessary to run the warehouse.

Chapter 2
Engineering or Industrial Optimization Methods

2.1 System Engineering Theory and Method

2. 1 Professional Terms, Words and Phrases, Sentence Illustration

1. Introduction

Definition of SE requires an understanding of its two constituent terms: system and engineering.

(1) Definition of Engineering

Engineering students often graduate without being introduced to the root term that provides the basis for their formal education. To illustrate this point, consider a conversational example.

The term engineering originates from the Latin word "ingenerare", which means "to create". Its first known use is traceable to 1720. Let's introduce a couple of example definitions of Engineering:

- Engineering——"The profession in which knowledge of the mathematical and natural sciences gained by study, experience, and practice is applied with judgment to develop ways to utilize economically the materials and forces of nature for the benefit of mankind".

- Engineering——"The application of science and mathematics by which the properties of matter and the sources of energy in nature are made useful to people".

The definition of Engineering above originates from earlier definitions by the Accreditation Board for Engineering and Technology (ABET), which accredits engineering programs in the United States. ABET evolved the definition from its founding in 1932 until 1964. It continued to appear in ABET publications from 1964 through 2002.

Two key points emerge from the introduction of these definitions:

- Firstly, you need to understand the definition and scope of your profession.

- Secondly, on inspection, these definitions might appear to be a mundane academic discussion. The reality is that these definitions characterize the traditional view of engineering. That is, engineering the "Box" paradigm or "Box" engineering that contributes to systems, products, or services failures attributed to "human error" or are considered by the user to be failures due to a lack of usability. This is a critical staging point in differentiating the scope of the SE—"Engineering the (User-Equipment) System, which includes the (Equipment) Box", versus traditional "Box" engineering. In that context, SE exemplifies the cliché "Learning to think outside the (Engineering) box" to develop systems, products, and services that users actually need, can use, and lead to a reduction in human errors that contribute to system failures. As a result, this impacts enterprise system reputation, profitability, customer satisfaction, marketplace perceptions, and subsequently shareholder value.

（2）Definition of System Engineering（SE）

Substantive content must always precede grammar to achieve successful results. Avoid negotiating content for the sake of achieving grammatical elegance and eloquence unless it precludes misinterpretation.

There are a number of ways to define SE, each dependent on an individual's, project's, or Enterprise's business domain, perspectives, and experiences. SE means different things to different people. You will discover that even your own views of SE will evolve over time. So, if you have a diversity of perspectives and definitions, what should you do? What is important is that you, project teams, or your enterprise should:

- Establish a consensus definition for SE.
- Document or reference the SE definition in enterprise command media to serve as a guide for all.

For those who prefer a brief, high-level definition that encompasses the key holistic aspects of SE—"Engineering the System"—consider the following definition:

- System Engineering—The multi-disciplined application of analytical, mathematical, and scientific principles for formulating, selecting, developing, and maturing an optimal solution from a set of viable candidates that has acceptable risk, satisfies user operational need (s), and minimizes development and life cycle costs while balancing stakeholder interests.

2. Methodology

（1）The"A" and the "B" Paradigms in Systems Engineering

The SDP has evolved into two process paradigms, the"A" paradigm and the "B" paradigm shown in Figure 2-1. The two paradigms are summarized as follows.

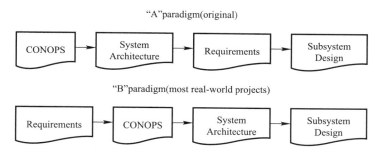

Figure 2-1　The "A" and the "B" paradigms of systems engineering

（2）The"A" paradigm

- Begins with the systems engineering activities performed in the needs identification state of the SDP ; the"A" column in the Hitchins-Kasser-Massie Framework（HKMF）.
- Is the original systems engineering paradigm which begins with a focus on converting a problematic or undesirable situation to a FCFDS and creating the CONOPS. Examples of the"A" paradigm CONOPS include the "to be" view in Business Process Reengineering（BPR）and the

conceptual model in Checkland's Soft Systems Methodology (SSM).

Research into the systems engineering literature found that successful projects such as the NASA Apollo program were characterized by a common vision of the purpose and performance of the solution systems among the customers, users and developers; namely a paradigm that began in the needs identification state of the SDP. Moreover, the common vision related to both the mission and support functions performed by the solution system program. Perceptions from the Generic HTP outside the systems engineering literature support the research with similar findings in the process improvement and quality literature. In addition, BPR creates and disseminates/communicates a "to-be" model of the operation of the conceptual reengineered organization before embarking on the change process.

(3) The "B" Paradigm

The "B" paradigm begins in the systems requirements state of the SDP; the "B" column in the HKMF. Many systems and software engineers have been educated to consider the systems engineering activities in column B of the HKMF as the first state in the SDP. For example:

• Requirements are one of the inputs to the "systems engineering process".

• In one postgraduate class at University of Maryland University College, the instructor stated that systems engineering began for him when he received a requirements specification.

The "B" paradigm is inherently flawed. This is because even if systems and software engineers working in a paradigm that begins in HKMF column B could write perfectly good requirements, they still cannot determine if the requirements and associated information are correct and complete because there is no reference for comparison to test the completeness. Consequently, efforts expended on producing better requirements in the "B" paradigm have not, and will not, alleviate the situation. The situation cannot be alleviated because the situation is akin to participating in Deming's red bead experiment, which demonstrates that errors caused by workers operating in a process are caused by the system rather than the fault of the workers. Recognition that the "B" paradigm is inherently flawed is not a new observation. For example:

• A proposal to reduce human error in producing requirements by analysing requirements using an approach of creating scenarios as threads of behaviour through a use case, and adopting an object-oriented approach; namely they proposed a return to the "A" paradigm.

• Stand-alone requirements make it difficult for people to understand the context and dependencies among the requirements, especially for large systems and so use cases should be used to define scenarios.

• One of the two underlying concepts of MBSE is to develop a model of the system to allow various stakeholders to gain a better understanding of how well the conceptual system being modelled could remedy the problem, before starting to write the requirements.

3. Introduction to the "S" Metamodel

Engineering disciplines such as ME, EE, ChE, CE, and so forth are based on underlying models of phenomena (mechanical, electrical, chemical, etc.) that are the fruits of physical sciences, mathematics, and philosophy. Newton's laws of motion, Maxwell's equations, and other underlying models describe aspects of the nature of subject systems, not engineering procedures for those systems, while opening up many procedural avenues that operate within the constraints of those underlying models of nature. In a similar fashion, the "S" Metamodel describes the underlying "systemic" aspects of systems of interest, based on the fruits of science and mathematics. In the tradition of those same physical sciences, these underlying models (whether specific to one technical discipline or systems in general) seek the "smallest model" capable of (verifiably) describing or explaining the phenomena of interest.

The rise of a number of MBSE methodologies and system representation standards has provided many of the needed elements of that underlying smallest model framework, and the "S" Metamodel builds on those while adding some important missing aspects and compressing redundant ones. Throughout, this is in the spirit of seeking out the smallest (simplest) verifiable model necessary to describe systems for purposes of engineering and science.

Figure 2-2 is a simplified summary of some of the key portions of the "S" Metamodel. This diagram is not the sort that is produced in a related engineering project (illustrated in Figure 2-3), but instead is a representation of the underlying classes and relationships on which those project-specific models are based. Those project-specific models may be in any modeling language (including, but not limited to, SysML, IDEF, or others) and supported by any engineering tool or information system, as in Figure 2-3.

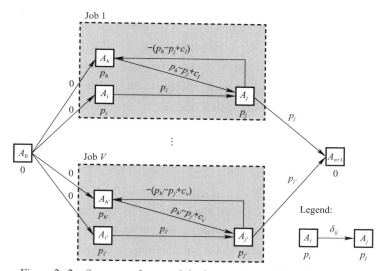

Figure 2-2   Summary of some of the key portions of the S* Metamodel

The conceptual awareness extract of Figure 2-2 is a simplified representation of selected "S" Metaclasses and key relationships that connect them/the formal "S" Metamodel is represented in Unified Modeling Language (UML)/and summarizes some of the most important "S" Metamodel concepts. Additional references are listed at the end of the chapter.

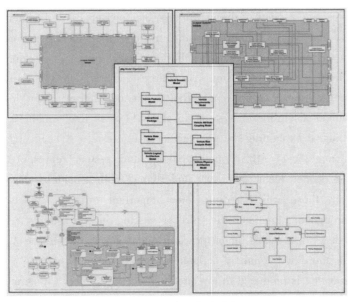

Figure 2-3　Example S* Model extracts

In reading Figure 2-2:

● The color coding provides an informal reminder of stereotypes mapping informal modeling languages (e. g. , SysML) and related views—especially for nontechnical views and viewers.

● *A feature* is an aspect of the behavior or performance of a system that has stakeholder value, described in the concepts and terminology of that stakeholder, and serving as the basis of selection of systems or system capabilities by or on behalf of the stakeholder. Features are parameterized by feature attributes, which have subjective stakeholder valuations.

● (*Functional*) *Interaction* means the exchange of energy, force, mass, or information between system components, each of which plays a (Functional) Role in that interaction. This is the traditional systems engineering "function" performed by a given system.

● *Functional roles* are described solely by their behavior and parameterized by *role attributes* that have objective technical valuations.

● *Requirements statements* are prose or other descriptions of the behavior of functional roles during interactions. They are the prose descriptive equivalent to the roles they describe, and are parameterized by requirements attributes which are identical to the related role attributes.

It is important to remember that these concepts are underlying metamodel concepts. Practical S* Models are represented using whatever modeling languages and tools may be of value. Figure 2-3 illustrates selected SysML views of a vehicle S* Model.

2. 2　Operations Research

1. Introduction

Operations Research can be defined as the use of quantitative methods to assist analysts and decision-makers in designing, analyzing, and improving the

2. 2Professional
Terms, Words and
Phrases, Sentence
Illustration

performance or operation of systems. The systems being studied may be any kind of financial systems, scientific or engineering systems, or industrial systems; but regardless of the context, practically all such systems lend themselves to scrutiny within the systematic framework of the scientific method.

The field of Operations Research incorporates analytical tools from many different disciplines, which can be applied in a rational way to help decision-makers solve problems and control the operations of systems and organizations in the most practical or advantageous way. The tools of Operations Research can be used to optimize the performance of systems that are already well-understood, or to investigate the performance of systems that are ill-defined or poorly understood, perhaps to identify which aspects of the system are controllable (and to what extent) and which are not. In any case, mathematical, computational, and analytical tools and devices are employed merely to provide information and insight; and ultimately, it is the human decision-makers who will utilize and implement what has been learned through the analysis process to achieve the most favorable performance of the system.

The ideas and methodologies of Operations Research have been taking shape throughout the history of science and mathematics, but most notably since the Industrial Revolution. In various ways, all of human knowledge seems to play a role in determining the goals and limitations underlying the decisions people make. Physical laws (such as gravity and the properties of material substances), human motivations (such as greed, compassion, and philanthropy), economic concepts (supply and demand, resource scarcity, division of labor, skill levels, and wage differentials), the apparent fragility of the environment (erosion, species decline), and political issues (territorial aggression, democratic ideals) all eventually are evident, at least indirectly, in the many types of systems that are studied using the techniques of Operations Research. Some of these are the natural, physical, and mathematical laws that are inherent and that have been discovered through observation, while others have emerged as a result of the development of our society and civilization. Within the context of these grand themes, decision-makers are called upon to make specific decisions—whether to launch a missile, introduce a new commercial product, build a factory, drill a well, or plant a crop.

Operations Research (also called Management Science) became an identifiable discipline during the days leading up to the Second World War. In the 1930s, the British military buildup centered around the development of weapons, devices, and other support equipment. The buildup was, however, of an unprecedented magnitude, and it became clear that there was also an urgent need to devise systems to ensure the most advantageous deployment and management of material and labor.

Some of the earliest investigations led to the development and use of radar for detecting and tracking aircraft. This project required the cooperative efforts of the British military and scientific communities. In 1938, the scientific experts named their component of this project operational research. The term operations analysis was soon used in the U.S. military to refer to the work done by teams of analysts from various traditional disciplines who cooperated during the war.

Wartime military operations and supporting activities included contributions from many scientific fields. Chemists were at work developing processes for producing high octane fuels; physicists were developing systems for the detection of submarines and aircraft; and statisticians were making contributions in the area of utility theory, game theory, and models for various strategic and tactical problems. To coordinate the effectiveness of these diverse scientific endeavors, mathematicians and planners developed quantitative management techniques for allocating scarce resources (raw materials, parts, time, and labor) among all the critical activities in order to achieve military and industrial goals.

The new analytical research on how best to conduct military operations had been remarkably successful, and after the conclusion of the Second World War, the skill and talent of the scientists that had been focused on military applications were immediately available for redirection to industrial, financial, and government applications. At nearly the same time, the advent of high speed electronic computers made feasible the complex and time consuming calculations required for many operations research techniques. Thus, the methodologies developed earlier for other purposes now became practical and profitable in business and industry.

In the early 1950s, interest in the subject was so widespread, both in academia and in industry, that professional societies sprang up to foster and promote the development and exchange of new ideas. The first was the Operational Research Society in Britain. In the U.S., the Operations Research Society of America (ORSA) and The Institute of Management Science (TIMS) were formed and operated more or less as separate societies until the 1990s. These two organizations, however, had a large and overlapping membership and served somewhat similar purposes, and have now merged into a single organization known as INFORMS (Institute for Operations Research and the Management Sciences). National societies in many other countries are active and are related through IFORS (the International Federation of Operational Research Societies). Within INFORMS, there are numerous special interest groups, and some specialized groups of researchers and practitioners have created separate societies to promote professional and scholarly endeavors in such areas as simulation, transportation, computation, optimization, decision sciences, and artificial intelligence. Furthermore, many mathematicians, computer scientists and engineers have interests that overlap those of operations researchers. Thus, the field of Operations Research is large and diverse. As will be apparent from the many illustrative applications presented throughout this book, the quantitative analysis techniques that found their first application nearly a hundred years ago are now used in many ways to influence our quality of life today.

2. Phases of Operation Research

Operations Research is a logical and systematic approach to provide a rational basis for decision making. The phase and processes of OR study must also be quite logical and systematic. There are six important steps in OR study, but it is not necessary that in all the studies each and every step is invariably present. These steps are arranged in following logical order.

Step 1   Observe the Problem Environment:

Step 1 in the process of OR study is observing the problem environment. The activities that constitute this step are visits, conferences, observations, research and so on. With the help of such activities, the OR scientist gets sufficient information and support to proceed and is better prepared to formulate the problem.

Step 2　Analyse and Define the Problem

Step 2 is analysing and defining the problem. In this step not only the problem is defined, but also uses, objectives and limitations of the study are stressed in the light of the problem. The end result of this step is a clear grasp of need for a solution and understanding its nature.

Step 3　Develop a Model

Step 3 is to construct a model. A model is representation of some real or abstract situation. Operations Research models are basically mathematical models representing systems, processes or environment in the form of equations, relationships or formulate. The activities in this step include defining interrelationships among variables, formulating equations, using known OR models or searching suitable alternate models. The proposed model may be field tested and modified in order to work under environmental constraints. The model may also be modified if the management is not satisfied with the answer that it gives.

Step 4　Select an Appropriate Data Input

Garbage in and garbage out is a famous saying. No model will work appropriately if data input is not appropriate. Hence, tapping the right kind of data is a vital step in OR process. Important activities in this step are analyzing internal-external data and facts, collecting opinions using computer data banks. The purpose of this step is to have a sufficient input to operate and test the model.

Step 5　Provide a Solution and Test Reasonableness

Step 5 in OR process is to get a solution with the help of a model and data input. Such a solution is not implemented immediately. First, the solution is used to test the model and to find limitations, if any. If the solution is not reasonable or if the model is not behaving properly, updating and modification of the model is considered at this stage. The end result of this step is a solution that is desirable and supports the current organizational objective.

Step 6　Implement the Solution

Implementation of the solution obtained in previous step is the last step of OR process. In OR the decision-making is scientific and implementation of decision involves so many behavioral issues. Therefore, the implementing authority has to resolve the behavioral issues. He has to sell the idea of use of OR not only to the workers but also to the superiors. Distance between management and OR scientist may offer a lot of resistance. The gap between one who provides a solution and one who wishes to use it should be eliminated. To achieve this, OR scientist as well as management should play a positive role. A properly implemented solution obtained through OR techniques results in improved working and wins the management support.

3. Methods or Tools

The Simplex method is a general solution method for solving linear programming problems. It was developed in 1947 by George B. Dantzig and, with some modifications for efficiency, has become the standard method for solving very large linear programming problems on computers. Most real problems are so large that a manual solution via the Simplex method is impractical, and these problems must be solved with Simplex programs implemented on a computer. Small problems, however, are quite useful in demonstrating how the Simplex method operates; therefore, we will use such problems to illustrate the various features of the method.

The Simplex method is an iterative algorithm that begins with an initial feasible solution, repeatedly moves to a better solution, and stops when an optimal solution has been found and, therefore, no improvement can be made.

To describe the mechanics of the algorithm, we must specify how an initial feasible solution is obtained, how a transition is made to a better basic feasible solution, and how to recognize an optimal solution. From any basic feasible solution, we have the assurance that, if a better solution exists at all, then there is an adjacent solution that is better than the current one. This is the principle on which the Simplex method is based; thus, an optimal solution is accessible from any starting basic feasible solution.

We will use the following simple problem as an illustration as we describe the simplex method:

$$\text{maximize} \qquad z = 8x_1 + 5x_2 \qquad\qquad (2-1)$$
$$\text{subject to} \qquad x_1 \leqslant 150 \qquad\qquad (2-2a)$$
$$x_2 \leqslant 250 \qquad\qquad (2-2b)$$
$$2x_1 + x_2 \leqslant 500 \qquad\qquad (2-2c)$$
$$x_1, x_2 \geqslant 0 \qquad\qquad (2-2d)$$

The standard form for this problem is:

$$\text{maximize} \qquad z = 8x_1 + 5x_2 + 0s_1 + 0s_2 + 0s \qquad\qquad (2-3)$$
$$\text{subject to} \qquad x_1 + s_1 = 150 \qquad\qquad (2-4a)$$
$$x_2 + s_2 = 250 \qquad\qquad (2-4b)$$
$$2x_1 + x_2 + s_3 = 500 \qquad\qquad (2-4c)$$

Zero coefficients are given to the slack variables in the objective function because slack variables do not contribute to z. The constraints constitute a system of $m = 3$ equations in $n = 5$ unknowns. In order to obtain an initial basic feasible solution, we need to select $n - m = 5 - 3 = 2$ variables as non-basic variables. We can readily see in this case that by choosing the two variables x_1 and x_2 as the non-basic variables, and setting their values to zero, then no significant computation is required in order to solve for the three basic variables: $s_1 = 150$, $s_2 = 250$, and $s_3 = 500$. The value of the objective function at this solution is 0.

In fact, a starting solution is just this easy to obtain whenever we have m variables, each of which has a coefficient of one in one equation and zero coefficients in all other equations (a unit vector of coefficients), and each equation has such a variable with a coefficient of one in it. Thus, whenever a slack variable has been added to each constraint, we may choose all the slack variables as the m basic variables, set the remaining $(n-m)$ variables to zero, and the starting values of the basic variables are simply given by the constants b on the right hand sides of the constraints. For cases in which slack variables are not present and, therefore, do not provide a starting basic feasible solution.

Once we have a solution, a transition to an adjacent solution is made by a pivot operation. A pivot operation is a sequence of elementary row operations (see the Appendix) applied to the current system of equations, with the effect of creating an equivalent system in which one new (previously non-basic) variable now has a coefficient of one in one equation and zeros in all other equations.

During the process of applying pivot operations to a linear programming problem, it is convenient to use a tabular representation of the system of equations. This representation is referred to as a Simplex tableau.

In order to conveniently keep track of the value of the objective function as it is affected by the pivot operations, we treat the objective function as one of the equations in the system of equations, and we include it in the tableau. In our example, the objective function equation is written as:

$$1z - 8x_1 - 5x_2 - 0s_1 - 0s_2 - 0s_3 = 0 \qquad\qquad (2-5)$$

The tableau for the initial solution is as follows (Table 2-1).

The tableau for the initial solution　　　　　　　　　　Table 2-1

Basis	z	x_1	x_2	s_1	s_2	s_3	Solution
z	1	-8	-5	0	0	0	0
s_1	0	1	0	1	0	0	150
s_2	0	0	1	0	1	0	250
s_3	0	2	$\boxed{1}$	0	0	1	500

The first column lists the current basic variables. The second column shows that z is (and will always be) a basic variable; and because these elements will never change, they really do not need to be explicitly maintained in the tableau. The next five columns are the constraint coefficients of each variable. And the last column is the solution vector; that is, the values of the basic variables. Using this representation of a current solution, we can now describe the purpose and function of each iteration of the Simplex method for a maximization problem.

Observe that the objective function row represents an equation that must be satisfied for any feasible solution. Since we want to maximize z, some other (non-basic) term must decrease in order to offset the increase in z. But all of the non-basic variables are already at their lowest value, zero. Therefore, we want to increase some non-basic variable that has a negative coefficient. As a simple rule, we will choose the variable with the most negative coefficient, because making this variable basic will give the largest (per unit) increase in z (Refer to Steps 1 and 2 in the following).

The chosen variable is called the entering variable, that is, the one that will enter the basis. If this variable increases, we must adjust all of the equations. Specifically, increasing the non-basic variable must be compensated for by using only the one basic variable in each row (having a coefficient of one). If the non-basic coefficient is negative, the corresponding basic variable increases. There is no limit to how much we can increase this. Clearly, if all coefficients are negative (or zero), then we can increase the non-basic variable, and hence the value of z, indefinitely. In this case, we say that the problem is unbounded, and there is no maximum solution.

If one or more of the coefficients are positive, then increasing the entering variable must be offset by a corresponding decrease in the basic variable. Specifically, if $a_{ik} > 0$, for basic variable x_i the non-basic column of x_k, then the new value of x_i, after x_k is increased, will be

$$x_i = b_i - a_{ik}x_k \tag{2-6}$$

But $x_i \geqslant 0$; therefore, we can increase x_k only to that point where

$$x_k = \frac{b_i}{a_{ik}} \tag{2-7}$$

Define $\theta_i = b_i / a_{ik}$ for all equations i for which $a_{ik} > 0$. Because we want to maximize the increase in x_k, we increase precisely to the point at which some basic variable first becomes zero (the minimum value of θ_i). That variable now leaves the basis, and is called the leaving variable (Refer to Steps 3 and 4 in the following).

The Simplex method can be summarized succinctly as follows:

Step 1: Examine the elements in the top row (the objective function row). If all elements are $\geqslant 0$, then the current solution is optimal; stop. Otherwise go to Step 2.

Step 2: Select as the non-basic variable to enter the basis that variable corresponding to the most negative coefficient in the top row. This identifies the pivot column.

Step 3: Examine the coefficients in the pivot column. If all elements are $\leqslant 0$, then this problem has an unbounded solution (no optimal solution); stop. Otherwise go to Step 4.

Step 4: Calculate the ratios $\theta_i = b_i / a_{ik}$ for all $i = 1, \dots, m$ and for which $a_{ik} > 0$. where a_{ik} is the i-th element in the pivot column k. Then select

$$\theta = \min\{\theta_i\} \tag{2-8}$$

This identifies the pivot row and defines the variable that will leave the basis. The pivot element is the element in the pivot row and pivot column.

Step 5: To obtain the next tableau (which will represent the new basic feasible solution), divide each element in the pivot row by the pivot element. Use this row now to perform row operations on the other rows in order to obtain zeros in the rest of the pivot column, including the z row. This constitutes a pivot operation, performed on the pivot element, for the purpose of creating a unit vector in the pivot column, with a coefficient of one for the variable chosen to enter the basis.

When we apply these steps to the initial tableau in our example problem, we select x_1 (with the most negative coefficient on the z row) as the entering variable (Table 2-2):

We compute

The tableau for the first iteration   Table 2-2

Basis	z	x_1	x_2	s_1	s_2	s_3	Solution
z	1	-8	-5	0	0	0	0
s_1	0	1	0	1	0	0	150
s_2	0	0	1	0	1	0	250
s_3	0	2	1	0	0	1	500

$$\theta_1 = \frac{150}{1} = 150 \tag{2-9}$$

$$\theta_3 = \frac{500}{2} = 250 \tag{2-10}$$

and select the minimum $\theta = \theta_1$. Therefore, the leaving variable is the one corresponding to the first basic variable s_1. A pivot operation on the pivot element then produces the next tableau which shows the new basic feasible solution (Table 2-3).

The tableau for the second iteration   Table 2-3

Basis	z	x_1	x_2	s_1	s_2	s_3	Solution
z	1	0	-5	8	0	0	1200
x_1	0	1	0	1	0	0	150
s_2	0	0	1	0	1	0	250
s_3	0	0	1	-2	0	1	200

The solution represented by this tableau is $x_1 = 150, s_2 = 250, s_3 = 200$, $x_2 = 0, s_1 = 0$, $z = 1200$.

In the next iteration, x_2 is chosen as the entering variable. Based on the ratios $\theta_2 = 250/1$ and $\theta_3 = 200/1$ we select $\theta = \theta_3$, therefore, the third basic variable s_3 leaves the basis. The pivot element is shown in the previous tableau. A pivot operation produces the new tableau (Table 2-4):

The tableau for the third iteration   Table 2-4

Basis	z	x_1	x_2	s_1	s_2	s_3	Solution
z	1	0	0	-2	0	5	2200
x_1	0	1	0	1	0	0	150
s_2	0	0	0	2	1	-1	50
x_2	0	0	1	-2	0	1	200

The solution represented by this tableau is $x_1 = 150, s_2 = 50$, $x_2 = 200, s_1 = 0, s_3 = 0$ and z is now 2200.

From this tableau, we can now select s_1 as the entering variable. We compute $\theta_1 = 150/1$ and $\theta_2 = 50/2$, choose $\theta = \theta_2$, therefore, designate s_2 as the leaving variable. The resulting tableau after a pivot operation is shown in Table 2-5.

Table 2-5

Basis	z	x_1	x_2	s_1	s_2	s_3	Solution
z	1	0	0	0	1	4	2250
x_1	0	1	0	0	$-1/2$	$1/2$	125
s_1	0	0	0	1	$1/2$	$-1/2$	25
x_2	0	0	1	0	1	0	250

Because all of the objective function row coefficients are non-negative, the current solution is optimal. The decision variables area:

$$x_1 = 125$$
$$x_2 = 250$$

and the optimal objective function value, denoted as z^*, is:

$$z^* = 8x_1 + 5x_2 = 8(125) + 5(250) = 2250 \qquad (2-11)$$

The values of the slack variables at optimality also provide useful information. The slack variable s_1 for the first constraint has a value of 25, indicating that there is a difference of 25 in the right and left sides of the constraint; thus, $x_1 = 125$ is 25 less than 150. This can typically be interpreted to mean that some resource corresponding to constraint 1 is not fully consumed at optimality; such a constraint is sometimes referred to as a nonbinding constraint. Since s_2 and s_3 are non-basic and, therefore, have a value of zero, we can see that the second and third constraints are met as equalities. These resources are used to capacity at optimality, and these constraints are sometimes called binding constraints.

If we examine a graphical representation of the feasible region of this linear programming problem in, we can observe the progression from extreme point A (initial solution) to extreme point B, then C, and finally the optimal solution at point D. Extreme points F and G are infeasible, and point E is a basic feasible solution but is not examined by the Simplex method.

In summary, let us briefly review the steps of the Simplex algorithm and the rationale behind each step. Negative coefficients, corresponding to non-basic variables, in the objective function row indicate that the objective function can be increased by making those associated variables basic (non-zero). If in Step 1 we find no negative element, then no change of basis can improve the current solution. Optimality has been achieved and the algorithm terminates.

Otherwise, in Step 2, we select the non-basic variable to enter the basis that has the greatest potential to improve the objective function. The elements in the objective function row indicate the per unit improvement in the objective function that can be achieved by increasing the non-basic variables. Because these values are merely indicators of potential and do not reveal the actual total improvement in z, ties are broken arbitrarily. In actual practice, choosing the most negative coefficient has been found to use about 20% more iterations than some more sophisticated criteria, such as are suggested by Bixby in 1994 (Figure 2-4).

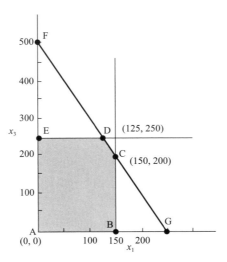

Figure 2-4   Simplex steps

The basic variable to be replaced in the basis is chosen, in step 4, to be the basic variable that reaches zero first as the entering variable is increased from zero. We restrict our examination of pivot column elements to positive values only (Step 3), because a pivot operation on a negative element would result in an unlimited increase in the basic variable. If the pivot column elements are all negative or zero, then the solution is unbounded and the algorithm terminates here. Otherwise, a pivot operation is performed as described in Step 5.

The Simplex tableau not only provides a convenient means of maintaining the system of equations during the iterations of the algorithm, but also contains a wealth of information about the linear programming problem that is being solved. In the following section, we will see various computational phenomena (indicating special problem cases) that may arise during the application of the Simplex method, as well as information that may be obtained from an optimal tableau.

4. Models

This section deals with the graphical solution of a two-variable LP.

Example 2-1 (The Reddy Mikks Company)

Reddy Mikks produces both interior and exterior paints from two raw materials, M_1 and M_2. The following table (Table 2-6) provides the basic data of the problem:

	The basic data		Table 2-6
Raw material	Tons of raw material per ton of		Maximum daily availability (tons)
	Exterior paint	Interior paint	
Raw material, M_1	6	4	24
Raw material, M_2	1	2	6
Profit per ton ($1000)	5	4	—

The daily demand for interior paint cannot exceed that for exterior paint by more than 1 ton.

Also, the maximum daily demand for interior paint is 2 tons.

Reddy Mikks wants to determine the optimum (best) product mix of interior and exterior paints that maximizes the total daily profit.

All OR models, LP included, consist of three basic components:

(1) Decision variables that we seek to determine.

(2) Objective (goal) that we need to optimize (maximize or minimize).

(3) Constraints that the solution must satisfy.

The proper definition of the decision variables is an essential first step in the development of the model. Once done, the task of constructing the objective function and the constraints becomes more straightforward.

For the Reddy Mikks problem, we need to determine the daily amounts of exterior and interior paints to be produced. Thus the variables of the model are defined as:

$$\begin{cases} x_1 = \text{Tons produced daily of exterior paint} \\ x_2 = \text{Tons produced daily of interior paint} \end{cases} \quad (2-12)$$

The goal of Reddy Mikks is to maximize (i. e. , increase as much as possible) the total daily profit of both paints. The two components of the total daily profit are expressed in terms of the variables x_1 and x_2 as:

$$\begin{cases} \text{Profit from exterior paint} = 5x_1 (\text{thousand}) \text{ dollars} \\ \text{Profit from interior paint} = 4x_2 (\text{thousand}) \text{ dollars} \end{cases} \quad (2-13)$$

Letting z represent the total daily profit (in thousands of dollars), the objective (or goal) of Reddy Mikks is expressed as

$$\text{Maximize } z = 5x_1 + 4x_2 \quad (2-14)$$

Next, we construct the constraints that restrict raw material usage and product demand. The raw material restrictions are expressed verbally as

$$\begin{pmatrix} \text{Usage of a raw material} \\ \text{by both paints} \end{pmatrix} \leqslant \begin{pmatrix} \text{Maximum raw material} \\ \text{availability} \end{pmatrix} \quad (2-15)$$

The daily usage of raw material M_1 is 6 tons per ton of exterior paint and 4 tons per ton of interior paint. Thus,

$$\text{Usage of raw material } M_1 \text{ by both paints} = 6x_1 + 4x_2 \text{ tons/day} \quad (2-16a)$$

In a similar manner,

$$\text{Usage of raw material } M_2 \text{ by both paints} = 1x_1 + 2x_2 \text{ tons/day} \quad (2-16b)$$

The maximum daily availabilities of raw materials M_1 and M_2 are 24 and 6 tons, respectively. Thus, the raw material constraints are:

$$\begin{cases} 6x_1 + 4x_2 \leqslant 24 \ (\text{Raw material } M_1) \\ x_1 + 2x_2 \leqslant 6 \ (\text{Raw material } M_2) \end{cases} \quad (2-17)$$

The first restriction on product demand stipulates that the daily production of interior paint cannot exceed that of exterior paint by more than 1 ton, which translates to:

$$x_2 - x_1 \leqslant 1 (\text{Market limit}) \quad (2-18)$$

The second restriction limits the daily demand of interior paint to 2 tons-that is,

$$x_2 \leqslant 2 \,(\text{Demand limit}) \qquad\qquad (2\text{-}19)$$

An implicit (or " understood-to-be") restriction requires (all) the variables, x_1 and x_2, to assume zero or positive values only. The restrictions, expressed as $x_1 \geqslant 0$ and $x_2 \geqslant 0$, are referred to as nonnegativity constraints.

The complete Reddy Mikks model is

$$\text{Maximize } z = 5x_1 + 4x_2 \qquad\qquad (2\text{-}20)$$

subject to

$$\begin{cases} 6x_1 + 4x_2 \leqslant 24\,(1) \\ x_1 + 2x_2 \leqslant 6\,(2) \\ -x_1 + x_2 \leqslant 1\,(3) \\ x_2 \leqslant 2\,(4) \\ x_1, \ x_2 \geqslant 0\,(5) \end{cases} \qquad\qquad (2\text{-}21)$$

Any values of x_1 and x_2 that satisfy all five constraints constitute a feasible solution. Otherwise, the solution is infeasible. For example, the solution $x_1 = 3$ tons per day and $x_2 = 1$ ton per day is feasible because it does not violate any of the five constraints; a result that is confirmed by using substituting ($x_1 = 3$, $x_2 = 1$) in the left-hand side of each constraint. In constraint (1), we have $6x_1 + 4x_2 = (6 \times 3) + (4 \times 1) = 22$, which is less than the right-hand side of the constraint ($= 24$). Constraints 2 to 5 are checked in a similar manner (verify!). On the other hand, the solution $x_1 = 4$ and $x_2 = 1$ is infeasible, because it does not satisfy at least one constraint. For example, in constraint (1), $(6 \times 4) + (4 \times 1) = 28$, which is larger than the right-hand side ($= 24$).

The goal of the problem is to find the optimum, the best feasible solution that maximizes the total profit z. First, we need to show that the Reddy Mikks problem has an infinite number of feasible solutions, a property that is shared by all nontrivial LPs. Hence the problem cannot be solved by enumeration.

Remarks: The objective and the constraint function in all LPs must be linear. Additionally, all the parameters (coefficients of the objective and constraint functions) of the model are known with certainty.

2.3   System Simulation

1. Introduction

System simulation is a general type of modeling that deals with the dynamic behavior of a system or its components. It uses a numerical computation technique for conducting experiments with a software model of a physical system, function, or process. Because simulation can embody the physical features of the system, it

2.3 Professional Terms, Words and Phrases, Sentence Illustration

is inherently less abstract than many forms of modeling discussed in the previous section. On the other hand, the development of a simulation can be a task of considerable magnitude.

In the development of a new complex system, simulations are used at nearly every step of the way. In the early phases, the characteristics of the system have not yet been determined and can only be explored by modeling and simulation. In the later phases, estimates of their dynamic behavior can usually be obtained earlier and more economically by using simulations than by conducting tests with hardware and prototypes. Even when engineering prototypes are available, field tests can be augmented by using simulations to explore system behavior under a greater variety of conditions. Simulations are also used extensively to generate synthetic system environmental inputs for test purposes. Thus, in every phase of system development, simulations must be considered as potential development tools.

There are many different types of simulations and one must differentiate static from dynamic simulations, deterministic from stochastic (containing random variables), and discrete from continuous. For the purposes of relating simulations to their application to systems engineering, this section groups simulations into four categories: operational, physical, environmental, and virtual reality simulation. All of these are either wholly or partly software based because of the versatility of software to perform an almost infinite variety of functions. Computer-based tools also perform simulations at a component or sub-component level, which will be referred to as engineering simulation.

(1) Operational Simulation

In system development, operational simulations are primarily used in the conceptual development stage to help define operational and performance requirements, explore alternative system concepts, and help select a preferred concept. They are dynamic, stochastic, and discrete event simulations. This category includes simulations of operational systems capable of exploring a wide range of scenarios, as well as system variants.

(2) System Effectiveness Simulation

During the concept exploration and concept definition phases of system development, the effort is focused on the comparative evaluation of different system capabilities and architectures. The objective is first to define the appropriate system performance requirements and then to select the preferred system concept to serve as the basis for development. A principal vehicle for making these decisions is the use of computer system effectiveness simulations, especially in the critical activity of selecting a preferred system concept during concept definition. At this early point in the system life cycle, there is neither time nor resources to build and test all elements of the system. Further, a well-designed simulation can be used to support the claimed superiority of the system concept recommended to the customer. Modern computer display techniques can present system operation in realistic scenarios.

The design of a simulation of a complex system that is capable of providing a basis for comparing the effectiveness of candidate concepts is a prime system engineering task. The simulation itself is likely to be complex in order to reflect all the critical performance factors. The evaluation of system performance also requires the design and construction of a simulation of the operational environment that realistically challenges the operational system's capabilities. Both need to be variable to explore different operational scenarios, as well as different system features.

A functional block diagram of a typical system effectiveness simulation is illustrated in

Figure 2-5. The subject of the simulation is an air defense system, which is represented by the large rectangle in the center containing the principal subsystems detect, control, and engage. At the left is the simulation of the enemy force, which contains a scenario generator and an attack generator. At the right is the analysis subsystem, which assesses the results of the engagement against an expected outcome or against results from other engagements. The operator interface, shown at the bottom, is equipped to modify the attacking numbers and tactics and also to modify the performance of these system elements to determine the effects on system effectiveness.

The size and direction of system effectiveness variations resulting from changes in the system model should be subjected to sanity checks before acceptance. Such checks involve greatly simplified calculations of the system performance and are best carried out by analysts not directly responsible for either the design or the simulation.

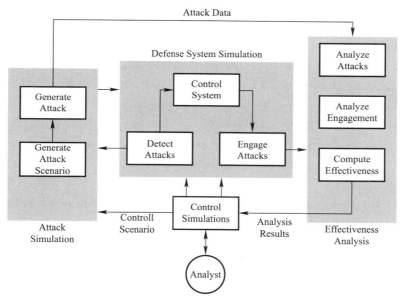

Figure 2-5   System effectiveness simulation

(3) Mission Simulation

The objective of the simulations referred to as mission simulations is focused on the development of the operational modes of systems rather than on the development of the systems themselves. Examples of such simulations include the conduct of air traffic control, the optimum trajectories of space missions, automobile traffic management, and other complex operations.

For example, space missions to explore planets, asteroids, and comets are preceded by exhaustive simulations of the launch, orbital mechanics, terminal maneuvers, instrument operations, and other vital functions that must be designed into the spacecraft and mission control procedures. Before design begins, an analytical foundation using simulation techniques is developed.

Such simulations model the vehicles and their static and dynamic characteristics, the information available from various sensors, and significant features of the environment and, if appropriate, present these items to the system operator's situation displays mimicking what they would see in real operations. The simulations can be varied to present a variety of possible scenarios, covering the range of expected operational situations. Operators may conduct "what if" experiments to determine the best solution, such as a set of rules, a safe route, an optimum strategy, or whatever the operational requirements call for.

(4) Engineering Simulation

At the component and sub-component level, there are engineering tools that are extensions of mathematical models. These are primarily used by design specialists, but their capabilities and limitations need to be understood by systems engineers in order to understand their proper applications.

Electronic circuit design is no longer done by cut-and-try methods using breadboards. Simulators can be used to design the required functionality, test it, and modify it until the desired performance is obtained. Tools exist that can automatically document and produce a hardware version of the circuit.

Similarly, the structural analysis of complex structures such as buildings and bridges can be done with the aid of simulation tools. This type of simulation can accommodate the great number of complicated interactions among the mechanical elements that make up the structure, which are impractical to accomplish by analysis and testing.

System simulations deal with the dynamic behavior of systems and system elements and are used in every phase of system development. Management of simulation effort is a system engineering responsibility.

Computer "war games" are an example of operational simulations, which involve a simulated adversarial system operated by two teams of players. They are used to assess the operational effectiveness of tactics and system variants.

System effectiveness simulations assess alternative system architectures and are used during conceptual development to make comparative evaluations. The design of effectiveness simulations is itself a complex system engineering task. Developing complex simulations such as these must seek a balance between fidelity and cost since such simulations can be systems in their own right. Scope must be controlled to obtain effective and timely results.

Physical or physics based simulations are used in the design of high-performance vehicles and other dynamic systems, and they can save enormous amounts of development time and cost.

Hardware in the loop simulations include hardware components coupled to computer-driven mechanisms. They are a form of physical simulation, modeling dynamic operational environments.

Environmental simulations subject systems and system elements to stressful conditions. They generate synthetic system environments that test systems' conformance to operational requirements.

Finally, computer-based engineering tools greatly facilitate circuit design, structural analysis, and other engineering functions.

2. Methods

Computer-aided simulation has been an important area of research and development in recent years, where new methodologies and tools are continuously developed leading to efficient simulators. However, most efforts have been focused on low-level simulation rather than on high level models. Importantly, conventional computer systems have become significantly complex, prohibiting the use of low-level models, which need significant computing resources for simulation, and requiring development of higher-level (more abstract) simulation models.

A typical low-level system simulator uses one of two main simulation methodologies: trace-driven and execution-driven. In trace-driven simulation, the simulator uses as input to the system model an input trace, which has been collected during an earlier operation of the system (or a similar system), e. g. an address trace obtained from a previous execution of a program. This simulation methodology is based on the assumption that, the operation of the system with the input trace constitutes a representative and repeatable operation of the analyzed system. Trace-driven simulation has been proven an indispensable tool for evaluation of single processors (uniprocessor systems) and the analysis of cache memories. However, it is not well suited for multiprocessor system simulation, because it cannot model and analyze synchronization and contention of multiprocessor systems, due to its inflexibility to change the order of instruction execution.

Execution-driven simulation is an alternative simulation method, which uses application executables (binary code) as input to the simulator instead of traces. It captures the effects of synchronization and contention and allows them to influence the course of simulation, but is quite slow, in general. There exist, however, two restricted forms of execution-driven simulation, which can be efficient in some cases: (i) direct-execution and (ii) detailed execution-driven simulation. Direct-execution simulation simulates only portions of applications and executes the remaining application portions directly on the simulation host machine; for example, most direct-execution simulators for shared-memory systems simulate only the memory subsystem of the multiprocessor. Thus, direct-execution simulation leads to faster simulation time. However, despite its efficiency and higher accuracy over trace-driven simulation, it is inadequate, in general, to simulate current processors because of their high degree of instruction-level parallelism, which requires detailed system modeling. Detailed execution-driven simulation overcomes the limitations of direct-execution simulation for systems with a high degree of instruction-level parallelism by modeling the entire system (processor) in detail. In order to make such a simulator efficient, the designer makes a significant trade-off between accuracy, simulation speed and simulation development effort.

Simulation methodologies are categorized not only according to the level (high or low) of the simulation models and the used metric, but according to the model of time they employ. System models are classified into three categories, according to the time model: continuous, discrete and combined.

In continuous time simulators, time flows in a continuous fashion (time is continuous) and system state changes continuously over time. Such simulators make extensive use of mathematical formulae to describe system behavior. The use of these mathematical equations leads to significantly high requirements for computational resources for simulation execution, which in turn, makes these simulators slow for small models and computationally prohibitive for complex systems. Due to this, continuous simulators are typically used for simulation of computer systems with relatively small numbers of components, which can be described at a low level of abstraction.

Discrete-event simulators are used to simulate components that operate at higher-level of abstraction, where time is continuous and discrete. Discrete-event models are based on events, where an event is an action that causes an instant transition of the system state; system state remains unchanged between two successive events. Discrete-event modeling can lead to system models that are quite accurate, as experience has shown, and efficient, due to fewer required calculations. Thus, discrete-event simulators are preferred over continuous ones.

Continuous and discrete-event modeling can be combined and lead to, so called, combined models. This type of modeling is used for computer systems in which discrete actions (events) influence continuous subsystems. The philosophy of combined modeling is the differentiation between continuous processes, that may be active between events, and discrete processes, that are activated by events: continuous processes cause continuous change of the system state, while discrete processes cause discrete changes. Combined modeling is a promising simulation technique suitable for complex and hybrid computer systems taking advantage of the accuracy of discrete-event modeling and the low-level abstraction of continuous modeling.

Discrete-event modeling is the most popular simulation technique for complex computer system architectures. The discrete-event simulator of a system is developed using three basic components: a simulation platform, the application logic (system model description) and general functions for input/output. There exist several approaches for discrete-event simulation, which differ in the method that represents the application logic. Some popular current methods are: the activity, the object-oriented and the event methods.

In discrete-event modeling with the activity method, each object (entity) of the simulator corresponds to an activity. Each activity is described by specifying its transitions and for each transition there is a description of the operations performed by the entities. The activity method has the advantage of simplicity, but it is often inefficient.

In the object-oriented method for discrete-event simulation, system entities are mapped to objects of the simulator. The distinct objects are identified and modeled; then, they are coupled to create sub-models and, finally, the entire model of the computer system is generated. This coupling is enhanced by object intercommunication and resource sharing, which are controlled by each object individually. The object-oriented method has the benefits of object-oriented programming, leading to high reusability and efficiency.

The method most commonly used for discrete-event simulation is the event method. In this method, each entity is modeled with some attributes. In addition, an entity corresponds to a start-activity event and an end-activity event. Events may occur synchronously or asynchronously. In event-driven discrete-event simulators, events occur asynchronously and at irregular intervals, while, in cycle-based discrete-event simulators, all changes in system state may be synchronized to a single clock. These two approaches of event occurrence can be combined by considering each clock tick as a simulation event.

In addition to the recent advances in simulation methodologies and modeling techniques for computer systems, a large number of simulation tools have been developed. These tools are developed either in software or in hardware, depending on the level of simulation. Software simulation tools are, typically, software libraries which are used with existing programming languages, like CSIM, Simjava and Silk, although there also exist programming languages that have been developed specifically for simulation, such as GPSS and SIMSCRIPT. Visual tools and environments, like Labview and Silk, enable efficient simulator construction. Hardware simulation tools are mostly used in conjunction with tools for design and development of computer systems, rather than in a stand-alone fashion.

Simulation tools are either general-purpose or special-purpose. Existing tools are mostly general-purpose, independent of the simulated systems and application, but differentiated by the simulation methodology and model they adopt. Special-purpose tools have been developed for specific applications, such as the ones for network simulation, and queuing network simulation, with an emphasis on graphical interfaces.

3. Models

(1) Continuous-Variable and Discrete-Event Models

Models commonly used in the physical sciences, engineering and biology often involve variables which are continuous functions of time. One example is in applied mechanics, where equations of motion may be derived from the application of Newton's laws of motion and involve quantities such as position, velocity and acceleration which may be defined as continuous functions. Similarly, in modeling electrical circuits involving resistors, capacitors and inductors, equations may be written down from Ohm's law and Kirchhoff's laws describing currents and voltages within a given electrical network as continuous functions of time. They are continuous-variable models and involve mathematical descriptions based on differential equations.

A second class of mathematical description, known as discrete-event models, is also important in certain types of computer simulation application. Changes in discrete systems take place either periodically or in a random fashion. Between the events which mark these changes all the variables of the system remain constant. One example of a discrete system in which changes take place periodically arises in the modeling of a digital computer used for real-time signal processing or direct digital control. In this case a continuous variable is sampled periodically using some form of analog to digital converter, and calculations are performed on the discrete numbers which have been input to the computer from the converter. The system cannot be modeled entirely using differential equations owing to the discrete nature of the processing actions within the computer and a difference equation type of formulation is necessary for the model of the computer and the associated analog to digital converters. Problems of discrete systems in which events occur randomly have led to the development of a separate form of simulation methodology which is generally known as discrete-event simulation. Examples of areas of application for discrete-event simulation include traffic flow analysis of all kinds. For example, the times of arrival of vehicles at a set of road traffic signals and requests for connections in a telephone communication system are both cases of discrete events which can be regarded as occurring randomly. Event-oriented simulation of this kind is outside the scope of this book. Further details of such simulation methods may be found in any of the many available texts dealing with this specialized area.

（2）Types of Continuous-Variable Model

Mathematical descriptions involving continuous variables may be divided, in general terms, into two broad classes. These are models of data and models of systems.

The first of these classes involves mathematical descriptions which have been fitted to measured response data. The resulting models consist of mathematical functions, such as polynomials or exponentials, and the coefficients or constants appearing in these descriptions often have no direct link to recognizable elements of the real system. Statistical models and other forms of "black box" description come within this class. Such models simply express an observed relationship between two or more variables of the real system. They have an important role in fields such as control systems engineering where input-output descriptions, for example, transfer functions, can be derived from measurements and can provide a starting point for design calculations. They tend, however, to be of less value for the study of problems at the research level since they provide little information about the internal processes of the system.

Models of systems, the second of the classes being considered, are usually developed by applying established laws and principles together with simplifying assumptions and hypotheses about the structure and function of the system being considered. Such models are essentially explanatory in nature and reflect complex causal relationships. Although models of systems may involve descriptions in which particular attention is given to relationships between one measured variable (the "output") and another (the "input"), there are also internal variables which have counterparts in the real system. Unlike data models, which are based simply on observations, system models should incorporate all relevant available knowledge concerning the structure and parameters of the real system.

One of the most fundamental divisions, in terms of mathematics, is between linear and nonlinear system models. In a linear system model responses are additive in their effects and satisfy the principle of superposition. In other words, the output is directly proportional to the input, and doubling of the input leads to doubling of the output. In a nonlinear model the principle of superposition is not satisfied. It is important that questions of linearity should be considered carefully in the initial stages of model development and that assumptions of linearity should not be made without justification. The range of linear operation of the system, if any such range exists, has to be established by careful evaluation of what is known about the real system or by carrying out additional tests on the system.

Time invariance is a second important property which can provide a basis for classification of models of systems. A time-invariant system is one in which the observed performance of the system is independent of the times at which the observations are made. As with linearity, time invariance must be verified in some way before being adopted as a basis for model formulation.

Models which are both linear and time invariant are particularly important and receive considerable attention in most introductory textbooks in fields such as applied mathematics, systems engineering, automatic control, electrical circuit analysis and applied mechanics. Many practical systems do have properties which may be approximated in a satisfactory way by linear time-invariant descriptions, even if only for specified and restricted sets of conditions. Linear time invariant models are also very attractive because they can be analyzed using standard mathematical techniques. Nonlinear and time-varying dynamic models present far greater difficulty in terms of classical mathematical solutions based on paper and pencil methods. It is for this reason, and for this very important class of problems, that computer simulation techniques have become so important. Computer simulation methods and numerical modeling can provide insight into and solutions to problems for which no analytical solutions are currently available, except possibly in very special and restricted cases.

2.4 Game Theory

2.4 Professional Terms, Words and Phrases, Sentence Illustration

1. Introduction

Game theory is the name given to the methodology of using mathematical tools to model and analyze situations of interactive decision making. These are situations involving several decision makers (called players) with different goals, in which the decision of each affects the outcome for all the decision makers. This interactivity distinguishes game theory from standard decision theory, which involves a single decision maker, and it is its main focus. Game theory tries to predict the behavior of the players and sometimes also provides decision makers with suggestions regarding ways in which they can achieve their goals. The foundations of game theory were laid down in the book *The Theory of Games and Economic Behavior*, published in 1944 by the mathematician John von Neumann and the economist Oskar Morgenstern. The theory has been developed extensively since then and today it has applications in a wide range of fields. The applicability of game theory is due to the fact that it is a context-free mathematical toolbox that can be used in any situation of interactive decision making. A partial list of fields where the theory is applied, along with examples of some questions that are studied within each field using game theory, includes:

(1) Theoretical Economics

A market in which vendors sell items to buyers is an example of a game. Each vendor sets the price of the items that he or she wishes to sell, and each buyer decides from which vendor he or she will buy items and in what quantities. In models of markets, game theory attempts to predict the prices that will be set for the items along with the demand for each item, and to study the relationships between prices and demand. Another example of a game is an auction. Each participant in an auction determines the price that he or she will bid, with the item being sold to the highest bidder. In models of auctions, game theory is used to predict the bids submitted by the participants, the expected revenue of the seller, and how the expected revenue will change if a different auction method is used.

（2）Networks

The contemporary world is full of networks; the Internet and mobile telephone networks are two prominent examples. Each network user wishes to obtain the best possible service (for example, to send and receive the maximal amount of information in the shortest span of time over the Internet, or to conduct the highest-quality calls using a mobile telephone) at the lowest possible cost. A user has to choose an Internet service provider or a mobile telephone provider, where those providers are also players in the game, since they set the prices of the service they provide. Game theory tries to predict the behavior of all the participants in these markets. This game is more complicated from the perspective of the service providers than from the perspective of the buyers, because the service providers can cooperate with each other (for example, mobile telephone providers can use each other's network infrastructure to carry communications in order to reduce costs), and game theory is used to predict which cooperative coalitions will be formed and suggests ways to determine a "fair" division of the profit of such cooperation among the participants.

（3）Political Science

Political parties forming a governing coalition after parliamentary elections are playing a game whose outcome is the formation of a coalition that includes some of the parties. This coalition then divides government ministries and other elected offices, such as parliamentary speaker and committee chairmanships, among the members of the coalition. Game theory has developed indices measuring the power of each political party. These indices can predict or explain the division of government ministries and other elected offices given the results of the elections. Another branch of game theory suggests various voting methods and studies their properties.

（4）Military Applications

A classical military application of game theory models a missile pursuing a fighter plane. What is the best missile pursuit strategy? What is the best strategy that the pilot of the plane can use to avoid being struck by the missile? Game theory has contributed to the field of defense the insight that the study of such situations requires strategic thinking: when coming to decide what you should do, put yourself in the place of your rival and think about what he/she would do and why, while taking into account that he/she is doing the same and knows that you are thinking strategically and that you are putting yourself in his/her place.

（5）Inspection

A broad family of problems from different fields can be described as two player games in which one player is an entity that can profit by breaking the law and the other player is an "inspector" who monitors the behavior of the first player. One example of such a game is the activities of the International Atomic Energy Agency, in its role of enforcing the treaty on the Non-Proliferation of nuclear weapons by inspecting the nuclear facilities of signatory countries. Additional examples include the enforcement of laws prohibiting drug smuggling, auditing of tax declarations by the tax authorities, and ticket inspections on public trains and buses.

(6) Biology

Plants and animals also play games. Evolution "determines" strategies that flowers use to attract insects for pollination and it "determines" strategies that the insects use to choose which flowers they will visit. Darwi's principle of the "survival of the fittest" states that only those organisms with the inherited properties that are best adapted to the environmental conditions in which they are located will survive. This principle can be explained by the notion of Evolutionarily Stable Strategy, which is a variant of the notion of Nash equilibrium, the most prominent game-theoretic concept. The introduction of game theory to biology in general and to evolutionary biology in particular explains, sometimes surprisingly well, various biological phenomena.

Game theory has applications to other fields as well. For example, to philosophy it contributes some insights into concepts related to morality and social justice, and it raises questions regarding human behavior in various situations that are of interest to psychology. Methodologically, game theory is intimately tied to mathematics: the study of game-theoretic models makes use of a variety of mathematical tools, from probability and combinatorics to differential equations and algebraic topology. Analyzing game-theoretic models sometimes requires developing new mathematical tools.

Traditionally, game theory is divided into two major subfields: strategic games, also called noncooperative games, and coalitional games, also called cooperative games. Broadly speaking, in strategic games the players act independently of each other, with each player trying to obtain the most desirable outcome given his or her preferences, while in coalitional games the same holds true with the stipulation that the players can agree on and sign binding contracts that enforce coordinated actions. Mechanisms enforcing such contracts include law courts and behavioral norms. Game theory does not deal with the quality or justification of these enforcement mechanisms; the cooperative game model simply assumes that such mechanisms exist and studies their consequences for the outcomes of the game.

2. Addressing Theoretical Concerns

Occasionally, game theorists examine questions that arise from the work of other game theorists. The most famous example of this is work on the Prisoners' Dilemma. Many scholars have questioned why cooperation did not arise in the Prisoners' Dilemma given that both actors would be better off cooperating than defecting. As illustrated in the Matrix below, both players have an incentive to defect since, regardless of the other player's action, each gains a higher pay-off by defecting. However, mutual defection leaves each player worse off than mutual cooperation.

A Prisoners' Dilemma

		Player 2	
		Cooperate	*Defect*
Player 1	*Cooperate*	3,3	1,4
	Defect	4,1	2,2

While the logic of the Prisoners' Dilemma tells us that defection is the equilibrium strategy, many people have noted situations where real world actors seemed to find themselves in situations that resembled the Prisoners' Dilemma and still cooperated. How could this cooperation arise? This problem is most evident in international relations. In an anarchic world without central authority, why do we see so much cooperation amongst egoistic states? This is the central question that drew Axelrod to this problem.

Axelrod popularized a solution to this problem by considering what would happen when the Prisoners' Dilemma game is iterated. This solution, however, does not work with a game that is iterated a finite number of times and each player is certain of the number of repetitions. In this case, neither player will have an incentive to try to induce cooperation by cooperating themselves. This arises from the fact that there is a known end to the interactions. To illustrate this, let us examine a situation where the Prisoners' Dilemma is repeated three times. Examining the final interaction first, neither player has an incentive to cooperate at this stage because the sole reason to cooperate was to encourage cooperation at a later stage. At the final stage, there is no incentive to encourage further cooperation since it is not possible. As such, each player will defect at this stage. What happens in the second round? In the second round, neither player has an incentive to try to invoke cooperation in the final round since we have already discovered that neither player will cooperate in the final round. As such, both will defect. This same reasoning can be used to show that each player will defect in the first period.

Axelrod found that if the game is repeated an infinite number of times and if each player's discount rate is at a sufficient level, cooperation can arise. This should not be interpreted that repetition always induces cooperation as an equilibrium in a repeated Prisoners' Dilemma. Rather, it is one of the possible equilibria. Moreover, drawing from the results of a series of computer tournaments, Axelrod discussed those strategies most effective in promoting mutual cooperation. He argued that Tit-for-Tat was an especially effective strategy for supporting mutual cooperation. This strategy, which calls for a player to always start cooperating and then mimic the other player's action from the previous round, allows cooperation to evolve and, at the same time, does not encourage players to exploit the cooperative play of another actor. This theoretical solution spawned a sizable literature, especially in international relations, concerning the effect of repetition and reciprocity on cooperation.

3. Models

A model of a specific "slice of life" in game theory terms is a purely imaginary object. The social reality, by its very nature, bristles with complexity and can be grasped only vaguely; it is therefore replaced by an idealized and deliberately simplified formal structure which is amenable to purely logical analysis. The conclusions of such an analysis apply not to the social reality itself but to an abstraction based upon certain properties which it is thought to possess. These conclusions are true provided only that they are logically consistent; their truth has nothing to do with their correspondence to the original social reality. If the abstract model does not correspond with reality in important details, however, it is of little practical value, and this is also the case if it does not yield insights that transcend our commonsense understanding of the social reality which it is intended to represent. Isaac Newton postulated unreal objects which have mass but no size and are attracted to one another according to a simple formula. Game theorists postulate unreal decision makers who are rational and error-free and choose options according to specified principles. The power of either theory to account for the behaviour of real objects or decision makers under various conditions can be tested through experiments.

The autonomous decision makers in a game are called layers. From the examples in the previous section, it is clear that the players may correspond to individual human beings or corporate decision-making bodies, and in some applications of the theory the players represent non-human animals. The essential quality of any player is the ability to choose, in other words to make decisions. These decisions or choices are sometimes called moves.

In some games, the moves made by ordinary decision makers do not lead to definite outcomes; the outcomes may partly depend upon the invisible hand of chance. In order to handle games like these, a fictitious player called Nature is invoked, and it is usually assumed that Nature moves disinterestedly according to the laws of probability. Poker is a typical example: provided that the cards are properly shuffled, Nature makes the first move by arranging the deck in a particular order, each possible arrangement occurring with equal probability. In many non-recreational games, Nature also plays a part.

A game must involve at least two players, one of whom may be Nature in the widest interpretation of game theory, otherwise there can be no interdependence of choice, and the total number of players is assumed to be finite except in esoteric applications of the theory. Each player must, in addition, have at least two options from which to choose; an agent with only one way of acting has no effect on the outcome of the game and can safely be ignored. In defining a player's options it is important to realize that doing nothing is sometimes a definite move, provided that there is at least one other option available.

The rules of the game determine what options are available to each player at each move, and the outcomes associated with any complete set of moves by all the players. The rules of chess, for example, define the permissible moves and the three possible outcomes: White wins, Black wins, or Draw.

2.5 Decision Analysis

1. Introduction

Decision analysis, also called statistical decision theory, involves procedures for choosing optimal decisions in the face of uncertainty. In the simplest situation, a decision maker must choose the best decision from a finite set of alternatives when there are two or more possible future events, called states of nature, that might occur. The list of possible states of nature includes everything that can happen, and the states of nature are defined so that only one of the states will occur. The outcome resulting from the combination of a decision alternative and a particular state of nature is referred to as the payoff.

2.5 Professional Terms, Words and Phrases, Sentence Illustration

Decision theory, in statistics, a set of quantitative methods for reaching optimal decisions. A solvable decision problem must be capable of being tightly formulated in terms of initial conditions and choices or courses of action, with their consequences. In general, such consequences are not known with certainty but are expressed as a set of probabilistic outcomes. Each outcome is assigned a "utility" value based on the preferences of the decision maker. An optimal decision, following the logic of the theory, is one that maximizes the expected utility. Thus, the ideal of decision theory is to make choices rational by reducing them to a kind of routine calculation.

When probabilities for the states of nature are available, probabilistic criteria may be used to choose the best decision alternative. The most common approach is to use the probabilities to compute the expected value of each decision alternative. The expected value of a decision alternative is the sum of weighted payoffs for the decision. The weight for a payoff is the probability of the associated state of nature and therefore the probability that the payoff occurs. For a maximization problem, the decision alternative with the largest expected value will be chosen; for a minimization problem, the decision alternative with the smallest expected value will be chosen.

Decision analysis can be extremely helpful in sequential decision-making situations—that is, situations in which a decision is made, an event occurs, another decision is made, another event occurs, and so on. For instance, a company trying to decide whether or not to market a new product might decide to test the acceptance of the product using a consumer panel. Based on the results of the consumer panel, the company will then decide whether or not to proceed with further test marketing; after analyzing the results of the test marketing, company executives will decide whether or not to produce the new product. A decision tree is a graphical device that is helpful in structuring and analyzing such problems. With the aid of decision trees, an optimal decision strategy can be developed. A decision strategy is a contingency plan that recommends the best decision alternative depending on what has happened earlier in the sequential process.

2. The Hierarchy of Decision Analysis

It is informative to place decision analysis in the hierarchy of techniques that have been developed to treat decision problems. We see that a decision analysis requires two supporting activities. One is a lower order activity that we call alternative evaluation; the second, a higher order activity that we call goal setting. Performing a decision analysis requires evaluating alternatives according to the goals that, have been set for the decision. The practitioners of operations research are quite experienced in alternative evaluation in both industrial and military contexts. In fact, in spite of the lip service paid to objective functions, only rare operations researchers have had the scope necessary to consider the goal-setting problems.

All mankind seems inexpert at goal setting, although it is the most important problem we face. Perhaps the role of decision analysis is to allow the discussion of decisions to be carried on at a level that shows the explicit need for goals or criteria for selection of the best alternative. We need to make goals explicit only if the decision maker is going to delegate the making of the decision or if he is unsure of his ability to be consistent in selecting the best alternative. We shall not comment on whether there is a trend toward more or less delegation of decision making. However, it is becoming clear to those with decision-making responsibilities that the increasing complexity of the operations under their control requires correspondingly more formal approaches to the problem of organizing the information that bears on a decision if inconsistent decisions are to be avoided.

The history of the analysis of the procurement of military weapons systems points this out. Recent years have shown the progression of procurement thinking from effectiveness to cost effectiveness. In this respect the military authorities have been able to catch up in their decision-making apparatus to what industry had been doing in its simpler problems for years. Other agencies of government are now in the process of making the same transition. Now all must move on to the inclusion of uncertainty, to the establishment of goals that are reflected in risk and time preferences.

These developments are now on the horizon and in some cases in sight; for example, although we have tended to think of the utility theory as an academic pursuit, one of our major companies was recently faced with the question, "Is 10 million dollars of profit sufficient to incur one chance in 1 million of losing 1 billion dollars?" Although the loss is staggering, it is realistic for the company concerned. Should such a large company be risk-indifferent and make decisions on an expected value basis? Are stockholders responsible for diversifying their risk externally to the company or should the company be risk-averting on their behalf? For the first time the company faced these questions in a formal way rather than deciding the particular question on its own merits and this we must regard as a step forward.

Decision analysis has had its critics, of course. One said, "In the final analysis, aren't decisions politically based?" The best answer to that came from a high official in the executive branch of our government who said, "The better the logical basis for a decision, the more difficult it is for extraneous political factors to hold sway." It may be discouraging in the short run to see logic overridden by the tactical situation, but one must expect to lose battles to win the war.

Another criticism is, "If this is such a good idea, why haven't I heard of it before?" One very practical reason is that the operations we conduct in the course of a decision analysis would be expensive to carry out without using computers. To this extent decision analysis is a product of our technology. There are other answers, however. One is that the idea of probability as a state of mind and not of things is only now regaining its proper place in the world of thought. The opposing heresy lay heavy on the race for the better part of a century. We should note that most of the operations research performed in the Second World War required mathematical and probabilistic concepts that were readily available to Napoleon. One wonders about how the introduction of formal methods for decision making at that time might have affected the course of history.

3. Methods or Tools

Decision analysis as a procedure for analyzing a decision is described below. This procedure is not an inviolable method of attacking the problem, but is a means of ensuring that essential steps have been consciously considered. The Figure 2−6 describes decision analysis in the broadest terms. The procedure is iterative and comprises three phases. The first is a deterministic phase, in which the variables affecting the decision are defined and related, values are assigned, and the importance of the variables is measured without any consideration of uncertainty. The second, or probabilistic, phase introduces probability assignments on the important variables and derives associated probability assignments on values. This phase also introduces the assignment of risk preference, which provides the best solution in the face of uncertainty. The third, or informational, phase reviews the results of the last two phases to determine the economic value of eliminating uncertainty in each of the important variables in the problem. In some ways, this is the most important phase because it shows just what it could cost in dollars and cents not to have perfect information. A comparison of the value of information with its cost determines whether additional information should be collected. If there are profitable further sources of information, then the decision should be together the information rather than to make the primary decision at this time. Thereupon will follow the design and execution of the information-gathering programs, whether it be a market survey, a laboratory test, or military field trials.

The information that results from this program may change the model and the probability assignments on important variables. Therefore, the original three phases must be performed once more. However, the additional work required to incorporate the modifications should be slight and the evaluation rapid. At the decision point, it may again be profitable to gather new information and repeat the cycle or it may be more advisable to act. Eventually, the value of new analysis and information-gathering will be less than its cost, and the decision to act will then be made.

This procedure will apply to a variety of decision situations: in the commercial area, to the introduction of a new product or the change in design of an old one; in the military area, to the acquisition of a new weapon or the best defense against that of a potential enemy; in the medical area, to the selection of a medical or surgical procedure for a patient; in the social area, to the regulation and operation of public utilities; and finally, in the personal area to selection of a new car, home or career. In short, the procedure can be applied to any decision susceptible to logical analysis.

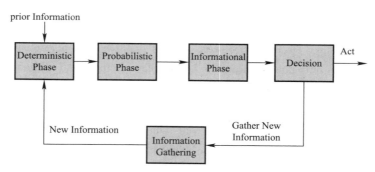

Figure 2-6　The decision analysis cycle

4. The Decision Model

The story of valuation begins with the frame, a scope that defines the valuation problem within its technical and economic context. This is a crucial step because whatever follows will one way or another relate to this frame. Think of it as a distinction that separates the valuation problem from all the outside factors; something that helps you decide what goes into valuation. Without a proper frame, the formulation may become too narrow to be useful or too wide to be affordable.

Consider for example a project consisting of drilling a production well into an oil-bearing formation. It will be a deviated well that the engineers hope will penetrate the right place in the formation. In the framing meeting, one manager argues that "while we are in the vicinity why not drilling a side-track well that explores a nearby prospect?" The proposed side-track costs only a fraction of an individual exploration well and does not introduce any added risks (Figure 2-7).

The suggestion stirs up the discussion with many others pointing out the pros and cons of this sidetrack. Some praise the suggestion because they believe it leads to useful information at low cost. It would be good for business. Others call it a bad suggestion as it delays the much-needed production. They desperately need to generate income as soon as possible and fill the empty export pipeline.

Before the discussion is confused, they had better refer to the frame. A proper frame clarifies the decision making by addressing the production timeliness and future exploration plans. It settles the side-track discussion by showing a viewpoint on how to measure its overall costs and benefits.

A good frame is a powerful element of any decision. It not only settles the irrelevant arguments, but also directs the analysis efforts. It directs the resources we would spend on data collection and analysis. Consider the millions-dollar implicit losses in terms of lost time and missed opportunities just because the analysis teams focused on a wrong frame of decision. Losses that they could entirely avoid only if they had spent more time on the framing of their decisions and less on confused modelling and number crunching. As Peter Drucker mentioned, "the true dangerous thing is asking the wrong question".

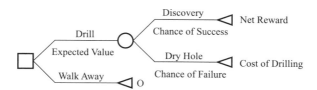

Figure 2-7   A simple decision tree model showing the decision to drill an exploration well

2.6   Reading Material

1. All Models Are Wrong, Some Are Useful

The logical precept about models being "abstractions of reality" especially applies to the upstream petroleum business. To make any decision, we first need a description of the real situation. We need a definition of the problem and an understanding of the uncertainty. In the end, the quality of our decision-making cannot exceed the quality of our models.

In making models, we need to simplify. Our models display only aspects of the reality but could not (and should not) reflect everything. The goal is to build useful (not realistic) models. Therefore, we select only the key aspects to show. As such, all models are simplification.

Our earlier discussion on the key aspects of hydrocarbon value chain is a good start, but by no means an exhaustive checklist. Each investment opportunity is unique and calls for its own purpose-built decision model. The investments may even depend on an entirely dissimilar set of factors and justify their own detailed study. But we hope that a general understanding helps.

For example, time constraints in a project could cut the possibility of further data acquisition. Then the drilling decision should be based on the current state of knowledge and not on the possibility of further resolution. Unlike an unconstrained project, here we work with a different frame of decision. Even though projects have comparable patterns, for analysis of any project we recommend defining a frame and finding the key uncertainties. As we learn about the value drivers, we should revert to the frame and revise.

2. The Time Constraints

Most petroleum exploration and development are within licenses. These are government-issued allowances giving a client the right to explore and develop. The terms of the licenses usually specify data acquisition (like seismic surveys and drillings) during a specific period. The client (oil company) also pays an area fee per square kilometers and per year. In a specific project, depending on how far we are within the license, the terms and conditions could impose a constraint on exploration schedule.

Other than these regulatory constraints, availability of resources (including budget, labor, or technology hardware) could also impose a time constraint. The period from discovery to first oil, called the lead time, is particularly important. During this period, companies select a development concept and execute it. In almost any project, this period needs the largest capital. With large outlay and no income, it is no surprise that all companies aim to shorten their projects' lead time.

At the time of exploration drilling, the lead time and project schedule are just assumptions. Yet, because of the effect of time on discounting, such assumptions deeply influence the value. Even with the known track-record of oil industry's underestimating cost and completion time still a good guide to realistic assumptions is the experts' insight and past experiences—the only sources of insight ever available.

With the improved understanding, the frame of our decision models could either shrink or expand. The limiting time constraints was an example of shrinkage. With limited time, we learned that we would have a limited decision space. The frame of a drilling decision could expand to include opportunities beyond. For example, drilling a well could bring to light further options, including the joint development scheme with a nearby prospect. We could also think of the "upside potentials" of drilling a well as it may open a new play with further exploration targets.

Chapter 3
Construction Project Management

3.1 Construction Project

1. Introduction

3.1 Professional Terms, Words and Phrases, Sentence Illustration

Construction projects are intricate, time-consuming undertakings. The total development of a project normally consists of several phases requiring a diverse range of specialized services. In progressing from initial planning to project completion, the typical job passes through successive and distinct stages that demand input from such disparate areas as financial organizations, governmental agencies, engineers, architects, lawyers, insurance and surety companies, contractors, material and equipment manufacturers and suppliers, and construction craft workers.

During the construction process itself, even a project of modest proportions involves many skills, materials, and literally hundreds of different operations. The assembly process must follow a natural order of events that constitutes a complicated pattern of individual time requirements and restrictive sequential relationships among the project's many segments. To a great extent, each construction project is unique—no two jobs are ever exactly the same. In its specifics, each structure is tailored to suit its environment, arranged to perform its own particular function, and designed to reflect personal tastes and preferences. The vagaries of the construction site and the possibilities for creative and utilitarian variation of even the most standardized building product combine to make each construction project a new and different experience. The contractor sets up its "factory" on the site and, to a large extent, custom builds each structure.

Construction is subject to the influence of highly variable and sometimes unpredictable factors. The construction team, which includes architects, engineers, craft workers, specialty contractors, material suppliers, and others, changes from one job to the next. All the complexities inherent in different construction sites—such as subsoil conditions, surface topography, weather, transportation, material supply, utilities and services, local specialty contractors, labor conditions, and available technologies—are an innate part of construction project.

The character of construction projects, typified by their complexity and diversity and by the nonstandardized nature of their production, is a result of variable inputs operated on by standard processes yielding a unique product. The use of prefabricated modular units is somewhat limiting this variability, but it is unlikely that field construction will ever be able to adapt completely to the standardized methods and product uniformity of assembly line production. To the contrary, many manufacturing processes are moving toward mass customization, or "one-off" production and adopting many of the project management tools originating in the construction industry.

A construction project is made up of many small components that are integrated to form a single complex project. To have a successful project, various characteristics of that project, including time, quality, cost, and safety, need to be managed.

Construction projects are dynamic and complex, requiring skilled and competent managers for successful execution. Construction project managers employ a variety of models to understand projects, including cost models, time-based models, graphical models, and production models.

2. Methods of Construction Project

Although the details of record keeping vary considerably among construction firms, there is a basic accounting logic and a set of fundamental accounting procedures that are common to companies in the construction industry. The primary basis of a contractor's accounting system centers on the determination of income and expense from each of its construction projects and the cost of the operations of its office staff and management. That is, the performance of each construction project is treated as a separate profit center. In an accounting sense, a profit center is any group of associated activities whose profit or loss performance is separately measured and analyzed.

In a construction company, the original estimate of costs pertaining to each contracted construction project becomes the basis for a budget for that project. As costs are incurred on the project, they are accounted for and are charged against the project activities or work items to which they pertain. Cost summaries and reports are regularly generated throughout the life of a project, and costs incurred are compared to the project budget. Management analysis follows and forms the basis for management action to assure insofar as possible that the project will be completed within the budget. Figure 3-1 illustrates the cycle of cost estimating, cost accounting, and cost control, and the record-keeping functions that accompany.

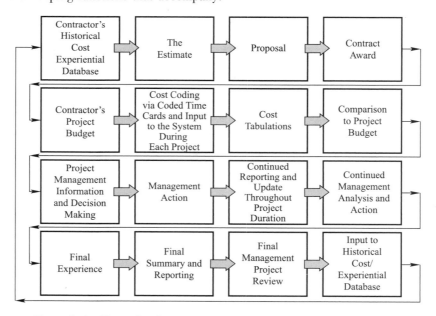

Figure 3-1   The cycle of cost estimating, cost accounting, and cost control

It is customary that the keeping of most of a contractor's business accounts be concentrated in the home office. However, on large projects and on some cost-plus contracts, a subsidiary set of accounts is frequently maintained in a field office where the record keeping pertaining to that project is accomplished. In this process however, the controlling accounts or master accounts for such projects are incorporated into a master set of accounting records that are maintained in the contractor's central office.

The two basic accounting methods employed by contractors in the conduct of their business are the cash method and the accrual method. In the cash method, income is taken into account only when cash is actually received, and expense is taken into account only when cash is actually expended. The cash method is a simple and straightforward form of income recognition, and no attempt is made in this method to match individual revenue payments received with the accompanying expenses.

The cash accounting method is used principally by small businesses, nonprofit organizations, and by some professional people for their personal records. Many small construction contractors use the cash method because of its simplicity, and because of the fact that tax liability for contract profits is recognized only when payment has actually been received. If a construction company performs only small projects, and maintains little or no materials inventory, and owns no capital equipment of consequence, the cash method is usually adequate.

However, for most construction companies the cash method does not work to the advantage of the contractor. For example, the cash method of accounting does not recognize depreciation of equipment and other capital assets because depreciation involves no recognition of cash income or outgo. Additionally, and importantly, income that has been earned but not received and expenses that have been incurred but not paid as of the end of a reporting period are not recorded or reflected in the company records in the cash method of accounting. An income statement, which is a summary document showing the company's revenue and expenses for a certain period of time, with profit or loss expressed as the difference between the expenses and revenue that is prepared on a cash accounting basis, will not present a realistic indication of true profit or loss for the company.

Similarly, a balance sheet, which is a summary of the company's assets, liabilities, and net worth at a certain point in time that does not reflect income earned but not yet paid and expenses incurred but not yet paid, does not accurately reflect the company's true financial condition. Income statements and balance sheets absent this information are therefore of limited value to management in assessing the financial condition of the company, and are entirely inadequate for use by lenders, sureties, and others outside the company who have an interest in a depiction of the company's financial position.

The accrual method is the second basic accounting procedure, and is the one most commonly used by all but the smallest construction companies. Under the accrual method of accounting, income is actually taken into account in the fiscal period during which it is earned, regardless of whether payment has actually been received. Similarly, items of expense are entered into the accounts as the expenses are incurred, whether or not they have actually been paid during the reporting period. The accrual method of accounting and income recognition is also more complicated, because by this method a connection is maintained on a continuous basis between the revenues earned and the associated expenses. The accrual accounting method requires a more elaborate system of accounting procedures and records. However, the accrual method is generally accepted as the accounting method that provides the most accurate and realistic portrayal of the financial condition of a business enterprise at any moment in time.

3. Models

As in a construction project, the SCOR model provides a set of tools to be used in developing the supply chain blueprint (Figure 3-2).

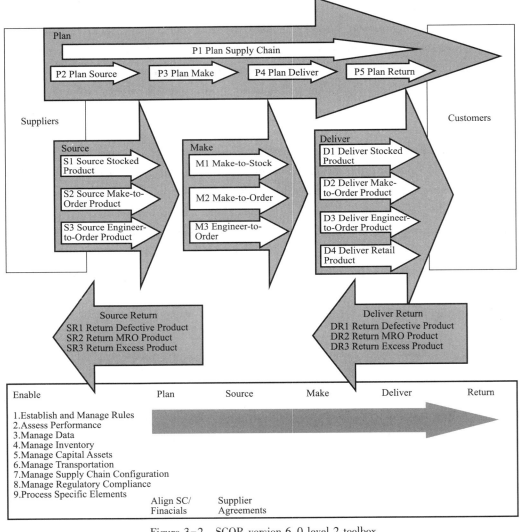

Figure 3-2   SCOR version 6. 0 level 2 toolbox

While the SCOR model is the only framework of its kind for developing a supply chain architecture, other complementary initiatives have emerged that focus on industry-specific practices and implementation level detail, such as data standards. Two such initiatives that have been adopted widely in recent years are Collaborative Planning, Forecasting, and Replenishment (CPFR) and RosettaNet.

We will be focusing on the SCOR model because, to our knowledge, it is the most widely accepted supply chain reference model in use. In fact, it is being adopted by the largest supply chain organization in the world, the U. S. Department of Defense.

Through its structure and method, the SCOR model makes what might be a monumental undertaking—creating a supply chain architecture—a manageable task. As in a construction project, the SCOR model provides a set of tools to be used in developing the supply chain blueprint.

(1) The Top Three Levels of the SCOR Model

The SCOR model has four levels of detail, the first three of which—processes, subprocesses, and activities—are described in the model. Operable processes, or level 4, are detailed workflow-level tasks and are always customized to an organization's specific strategy and requirements. As such, they are not included in the published version of the model.

Starting with level 1 and ending with level 3, the content of the SCOR model can be used to translate business strategy into a supply chain architecture designed to achieve your specific business objectives. The exact order in which you use the different levels of the SCOR model will depend on your specific business needs and starting point.

(2) SCOR Level 1

At level 1, you confirm how business processes will align with your high level business structure (business units, regions, etc.) and supply chain partners and refine your supply chain's strategic objectives—the business priorities that your supply chain must support. Level 1 focuses on the five major supply chain processes (plan, source, make, deliver, and return). Using these processes, the alignment between process and organizational domains can be established to describe where processes must be standardized across entities. Choices at level 1 drive information systems costs because different processes across business units typically involve multiple applications and the associated implementation and maintenance costs. In addition, level 1 decisions also will determine whether an organization will be able to implement certain business practices. For example, does the source process need to be standardized between two business units or are differences justified? If the goal is to consolidate volume across multiple business units to gain leverage with suppliers, standardization of a good part of the source process will be needed.

Once business processes and organizational domains are aligned, setting performance targets for these key process areas is an important next step. The SCOR model provides a supply chain scorecard for setting and managing supply chain performance targets across the organization. This step is one of the most critical and difficult activities in supply chain design because of the need to gain internal consensus on targets and priorities. It is driven by your supply chain strategy.

As an example, one of our clients, a leader in the consumer electronics industry, was losing market share to competitors with a strong focus on specific market segments. The company had long been organized as a single, centralized business structure and recognized the need to transform to multiple, market-facing business units in order to compete effectively.

Once the new business units had been established, executive management reviewed both the strategic vision and the related supply chain requirements for each. Prior to the reorganization, all supply chain processes (plan, source, make, deliver, and return), supporting information systems, and assets had been shared. The company also had outsourcing policies that limited contract manufacturing to end-of-life products, as well as other rules that limited product customization to control unit costs and maximize inventory flexibility. Deciding which of these policies to keep and which to change was critical to establishing the new strategic boundaries for supply chain design.

In order to establish these boundaries, each business unit developed its own business strategy and performance objectives and then summarized the resulting implications for its supply chain. Given the critical importance of materials costs (up to 85 percent of product cost), product quality, and time to market, it was decided to maintain the shared plan, source, make, deliver, and return processes and assets while changes were made to inventory policies for each business unit to meet the specific service requirements of the different end markets.

(3) SCOR Level 2

At level 2, you refine your choice of supply chain processes and confirm how supply chain processes align with your infrastructure (physical locations and information technology). Also called the configuration level, level 2 involves developing and evaluating high-level options for the supply chain process architecture by choosing the "flavors" of plan, source, make, deliver, and return. This is done by selecting the relevant subprocesses—or process categories—based on your supply chain strategy, The selection of process categories will drive level 3 design because each category requires very different detailed activities.

For example, manufacturing companies have a number of options for how they will produce their products. They can build in anticipation of customer orders (make to stock), build only after a firm customer order is in hand (make to order), build to a semifinished level and complete the build after an order is received (configure to order), or build the product based on specifications that are unique to the customer and therefore require detailed engagement in advance of starting any work (engineer to order).

Once the process categories are chosen, they are used to describe existing supply chain configurations. This typically takes the form of a geographic map showing where your customers, suppliers, warehouses, factories, and order desks are and using the process categories to describe the major physical and informational flows. In essence, this is like taking an inventory of the processes in use today and where they occur.

Once you understand the current configurations, you can develop and test "to be" options. Be aware, however, that the SCOR level 2 analysis may show you that you cannot optimize what you want because of existing limitations, such as excessive transportation costs. In other words, you may not be able to execute all your "to be" requirements in the near term and will need to develop a road map to move progressively toward your target configuration.

One of our clients, an international aerospace company, was struggling to manage a complex web of relationships among its own sales, logistics, and manufacturing operations; several key subcontractors; and a major customer, an aircraft manufacturer. The company was a prime contractor in a commercial aircraft program. Ensuring on-time delivery of its subsystem to the customer's final assembly and testing facility required coordinating material, information, and financial flows with subcontractors located on three continents.

Supplier deliveries for the commercial jet program were increasingly late. And when the aircraft manufacturer asked to reschedule orders, the company had to contact its suppliers before providing a confirmation date—a process that took several weeks. Because of these problems, the company was struggling to maintain its credibility with a key account. It used the SCOR model to gain a greater understanding of the underlying problems.

The project team used the SCOR model to map order management, procurement, physical distribution, supply chain planning, and financial flows at the company, as well as all key interfaces with subcontractors. Each activity was associated with a SCOR level 2 process category. For the first time, the company had clear visibility of the subsystem's supply chain as a whole and was able to see which activities were performed by the company, the customer, and subcontractors. In addition, the use of standard process category definitions meant that each constituent was using the same definition for the processes for the first time.

Opportunities to simplify the supply chain were quickly apparent. For example, major subassemblies moved through multiple internal warehouses before being made available for final assembly. This caused significant delay yet added no additional value to the product. The level 2 process map showed the reason for this. All products were routed to a regional consolidation platform. Once they entered the platform, there was an official transfer of ownership from internal manufacturing to the aircraft program. The team realized that a change in process and supporting information systems would allow some product to be shipped directly to the final preparation point near the customer's assembly line, eliminating several weeks in the delivery cycle.

Interestingly, the visibility created by the SCOR process map also forced the company to rethink some long-held beliefs about what was causing customer service to be below desired levels. It had long thought that the order-management process—where orders were transferred automatically from the customer into one system and then manually rekeyed into another system for financial management before communication to suppliers—was the cause of order delays. The analysis showed that although rekeying added costs and introduced potential errors, the management of subcontractors was a much larger problem. The existing process included communication of planned requirements to key subcontractors as part of a formal ordering process, where the suppliers also confirmed quantities and delivery dates. But supplier updates regarding schedule slippages, as well as communication of changes in order volume from the prime contractor, were managed in a less formal manner. Some of the major changes defined by the team included new roles for procurement, monthly subcontractor planning reviews, a process to adjust previously agreed-on plans, and business rules to guide manufacturing schedule changes at the subcontractor. The company's multimonth effort delivered dramatic results: Supplier on-time deliveries improved by more than 20 percent, and order confirmation times were cut sharply. Today, the company can confirm customer orders in two to three days rather than two to three weeks, and customer confidence has been restored.

(4) SCOR Level 3

SCOR level 3 is also called the process-element level; this is where you can complete your supply chain architecture by adding operational detail to your SCOR level 2 design. Within SCOR level 3 you will find specific business practices, associated metrics, and guidance about the information systems needed to support the process—in terms of both functionality and supporting data. The tools you'll need to do this work have been assembled for you already. You will develop "as is" maps illustrating the alignment between processes, locations, and organizations. These maps typically will show where inventory is located, the lead times between process elements, and the alignment between process elements and supply chain information systems.

By applying basic lean principles, the level 3 "as is" analysis can reveal a number of improvement opportunities driven by the configuration, including reducing process and information systems complexity, creating better linkages between end-customer demand and end production, eliminating similar activities conducted in multiple locations, and reducing wait time and the associated inventory and customer lead times.

In addition to analyzing the overall configuration, you also will consider best practices, applications, metrics, and organizational models as part of your level 3 "to be" design. By analyzing your current capabilities versus your "to be" design, you'll understand the implications for the existing processes and information systems. Typical information systems implications include system gaps, missing data, and insufficient integration between information systems. Then you can evaluate each "to be" option based on the business criteria set at SCOR level 1 and choose which to develop at the operable level (level 4) of detail needed for a real working solution.

Case in point: We worked with a large retailer that needed to reduce inventory levels without sacrificing service. The company has hundreds of retail locations, ranging from megastores to neighborhood grocery outlets. It had grown through acquisition, and as new acquisitions were made, the acquired businesses were established as independent business units. Some functions were shared, including purchasing, warehouse management, and accounting. For the most part, however, each business unit was allowed to operate independently, maintaining its own processes and information systems. This practice led to very high information-systems costs due to different applications, each requiring dedicated, ongoing support.

The company had been frustrated by several failed efforts to improve its overall performance; it had spent months mapping its key processes and analyzing the resulting improvement opportunities. Still, the project team was not able to reach agreement on the "to be" supply chain. The major roadblock was the lack of an overall architecture. Team members were not even able to agree on which processes were part of the supply chain and which were not! Moreover, processes within specific functions were well defined, but those which cut across functions, such as supply chain planning, were not.

To break the deadlock, the team used SCOR level 3 to map its current processes. An analysis of the deliver process elements showed that the physical supply chain was highly optimized in terms of warehousing operations and that highly developed processes were in place to ensure the best handling of its products from suppliers to retail locations. Examination of warehouse practices revealed the adoption of many leading-edge warehouse management practices, such as picking and order preparation using voice-recognition technology.

An analysis of the plan and source process elements revealed that the supply chain had been optimized to move high volumes of consumer favorites that were purchased every day in predictable volumes. The team closely examined how demand was calculated at each level of the supply chain, starting with the retail store, moving back to the warehouse, and finally moving on to the supplier.

Using plan source process elements (Figure 3-3), the team realized that information on actual sell-through at the store was not used in planning requirements for suppliers and that each store placed orders on the warehouses based on its best view of demand. Using the P 2.1 process element—identify, prioritize, and aggregate product requirements—the team saw that distribution warehouses that supplied the retail outlets were pulling inventory from suppliers based on historical demand patterns for all products—which was fine as long as demand was consistent with historical levels.

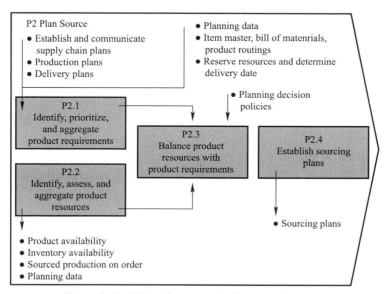

Figure 3-3   Using plan source for better performance

In actuality, of course, demand patterns for many products were highly variable, particularly in the cases of new products, store-level promotions, and the periodic introduction of seasonal merchandise. These events distorted demand patterns, creating a baseline demand that was appropriate only for a specific time period. This meant under supply at the beginning of a promotion and oversupply at the end. The team realized that major changes would be required to planning, including the introduction of collaborative planning with suppliers during promotions and new product introductions.

Making the change to the plan process would have a major impact on existing information systems. And gaining full acceptance of the new process architecture would require involvement of a broader team. Following its initial work using SCOR level 3, the company initiated an enterprise project involving both business managers and information systems managers to further develop the new process and information systems architecture.

As can be seen by these examples, SCOR provides a structured approach to developing a supply chain architecture. SCOR's top-down approach, which moves progressively into more detail, allows you to see the big picture before moving into greater levels of detail. And the model's hierarchical structure, which breaks down processes into subprocesses and activities, means that companies can see how changes will affect the existing supply chain operations. This helps to clarify risks, needed resources, and implementation timelines. For typical benefits of using SCOR, see Figure 3-4.

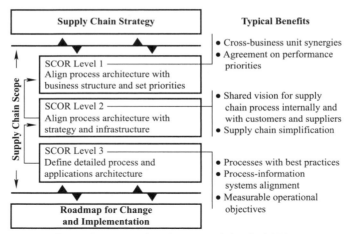

Figure 3-4 Benefits of using each level of SCOR

3.2 Bidding, Design, Procurement and Site Construction Management

1. Design

(1) The BIM Process Intends to Achieve Creating an Open and Collaborative Design Process

The design team and other parties involved in the construction project did not work together, they would only focus on their own small part with little to no communication or consideration for the other members of the design and construction team. This attitude lead to the projects not meeting the client's needs fully, as the Latham and Egan reports stated, because the design team was not working together

3.2 Professional Terms, Words and Phrases, Sentence Illustration

with the end result in mind.

BIM intends to turn this approach around, by promoting early and constant communication and collaboration between all the parties involved in the design, and construction process. As well as getting the Facilities Management team (FM) involved at an early stage, so they can start to understand what they will be maintaining. This early involvement of the FM team is part of the Government Soft Landings scheme (GSL).

This collaboration between the whole design team is aimed at getting the team to function as one, rather than as individual sections, so the design process can be more easily controlled and effective workflows can be implemented. The end result of this should be a building which fully meets the client's needs and expectations, as well as being fully functional to meet its users/ occupies needs.

(2) Levels of BIM

① BIM Level 0

Level 0 is the next step up from hand drafting, where 2D CAD tools are used to create details, which are then distributed out via paper copy or electronic paper copy (e. g. a PDF document). The main standards which relate to this level are:

● BS 1192-5-Construction drawing practice: Guide for structuring and exchanging of CAD data.

● BS 7000-4-Design management systems: A guide to managing design in construction.

② BIM Level 1

This level looks at CAD packages that are capable of 3D modelling, where 2D details and drawings are generated from the 3D model. The drawings created are shared via a Common Data Environment (CDE), which is a datapool that the whole design team has access to and shares their information through. However, the design team do not have to share their 3D models at Level 1, which is why this stage is also referred to as "lonely BIM". The standards which relate to this level include those stated in level 0 and the following:

● BS 1192-Collaborative production of architectural, engineering and construction information (Which supersedes BS 1192-5).

● BS 8541-2-Library objects for architecture, engineering and construction. Recommended 2D symbols of building elements for use in building information modelling.

③ BIM Level 2

Level 2, sometimes also referred to as "proprietary BIM" (pBIM), utilises 3D CAD packages with intelligence and the ability to add and structure information, as discussed earlier, in the form of BIM authoring tools. Level 2 also involves collaboration between the whole design team by sharing their details and models via a CDE, which allows for the creation of a federated 3D model. A federated model is a collection of all the models produced by all the different design teams on a project, which are pulled together to create one whole building model, which is a virtual simulation of the proposed construction/building. The federated model can be used for clash and problem detection, analysis, time scheduling and costing for the whole project (which are also referred to as the dimensions of BIM). The standards which relate to BIM Level 2, include all previously stated in Levels 0 and 1 (except those which have been superseded) and the following:

- PAS 1192-2-Specification for information management for the capital/delivery phase of construction projects using BIM.
- PAS 1192-3-Specification for information management for the operational phase of assets using BIM.
- BS 1192-4-Collaborative production of information. Fulfilling employers information exchange requirements using COBie.
- PAS 1192-5-Specification for security-minded building information modelling, digital built environments and smart asset management.
- BS 8541-1-Library objects for architecture, engineering and construction. Identification and classification.
- BS 8541-3-Library objects for architecture, engineering and construction. Shape and measurement.
- BS 8541-4-Library objects for architecture, engineering and construction. Attributes for specification and assessment.
- BS 8541-5-Library objects for architecture, engineering and construction. Assemblies.
- BS 8541-6-Library objects for architecture, engineering and construction. Product and facility declarations.

④ BIM Level 3

Level 3 BIM, which is also referred to as Digital Built Britain (DBB) and "integrated BIM" (iBIM), does not yet have a set definition for what it is, as it is still in development. The idea of what DBB will be is a fully integrated and collaborative process, which will be enabled by web-based technologies, through which all the design teams on a project can work on the building model simultaneously. This process is also intended to fully utilise the dimensions of BIM, which will be explained in the next section.

2. Procurement

Procurement refers to the ordering, expediting, and delivering of key project equipment and materials, especially those that may involve long delivery periods. This function may or may not be handled separately from the construction process itself. Construction is, of course, the process of physically erecting the project and putting the materials and equipment into place, and this involves providing the manpower, construction equipment, materials, supplies, supervision, and management necessary to accomplish the work.

This stage moves toward conclusion with substantial completion of the project when the owner gains beneficial use of the facility. The conclusion of the project occurs when the terms of all contracts are fulfilled and the contracts are closed out. This closeout cycle is often part of a commissioning process that accomplishes many things, including bringing the facility on line, facilitating owner occupancy and turnover of facility operations to the owner, and closing out of all construction contracts. Many contractors follow the final closeout of the project with an internal postproject review from which the contractor gleans a great deal of information that helps to improve company processes and hence to mold the evolution of the company.

Methods and Model of Procurement:

(1) Bids (Purchases that exceed the bid threshold— $ 36,000)

This method is used for contracts for goods, materials, services and public work projects that exceed the bid threshold of $ 36,000.

Examples

Building Services Department	Technology
Plumbing, Electrical, HVAC work	Computer Supplies/Equipment
Custodial Supplies	Printers/Computer
Public Works Project	lnteractive Boards
Food Services Department	Title 1 Testing
Groceries and Canned Goods	Test Scoring Services
Pest Control Services	
Baking Goods—Rolls, Bread	Athletics
	Footwear
District	Athletic Supplies/Equipment
Furniture	Physical Ed Supplies/Equipment
AV Equipment	
Calculators	

Lowest Responsible Bidder

The common thread of all these bids is that the district has to award the bid to the lowest responsible bidder which means the lowest price.

(2) Quotations (Purchases that fall between $ 5,400 and $ 35,999)

This method of procurement is used for contracts for goods, materials, services and public work projects that in the aggregate between $ 5,400 and $ 35,999.

Examples:

Athletic Wear	Fitness Equipment
Athletic Trainer Supplies	Instrument Reeds
Dry Cleaning Services	Payroll Checks
Fax Machines Supplies	

Again, as with bids, the contract is awarded based upon the lowest price.

(3) Request for Proposal—RFP

The RFP method is designed to award the contract to the vendor based upon a list of criteria which include:

- Management Criteria

> Business organization; staffing

> Experience

> Knowledge of district

● Technical Criteria

> Submission of narrative how firm will provide services; planned approach; measurable results

> Understanding how services will be provided

● Cost Criteria

> Fee proposal submission; cost analysis

The contract for an RFP contract does not; I repeat does not have to be given to the respondent who submits the lowest price. The district administrator provides an evaluation scoring of each respondent using the criteria as a basis of award.

(4) Other Procurement Methods

State Contract Purchasing, Emergency Contracts, Cooperative Purchasing Agreements, Shared Services Agreements, Sound Business Practices.

3. Management of Field Construction

Discussions up to this point have demonstrated that owners have the option of using many different project delivery systems to get their projects built. Regardless of the variability of these systems, however, one party assumes management responsibility for the field construction process. Depending on the methods used by the owner, this party may be the owner, the architect-engineer, a construction manager, or a general contractor.

The management of field construction customarily is done on an individual project basis, with a project manager being made responsible for all aspects of the construction. For large projects, a field office usually is established directly on the job site for the use of the project manager and staff. A good working relationship with a variety of outside persons and organizations, such as architects, engineers, owners, subcontractors, material and equipment suppliers, labor unions, and regulatory agencies, is an important part of guiding a job through to its conclusion. Field project management is directed toward pulling together all the diverse elements necessary to complete the project satisfactorily. Management procedures presented later will, in general, be discussed only as they apply to field construction, although they are equally applicable to the entire project, from concept to commissioning.

(1) Methods

Day-to-day construction in the field has little in common with the assembly line production of standardized products. Standard costs, time and motion studies, process flow charts, and line-of-balance techniques—all traditional management devices used by the manufacturing industries—have limited applicability to general construction. Historically, construction project management has been a rudimentary and largely intuitive process, aided by useful but inadequate adaptations from manufacturing.

Over the years, however, new scientific management concepts have been developed and applied. Application of these concepts to construction has resulted in the development of techniques for the control of construction cost, time, resources, and project finance, which recognize construction as a series of repetitive processes that can be managed and improved. The result is treatment of the entire construction process as a unified system. Comprehensive management control is applied from inception to completion of construction operations.

Construction project management starts at the point at which the contractor is brought into the project. Initial activities include development of a comprehensive construction budget and a detailed schedule of operations.

These cost-based and time-based models of the project establish the accepted cost and time goals used as a blueprint for the tangible construction operations. After the project has begun, monitoring systems are established that measure the actual costs and progress of the work at periodic intervals. The reporting system provides progress information that is measured against the planned targets. Comparison of field investments and progress with the established plan quickly reveals exceptions that must receive prompt management attention. In addition to using data from the system to design corrective action and exert control over project operations, the data can also be used to make corrected forecasts of costs and time to complete the work.

The process just described is often called management-by-exception. When applied to a given project, it emphasizes the prompt and explicit identification of deviations from an established plan or norm. Reports that highlight exceptions from the standard enable the manager to recognize quickly those project areas requiring attention. As long as an item of work is progressing in accordance with the plan, no action is needed, but there are always plenty of problem areas that do require attention. Management-by-exception devices are useful. In addition to cost and time, the project management system is necessarily concerned with the management of job resources, with safe execution of operations, and with project financial control. Resources in this context refer to materials, labor, construction equipment, and subcontractors. Resource management is primarily a process of advanced recognition of project needs, scheduling and expediting of the resources required to meet those needs, and adjusting the demands where necessary. Safe execution of construction operations involves the use of labor, tools, and construction equipment to properly install the materials and equipment brought to the workface in an incident-free environment. Project financial control relates to the responsibility of the project manager for the total cash flow generated by the construction work and the terms of the contract.

（2）Models

Having the field engineering office computerize their files and records for technical data, inspection records, field surveys, change orders, correspondence, and the like can save time and money. A CAD station tied into the home office system on design-build jobs also can be useful if the project is handling a lot of field changes. Having a few commonly used structural and civil design programs available can speed up the field engineer's response to requests for information in those areas. Having PCs in the CM's office and the administrative offices generally increases field office productivity and ensures professional-looking output. Handling the creation and flow of field-office paperwork by computers is virtually a must on today's information-driven projects. PCs equipped with modems have long since replaced the old teletype machines and are starting to cut into the need for separate facsimile machines. Continued combining of PCs with communications systems is expected to be the wave of the future for many computer applications.

Review Questions and Problems:

1. What are the whole processes included for a construction project?

2. What is the need for project management?

3.3 Time and Cost Management

3.3 Professional Terms, Words and Phrases, Sentence Illustration

1. Introduction

Project time and cost management are based on time and cost models developed for the project and an information system that will provide data for comparing expected with actual performance. The information system measures, evaluates, and reports job progress, comparing it with the planned performance expressed in the models. This keeps the project manager apprised of the nature and extent of any deviation. When deviations do occur, the manager identifies the cause or causes of the deviation, develops corrective action that can be taken to correct the deviation, and then executes whatever action is considered feasible and effective to correct the situation. The manager then verifies the effectiveness of the corrections in future reports. Costs and time can get out of hand quickly on construction projects where production conditions are volatile. Job monitoring must detect such aberrations quickly.

Cost and time control information must be timely, with little delay between fieldwork and management review of performance. This timely information gives the project manager a chance to evaluate alternatives and take corrective action while an opportunity still exists to rectify problem areas.

In a sense, all management efforts are directed toward cost control because expedient completion of safe and high-quality projects represents both construction savings for the contractor and beneficial usage for the owner. In practice, however, time and cost management are spoken of and applied as separate, although interrelated, procedures. One aspect of this separation is the difference in job breakdown structure used for time-control and cost-control purposes. The distinctive character of the two procedures requires that the project be divided into two different sets of elements: project components for time control and work classifications for cost control.

The realities of a field project make the strict control of every detail unattainable in a practical sense. Consequently, it must be recognized that the time and cost management methods discussed in this book are imperfect procedures, affording results of reasonable accuracy to managers whose powers to control are far from absolute. Project management procedures offer no panacea for construction problems. They provide no magic answers, and the management information generated is no better than the quality of the input data. Nevertheless, a reasonably good basis is established for informed decision making.

2. Method of Time and Cost Management

The computer is an invaluable tool to assist project managers in accomplishing many tasks.

However, there are still many problems that are not suitable for computer solution. One of those tasks is project shortening, for which the computer does not normally serve as an adequate stand-alone device. Manual methods, relying on human insight and judgment, continue to play a commanding role in the process. The project time acceleration procedures discussed herein describe and emphasize such an approach. This does not mean that the computer plays a trivial supporting role, since management and computer can work together to achieve the best solution possible. The manager can originate and pass on matters of judgment, and the computer can process the decisions made by project management. The process of least-cost shortening of actual construction networks can become enormously complex. Multiple critical paths can appear and make the shortening process a very complicated procedure. The number of possible expediting combinations to be tested, if an optimal solution is to be achieved, can become very large. It must be recognized, therefore, that the usual manual time reduction will certainly not always provide project management with truly optimal expediting combinations. However, mathematical precision with imprecise data is neither the only nor necessarily the most important consideration involved in such a process. Of necessity, the actual accomplishment of time reduction in practice must be concerned with a number of practical considerations beyond the matter of buying the most time for the least money. Manual solutions for project time reductions, while perhaps not optimal, do provide invaluable guidance to the project manager in making decisions about whether expediting is practical and, if so, how to proceed. In most cases, guidance on how to make intelligent choices of time-reduction actions is as valuable as a theoretically optimal solution. Input data are uncertain, conditions change from day to day, and construction is simply not an exact or a completely predictable process. Even the critical path of a given network may change its routing occasionally as the work progresses. Project managers strive to find practical, reasonable answers rather than seek to achieve perfection. Expediting a project manually makes it possible to inject value judgments into the process and affords the project manager an intuitive feel for the effect of expediting actions on other aspects of the project. In addition, a project time-reduction study can easily include the critical evaluation of time gained by revisions in job logic as well as that gained by shortening individual activities. The manual accomplishment of project time reduction is directed entirely toward reducing the length of the applicable critical path or paths. This is a step-by-step process using time-reduction measures that are considered feasible and best suited to the job context. These may be changed in the job plan, the shortening of individual activities, or both. The usual procedure is to gain each increment of time with the least possible increase in direct cost. Where other job factors are of greater importance than incremental cost, shortening steps are taken in whatever order project management believes is in the overall best interest of the work.

In an environment of constant change, the established time goals of a construction project must be met. To that end, the time management sequence shown in Figure 3 − 5 is repeated regularly over the life of the project. The current operational plan and schedule, consonant with established project time constraints, underpin the time management system. Based on the latest version of the job network, produce a work schedule with calendar dates given for the start and finish of each project activity. This schedule is used for the day-to-day time control of the project. Such a system constitutes an effective early-warning device for detecting when and where the project may be falling behind schedule. The work plan, however, must respond to changing conditions if project objectives are to be accomplished successfully. The monitoring phase of time management involves the periodic measurement of actual job progress in the field and its comparison with the planned objectives. Project monitoring, therefore, involves the determination of work quantities put into place and the reporting of this information in a format suitable for its comparison with the programmed job schedule. Network activities constitute a useful and convenient basis for progress measurement and reporting. At regular intervals, the stage of project advancement is observed and reported. As of each cutoff date, note is made of those activities that have been completed and the degree of completion of those activities that are in progress. Review of this information by project management discloses where the project currently is ahead or behind schedule and by how much. Critical activities, and those with low float values, are monitored very closely because of their strategic importance in keeping the project on schedule. Corrective action to expedite lagging work items is taken after analysis of the reported progress data reveals what options are available. No project plan or schedule can ever be perfect, and deviations will inevitably develop as the project progresses. As a result, the baseline version of the schedule will become increasingly inaccurate and unrealistic as changes, slippages, and other logic and schedule aberrations occur. Consequently, the network must be corrected as needed, and calculations must be updated occasionally so that the current job schedule reflects actual job experience to date. These updates often reveal shifts in critical paths and substantial changes in the floats of activities. The latest updated schedule reflects the actual current job conditions and the updated plan based upon those job conditions. It constitutes the current basis for project time control.

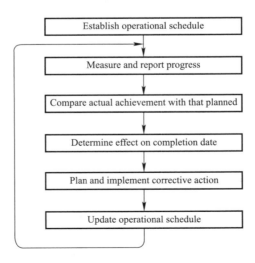

Figure 3-5   Time management cycle

3. Model of Time and Cost Management

（1）Six Sigma（1990 and Beyond）

Six Sigma is a quality improvement methodology with the ideal outcome of reaching zero defects. It can be considered the next evolution of total quality management. In the late 1980s Motorola began implementing the Six Sigma methodology under CEO Bob Galvin, and the company became a quality leader in industry. General Electric（GE）followed shortly after and achieved similar successes; GE successes with Six Sigma led to a rapid proliferation of the Six Sigma methodology in industry.

Six Sigma primarily functions in three different ways: as a metric, management system, and methodology. As a metric, Six Sigma is a scale of a company's quality level; for an organization to have a "Six Sigma level" of quality, the company must only have 3.4 defects per one million opportunities（DPMO）or less. As a management system, Six Sigma pulls the concepts of Six Sigma into a corporate business strategy. As a methodology, Six Sigma is represented by the DMAIC model. DMAIC is the acronym for define, measure, analyze, improve, and control. The major advances of the Six Sigma methodology over total quality management relate to:

① The establishment of stretch goals to achieve zero defects.

② The creation of the DMAIC process improvement cycle.

③ The heavy use of statistics and data to make management decisions and reduce variation in processes.

In addition to these advances, the Six Sigma field has also designated various levels of personal expertise in applying Six Sigma: green belt（novice to Six Sigma with some experience in Six Sigma projects）, black belt（expert in applying and leading Six Sigma improvement projects）, and master black belts（organization leaders who oversee all Six Sigma efforts and execution plans within an organization）. These personal designations are typically granted by a third party, such as a professional society or educational institute or may be granted via a certification process within the organization applying Six Sigma.

（2）Lean Six Sigma（2005 and Beyond）

Lean Six Sigma is a managerial concept combining Lean and Six Sigma and focuses on simultaneous quality improvements and cost reductions for an organization, product, or process. The Lean Six Sigma concept was first introduced in 2002 by Michael George in the book titled *Lean Six Sigma: Combining Six Sigma with Lean Production Speed*. The combination of Lean and Six Sigma laid the foundation to combat the largest criticisms of Lean and Six Sigma as stand-alone methodologies, specifically for Lean that it was not concerned with the quality of the product and for Six Sigma that it was not concerned with cost reductions. Before the introduction of Lean Six Sigma, many managers viewed quality improvements and cost reduction initiatives as mutually exclusive ventures; the Lean Six Sigma concept opened the door to the fact that both can and should be implemented simultaneously.

In a perfect world, an organization will have all parts of its business running smoothly and efficiently. Obviously this is rarely the case—which is why organizations employ specialists that continuously improve operations regardless of changes to the economic environment, competitor behavior, or integration of new IT platforms. In the change management hierarchy, the Lean and Six Sigma practitioners need to work closely with the BPM team because they are responsible for analyzing those models developed by the process analysts.

In a manufacturing or service organization, the Lean practitioners will usually be responsible for optimizing visual management processes. Imagine you work on a floor with eighty staff members, and there are only two printers located on the other side of the floor. In order for you to print out a document, you need to walk across the room, take your document off the printer, and return to your desk. The Lean team will assess the time taken to complete that task, and, if necessary, move that printer closer to you and your colleagues to minimize the wasted time spent walking across the room. This example may seem trivial to many people who work in low tempo environments, but it's highly applicable to teams that work in call centers, processing hubs, or anywhere where speed and time is critical to the work. Therefore, the Lean team needs the process models to identify where visual obstacles occur and determine opportunities for improvement.

Likewise, the Six Sigma practitioners also need process models to measure the cost and time involved in completing a process from end to end (one that starts with the customer and ends with the customer). Six Sigma practitioners will usually take a process model and add in the time and cost associated with completing a single process in an end-to-end model. They are then able to use statistical analysis to determine cycle times as well as chokepoints that slow down a process from running at optimum efficiency.

Review Questions and Problems:

How can managers minimize costs?

3.4　Planning and Scheduling

1. Planning

The key construction activities that we need to plan, organize, and control lie at the very heart of the total construction management system.

3.4 Professional Terms, Words and Phrases, Sentence Illustration

（1）Definitions

Planning is a bridge between the experience of the past and the proposed action that produces a favorable result in the future. Planning is a precaution by which we can reduce undesirable effects or unexpected happenings and thereby eliminate confusion, waste, and loss of efficiency. Planning is the prior determining and specifying of the factors, forces, effects, and relationships necessary to reach the desired goals. The first definition reminds us to make use of our prior experience, often gained from past mistakes, to avoid repeating them in our present endeavor. It also says that we should not reinvent the wheel on each new project. The second definition cites the advantages of increased productivity by planning the unexpected and undesirable happenings out of existence before starting to work. The third one stresses making a conscious effort to find and control the variables in a capital project. We must do that before starting work if we are to meet our project goals. It also indicates the need for an organizational phase if we are to execute the plan. All of the definitions point to the obvious conclusion that the first move on any project assignment is to do the necessary planning. Furthermore, that applies to every one of your activities throughout the project!

Planning is the process of devising of workable scheme of operations that, when put into action, will accomplish an established objective. The most time-consuming and difficult aspect of the job management system—planning—is also the most important. It requires an intimate knowledge of construction methods combined with the ability to visualize discrete work elements and to establish their mutual interdependencies. If planning were to be the only job analysis made, the time would be well spent. Construction planning, as well as scheduling, must be done by people who are experienced in and thoroughly familiar with the type of fieldwork involved. Significant learning takes place during the planning phase of a project. Therefore, the people doing the planning are in the best position to manage the work. The project network and the management data obtained from it will be realistic and useful only if the job plan is produced and updated by those who understand the job to be done, the ways in which it can be accomplished, and the job-site conditions. Those executing the work in the field are most likely to be committed to ensuring that the work is done according to the plan if they participate in the planning process. To construct the job network, information must be sought from many sources. Guidance from key personnel involved with the project, such as estimators, the project manager, the site superintendent, and the field engineer, can be obtained from a planning meeting or perhaps a series of meetings. The network serves as a medium whereby the job plan can be reviewed, criticized, modified, and improved. As problems arise, consultations with individuals can clear up specific questions. The important point here is the need for full group participation in the development of the network, and collective views must be solicited. Participation by key subcontractors and suppliers is also vital to the development of a workable plan. Normally, the prime contractor sets the general timing reference for the overall project. Individual subcontractors then review the portions of the plan relevant to their work and help develop additional details pertaining to their operations. An important side effect is that this procedure brings subcontractors and the prime contractor together to discuss the project. Problems are detected early, and steps toward their solutions are started well in advance. It must be recognized that the project plan represents the best thinking available at the time it is conceived and implemented. However, no such scheme is ever perfect, and the need for change is inevitable as the work progresses. Insight and greater job knowledge are acquired as the project evolves. This increased cognizance necessarily results in corrections, refinements, and improvements to the operational plan. The project program must be viewed as a dynamic device that is continuously modified to reflect the progressively more precise thinking of the field management team.

（2）Methods

Construction planning may be said to consist of five steps:

① A determination of the general approach to the project.

② Breakdown of the project into job steps or "activities" that must be performed.

③ Ascertainment of the sequential relationships among these activities.

④ Graphic presentation of this planning information in the form of a network.

⑤ Endorsement by the project team.

Two different planning methodologies are presented : beginning-to-end planning and top-down planning. Beginning-to-end planning breaks the job into steps or activities, starting with mobilization of the project, and proceeds step-by-step through the project to completion. This method presumes some level of detail from the beginning or starts with limited detail and adds detail as planning proceeds. Top-down planning, sometimes referred to as work breakdown structure, starts with the overall project, breaking it into its major pieces, then breaking the major pieces into their component pieces. This process continues until the pieces are of sufficient detail to satisfy the complexity of the project. Both methods arrive at the same result : job activities that can be used to form a graphical logic diagram.

Project planning is central to project management. Planning takes place at all stages. When owners want a new facility, they put together a plan to acquire what they need, the plan is typically very simple in concept (though it may be quite complex in execution), consisting of a few steps :

① Identify the need as clearly as possible.

② Determine a budget and completion date.

③ Bring together a team that can design and build the facility.

④ Monitor the process throughout the project's schedule. (construction project management)

Planning is the first step in the process of construction time control. On the basis of a detailed study of job requirements, planning establishes what is to be done, how it is to be done, and the order in which it will proceed. The planning function is accomplished by dividing the project into many components or time-consuming steps, called activities, and establishing the sequence in which they will be performed. An example of an activity might be "Install boiler" or "Set bar joists." The results of project planning are shown graphically in the form of a network diagram. This diagram can be drawn using either of two different graphical notation systems, "precedence" or "arrow." Since precedence notation has become the predominant way to represent schedule networks, it is emphasized herein and is used throughout for discussion purposes. However, since older schedules in arrow diagram formatting are still encountered, examples of arrow networks will be found on the companion website.

A detailed time study of the planning network is then conducted, with adjustments to the plan being made as necessary to meet the project milestone and completion dates. Some selective shortening of key construction activities may be in order at this point. Manpower and construction equipment requirements are evaluated for individual job activities, with adjustments made to minimize unbalanced or conflicting demands. On the basis of these studies, the contractor establishes a calendar-date schedule of the anticipated start and finish times for each activity. The resulting time schedule, subject to periodic revision and correction during construction, is the essential basis for the day-to-day time control of the project. Such a schedule serves as an exceptionally effective early-warning device for detecting when and where the project is falling behind and the impact that the delays will have on the project as a whole.

2. Scheduling

（1）Introduction

Until about 1960, projects were scheduled using bar charts. Henry Gantt worked out a system of notation for creating such charts and using them to report progress, so they are commonly called Gantt charts. A simple example is shown in Figure 3-6.

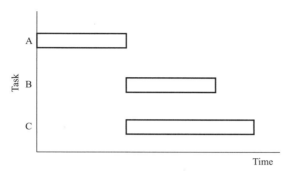

Figure 3-6　A Simple Gantt Chart

This is the way Gantt charts were drawn before 1960. Notice that the chart gives no indication of whether Tasks B and C depend on the completion of Task A or whether they just coincidentally start when A is completed. This means that if Task A slips, we can't tell what impact it will have on subsequent tasks.

For that reason, a method of showing such dependencies was developed in the late 1950s. The relationships among tasks were shown using arrow diagrams. Two different forms were developed. One was called Critical Path Method (CPM), and the other was called Program Evaluation and Review Technique (PERT). The difference between the two systems is that PERT makes use of a calculated task duration and allows you to estimate probabilities of completing work, whereas CPM just makes use of estimated task durations with no regard for probabilities.

Both systems allow you to determine which series of activities (or path) in a project will take the longest time to complete. When the project is scheduled to end at the point where the critical path ends, it will have no latitude. Shorter paths, however, will have latitude, which is called either slack or float. The slack or float provides some protection from unexpected events or from inaccurate estimates. You never want to have a schedule that has no float, as the risk that you won't meet your completion date is extremely high.

In addition to there being two systems, there are two forms of notation. One is called Activity On-Arrow (AOA), and the other is called Activity On-Node (AON). In AOA notation, the arrow represents the work to be done, and the circle represents an event—either the beginning of another activity or the completion of a previous one. This is shown in Figure 3-7.

For AON notation, a box (or node) is used to show the task itself, and the arrows simply show the sequence in which work is done. This is shown in Figure 3-8.

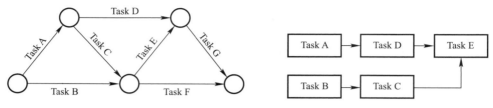

Figure 3-7 Activity-on-Arrow Notation   Figure 3-8 Activity-on-Node Notation

Since both systems get the same schedule results, it makes no difference which one is used. However, most software produces only one of them, and it is usually AON. A few programs, such as Primavera, allow you to choose the system you prefer.

Arrow diagrams allow you to determine whether it is possible for a task to start at a certain time. When you create a large schedule using bar charting, you may inadvertently show tasks starting before a predecessor is finished, and if this isn't possible, then your schedule won't work. This was one of the main reasons why CPM and PERT were created in the first place. So, if you want to create a schedule that will work, you should always work out the interdependencies among all of the activities in a project.

Scheduling is concerned with the allocation of scarce resources to activities with the objective of optimizing one or more performance measures. Depending on the situation, resources and activities can take on many different forms. Resources may be machines in an assembly plant, CPU, memory and I/O devices in a computer system, runways at an airport, mechanics in an automobile repair shop, etc. Activities may be various operations in a manufacturing process, execution of a computer program, landings and take-offs at an airport, car repairs in an automobile repair shop, and so on. There are also many different performance measures to optimize. One objective may be the minimization of the makespan, while another objective may be the minimization of the number of late jobs.

The study of scheduling dates back to 1950s. Researchers in operations research, industrial engineering, and management were faced with the problem of managing various activities occurring in a workshop. Good scheduling algorithms can lower the production cost in a manufacturing process, enabling the company to stay competitive. Beginning in the late 1960s, computer scientists also encountered scheduling problems in the development of operating systems. Back in those days, computational resources (such as CPU, memory and I/O devices) were scarce. Efficient utilization of these scare resources can lower the cost of executing computer programs. This provided an economic reason for the study of scheduling.

The scheduling problems studied in the 1950s were relatively simple. A number of efficient algorithms have been developed to provide optimal solutions. Most notable are the work by Jackson, Johnson, and Smith. As time went by, the problems encountered became more sophisticated, and researchers were unable to develop efficient algorithms for them. Most researchers tried to develop efficient branch-and-bound methods that are essentially exponential time algorithms. With the advent of complexity theory, researchers began to realize that many of these problems may be inherently difficult to solve. In the 1970s, many scheduling problems were shown to be NP-hard.

In the 1980s, several different directions were pursued in academia and industry. One direction was the development and analysis of approximation algorithms. Another direction was the increasing attention paid to stochastic scheduling problems. From then on, research in scheduling theory took off by leaps and bounds. After almost 50 years, there is now an astounding body of knowledge in this field.

(2) Method of Scheduling

In the design-build or turnkey approach, the contractor is responsible for scheduling the complete project, including the design, procurement, and construction. Here we will concentrate on scheduling the construct-only approach, to avoid confusing our construction-oriented efforts in this chapter. There are two other commonly used contracting options to cover; namely the construct-only based on compete design, and the third party constructor working with the owner's design firm. The only basic difference between these two options is the handling of the design-construction interface, which is relatively straightforward. Also, the problem of differences in process versus nonprocess types of projects does not assert itself in our scheduling discussions. Experienced CM practitioners in each project arena know the specific technologies that require special scheduling attention. Any major differences will be clarified in the general discussion.

(3) Project Execution and Scheduling Philosophy

Construction execution and scheduling philosophy are two items that greatly affect the preparation of the construction schedule. The construction execution philosophy is actually the construction master plan. The plan lays down the basic ground rules for construction execution. It also answers such questions as: What is the construction scope? Will design be completed or concurrent? Who does procurement? Will we self-perform or subcontract construction? Each answer affects the selection of a suitable scheduling approach and format. Scheduling philosophy refers to the selection of the scheduling system. For example: Will we use bar charts or CPM? How often will the schedule be cycled? How many activities are there? Do we have trained people for that type of schedule? What are the contractual requirements for progress reporting? These questions must be decided along with the contracting basis prior to the first scheduling meeting. It's the CM's responsibility to establish those two philosophies and to get management approval on them. Changing either of the philosophies later can be very expensive and disruptive of the project work. As a major part of the project master plan, the construction schedule must also dovetail with the other major project activities such as design and procurement. The construction schedule should also reflect the start-up sequence of the various units making up the facility. Naturally, units that start up first must finish first. The reliability of the construction schedule is a function of the degree of design completion available when the schedule is made. That is no problem in the case where design is completed before bidding the construction. In other project execution modes, design should be 30 to 50 percent complete if a reliable operational construction schedule is to be prepared. On small projects, the construction milestone schedule may be the only one used. On larger projects, the construction schedule serves as the basis for making more detailed weekly work plans in the field for each major activity. In any case, the approved construction schedule is the fundamental working document used by the owner and the contractor to set the major milestones and monitor the actual construction progress.

(4) Project Scheduling Model

① Activities and Temporal Constraints

Let J be the given set of production orders or jobs $\ell = 1, \ldots, v$ for individual ingots. Each job ℓ consists of the four operations melting the ingredients in the potroom, changeover of the mould, casting the melt from the potroom into the casting unit, and cooling the ingot in die casting unit. For what follows we consider the execution of the jobs $\ell \in J$ as a project, where we associate the operations of jobs $\ell \in J$ with the n activities $A_1 \ldots, A_n$ of the project. We define the activities in such a way that during their execution they have constant requirements for the production facilities. Accordingly, the set of activities $\mathcal{A}$ consists of three subsets $\mathcal{A}_1$, $\mathcal{A}_2$ and $\mathcal{A}_3$ which for every job ℓ contain the three activities corresponding to the melting plus casting in a potroom, the exchange of the mould, and the casting plus cooling in a casting unit of the casting system (Figure 3-9). The dummy activities A_0 and A_{n+1} represent the start and the completion of the production. The duration of activity A_i is denoted by p_i, where $p_0 = p_{n+1} = 0$. The duration p_i of a changeover activity $A_i \in \mathcal{A}_2$ depends on the sequence in which the jobs are processed on the casting unit. If job ℓ and the job ℓ' preceding ℓ on the casting unit require different moulds, p_i equals the setup time S_ℓ for installing the mould belonging to ℓ. Otherwise, the mould need not be replaced, and p_i is equal to zero.

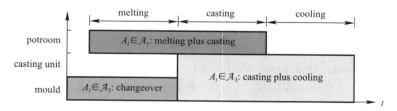

Figure 3-9   Activities A_i of the project

Since the jobs can be performed in alternative casting systems, we define a set M_i, of alternative execution modes m for each activity $A_i \in \mathcal{A}$ along with corresponding binary decision variables x_i^m, which are equal to 1 if activity A_i is executed in mode m and equal to zero otherwise. Vector $x = (x_i^m)_{A_i \in \mathcal{A}, m \in M_i}$ is referred to as a mode assignment. The mode-assignment constraints.

$$\sum_{m \in M_i} x_i^m = 1 (A_i \in \mathcal{A}) \qquad (3-1)$$

Say that each activity has to be carried out in exactly one mode. In addition, we have to ensure that all activities belonging to one and the same job ℓ are carried out in the same casting system. Let $\mathcal{A}^l \subseteq \mathcal{A}$ be the set of activities belonging to job ℓ. The condition is formulated as the mode-identity constraints:

$$\sum_{m \in M_i \cap M_j} x_i^m x_j^m = 1 \, (\ell \in J; A_i, A_j \in \mathcal{A}^\ell) \tag{3-2}$$

Note that in our case it holds that $M_i = M_j$ for all A_i, $A_j \in \mathcal{A}^\ell$ so that Formula (3-2) could also be written in the form $(x_i^m)_{m \in M_i} = (x_j^m)_{m \in M_j}$.

The following temporal constraints arise from technological requirements. Consider the melting plus casting activity the changeover activity A_h, and the casting plus cooling activity A_j of a job $\ell \in J$. By definition, activities A_h and A_j are pulled tight. Let C_ℓ denote the cooling time for job ℓ. Then we have a minimal time lag $\delta_{hj}^{\min} = p_h - p_j + C_\ell$ and an equally large maximal time lag $\delta_{hj}^{\min} = p_h - p_j + C_\ell$ between the starts of activities A_h and A_j. In addition, the mould has to be installed before the casting. This precedence relationship between activities A_i and A_j gives rise to the minimal time lag $\delta_{ij}^{\min} = p_i$. The conditions that no activity is started before the production start nor completed after the production end can be ensured by introducing the minimal time lags $\delta_{0h}^{\min} = \delta_{0i}^{\min} = 0$ and $\delta_{j(n+1)}^{\min} = p_j$.

The activity-On-Node network G depicted in Figure 3-10 illustrates the activities and prescribed time lags of the project. Each activity A_i is identified with a node of the network. Thus, the node set V of the network coincides with the set $\mathcal{A} \cup \{A_0, A_{n+1}\}$ of all real and dummy activities. For each minimal time lag $\delta_{ij}^{\min}$, network G contains an arc (A_i, A_j) with initial node A_i, terminal node A_j, and weight $\delta_{ij} = \delta_{ij}^{\min}$. A maximal time lag $\delta_{ij}^{\max}$ is represented as an arc (A_j, A_i) with initial node A_j, terminal node A_i, and weight $\delta_{ij} = -\delta_{ij}^{\max}$.

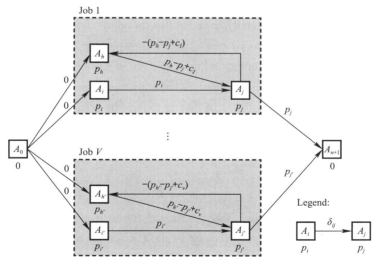

Figure 3-10   Activity-On-Node network G

Now let $S_i \geq 0$ denote the decision variable providing the start time of activity $A_i \in V$. A vector (S, x) with $S = (S_i)_{A_i \in V}$ is called a (production) schedule. By convention, we set $S_0 := 0$, and thus S_{n+1} equals the production makespan. We say that a schedule (S, x) is mode-feasible if mode assignment x satisfies the mode-assignment and mode-identity constraints (3-1) and (3-2). Schedule (S, x) is called time-feasible if S complies with the temporal constraints.

$$S_j - S_i \geqslant \delta_{ij}((A_i, A_j) \in E) \qquad (3-3)$$

where E is the arc set of network G. For $\delta_{ij} = p_i$, inequality. (3-3) is also called a precedence constraint. It is well-known that a time-feasible schedule exists if and only if G does not contain any cycle of positive length. In our case, the latter condition is always met because all cycles have length zero.

② Resource Constraints

In this section, we are concerned with the resource constraints of the production scheduling problem. Basically, all production facilities (potrooms, casting units and moulds) correspond to renewable resources. The set of renewable resources is denoted by $\mathcal{R}$ and B_k, stands for the capacity of renewable resource $R_k \in \mathcal{R}$.

An activity $A_i \in \mathcal{A}$ takes up b_{ij}^m units of resource $R_k \in \mathcal{R}$ if A_i is executed in mode $m \in M_i$. By $\mathcal{A}_k(x) := \{ A_i \in \mathcal{A} | \sum_{m \in M_i} b_{ik}^m x_i^m > 0 \}$ we denote the set of all activities being executed on resource R_k given mode assignment x. We call a schedule (S, x) capacity-feasible if for each renewable resource $R_k \in \mathcal{R}$, no more than B_k units of R_k are required simultaneously, i. e. ,

$$\sum_{\substack{A_i \in \mathcal{A}_k(x) : m \in M_i \\ S_i \leqslant t < S_i + p_i}} \sum b_{ik}^m x_i^m \leqslant B_k (R_k \in R; t \geqslant 0) \qquad (3-4)$$

In a potroom, only one alloy can be melted at a time. This condition can be taken into account by using the concept of batching machines and incompatible job families discussed in studies on machine scheduling. Let $\mathcal{R}^\beta \subseteq \mathcal{R}$ denote the set of batching machines and let φ_i designate the family of activity A_i. Family φ_i identifies the alloy and length of the ingot belonging to activity A_i. Recall that in a casting system, two melting plus casting activities A_i, $A_j \in \mathcal{A}_1$ can only be processed in parallel if the corresponding ingots are of the same alloy and length since the melt is cast in all casting units simultaneously. A batching machine has to be operated in such a way that the activities running in parallel must belong to the same family and must be started at the same time. Accordingly, a schedule (S, x) is called batching-feasible if

$$S_i = S_j \, and \, \varphi_i = \varphi_j (A_i, A_j \, with \, [S_i, S_i + p_i [\, \cap \, [S_j, S_j + p_j [\, \neq \phi \, and \, A_i A_j \in \mathcal{A}_k(x) \, for \, some \, R_k \in \mathcal{R}^\beta)$$

$$(3-5)$$

Each potroom is modeled as a batching machine $R_k \in \mathcal{R}^\beta$ whose capacity B_k equals the number of casting units belonging to the casting system. For the resource requirements we have $b_{ik}^m = 1$ if $A_i \in \mathcal{A}_1$ and if in mode m, activity A_i is executed in the potroom of resource R_k.

Next, we consider the changeover of the mould and the casting process. As previously stated in section 3. 1, the casting requires the mould of the desired cross-section to be installed on the casting unit. Obviously, it is not possible to use the installed mould for processing another ingot before the casting has been completed. To model the latter requirement, we introduce a set $\mathcal{R}^\alpha \subseteq \mathcal{R}$ of allocatable resources. The b_{ik}^m units of allocatable resource $R_k \in \mathcal{R}^\alpha$ processing an activity $A_i \in \mathcal{A}$ in mode $m \in M_i$ remain occupied from the start of a given allocating activity $A_{h(i)}$ up to the completion of activity A_i, where for simplicity we assume that $A_{h(i)} \notin \mathcal{A}_k(x)$.

A schedule (S, x) is called allocation-feasible if, at any point in time, no more than B_k units of a resource $R_k \in \mathcal{R}^{\alpha}$ are allocated, i. e. ,

$$\sum_{\substack{A_i \in \mathcal{A}_k(x): \\ S_{h(i)} \leqslant t < S_i + p_i}} \sum_{m \in M_i} b_{ik}^m x_i^m \leqslant B_k (R_k \in \mathcal{R}^{\alpha}; t \geqslant 0) \tag{3-6}$$

Moulds of the same type form an allocatable resource $R_k \in \mathcal{R}^{\alpha}$ with capacity B_k being equal to the number of moulds of that type. Each casting plus cooling activity A_i requires one unit of the allocatable resource $R_k \in \mathcal{R}^{\alpha}$ corresponding to the mould type needed, i. e. , $b_{ik}^m = 1$ for all $A_i \in \mathcal{A}_3$ and all $m \in M_i$, The mould is allocated to activity A_i at the start of the corresponding changeover activity $A_{h(i)} \in \mathcal{A}_2$.

We now turn to resources that have to be changed over between consecutive activities. Let $\mathcal{R}^{\gamma} \in \mathcal{R}$ denote the set of those changeover resources. Given a schedule (S, x), let A_i, $A_j \in \mathcal{A}_k(x)$ be two activities sharing some changeover resource $R_k \in \mathcal{R}^{\gamma}$, and let ϑ_{ij}^k denote the time needed for changing over a unit of resource R_k from A_i to A_j. ϑ_{ij}^k and $\vartheta_{i(n+1)}^k$ are the initial setup and terminal tear-down times for resource R_k. We assume that the changeover times satisfy the weak triangle inequalities:

$$\vartheta_{hi}^k + p_i + \vartheta_{ij}^k \geqslant \vartheta_{hj}^k [R_k \in \mathcal{R}^{\gamma}; A_h, A_i, A_j \in \mathcal{A}_k(x) \cup \{A_0, A_{n+1}\}] \tag{3-7}$$

Now consider the set:

$$P_k(S, x) = \{(A_i, A_j) \mid A_i \in \mathcal{A}_k(x) \cup \{A_0\}; A_j \in \mathcal{A}_k(x) \cup \{A_{n+1}\}; S_j \geqslant S_i + p_i + \vartheta_{ij}^k\} \tag{3-8}$$

of all pairs (A_i, A_j) for which the time span between the completion of activity A_i and the start of activity A_j is sufficiently long for a changeover on R_k. Let f_{ij}^k for $(A_i, A_j) \in P_k(S, x)$ denote the decision variable which is equal to 1 precisely if A_i and A_j are to be processed consecutively on some unit of resource R_k, and equal to zero, otherwise. $f_{ij}^k = 1$ causes a changeover time of ϑ_{ij}^k time units between the completion of A_i and the start of A_j. There exists a feasible assignment of the activities $A_i \in \mathcal{A}_k(x)$ to the individual units of resource R_k observing the changeover times if and only if first,

$$\sum_{(A_j, A_i) \in P_k(S, x)} f_{ji}^k = \sum_{(A_i, A_j) \in P_k(S, x)} f_{ij}^k = 1 [R^k \in \mathcal{R}^{\gamma}; A_i \in \mathcal{A}_k(x)] \tag{3-9}$$

and second,

$$\varphi_k(S, x) := \sum_{(A_0, A_j) \in P_k(S, x)} f_{0j}^k \leqslant B_k \in (R_k \in \mathcal{R}^{\gamma}) \tag{3-10}$$

It is shown that the problem of minimizing $\varphi_k(S, x)$ subject to equations $(3-9)$ represents a minimum-flow problem in the precedence graph of strict order $P_k(S, x)$.

We call a schedule (S, x) changeover-feasible if for all $R_k \in \mathcal{R}^{\gamma}$ there exist flows $f^k = (f_{ij}^k)_{(i,j) \in P_k(S, x)}$ satisfying conditions $(3-9)$ and $(3-10)$.

We associate each group of casting units belonging to one casting system with a changeover resource $R_k \in \mathcal{R}^{\gamma}$ whose capacity B_k equals the number of casting units in the system. If casting plus cooling activity A_i is executed in the mode $m \in M_i$ belonging to the casting system of resource

R_k, A_i requires one unit of resource R_k, i. e. , $b_{ik}^m = 1$. If jobs ℓ and ℓ' use the different mould types, the changeover time between the respective casting plus cooling activities A_i, $A_j \in \mathcal{A}_3$ on R_k is equal to the time needed for installing the mould for job ℓ' i. e. , $\vartheta_{ij}^k = s_{\ell'}$. Otherwise, the changeover time is equal to zero. The duration of the corresponding changeover operation $A_h \in \mathcal{A}_2$ of job ℓ' is $p_h = \vartheta_{ij}^k$.

The last resource constraint to be modeled emanates from the technological requirements that, first, only one of the casting units belonging to a casting system can be changed over at a time and, second, a mould cannot be installed into any casting unit during casting or cooling. These conditions are modeled by defining an extra renewable resource $R_k \in \mathcal{R}$ for each casting system, where again capacity B_k is chosen to be equal to the number of casting units of the casting system. Resource R_k is taken up by the changeover and casting plus cooling activities A_i and A_j of those jobs ℓ which in mode assignment x are performed on the casting system associated with R_k. We set $b_{ik}^m = B_k$ and $b_{jk}^m = 1$, where m is the mode corresponding to the respective casting system. Then constraints (3-4) ensure that no two casting units can be changed over in parallel and that up to B_k casting plus cooling operations A_j can be processed simultaneously, but no operation can be processed while one of the units is changed over.

3.5　Reading Material

The New Production Model

Although construction projects are typically one of a kind, similar construction operations are repeated on many projects. Most any building project and many heavy civil projects have concrete work. Most heavy civil projects have a significant portion of earthwork, as does any new building project. It is important to plan efficient field operations. Though each field operation can be studied individually as the project moves forward, many efficiencies with broader impact can be incorporated into the initial production planning process. For example, opportunities may be found for prefabrication, which can lead to efficiency through assembly-line techniques. On the highway bridge, it is determined that the abutment forms could be prefabricated and brought to the site ready for installation. In building construction where there is a great deal of repetition in projects such as office buildings, hotels, and multistory residential facilities, there are significant opportunities for prefabrication, resulting in field assembly of components rather than "stick building". In addition to saving time, prefabrication can often result in safer field operations with higher quality and lower costs.

Fundamental to planning efficient production methods is simplifying each step of the process. This starts with simplifying the drawings. Construction plans have traditionally been terse and diagrammatic. Dimensions are given once. Typical details are drawn with exceptions shown in a schedule or table. High rates of production require that the details be spelled out for each step of the work. Rather than have craftspeople search through the drawings for the location of inserts, weld plates, and dimensions, this information is typically shown on a shop drawing.

Significant changes are occurring to traditional construction drawings with the advent of

Building Information Modeling (BIM). Instead of paper drawings, the design of most projects has moved to digital models based on advanced versions of Computer-Aided Design (CAD) software. Currently, even though the design is in a digital format, the final product of the design is often still printed. But there is a growing trend toward digital-only documents. BIM has expanded the traditional two-dimensional CAD computer model to three dimensions, enabling the project to be rotated and moved so that it can be viewed from any point, internal or external. BIM then adds the fourth dimension of time so that sequencing of the construction operations can be studied and the schedule can be incorporated into the BIM model. Finally, BIM has the capability of adding what some refer to as the fifth dimension, the verbal definition of installed items. This includes specifications and other pertinent information, such as installation guidelines and production costs. BIM is taking on the role of becoming a repository for all information about the project from all stakeholders in a single large digital model.

Because of the integrated nature of the BIM model bringing together information from many sources into a single model, it is changing the very nature of the relationships among participants in a construction project. Traditionally, the architect-engineer provided the design for a project and retained the intellectual property rights to the design. The general contractor and various specialty contractors provided information on cost and schedule and protected proprietary information, especially related to costs. In a BIM environment, all of this information from the various participants in the project is being entered into the single BIM model, so information is shared. Even more significant, risk is shared. In this highly interrelated environment, a new contractual basis is required, leading to the emergence of a project delivery system that has become known as Integrated Project Delivery (IPD).

As BIM becomes more prevalent, it will change the way project managers and field supervisors do their jobs. Installation details that were accessed on shop drawings will be accessed on tablet computers and even smartphones. Planning and updating can be extended literally until the point of installation and adjusted based on real-time field conditions. This means the balance of responsibilities between the project manager and the field supervisor will evolve with more, higher-level decisions being made in real time in the field. Meanwhile, while project managers are delegating more decisions to the field, they are also working much more closely with the other stakeholders in the project through the shared risk and reward of the IPD contract.

Chapter 4
Modern Evaluation Technique of Project Management

4. 1　Project Management and Evaluation

1. Introduction

The goal of project management is to deliver a result that meets an agreed schedule, budget, and level of quality. There are many methodologies or frameworks proposed to underpin project performance, such as the following well-known frameworks:

4. 1 Professional Terms, Words and Phrases, Sentence Illustration

- Critical Chain Project Management (CCPM).
- Extreme Project Management (XPM)/mega project.
- Lean Project Management.
- Projects in Controlled Environments (PRINCE2).
- Project Management Body of Knowledge (PMBOK).
- Scrum.
- Waterfall or Stage Gate.

Many firms utilize the stage-gate process as their project management framework. The stage-gate process is a decision-driven methodology for managing a project throughout its life cycle. Each stage represents a series of activities to increase the level project definition, ending with a gate where the work completed during the stage is reviewed against predetermined criteria. The gates are formal decision points to allow management to review the project and decide if it should proceed to the next development phase, recycle the work, or be canceled.

There is no set rule as to the number of stages; however, a standard process usually has no more than six. The steps for a typical four-stage process are as follows:

(1) Feasibility study to first assess a project's economic, operational, and technical feasibility, then to evaluate as a wide number of realistic concept options as possible, and then to select the best concept.

(2) Concept selection [pre-front-end engineering design (pre-FEED)] to further develop the selected concept and make it ready to start engineering definition.

(3) Engineering definition [front-end engineering design (FEED)] to fully define the selected concept so that it is absolutely clear what the project is and how it will be executed, as well as the detailed cost and schedule.

(4) Execution or implementation, handover, and completion (IHC) to execute the project as defined, with tight project controls in order to achieve the final investment decision

commitments made in Stage 3.

Each project stage requires the completion of various deliverables that collectively reflect project maturity from initiation to completion. At each gate, the relevant authority decides if the project has completed all of the deliverables required to proceed to the next stage, if the project is still aligned with business objectives, and if risks to delivery are being properly managed. If so, then approval to proceed to the next phase if given; if not, the project is either recycled for further definition or terminated.

However, many times in the early phases of project development, critical issues are not properly addressed, such as clarity regarding roles and responsibilities, alignment of goals and objectives, and clearly defined requirements. Addressing these issues can create conflict, so they are ignored to avoid any interference with meeting gate approval timing, with the assumption that gaps will be addressed in the next stage. Unfortunately, "kicking the can down the road" tends to make things worse as the project proceeds through the development process.

The Project Management Institute (PMI) formally defines project management as follows: "The application of knowledge, skills, tools and techniques to project activities to meet the project requirements." Even though that definition is open to broad interpretation, its detail is not full. Project Management is an organized common-sense approach that utilizes the appropriate client involvement in order to meet sponsor needs and deliver the expected incremental business value.

This definition is a marked change from any readers may have seen before. First, it is the only definition that explicitly refers to business value. Business value is the responsibility of the client through their requirements statements. The project manager is responsible for meeting those requirements. Meeting requirements is the cause and incremental business value is the effect. Second, and equally important in the definition through the common-sense term is the implication that effective project management is not a "one size fits all" approach. Because it is a "common-sense approach", it must adapt to the changing project conditions. Third, it is essential that you clearly understand requirements. Requirements and their documentation will establish the project characteristics and be your guide to choosing and adapting the project-management approach you will be using.

2. Model

Choosing and adapting the best-fit PMLC model is a subjective decision based on several variables. Figure 4-1 is a display of the decision process.

Although anyone may have easily arrived at a best-fit approach and best-fit PMLC model based on the confidence you have with the RBS and the degree of completeness of the WBS, there is more work to be done before you can proceed with the project. First you have to assess the impact; Second, you have to make the necessary adjustments to the chosen PMLC model to account for that impact. The factors discussed here are those that might affect, and even change one's choice of the best-fit PMLC model.

(1) Total Cost

As the total cost of the project increases, so does its business value and so does its risk.

Whatever PMLC model you have chosen, you might want to place more emphasis on the risk management plan than is called for in the chosen model. If one of the team members isn't already responsible for managing risk, appoint someone. Losses are positively correlated with the total cost, so you should be able to justify spending more on your mitigation efforts than you would for a project of lesser cost.

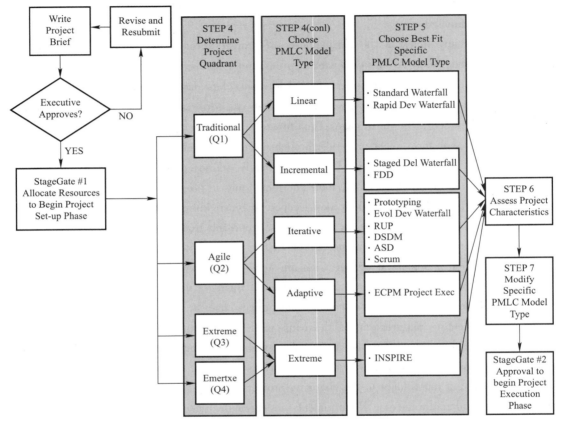

Figure 4-1　PMLC model choice process

(2) Duration

A longer duration project brings with it a higher likelihood of change, staff turnover, and project priority adjustments. None of these are for the good of the project. Make sure the client understands the implications of the Scope Bank and how to manage their own scope change requests. Staff turnover can be very problematic. Put more emphasis on the mitigation plans for dealing with staff turnover. Project priority changes are beyond one's control. That needs to be on an aggressive schedule to the extent possible.

(3) Market Stability

Any venture into a volatile market is going to be risky. One could postpone the project until the market stabilizes, or one could go forward but with some caution. One way to protect the project would be to implement deliverables incrementally. A time-box comprising shorter increments than originally planned might make sense, too. As each increment is implemented, revisit the decision to continue or postpone the project.

(4) Technology

Technology is changing at an increasing rate. It is not only difficult to keep up with it, but it is difficult to leverage it to your best advantage. If the current technology works, stick with it. If the new technology will leverage you in the market, you might want to wait but make sure you can integrate it when it is available. Don't forget that the competition will be doing the same, so rapid response is to one's advantage.

(5) Business Climate

The more volatile the business climate, the shorter the total project duration should be. For APM projects, the cycle time-boxes could also be shorter than typically planned. Partial solution releases will have a higher priority than they would in business climates that are more stable.

Review Questions and Problems:

1. What is the project management?

2. Please give some recommendations about project evaluation.

4.2   Resource Management

4.2 Professional Terms, Words and Phrases, Sentence Illustration

1. Introduction

Grid resource management controls how to provide the available capacity of resources and services in a grid system for other entities including users, applications, services, middleware, etc. In a service-oriented manufacturing grid (MGrid) architecture, resources can no longer be narrowly understood as physical entities, rather they refer to any manufacturing capabilities which can be shared and used in a networked manufacturing environment, including computational resources, equipment resources, human resources, public service resources, material resources, user information resources, application system resources, technical resources, and so forth.

MGrid resource service management allocates the submitted manufacturing tasks or resource service requests to appropriate resources within the shortest amount of time and with the highest benefit to both resource provider and demander. It achieves this by searching the qualified resource service in MGrid according to a user's QoS requirement, and realizing the mapping from QoS requirements to resource capabilities. Therefore, an effective QoS management is especially important to resource management and resource optimal allocation. Regardless of the context, QoS management should address the following needs:

(1) Specifying QoS managements.

(2) Mapping QoS requirements to resource capabilities.

(3) Negotiating QoS with resource owners.

(4) Reserving and allocating resources.

(5) Monitoring parameters associated with QoS.

(6) Adapting to varying resource quality characteristics.

2. Models

In order to illustrate how the previous work can be used in MGrid resource service management, an MGrid-Ontology based resource service discovery is put forward as shown in Figure 4-2. Its brief work flow is described below.

(1) Service Publication

Step 1: The RSP (Resource Service Provider) publish their resource services to MGrid through corresponding user interface.

Step 2: Published resource services with OWL-S interfaces are then loaded into MGRSR (MGrid Resource Service Repository), in which the elements of resource service such as the service name, service description, service contact, and properties are registered with MGRSR.

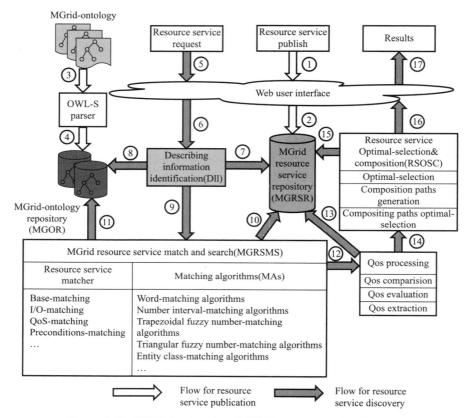

Figure 4-2   MGrid-Ontology based MGrid resource service discovery

Step 3: While publishing the resource service, the RSP may also publish resource service ontology which can be defined in OWL-S.

Step 4: The ontology is parsed by an OWL-S parser and loaded into the MGrid-Ontology Repository (MGOR). The MGOR is used by a reference engine to refer the semantic relationships of describing information when search and match service and query.

(2) Service Discovery

Step 5: The RSD (Resource Service Demander) submit their resource service requirements to MGrid through corresponding user interface. The requirements are formatted into expected resource service describing information and properties.

Step 6: The requirements are then forwarded to the DII (Describing Information Identification).

Step 7-8: DII accesses the MGRSR to identify and mark the properties of available resource services in MGRSR that are irrelevant to the properties used in the service requirements based on the MGrid-Ontology defined in MGOR.

Step 9: The requirements are then forwarded to MGRSMS (MGrid Resource Service Match and Search).

Step 10~11: MGRSMS invokes its interior components RS-Matcher (i. e. Resource Service Matcher) and MAs (i. e. Matching Algorithms), which access MGRSR to calculate the similarity of requested services and available resource services in MGRSR based on the MGrid-Ontology defined in MGOR.

Step 12: After Step 10~11, RSD's requirements are matched with their functional aspect. But the quality of the discovered resource service is out of consideration. In addition, the discovered resource service qualified for RSD's functional requirements may be far more than one. How to select the optimal one is another issue that has to be addressed during resource service scheduling. Hence, MGRSMS forwards its results to the component QoS processing, which in turn filters functionally matched resource services with nonfunctional aspect (i. e. QoS) after QoS processing, including QoS extraction, QoS evaluation, QoS comparison and so on.

Step 13: QoS processing accesses MGRSR and extracts related QoS information of the discovered resource services by invoking interior components QoS extraction, then evaluates and compares extracted QoS properties by invoking internal services QoS evaluation and QoS comparison.

Step 14: A list of discovered resource services that are marked with their non-functionally matched degree is forwarded to RSOSC (Resource Service Optimal-Selection and Composition).

Step 15: In an MGrid system, the requirements (or resource service request) of RSD can be classified into two kinds: ① Single Resource Service Request Task (SRSR Task), which can be completed by invoking only one resource service, and ② Multi-Resource Services Request Task (MRSR Task), which is completed by invoking several resource services in a certain sequence. For an SRSR Task, the system searches out the resource services that qualified for its function requirements and selects the optimal one to execute. For an MRSR Task, in addition to the search for all qualified resource services according to each subtask, the system has to select one candidate resource service for each subtask and generate a new Composite Resource Service (CRS); the system then has to select the optimal resource service composite path from all possible paths to execute the task with the given multi-objective and multiconstraint. Therefore, RSOSC is designed to address the above issues.

Step 16~17: The final results are then presented to the user via the corresponding web user interface of MGrid.

Review Questions and Problems:

What are the benefits of Grid resource management? how it can be applied in constructing project management?

4.3 Risk Management

A risk is something that might happen in the future and which may threaten success. The sooner a potential risk is identified, the sooner the unexpected of action can be determined to remove or at least minimize it. A risk is assessed on:

- the probability of something happening.
- the impact it would have.
- the action necessary to avoid it.

4.3 Professional Terms, Words and Phrases, Sentence Illustration

When it comes to form ideas about how to tackle the project, do a risk analysis to anticipate any future problems. The first stage of a risk analysis is to identify the kind of risks one may face. Often the best way to do this is to involve all members of the project team in a risk assessment workshop, taking each of the areas in the table below as your agenda. Try to be as thorough as possible when brainstorming, it can be very easy to overlook potential threats. Anyone may come across the following types of risk (Table 4−1):

Types of risks   Table 4−1

Risk	What is it?	Questions to ask
Reputational (your brand)	This occurs when a company's image is tarnished by an unpopular action	• Will it harm perception of your company if you carry out this project (e.g. by your customers/shareholders)? • Does it fit with products/services you already provide?
Operational	This arises if the project requires processes that your business can't support, or it is designed incorrectly through lack of expertise.	• Will any processes incur increased volumes of work or business? If so, can your company cope? • Have new systems been designed for and communicated to the right areas and people? • Might you have to reorganize any area or department of your company?
Political	These might include changes in tax laws, public opinion, government policy or foreign influence.	• How likely are any of these possibilities? • Would any of them significantly affect the success of your project (e.g. if a foreign exchange rate rose or fell dramatically)?
"Acts of God"	These encompass natural/external events, such as floods, storms, diseases and so on.	• Would your project be adversely affected by any of these (e.g. if it involves building work)? • If so, would changing the timing of the project make a difference (e.g. summer rather than winter)?
People	This could include changes to working conditions or the need to employ new/extra staff.	• Will employees accept changes to working conditions? • If you need extra staff, can the skills easily be found, and can you afford them? • How would you manage if a key person leaves or is ill?

continued

Risk	What is it?	Questions to ask
Premises and business continuity	if the project causes a problem with your premises, people or systems, this might threaten your company's whole business.	• Can you operate the project in your existing premises/locations? • If operating the project breaks a key system or process, will this cause your company to cease business (temporarily or permanently)?
Technical	Risks might include advances in technology, technical failure, etc.	• Does the technology you're intending to use fit with what you have already? • Are any new systems sufficiently flexible/scalable?
Financial	Areas indude business failure, stock market, unemployment, etc.	• Could any of these spell disaster for your project? • Who would be affected?

Risk, in general terms, can be viewed as the implications of an activity, along with its associated uncertainties on an outcome. PMI (Project Management Institute) has defined risk as "an uncertain event or condition that, if it occurs, has a positive or negative effect on a project's objectives". PMI has separated project risk into two categories: individual project risk and overall project risk. Individual risks tend to be those managed on a day-to-day basis and may not have a direct impact on the project cost, schedule, scope, and/or quality. Some examples of individual risks would be a delay in material arrival to a job site, weld rejection rate, productivity of labor, etc. Overall project risk is the aggregate effect of uncertainty on the project as a whole and deals with the broader project environment, such as labor action, social unrest, commodity price fluctuation, etc. Consequently, risk should be regarded as a persistent presence for the duration of any activity. The SRA has defined risk management as "activities to handle risk such as prevention, mitigation, adaptation or sharing" that "often include trade-offs between costs and benefits of risk reduction and choice of a level of tolerable risk". To accomplish this, a cyclic process with the following steps is used:

(1) Identify risks.

(2) Assess and prioritize risks.

(3) Group risks by risk breakdown structure (RBS) category.

(4) Identify leading and lagging indicators and risk responses.

(5) Monitor, close out, and adjust as required.

Project risk has been studied through many lenses, such as Bayesian methods, systems dynamics, neural networks, fuzzy logic, and the analytical hierarchy process. However, these approaches have assumptions that are limiting. For instance, the analytical hierarchy process assumes that the risks act in isolation, and Bayesian methods do not consider closed-loop systems. Although project risk management has been recognized as an integral part of project management for decades and has experienced many analytical advances, many projects still do not meet their objectives. This performance gap has been attributed to an overemphasis on techniques rather than effective identification and assessment of risks, as well as utilizing approaches that are steeped in linear sequential thinking.

4.4 Market and Business Process Management

1. Business Process Management

4.4 Professional Terms, Words and Phrases, Sentence Illustration

Googling the term "Business Process Management" in May 2008 yields some 6.4 million hits, the great majority of which (based on sampling) seem to concern the so-called BPM software systems. This is ironic and unfortunate, because in fact IT in general, and such BPM systems in particular, is at most a peripheral aspect of Business Process Management. In fact, Business Process Management (BPM) is a comprehensive system for managing and transforming organizational operations, based on what is arguably the first set of new ideas about organizational performance since the Industrial Revolution.

BPM has two primary intellectual antecedents. The first is the work of Shewhart and Deming on statistical process control, which led to the modern quality movement and its contemporary avatar, Six Sigma. This work sought to reduce variation in the performance of work by carefully measuring outcomes and using statistical techniques to isolate the "root causes" of performance problems-causes that could then be addressed. Much more important than the details of upper and lower control limits or the myriad of other analytic tools that are part of quality's armamentarium are the conceptual principles that underlie this work: the core assumption that operations are of critical importance and deserve serious attention and management; the use of performance metrics to determine whether work is being performed satisfactorily or not; the focus on hard data rather than opinion to isolate the root causes of performance difficulties; the concept of blaming the process not the people, that performance shortcomings are rooted in objective problems that can be identified and dealt with; and the notion of never-ending improvement, that solving one set of problems merely buys an organization a ticket to solve the next round.

The other primary antecedent of BPM, my own work on Business Process Reengineering, had complementary strengths and weaknesses. On the one hand, at least in its early days, reengineering was positioned as an episodic rather than an ongoing effort; it lacked the continuous dimension of quality improvement. It also did not have as disciplined anapproach to metrics. On the other hand, it brought two new wrinkles to the process world. The first was its refined definition of process: end-to-end work across an enterprise that creates customer value. Here, putting a box on a shelf would not qualify as a meaningful process; it would merely be a small part of an enterprise process such as order fulfillment or procurement. Addressing large-scale, truly end-to-end processes means focusing on high-leverage aspects of the organization's operations and so leads to far greater results and impacts. In particular, by dealing with processes that cross functional boundaries, reengineering was able to attack the evils of fragmentation: the delays, nonvalue-adding overhead, errors, and complexity that inevitably result when work transcends different organizations that have different priorities, different information sources, and different metrics. The other new theme introduced by reengineering was a focus on process design as opposed to process execution. The design of a process, the way in which its constituent tasks are woven together into a whole, was not of much concern to the founders of the quality school; they made a tacit assumption that process designs were sound, and that performance difficulties resulted from defects in execution. Reengineering recognized that the design of a process in fact created an envelope for its performance, that a process could not perform on a sustained basis better than its design would allow. Should performance requirements exceed what the design was capable of, the old design would have to be discarded and a new one substituted in its place.

2. Process Management Cycle

Over the last decade, these two approaches to process performance improvement have gradually merged, yielding modern Business Process Management—an integrated system for managing business performance by managing end-to-end business processes. Figure 4-3 depicts the essential process management cycle. It begins at the bottom, with the creation of a formal process. This is not a minor, purely formal step. Many organizations find that certain aspects of their operations are characterized by wild variation, because they lack any well-defined end-to-end process whatsoever. This is particularly true of low-volume, creative processes such as product development or customer relationship management. In essence, they treat each situation as a one-off, with heroics and improvisation substituting for the discipline of a well-defined process. Such heroics are of course unreliable and unsustainable.

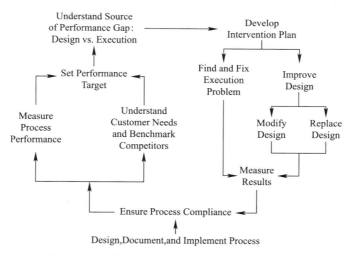

Figure 4-3   The essential process management cycle

Once a process is in place, it needs to be managed on an ongoing basis. Its performance, in terms of critical metrics that relate to customer needs and company requirements, needs to be compared to the targets for these metrics. Such targets can be based on customer expectations, competitor benchmarks, enterprise needs, and other sources. If performance does not meet targets, the reason for this shortcoming must be determined. Broadly speaking, processes fail to meet performance requirements either because of faulty design or faulty execution; which one is the culprit can generally be determined by examining the pattern of performance inadequacy. Pervasive performance shortcomings generally indicate a design flaw; occasional ones are usually the result of execution difficulties. If the fault lies in execution, then the particular root cause (such as inadequate training, or insufficient resources, or faulty equipment, or any of a host of other possibilities) must be determined. Doing so is a challenging undertaking, because of the large number of possible root causes; as a rule, however, once the root cause has been found, it is easy to fix. The opposite is true of design problems: they are easy to find (being indicated by consistently inadequate performance) but hard to fix (requiring a wholesale rethinking of the structure of the process). Once the appropriate intervention has been chosen and implemented, the results are assessed, and the entire cycle begins again.

This cycle is derived from Deming's PDCA (Plan Do Check Act) cycle (Deming 1986), with the addition of the attention to process design. Although this picture is quite simple, it represents a revolutionary departure for how enterprises are managed. It is based on the premise that the way to manage an organization's performance is not by trial and error, not by pushing people harder, and not through financial manipulation, but through the deliberate management of the end-to-end business processes through which all customer value is created. Indeed, BPM is a customer-centered approach to organizational management. Customers neither know nor care about the many issues that typically are at the center of most executives' attention: strategies, organizational designs, capital structures, succession plans, and all the rest. Customers care about one thing and one thing only: results. Such results are not acts of God or the consequence of managerial genius; they are the outputs of business processes, of sequences of activities working together. Customers, results, and processes form an iron triangle; an organization cannot be serious about anyone without being equally serious about the other two.

3. Payoffs of Process Management

Through process management, an enterprise can create high-performance processes, which operate with much lower costs, faster speeds, greater accuracy, reduced assets, and enhanced flexibility. By focusing on and designing end-to-end processes that transcend organizational boundaries, companies can drive out the nonvalue adding overhead that accumulates at these boundaries. Through process management, an enterprise can assure that its processes deliver on their promise and operate consistently at the level of which they are capable. Through process management, an enterprise can determine when a process no longer meets its needs and those of its customers and so needs to be replaced.

These operational benefits of consistency, cost, speed, quality, and service translate into lower operating costs and improved customer satisfaction, which in turn drive improved enterprise performance. Process management also offers a variety of strategic benefits. For one, process management enables companies to respond better to periods of rapid change (such as ours). Conventional organizations often do not even recognize that change is happening until it is reflected in financial performance, by which time it is too late; even should they recognize that change has occurred, they have no mechanism for responding to it in a disciplined fashion. Under a process management regime, by contrast, change is reflected in the decline of operational performance metrics, which are noted by the process management system; the design of the process is then the tool through which the organization can respond to this change. Process management also provides an umbrella for a wide range of other performance improvement initiatives, from globalization and merger integration to ERP implementation and e-business. Too many enterprises treat each of these phenomena as independent, which leads to a proliferation of uncoordinated and conflicting change initiatives. In fact, they are all either mechanisms for supporting high-performance processes or goals that can be achieved through them. Linking all of a company's improvement efforts under the common umbrella of process management, and managing them in an integrated fashion, leverages a wide range of tools and deploys the right tool to the right problem.

4. Enablers of Process

Despite its elegance and power, many organizations have experienced difficulties implementing processes and process management. For instance, an electronics company designed a new product development process that was based on crossfunctional product teams, but they were unable to successfully install it and get it operating. The reason, as they put it, is that "you can't overlay high performance processes on a functional organization". Traditional organizations and their systems are unfriendly to processes, and unless these are realigned to support processes, the effort will fail.

There are five critical enablers for a high-performance process; without them, a process will be unable to operate on a sustained basis.

(1) Process Design

This is the most fundamental aspect of a process: the specification of what tasks are to be performed, by whom, when, in what locations, under what circumstances, to what degree of precision, with what information, and the like. The design is the specification of the process; without a design, there is only uncoordinated individual activity and organizational chaos.

(2) Process Metrics

Most enterprises use functional performance metrics, which create misalignment, suboptimization, and confusion. Processes need end-to-end metrics that are derived from customer needs and enterprise goals. Targets need to be set in terms of these metrics and performance monitored against them. A balanced set of process metrics (such as cost, speed, and quality) must be deployed, so that improvements in one area do not mask declines in another.

(3) Process Performers

People who work in processes need a different set of skills and behaviors from those who work in conventional functions and departments. They need an understanding of the overall process and its goals, the ability to work in teams, and the capacity to manage themselves. Without these characteristics, they will be unable to realize the potential of end-to-end work.

(4) Process Infrastructure

Performers need to be supported by IT and HR systems if they are to discharge process responsibilities. Functionally fragmented information systems do not support integrated processes, and conventional HR systems (training, compensation, and career, etc.) reinforce fragmented job perspectives. Integrated systems (such as ERP systems and results-based compensation systems) are needed for integrated processes.

(5) Process Owner

In a conventional organization, no one is responsible for an end-to-end process, and so no one will be in a position to manage it on an end-to-end basis (i. e. carry out the process management cycle). An organization serious about its processes must have process owners: senior managers with authority and responsibility for a process across the organization as a whole.

Having some but not all of these enablers for a process is of little or no value. For instance, a well-designed process targeted at the right metrics will not succeed if performers are not capable of carrying it out or if the systems do not support them in doing so. Implementing a process in effect means putting in place these five enablers. Without them, a process may be able to operate successfully for a short term but will certainly fail in the long run.

5. BPM Capability for Process

The experiences of hundreds of companies show that not all are equally able to install these enablers and so succeed with processes and process management. Some do so effectively, while others do not. The root cause of this discrepancy lies in whether or not an enterprise possesses four critical capabilities that are prerequisites to its summoning the resources, determination, and skills needed to succeed with processes.

(1) Leadership

The absolute sine qua non for effective deployment of process management is engaged, knowledgeable, and passionate senior executive leadership of the effort. Introducing processes means introducing enormous change-realigning systems, authority, modes of operation, and more. There is no change that most organizations have experienced that can compare to the disruption that the transition to process brings. Unless a very senior executive makes it his or her personal mission, process will run aground on the shoals of inertia and resistance. Moreover, only a topmost executive can authorize the significant resources and changes that process implementation requires. Without such leadership, the effort is doomed; with it, all other problems can be overcome.

(2) Culture

A Chief Operating Officer once remarked to me, "When one of my people says he doesn't like process, he really means that he doesn't want to share power". Process, with its focus on customers, outcomes, and transcending boundaries is anathema to those who are focused on defending their narrow bit of turf. Process demands that people at all levels of the organization put the customer first, be comfortable working in teams, accept personal responsibility for outcomes, and be willing to accept change. Unless the organization's culture values these principles, processes will just roll off people's backs. If the enterprise culture is not aligned with these values, leadership must change the culture so that it does.

（3）Governance

Moving to process management, and institutionalizing it over the long run, requires a set of governance mechanisms that assign appropriate responsibilities and ensure that processes integrate with one another (and do not turn into a new generation of horizontal silos). In addition to process owners, enterprises need a process office (headed by a Chief Process Officer) that plans and oversees the program as a whole and coordinates process efforts, as well as a Process Council. This is a body consisting of the process owners, the executive leader, and other senior managers, which serves as a strategic oversight body, setting direction and priorities, addressing cross-process issues, and translating enterprise concerns into process issues. These mechanisms need to be put in place to manage the transition to process, but continue on as the essential management superstructure for a process-managed enterprise.

（4）Expertise

Implementing and managing processes is a complex and high stakes endeavor, not for the inexperienced or the amateur. Companies need cadres of people with deep expertise in process design and implementation, metrics, change management, program management, process improvement, and other relevant techniques. These people must have formal methodologies to follow and must be sustained with appropriate career paths and management support. While not an insuperable barrier, many organizations fail to develop and institutionalize this capability, and then unsurprisingly find themselves unable to carry out their ambitious programs.

Organizations without these four capabilities will be unable to make process management work, and must undertake urgent efforts to put them in place. Developing leadership is the most challenging of these; it typically requires the intervention of a catalyst, a passionate advocate of process with the ear of a potential leader, who must patiently familiarize the candidate with the concepts of process and their payoffs. Reshaping culture is not, despite myths to the contrary, impossible, but it does take time and energy. The other two are less difficult, but are often overlooked.

6. Principles of Process Management

It can be helpful to summarize the concepts of process management in terms of a handful of axiomatic principles, some obvious, some not, that together express its key themes.

（1）All work is process work. Sometimes the assumption is made that the concepts of process and process management only apply to highly structured, transactional work, such as order fulfillment, procurement, customer service, and the like. Nothing could be further from the truth. The virtues of process also adhere to developmental processes, which center on highly creative tasks, such as product development, demand creation, and so on. Process should not be misinterpreted as a synonym for routinization or automation, reducing creative work to simplistic procedures. Process means positioning individual work activities—routine or creative—in the larger context of the other activities with which it combines to create results. Both transactional and development processes are what is known as core processes—processes that create value for external customers and so are essential to the business. Organizations also have enabling (or support) processes, which create value for internal customers; these include hire to retire, information systems development, and financial reporting. Such processes have customers and create value for them (as must any process, by definition), but those customers are internal. The third category is governing processes, the management processes by means of which the company is run (such as strategic planning, risk management, and performance management). (Process management is itself a governing process!) All processes need to be managed as such and so benefit from the power of process management.

(2) Any process is better than no process. Absent a well-defined process design, chaos reigns. Individual heroics, capriciousness, and improvisation rule the day, and results are inconsistent and unsustainable. A well-defined process will at the least deliver predictable, repeatable results, and can serve as the staging ground for improvement.

(3) A good process is better than a bad process. This statement is not as tautological as it seems. It expresses the criticality of process design, that the caliber of a process design is a critical determinant of its performance, and that some processes are better designed than others. If a company is burdened with a bad process design, it needs to replace it with a better one.

(4) One process version is better than many. Standardizing processes across all parts of an enterprise presents a single face to customers and suppliers, yields profound economies in support services such as training and IT systems, allows the redeployment of people from one business unit to another, and yields a host of other benefits. These payoffs must be balanced against the intrinsically different needs of different units and their customers, but our bias should be in favor of standardization.

Even a good process must be performed effectively. A good process design is a necessary but insufficient prerequisite for high performance; it needs to be combined with carefully managed execution, so that the capabilities of the design are realized in practice.

(5) Even a good process can be made better. The process owner needs to stay constantly vigilant, looking for opportunities to make modifications to the process design in order to further enhance its performance. Every good process eventually becomes a bad process. No process stays effective forever in the face of change. Customer needs change, technologies change, competition changes, and what used to be a high level of performance becomes a poor one, and it is time to replace the formerly good process with a new one.

7. Methods and Tools

Depending on project type and specific requirements, there are different procedures how to use the SAP Business Process Management Methodology. Usually process optimization projects following the generic SAP BPM methodology can be split into following four phases: calibration, as-is analysis, to-be process design, and solution transformation. These phases are integrated into the overall SAP implementation method ASAP 7.0. Result of those phases is a Business Blueprint. This generic procedure is typically used in such projects, when neither a corporate process governance nor a process understanding is available (Figure 4-4).

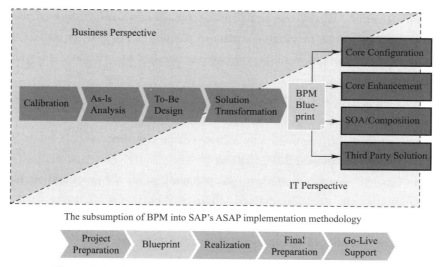

The subsumption of BPM into SAP's ASAP implementation methodology

Figure 4-4   Generic SAP business process management methodology

The phases in detail:

(1) The purpose of the calibration phase is to identify the business processes that are to be examined in detail. It features a comprehensive overview of the company's process landscape and the business success factors derived from the corporate strategy. On the basis of this information, criteria for evaluating business processes are defined and each process is assessed. The outcome of this phase is a prioritization of the processes to be analyzed.

(2) The overall goal of the as-is analysis is to understand business reality and its weaknesses, and develop solution ideas in order to finally define optimized to be processes. Understanding the business reality is a precondition for the later process optimization. The first step of the as-is analysis is to record relevant processes. Interviews and workshops are held to identify process steps and corresponding key performance indicators and process parameters. In a second steps process related weaknesses need to be determined and documented. Afterwards these areas should be analyzed more closely in order to identify root-causes and interdependencies. Based on identical causes the weaknesses shall be clustered and prioritized according to their potential for process improvement. This results in a list of most promising processes for to be process design.

(3) In the to-be process design phase initially concepts to eliminate the weakness cluster of the previous phase shall be developed and documented. Then appropriate to-be processes must be defined in order to realize the benefits from previous elaborated concepts. A precise description of all relevant process parameters is crucial. Defining to-be processes is an iterative procedure and the optimization potential shall be evaluated during this procedure by comparison of as-is and to-be processes. Usually such process changes also incorporate organizational adjustments. Therefore this phase results beside optimally defined and documented to-be processes in accompanying organizational changes.

(4) The last phase, the solution transformation, deals with the construction of to-be processes

within the IT infrastructure. IT systems, applications and services required to implement the to-be design shall be identified in the existing or a planned solution landscape. In an SAP environment the to-be processes will be mapped against corresponding standard software packages which results in following categories of SAP coverage:

- Processes supported by core configuration.
- processes supported by core enhancements (e. g. user exists).
- processes supported bycomposite applications/enterprise services.
- processes supported by non SAP solutions.

Finally a detailed target architecture is planned, and the required implementation, development, and integration steps are defined. In an SAP environment, the outcome corresponds to a SAP blueprint.

Due to already mentioned efficiency reasons, i. e. to decrease project duration and implementation costs SAP Consulting provides an accelerated procedure of the BPM methodology (Figure 4-5). This procedure utilizes "Business Best Practices" related to business processes, i. e. industry-specific predefined process descriptions provided by SAP Consulting. Therefore the usually time consuming as-is analysis can be reduced in most instances.

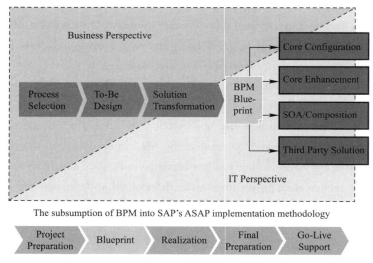

The subsumption of BPM into SAP's ASAP implementation methodology

Figure 4-5　Accelerated SAP business process management methodology

The procedure for business process optimization is structured in the following three phases: process selection, to-be design and solution transformation. Due to SAP's overall approach to reduce implementation costs and time the accelerated procedure will be presented in more detail.

8. Models (Six Sigma's Business Process Management Model)

Six Sigma as a management system incorporates the Business Process Management (BPM) model. The Six Sigma Management System treats the business process as its fundamental organizational building block. The business process is the operational unit that is measured, managed, and continuously improved through the Six Sigma Management System.

The BPM model is best understood when contrasted with the classic functional model of management. In this classic model, the building block of an organizational unit is the functional department. Before 1990, most American companies operated their businesses in functional silos and basically ignored the ideas of business process management. In the minds of functional management, process design involved writing policy and procedure manuals for functional departments to follow.

Motorola invented and pioneered Six Sigma in the late 1980s. In the 1990s, leading businesses, including Motorola, turned to process reengineering to compete in markets that were exploding with improvement in the variety and quality of customer choices. Markets had changed from supplier-driven, push-controlled to customer demand-controlled dynamics. As these leading companies experimented and developed their understanding of process management and redesign, their leaders' vision evolved from a focus on managing specialized functional divisions of labor to the focus on managing business processes. BPM became their fundamental operating model. Through years of effort and work with BPM, they invented continuous process improvement as an operational strategy that combined the strengths of the Six Sigma improvement methodology and the BPM model.

Motorola and a few other global technology giants led a dramatic change in the fundamentals of how goal-driven organizations are designed and operated. They fought against a 150-year practice of designing organizations exclusively with the hallowed building blocks of the discrete functional departments-accounting, manufacturing, marketing and sales, etc. Instead, these leaders chose the "business process" as their organizational building block. Through trial and success, these companies have demonstrated the supremacy of the business process as the fundamental building block and the management unit to measure and control in high performance companies.

The process was a more natural unit to manage in the manufacturing companies that led the revolution than in the service businesses and government agencies that have since adopted the continuous process improvement strategy. Motorola, GE, Raytheon, and others began their process improvement efforts in their manufacturing operations with a goal of improving the quality and reducing the cost of their products. In manufacturing, these companies all achieved a very impressive, breakthrough level of success that proved the viability of BPM and continuous process improvement using Six Sigma methods. Billions of dollars were saved and customers were delighted with the quality and value of the products they received. Allied Signal's Raymond C. Stark, Vice President of Six Sigma & Productivity, attributed Six Sigma practices with saving the company $1.5 billion between 1994 and 1998.

But, at Motorola and GE, the application of BPM and Six Sigma continuous process improvement was not limited to the manufacturing arena. GE launched a corporate wide quality improvement strategy in 1995 when Jack Welch, Chairman and CEO, committed GE's empire to reach Six Sigma quality by the year 2000. Welch was quoted in 1997 that he expected his managers to be "committed zealots" of Six Sigma. The following year the company credited Six

Sigma with adding $ 300 million to 1997 operating income.

In that time period, Motorola's leadership worldwide embarked on there design, in fact, the redefinition of the total set of core business processes that had to be managed and improved to compete and survive in the changing global marketplace.

Motorola's core business process redesign experience enhanced and extended the definition of a process from a "manufacturing process" to a true "business process". In the broadest sense, a process is a structure for action to achieve predetermined goals. The classic definition, from Thomas Davenport, in Process Innovation, 3 states that a process is: "A structured, measured set of activities designed to produce a specified output for a particular customer or market. ... A process is a specific ordering of work activities across time and place, with a beginning, an end, and clearly identified inputs and outputs."

The key elements in this definition include structured and measured activities done in a specific ordering. A process must be bounded by a beginning and an end with clearly identified inputs and outputs. Those elements of the definition of a process remain fundamental to all process improvement work, especially Six Sigma. However, from the Motorola experience, a "business process" has come to have even richer meaning and greater utility as aconceptual tool for process management and continuous process improvement.

The most fundamental characteristic of a "business process" is not the individual structured measured activity or its inputs and outputs. It is the synchronization and coordination of structured, measured activities that tie them into business processes. That synchronization and coordination is typically accomplished through managing the flow of information through the "business process".

This enhanced understanding of the "business process" allows organizations today to manage and improve core business processes and business service processes. A "service process" is seen as coordinated set of collaborative, transactional activities that deliver value to customers.

A "core business process" is typically strategic to the survival of an organization and is:

• Large, complex, and long-running. A single instance of a process such as "order fulfillment" or "design and develop new product" may run for months, or even years.

• Multi-dimensional, with end-to-end flows involving materials, information, and even internal and external business commitments.

• Widely distributed across traditional organizational boundaries both within and even between organizations.

When Motorola, GE, and other leaders began their efforts to redesign and redefine their businesses in terms of processes, their businesses were made up of processes in an organic or unmanaged state. These same organic process conditions continue to be encountered by every organization that is beginning the Six Sigma journey into process management and continuous process improvement.

Organic processes in their unmanaged state share many characteristics which make them difficult to deal with, at least initially.

- Cross-functional organic processes exist inside all large organizations, even those that are functionally managed. These processes are implicit, accepted, and mostly unmeasured, having evolved within the history of the organization.

- Organic processes are functional, producing some successful output units, but are uncontrolled and unreliable in terms of the quality and productivity they generate.

- Organic processes fiercely resist efforts at managed change, due to the threatening nature of moving from a trusted order to an unknown new order.

- Organic processes are difficult to see inside any organization that has not consciously designed or explicitly documented their processes.

- Organic processes interact with other processes. They divide and combine with one another as their undefined boundaries change.

- Organic processes evolve through: unplanned changes and series of small adjustments in their internal activities, and the acquisition or loss of process participants and their capabilities.

- Organic processes are often partially automated. For the sake of speed and reliability, routine or mundane activities are performed by computers wherever possible. Automated components of organic processes are normally the result of the one-to-one conversion of original manual activities into automated activities.

- In organic processes, people perform the tasks that are too unstructured to delegate to a computer or that require personal interaction with customers.

- Quality and productivity are often dependent on the intelligence, judgment, and efforts of individuals.

- People interpret formal and informal information flowing though the process, make judgments, and act to solve perceived internal or customer related problems.

- People modify processes to adapt to varying requirements. This makes processes dynamic and adaptive to demands from customers and unstable with variable output quality and quantity.

Through Six Sigma process improvement methodologies, organic processes are restructured, made explicit and visible, and ultimately, are brought under control. Motorola's people and leadership went through great struggles to accomplish this. Every Motorolan felt the stress of this enormous Six Sigma process redesign challenge, as safe traditional roles in organic processes were peeled away to build the new order of core process management. Today, as part of the Six Sigma Management System, leaders who are in charge of segments of Motorola's business operations are given the title of "Process Owner" and tasked with the continued maintenance and improvement of the processes they own.

The Six Sigma Management System has adopted BPM as the model for creating and deploying processes as fundamental organizational business units. Today, organizations that practice Six Sigma management treat their processes with great care and combine continuous process improvement with planned life-cycle process management. Managed processes have become critical proprietary intellectual property. Some say that managed processes are the business today and continuous process improvement will be the future of the business.

Review Questions and Problems：

1. What are the five critical enablers for a high-performance process?

2. Please talk about the relationship between the market and business process management.

4. 5　Investment Decision and Economic Evaluation

1. Introduction

The investment decision is concerned with the acquisition or disposal of investment assets. The assets may be real assets or financial assets. Real assets include land, buildings or interests in land and buildings, plant, machinery,

4. 5 Professional Terms, Words and Phrases, Sentence Illustration

stocks of material, etc., whilst financial assets are various forms of securities, deposits, debt instruments, etc. Most investors possess investment portfolios which are a mixture of financial and real assets and their interactions within the portfolio cannot be ignored.

The investor usually faces another set of problems, which is closely related to and emerging as the companion of the investment decision. These problems are to do with the decisions associated with the financing of the investment projects contemplated. The financing decision is expected to resolve the question of how much money should be raised, and in what ways, for the investment projects proposed. The financial markets provide the means through which the investor may have access to finance in various forms. The understanding of the money and capital markets therefore is extremely important to the investor if he is to resolve his funding problem in an optimal way.

The decision-making process requires the establishment of criteria against which investment projects and propositions could be evaluated; it also needs the existence of alternatives from which the selection is to be made or an order of preference be drawn up. The criteria and the alternatives will be perceived in value terms. In the world of investment, value is usually expressed in money terms. The fact is that the base of decision-making, relating to investment, is quantitative and therefore lends itself easily to rational treatment, although, in practice, the processes of investment decision-making are often irrational and riddled with inconsistencies.

The investment characteristics of property are significantly different from the characteristics of assets in other investment media. This is the reason why property is so useful and attractive for the purposes of diversification. On the other hand, such differing characteristics isolated property from the other media, in which tremendous strides were made in the development of decision-making methodology and the modernizing of investment and portfolio management techniques.

The full integration of property into the global investment portfolio depends on the full understanding of the investment characteristics of property not only in isolation, but also in the portfolio context.

A successful way to achieve the integration of property into the global investment portfolio is to collect all the property assets into a specialized property portfolio, then treat the property portfolio as a single asset in the global portfolio. The property portfolio is then assembled and managed by property experts who thoroughly understand the characteristics of the assets in their care. If the managers of property portfolios are also equipped with the understanding of the rationale of modern portfolio management practice, the efficiency of property portfolios as investment vehicles should be virtually guaranteed.

As the unitization and securitization of property assets gain ground, the complete integration of property into the global investment portfolio will occur, provided that the investment managers and property experts understand each other's problems and methodology.

The first step on the way to integration must be the recognition of the special investment characteristics of property, the understanding of the process of construction of property portfolios and the identification of the property portfolio problem.

The second step is the examination of the theory and methodology which have evolved in other investment media in order to see if that theory and methodology can be used or adapted for property investment and portfolio work.

Until quite recently, portfolio activity was regarded as an art, where intuition and "feel" dominated decision-making. Objective, quantitative analysis was not possible as the theoretical foundations were not yet laid. Modern portfolio theory was pioneered by Harry M. Markowitz, who in his article "Portfolio selection" laid down the theoretical foundations of the rational approach to the selection, analysis and management of investment portfolios. He postulated the concept of efficient diversification, and from his seminal work portfolio theory rapidly developed. Portfolio theory and the capital market theory now form a fairly coherent, theoretical framework ready for implementation in practice.

2. Theory (Indicators System)

Regardless of the method used, assessment of investment projects is accomplished by means of an indicators system. The system contains efficiency indicators designed in economic and technical specifics of the area in which the project is realized, with economic significance and relevance for the characterization and expression of purpose and investor interests. In formulating the system of indicators for evaluating projects is taken into account also the relative importance that decision-maker is giving one or other of the indicators of efficiency, compared with other possible indicators to use, develop or use of economic theory in practice.

Basically, a system of indicators of economic efficiency of investments, including between five and nine indicators (number of indicators = 7 ± 2) and its use of a draft choice ensure convenient, not much in terms of the exigencies of efficiency.

The decision to invest is born of necessity or interest to make an investment. Any decision to invest must be subordinated of the private finance objective, which of the maximization company value. The way in which an organization grow and develop, the ability to survive and even being competitive will depend on the ability to generate steady streams of ideas for new products, better products or lower costs, that is to get the best investment decisions. Such a decision is based on several considerations: "value system" (time value of money n), the economic context of the project, the perspective of investors, funding opportunities, risks, the forecast of the input and output flows, accounting of performance, as well as on various alternative investment opportunities with comparisons depending on available resources, generic comparisons called opportunity cost of investment.

3. Methods and Tools

Pay attention to the determination of project cost in the stage of feasibility study and investment decision. Feasibility study and investment decision-making are the source of project cost, and determination is the key to evaluate construction projects and carry out follow-up work. The key to doing a good job of the feasibility study report is to do a good job of market research, starting with input and output, to solve the problem of the economic "rationality" of the project. It should not only meet the planning requirements of the city where it is located, but also meet the use functions. It should not only consider the requirements of functional zoning and the spacing of buildings, but also consider saving land to the greatest extent. The layout should be compact and reasonable as far as possible, and the terrain and landform should be used separately to reduce the land cost. The depth of feasibility study should be standardized and standardized, and the research report should ensure its authenticity and scientificity. Investment estimation is an important basis for studying and analyzing the economic effect of development projects, and it is also the main basis for decision-making. The investment estimation should truly reflect the design intent and project content from the project scale and project content, and the cost composition should be complete and reasonable to ensure the estimation quality. Cost management personnel should start from the optimization of the construction plan and penetrate into the whole process of design. According to the principle of project cost management, they should reasonably predict the changes of various dynamic factors in the investment estimation, and try to make full investment without leaving a gap, so as to provide an important basis for investment decision-making.

The key to project investment control is in the investment decision-making and design stage. For a long time, China has generally ignored the cost control in the early stage of engineering construction projects, and often focuses on the construction stage to control the project cost. Although this is also effective, it is, after all, twice the effort. To effectively control the project cost, we must resolutely shift the focus to the early stage. At present, especially the key is to grasp the design and prepare for a rainy day, so as to achieve twice the result with half the effort. Therefore, the construction cost control of the construction unit should focus on the design stage, which is the fundamental to effectively control the construction project investment. How important the investment management in the design stage is to the cost management of the whole project.

Bidding is the main means to introduce competition mechanism and reduce project cost. The quality of the construction team is related to the success or failure of the project cost control of the construction unit and the owner's satisfaction with the development of enterprise products when they move in. Therefore, the construction enterprise is required to have sufficient technical strength, which not only enables the enterprise's own production and operation to achieve high efficiency, high quality and low consumption, but also enables the construction enterprise to have the strength to give reasonable discounts to the construction unit on the cost of project. At the same time, it is necessary to strictly grasp the bidding conditions of the project, carefully prepare the base bid price and bidding documents of the project, and do a good job in bid evaluation and award. The contract and construction period shall be determined through negotiation and negotiation based on the bid winning price. Public bidding or invitation bidding shall be adopted for project bidding. The terms of the bidding document should be rigorous, accurate and comprehensive.

As the professional agent of the construction unit in terms of contract and cost, cost engineers or consulting companies should give full play to their professional expertise, effectively control investment and ensure reasonable and best cost-effectiveness in the process of formulating contract conditions, selecting bidding methods and negotiating the contract amount according to corresponding laws and regulations. When negotiating the whole contract and the project contract price with the contractor, in addition to evaluating the rationality of the contractor's overall quotation based on the market price, it is particularly necessary to pay attention to the time value of funds to evaluate the balance of the contractor's quotation. At the same time, cost engineers or consulting companies should also abide by fair professional ethics to prevent deliberately lowering the contractor's price in accordance with the wishes of the industry. As far as the construction unit is concerned, it generally hopes that the project cost will be lower and better, but from the contract management of the construction industry, it can be seen that the apparent low price often leads to Jerry built work or frequent claims, and even leads to serious events such as delay and suspension. Therefore, reasonably formulating the base bid price and bid evaluation is an important means to ensure that the investment can be controlled. This not only ensures the reasonable interests of the contractor and is beneficial to the smooth progress of the project, but also indirectly protects the interests of the owner.

4. Models

To effectively control the investment in the design stage, we need to strengthen the control of the project investment as a whole, from passive response to active control, from post accounting to pre control, and quota design is an investment control method proposed according to the above requirements. The so-called quota design is not blindly saving investment, but controlling the preliminary design according to the approved feasibility study report and estimation, and controlling the construction drawing design according to the approved preliminary design documents. The quota design divides the funds into several units according to the different positions or functions of the structure. The designers design according to the limit to fully ensure the control role of the budget estimate and budget. Through technical and economic optimization, they scientifically pursue low investment on the premise of ensuring that the project meets the technical safety and functions. Using quota design in the process of highway construction projects is a powerful measure to control investment expenditure and effectively use funds. According to the investment approved in the previous stage, the design of the next stage is controlled with the control project as the main content, so as to effectively overcome and control the phenomenon of "Three Excesses".

The optimization of design scheme refers to the selection of the best design scheme with advanced technology and economic rationality through the comparison of various design schemes, so as to control the project investment and improve the effect of project investment. The general methods used in the optimization and comparison of design schemes of highway engineering construction projects include technical and economic analysis methods and value analysis methods. The technical and economic analysis method should not only consider the technical scheme of the project, but also pay more attention to the cost, that is, the combination of technology and economy. The minimum cost method and multi-objective optimization method are generally used in the analysis and comparison of design schemes. Value engineering is an activity process that studies how to obtain the required functions at a reasonable cost with the object of product function and production cost. It is a method that can effectively control the coordination between engineering cost and function with the goal of improving value and the core of function analysis. Value refers to the proportion between cost expenditure and acquisition.

The budget estimate document is a comprehensive document to determine the project investment. It not only reflects the construction scale of each project, but also stipulates the scope of economic activities of the project. At the same time, it also comprehensively observes the rationality of each project design and construction scheme. Through the preparation of design budget, the schemes of highway engineering projects can be compared, analyzed and evaluated, so as to select the most economical design scheme and make full use of the project investment. At the same time, we should strengthen the review of the design budget. The design unit should first conduct internal review of the prepared documents, and then review and submit them for approval according to the specified procedures. In addition, we should improve the professional technical level of cost personnel, improve the qualification access and assessment demonstration of project investment managers, strengthen training, improve the quality of personnel, and implement the professional qualification system of cost engineers.

Review Questions and Problems:

What is the difference between internal investment and foreign investment?

4.6 Finance and Internet Plus

1. Introduction

(1) Financial Control

4.6 Professional Terms, Words and Phrases, Sentence Illustration

Construction contracts normally require that contractors perform prescribed duties of a financial nature. For example, they are made responsible for certain aspects of the payment process. This can include project cost breakdowns, the forecasted schedule of progress payments, preparation or approval of periodic pay estimates, and documentation required for final payment. Construction contracts prescribe specific procedures to be followed by the contractor with regard to payment for extra work, extensions of time, processing of change orders, claims, and settlement of disputes.

The project manager is also responsible to the company for implementing and maintaining standard fiscal procedures. One of the most important of these is monitoring project cash requirements during the contract period. Even a highly profitable job will require a considerable amount of cash to meet payrolls, purchase materials, and meet other project obligations. The size and timing of these cash demands is a serious matter for the contractor, and appropriate financial forecasts must be made. In fact, one of the most common causes for construction companies failing is lack of operating cash, which puts the contractor out of business even if the companies have jobs that would be profitable if they could be completed. A system of disbursement control is needed to regulate and control payments to material vendors, subcontractors, and others.

Another aspect of financial control is that of maintaining a complete and detailed daily record of the project. Such a job log can be invaluable in the settlement of claims and disputes that may arise from the work. This job history includes names, dates, places, and documentation of everything that happens as well as everything that fails to happen.

(2) Progress Payments

Construction contracts typically provide that the owner shall make partial payments of the contract amount to the prime contractor as the work progresses. Payment at monthly intervals is the usual proviso. Depending on the type of work and contract provisions, the monthly pay requests may be prepared by the contractor, the architect-engineer, or the owner. In any event, a pay request is prepared periodically, and the cost of the work accomplished since the owner made the last payment to the contractor must be compiled. Typically, this compilation is done in practice by determining the total value of work actually performed to date and then subtracting the sum of the previous progress payments made by the owner.

The total value of work done to date is obtained in different ways, depending on the type of contract. Under lump-sum contracts, progress customarily is measured in terms of estimated percentages of completion of major job components. The quantities of work done on unit-price contracts are determined by actual field measurement of the bid items put into place. In either type of contract, materials stored onsite usually are taken into account, as well as any prefabrication or preassembly work that the contractor may have done at some location other than the job site.

In accordance with the terms of the contract, the owner usually retains a prescribed percentage of each progress payment. A retainage of 10 percent is common, although other percentages are also used. To an increasing extent, construction contracts provide that retainage shall be withheld only during the first half of the project. After that, if the work is progressing satisfactorily and with the consent of the surety, all subsequent progress payments are made in full, thus effectively reducing retainage to 5 percent by the end of the job. The retainage is held by the owner until the work receives final certification by the architect-engineer, the owner accepts the project, and the contractor submits any required affidavits and releases of lien. Final payment is then made to the contractor, including the accumulated retainage.

Negotiated contracts of the cost-plus variety usually provide for the contractor's submission of payment vouchers to the owner at specified intervals during the life of the contract. A common provision is weekly reimbursement of payrolls and monthly reimbursement of all other costs, including a pro rata share of the contractor's fee. It is not uncommon under this type of contract for the owner to pay all vouchers in full without deducting any percentage as retainage. Some contracts provide for the retention of a stated percentage of the contractor's fee. Others provide that the owner make full reimbursement to the contractor up to some designated percentage (80 percent sometimes is used) of the total estimated project cost. Further payments then are withheld until some specified amount of money has been set aside. The owner retains this reserve until the project has been satisfactorily completed.

(3) Internet Plus

In March 2015, the Chinese government unveiled Internet Plus, an action plan expected to push forward the Chinese economy. The plan aims to integrate mobile Internet, cloud computing, big data, and the Internet of Things (IoT) with traditional industries to promote economic restructuring, improve people's livelihoods, and even transform government functions. However, China's Internet Plus plan is still in early stages, and lacks an innovation-driven ecosystem as well as open and customizable platforms. In this article, we present Internet Plus's characteristics from six different perspectives. The plan faces several challenges, but also offers promising development trends.

(4) Internet Plus and Its Characteristics

Internet Plus is the integration of the internet and traditional industries through online platforms and IT; it is expected to push forward the Chinese economy by reforming innovation and economic structure. In general, the emerging Internet Plus in China has the following characteristics:

• Trans-boundary integration. Internet Plus involves economic subjects from different fields; thus, trans-boundary integration of the internet and traditional industries is the most important feature.

• Structure reformation. The information revolution, globalization, and the internet have broken existing social, economic, and even cultural structures; thus, a process of restructuring is needed in the Internet Plus era.

• An open and shared platform. An important objective of Internet Plus is to provide an open and shared innovation platform by dissolving the barriers that restrict innovation so that entrepreneurs have more opportunities to realize their innovations.

• Ubiquitous connection. By integrating Internet Plus with cloud computing, big data, and the IoT, everyone and everything will be connected, that is, people to people, people to objects, people to services, and objects to objects. Hence, ubiquitous connection will be an important feature.

Internet Plus must also be:

• Innovation driven. China's current resource-driven economy is unsustainable and must transform to an innovation-driven economic mode in the Internet Plus era, where internet thinking is adopted to motivate innovations.

• Human-centric. The internet's most fundamental power originates from its respect for humanity, the awe of the user experience, and its concern for human creativity. Therefore, because it represents the integration of the internet and traditional industries, humancentric product design and manufacturing is another feature of Internet Plus.

(5) Internet + Finance

Thanks to the strong innovative ability of internet companies, various internet finance modes have emerged in recent years, including online banking, online and mobile payment, peer-to-peer (P2P) lending, crowdfunding, and internet banks. For example, private Chinese online financial organizations, such as Alibaba's Yu' E bao and Tencent's Licaitong, have shaken the traditional financial markets monopolized by state-owned banks; the former raised 250 billion RMB in just seven months, and the latter attracted more than 10 billion RMB in only six working days. Meanwhile, there were more than 1500 P2P lending platforms in China as of 2014, with a total trading volume of 252. 8 billion RMB.

2. Methods and Tools

The payment management of engineering construction funds involves the vital economic interests of investors, participants and other parties, and is related to the investment management and control of construction projects. It is a very important basic work.

Formulate a reasonable plan for the use of project construction funds. Contractors of military engineering construction shall, in accordance with the requirements of the contract, stipulate the scope of use of special funds and determine that special funds shall not be misappropriated. Therefore, the relevant military departments should put forward requirements to the contractor in advance, and formulate the use plan of various special funds in the construction organization design according to the current specifications and standards, construction management level and technical level in combination with the project characteristics, operation environment and schedule requirements, so as to clarify the estimated proportion and purpose of special funds in the project construction.

Standardize the payment and use procedures of project funds. The contractor of military engineering construction shall apply for and allocate special funds for engineering construction in stages according to the actual needs of the project, the fund use plan and the completion schedule. In principle, the application and payment of progress payment can be carried out according to the proportion of the completed quantities of the project. The construction contractor shall maintain the progress of the project within the limited time required to allocate special project funds to submit the project price list required to be allocated to the supervision unit for approval. When the project progress appropriation is paid to 80%, it will no longer be paid. When the project is completely completed and reviewed, the final settlement payment can be made only after a certain quality deposit is withheld according to the regulations.

Implement fund control during project construction. In order to prevent the military engineering construction unit from increasing the amount of application for payment by changing the design and misrepresenting the project, the management personnel at the construction site must strictly review the completion progress. First, review the validity of visas. The acceptance visa and construction records of all concealed works shall be complete, and the actual quantities can be included in the calculation only after they are confirmed to be consistent with the as built drawings. Second, review the fairness of visa content. Judging from the current implementation of military engineering construction, there is a serious phenomenon of visa chaos. In order to avoid the increase of investment caused by unreasonable visas, the rationality, legitimacy and objectivity of the visa content should be carefully analyzed in the process of settlement review. If serious inaccuracies or unreasonable visas are found, they should be cancelled in time. Third, examine whether there is an increase in the cost of visas. Not all visa changes will cause cost changes. For example, before the change is implemented, only the elevation and plane position are changed. Some visas only further clarify the engineering practice, but will not cause cost increases, and can only be used as a reference for construction acceptance. It should be noted that during the construction process, if there are engineering changes, the relevant departments should handle the engineering change price in a timely manner in accordance with the contract and relevant regulations. The increase cost of funds shall be determined according to the relevant rates of the competent department, so as to serve as the basis for the payment of the progress payment of the project. When handling the completion settlement, the military engineering construction unit shall pay the project special funds based on the completion settlement price.

3. Models

Most business models are not static. The technology on which they rest and the environments in which they operate continually change. The firms and competitors who design them initiate or react to change. In responding to or initiating change to sustain or attain a competitive advantage, it is important to understand the nature of change so as to better take advantage of it in crafting and executing a business model. Where that change is from a new technology such as the internet, one of the first things to remember is that profiting from the new technology will take more than mastering the new technology. Profiting from a new technology depends both on how easy it is to imitate the new technology and the extent to which complementary assets are important and readily available. In short, it takes more than technology to make money from technology. It also takes complementary assets. Imitable or not, being able to develop the new technology is important since many firms that fail to profit from a new technology, despite having complementary assets, do so because they do not know how to develop the new technology. Various models have explored who is most likely to more effectively develop a new technology. The incremental/radical, architectural innovation, disruptive change, innovation value-added chain, and technology life cycle models all argue that the type of firm that can best exploit a technological change depends on the type of change. Table 4-2 summarizes the elements of these models.

Review Questions and Problems:

1. What are the responsibilities for a project financial manager?
2. Please talk about the characteristics of Internet Plus.

Summary of models   **Table 4-2**

Model	Key Points about Model	Implications for the Internet
Complementary assets	• It takes more than technology to profit from a technology. The imitability of the technology and complementary assets are also important. • Explains why inventors are not always the ones that profit from an innovation.	• Since the Internet is an imitable technology, we can expect bricks-and-mortar firms that have complementary assets to win bricks-and-mortar versus dot. com battles in those industries where such assets are important and difficult to acquire.
Incremental/Radical dichotomy	• Focuses on technological component of innovation. • Bundles component and architectural knowledge. • The type of technological change determines the type of firm that is able to exploit it. • Capabilities and cultures that are embedded in the old technology are likely to handicap firms in the face of radical technological change. Incumbents are more likely to exploit incremental technological changes while new entrants are more likely to exploit incremental changes	• Whether the internet is radical or incremental depends on the industry • Where the internet is radical, firms with capabilities and cultures that are embedded in the old technology run the risk of these capabilities handicapping internet efforts. Different organizational arrangements can alleviate the problem. • Complementary assets are likely to help bricks-and-mortar firms in battles with dot. coms
Architectural innovation	• Unbundles technological knowledge into component and architectural innovations. • Explains why incumbents fail at what appear to be incremental innovations—they are actually architectural innovations	• Can expect impact of the Internet to have a larger long-term effect on value chains of manufacturing companies than would appear at first glance. • Knowledge of interactions between value-chain functions likely to change enough to influence functional activities and firm performance.
Disruptive change	With disruptive technologies, • New markets are created by introducing new products or services. • The new products or services cost less than existing products or services • New products initially perform worse than existing products when judged by the performance metrics that existing mainstream customers value. Eventually. performance catches up. • The technology should be difficult to protect using patents	• This model suggests that the internet is a disruptive technology in many industries. In such industries, firms need organizational arrangements that allow for development of Internet resources, processes, and values without being handicapped by bricks-and-mortar resources, processes, and values. • Some firms may need to have separate Internet entities.

continued

Model	Key Points about Model	Implications for the Internet
Innovation value-added chain	• The impact of a technological change on co-opetitors may be just as important as that on focal firms. (Recall that co-opetitors are the suppliers, customers, and complementors with whom the firm must cooperate and compete.) • Explains why incumbents may fail at incremental innovations and why they may succeed at radical innovations	To really understand the impact of the Internet on a firm's business model, it is important to understand the impact on the firm's co-opetitors as well.
Technology life cycle	There are three phases in an innowation's life cycle: • In the fluid phase, firms place their bets: e. g., new entrants choose the profit sites in which they want to locate. • In the transitional phase, where a standard or dominant design defines a critical point in the life of an innovation, competition forces many firms to exit. • In the specific phase, firms may want to determine their competitive advantage and focus on it.	• We should have expected the dot. com boom and burst to take place although the timing was not predictable. • Firms that want to improve their chances of survival during a burst need a good business model.

4.7 Reading Material

1. Emerging Trends for Agile Project Management

Agile project management provides the opportunity to rapidly deliver software, services and products to satisfy the demands of ever-changing customer needs. The need to rapidly develop software and digital processes using agile methods has become increasingly important in order to compete in digital markets, indeed for many organizations it is becoming vital for their survival.

One of the trends is the provision of a continuous delivery of software and services. This approach uses concepts from agile methods and lean manufacturing, incorporating frequent releases and automation wherever possible. Regular feedback from customers ensures the quality of deployments and what is delivered actually meets customer needs.

Continuous delivery can be far more effective with the integration of development teams with delivery teams. Considerable further gains can be made if software, service and project delivery can be integrated with other business processes. The challenge for managers is to ensure that all relevant processes are optimized, providing an opportunity to reduce the cost and complexity of processes across the organization.

Agile projects are becoming increasingly data-driven to ensure that they are meeting the goals of the project and aligned to what the customer requires. The progress of projects is now often tracked real time, based on working software or solutions and feedback from customers. It is the governance and compliance aspects of project management that are increasing in importance in agile approaches, ensuring that process improvement, business goals and regulations are being met.

The following sections examine some of the major trends and challenges: understanding customer needs, use of data and visualizations, achieving collaboration across teams and providing teams with autonomy so they can select whichever lean and agile methods they consider add value to achieve the business strategy.

2. Delivering Enterprise Agility

Although there has been considerable success in software delivery using agile methods, the challenge now, as Rigby et al. (2016) outline in their *Harvard Business Review Article*, *Embracing Agility*, is that many organizations need to capitalize on agility across the organization. In an increasingly competitive market, it is necessary to gain the advantages of adaptability provided by agile processes. Evidence for the economic benefit has been shown by surveys extending back to 2007 by the Center for Information Systems Research (CISR) at MIT Sloan, indicating that agile firms can increase profits by 37%. In addition, Peter Weill and Stephanie Woerner (2016) have shown there is a significant increase inrevenue and profit margins for organizations that embrace digitalization and understand their customers better.

Research published by McKinsey showed that many organizations are using agile project management to deliver goods and services with greater efficiency. This also brings further challenges from "always on" customers who expect continual availability and reliability. To take advantage of new market opportunities and adapt dynamically requires not just adaptability within delivery pipelines but across the enterprise. As Ross, Weill and Robertson explain in their book, *Creating a Foundation for Business Execution*, to keep up with the changing business environment, it is also necessary to have flexibility within the digital processes and enterprise architecture. It is with agile project management that organizations can take advantage of these new digital business opportunities and accelerate time to market.

3. Understanding Business Value and Customer Value

Forming strategic partnerships and looking for ideas outside the organization is one way to accelerate innovation. This can be aided by more agile approaches allowing teams to decide how to structure these conversations and change how teams share information at the start of projects, via workshops or alternatively hackathons. These approaches provide an insight into the processes and value streams of different groups. For a customer, this may give further insight in their value stream, from their request to fulfillment of their order.

Agile processes are increasingly integrated with different perspectives so that the teams better understand the customer's journey. Customer needs are increasingly incorporated at an earlier stage, not just after the engineering solution, as we now often see, integrated with agile processes the mapping of the customer experience (CX). Processes need careful design and consideration, whether they are providing value for the business or customer, or both. For example, it is of limited value if, an APP helping a customer locate a store selling a product they want (via geo-location on their smart phone), if this system is not integrated into the supply chain and the store takes weeks to order the product. The whole supply chain needs to be considered. Mark Schwartz highlights in his book, *The Art of Business Value*, that managers need to ensure that the meaning of value is considered from the perspective of the business, partners and what the customer values.

Chapter 5
Information Technology and Management Information System

5.1 Management Information Systems

5.1 Professional Terms, Words and Phrases, Sentence Illustration

1. Information Systems

An Information System (IS) can be defined technically as a set of interrelated components that collect (or retrieve), process, store, and distribute information to support decision making, coordinating, and control in an organization. Information Systems may also help managers and workers analyze problems, visualize complex subjects, and create new products. Information Systems contain information about significant people, places, and things within the organization or in the environment surrounding it. Input, processing and output in an Information System produce the information that organizations need to make decisions, control operations, analyze problems, and create new products or services. Information Systems also require feedback, which is output that is returned to appropriate members of the organization to help them evaluate or correct the input stage.

Management Information Systems:

Just like finance, accounting, marketing, and many others, management information systems is a business function vitally important to the success of your organization. Formally, we define management information systems as follows:

Management Information Systems (MIS) deals with the planning for, development, management, and use of information technology tools to help people perform all tasks related to information processing and management. So, MIS deals with the coordination and use of three very important organizational resources—information, people, and information technology. Stated another way, people use information technology to work with information. And to do so they are involved in MIS. Ideally, of course, people use technology to support the goals and objectives of the organization as driven by competitive pressures and determined by appropriate business strategies. MIS helps them to do this.

2. Dimensions of Information Systems

To fully understand Information Systems, you will need to be aware of the broader organization, people, and information technology dimensions of systems (Figure 5−1) and their power to provide solutions to challenges and problems in the business environment. We refer to this broader understanding of Information Systems, which encompasses an understanding of the people and organizational dimensions of systems as well as the technical dimensions of systems, as

Information Systems literacy. The field of Management Information Systems (MIS) tries to achieve this broader Information Systems literacy. MIS deals with behavioral issues as well as technical issues surrounding the development, use, and impact of Information Systems used by managers and employees in the firm.

Figure 5-1　Information systems are more than computers

Using information systems effectively requires an understanding of the organization, people, and information technology shaping the systems. An information system provide a solution to important business problems or challenges facing the firm.

(1) Organizations

Information Systems are an integral part of organizations. And although we tend to think about information technology changing organizations and business firms, it is, in fact, a two-way street: The history and culture of business firms also affects how the technology is used and how it should be used. In order to understand how a specific business firm uses Information Systems, you need to know something about the structure, history, and culture of the company. Organizations have a structure that is composed of different levels and specialties. Information Systems are built by the firm in order to serve these different specialties and different levels of the firm. In addition, most organizations' business processes include formal rules that have been developed over a long time for accomplishing tasks. These rules guide employees in a variety of procedures, from writing an invoice to responding to customer complaints. Information Systems automate many business processes. What's more, organization has a unique culture, or fundamental set of assumptions, values, and ways of doing things, that has been accepted by most of its members. Parts of an organization's culture can always be found embedded in its Information Systems.

Organizations must treat information as any other resource or asset. It must be organized, managed, and disseminated effectively for the information to exhibit quality. Within an organization, information flows in four basic directions:

① Upward. Upward information flows describe the current state of the organization based on its daily transactions. When a sale occurs, for example, that information originates at the lowest level of the organization and is passed upward through the various levels. Along the way, the information takes on a finer level of granularity. Information granularity refers to the extent of detail within the information. At lower organizational levels, information exhibits fine granularity because people need to work with information in great detail. At the upper organizational levels, information becomes coarser because it is summarized or aggregated in some way. That is, strategic managers need sales by year, for example, as opposed to knowing the detail of every single transaction.

② Downward. Strategies, goals, and directives that originate at a higher level are passed to lower levels in downward information flows. The upper level of an organization develops strategies; the middle levels of an organization convert those strategies into tactics; and the lower levels of an organization deal with the operational details.

③ Horizontal. Information flows horizontally between functional business units and work teams. The goal here is to eliminate the old dilemma of "the right hand not knowing what the left hand is doing." All units of your organization need to inform other units of their processes and be informed by the other units regarding their processes. In general, everyone in a company needs to know everything relevant in a business sense (personal, sensitive data not included).

④ Outward/Inward. Information is communicated from and to customers, suppliers, distributors, and other partners for the purpose of doing business. These flows of information are really what electronic commerce is all about. Today, no organization is an island, and outward/inward flows can yield a competitive advantage.

Another organizational perspective on information regards what information describes. Information is internal or external, objective or subjective, and various combinations of these.

- Internal information describes specific operational aspects of an organization.
- External information describes the environment surrounding the organization.
- Objective information quantifiably describes something that is known.
- Subjective information attempts to describe something that is unknown.

Consider a bank that faces the decision about what interest rate to offer on a CD. That bank will use internal information (how many customers it has who can afford to buy a CD), external information (what rate other banks are offering), objective information (what is today's prime interest rate), and subjective information (what the prime interest rate is expected to be in the future). Actually, the rate other banks are offering is not only external information (it describes the environment surrounding the organization) but objective information (it is quantifiably known). Information usually has more than one aspect to it.

(2) People

A business is only as good as the people who work there and run it. Likewise with Information Systems—they are useless without skilled people to build and maintain them, and without people who can understand how to use the information in a system to achieve business objectives. Business firms require many kinds of skills and people, including managers as well as rank-and-file employees. As you will learn throughout this text, technology is relatively inexpensive today, but people are very expensive. Because people are the only ones capable of business problem solving and converting information technology into useful business solutions, we spend considerable effort in this text looking at the people dimension of Information Systems.

The single most important resource in any organization is its people. People set goals, carry out tasks, make decisions, serve customers, and, in the case of IT specialists, provide a stable and reliable technology environment so the organization can run smoothly and gain a competitive advantage in the marketplace. So, this discussion is all about you. In business, your most valuable as set is not technology but rather your mind. IT is simply a set of tools that helps you work with and process information. Technology really is just a mind support tool set. Technology such asspreadsheet software can help you quickly create a high-quality and revealing graph. But it can't tell you whether you should build a bar or a pie graph, and it can't help you determine whether you should show sales by territory or sales by salesperson. Those are your tasks, and that's why your business curriculum includes classes in human resource management, accounting, finance, marketing, and perhaps production and operations management.

Nonetheless, technology is a very important set of tools for you. Technology can help you be more efficient and can help you dissect and better understand problems and opportunities. So, it's as important for you to learn how to use your technology tool set as it's important that you understand the information to which you're applying your technology tools (Management Information Systems for the Information Age).

(3) Technology

Information technology is one of many tools managers use to cope with change and complexity. Computer hardware is the physical equipment used for input, processing, and output activities in an Information System. It consists of the following: computers of various sizes and shapes; various input, output, and storage devices; and telecommunications devices that link computers together. Computer software consists of the detailed, preprogrammed instructions that control and coordinate the computer hardware components in an Information System. Data management technology consists of the software governing the organization of data on physical storage media. Networking and telecommunications technology, consisting of both physical devices and software, links the various pieces of hardware and transfers data from one physical location to another. The world's largest and most widely used network is the Internet. The Internet has created a new "universal" technology platform on which to build new products, services, strategies, and business models. The World Wide Web is a service provided by the Internet that uses universally accepted standards for storing, retrieving, formatting, and displaying information in a page format on the Internet. Web pages contain text, graphics, animations, sound, and video and are linked to other Web pages. By clicking on highlighted words or buttons on a Web page, you can link to related pages to find additional information and links to other locations on the Web. All of these technologies, along with the people required to run and manage them, represent resources that can be shared throughout the organization and constitute the firm's Information Technology (IT) infrastructure. The IT infrastructure provides the foundation, or platform, on which the firm can build its specific Information Systems. Each organization must carefully design and manage its information technology infrastructure so that it has the set of technology services it needs for the work it wants to accomplish with Information Systems.

The third key resource for Management Information Systems (MIS) is information technology (IT), any computer-based tool that people use to work with information and support the information and information-processing needs of an organization. IT includes a cell phone or PDA that you use to obtain stock quotes, your home computer that you use to write term papers, large networks that businesses use to connect to one another, and the Internet that almost one in every six people in the world currently uses.

(4) Key Technology Categories

One simple—yet effective—way to categorize technology is as either hardware or software. Hardware is the physical devices that make up a computer. Software is the set of instructions that your hardware executes to carry out a specific task for you. So, your Blackberry is the actual hardware; and it contains software that you use to maintain your calendar, update your address book, check your e-mail, watch videos, obtain stock market quotes, and so on.

All hardware technology falls into one of the following six basic categories:

① An input device is a tool you use to enter information and commands. Input devices include such tools as keyboard, mouse, touch screen, game controller, and bar code reader.

② An output device is a tool you use to see, hear, or otherwise recognize the results of your information-processing requests. Output devices include such tools as printer, monitor, and speakers.

③ A storage device is a tool you use to store information for use at a later time. Storage devices include such tools as thumb drive, flash memory card, and DVD.

④ The Central Processing Unit (CPU) is the hardware that interprets and executes the system and application software instructions and coordinates the operation of all the hardware. RAM, or random access memory, is a temporary holding area for the information you're working with as well as the system and application software instructions that the CPU currently needs.

⑤ A telecommunications device is a tool you use to send information to and receive it from another person or computer in a network. If you connect to the Internet using a modem, the modem is a telecommunications device.

⑥ Connecting devices include such things as a USB port into which you would connect a printer, connector cables to connect your printer to the USB port, and internal connecting devices on the motherboard.

There are two main types of software: application and system. Application software is the software that enables you to solve specific problems and perform specific tasks. Microsoft Word, for example, can help you write term papers. From an organizational point of view, payroll software, collaborative software, and inventory management software are all examples of application software.

System software handles tasks specific to technology management and coordinates the interaction of all technology devices. System software includes network operating system software, drivers for your printer and scanner, operating system software such as Windows XP and Mac OS, and utility software such as anti-virus software, uninstaller software, and file security software.

If this is your first exposure to technology hardware and software, we suggest you explore Extended Learning Module A (Computer Hardware and Software).

As we have seen, management information systems really is all about three key organizational resources—the people involved, the information they need, and the information technology that helps them. MIS is about getting the right technology and the right information into the hands of the right people at the right time. To meet the technology and information needs of your organization, you must understand the industry in which you operate, build the appropriate business strategies, and then identify the important business processes that support the strategies. Finally, you select the right technologies.

3. Research Approach

Research methodology in the area of Information Systems (IS) can be categorized under different subjects and encompasses many areas, such as: Technology, Management, Political Science and Strategy. Research methodology can be classified in different ways, the most common and widely used are the qualitative approach and the quantitative approach. Therefore, the research approaches for Information Systems are qualitative approach and quantitative approach.

(1) Qualitative Approach

The qualitative research approach often depends on the interpretive or critical paradigm within social sciences to help researchers to study social and cultural phenomena; it is the approach that represents collect data depends on the field or life situation such as experiences, values, and behaviors of other people. On the other hand defined that the data in qualitative research come in form as words, phrases, sentences and narrations rather than numbers (non-numerical data), e. g. explanation, conversation, interviews and discussion, which makes the collected data of qualitative rich and holistic with strong potential for revealing complexity, through focusing on problems in their social and cultural environments. The qualitative approach method provides explanations to explore a particular phenomenon, theory building and capturing everyday life through data collection and analysis, which shifts the philosophical assumptions to appropriate research design and technique data.

(2) Quantitative Approach

The quantitative approach includes the interpretation of numeric data such as percentages, interval or ratio and using items of analysis such as graphs or diagrams to get perfect results. The quantitative approach can be described as an extreme of empiricism, which depends on control and explanation of the phenomenon. The quantitative researchers are more interested to measure about "how many?", "how often?", or "to what extent?". Quantitative research in the analysis of data depends on statistical principles, and this contrary to qualitative research, which is preferred when there is little research into the phenomenon needs to be investigated to be more understood. Table 5-1 outlines a summary of the strength and weaknesses of the qualitative research method and quantitative research method. In qualitative and quantitative approaches there are different methods of concept. Table 5-2 outlines the comparison between the two methods in terms of concepts, processes, and analysis.

Strengths and weaknesses of the qualitative and quantitative research methods

Table 5-1

Method	Strength	Weaknesses
Qualitative	• The qualitative analysis allows a complete, rich and detailed description. • Can be faster when compared to quantitative methods. • Does not reduce complex human experiences to numerical form and allows a good insight into a person's experiences and behavior. • Qualitative methods can be cheaper than quantitative research. • Ambiguities, which are inherent in human language, can be recognized in the analysis.	• Qualitative data is difficult to analyze and needs a high level of interpretative skills. • Good chance of bias. • Hard to draw brief conclusions from qualitative data. • Qualitative data faces difficulties in terms of comparison. • Low level of accuracy in terms of statistics.
Quantitative	• Quantitative analysis allows for the classifying of features, counting them, and constructing more complex statistical models in an attempt to explain what is observed. • Findings can be generalized to a larger population. • Allows researchers to analyze more easily because quantitative data is in numerical form. • Provides a high level of accuracy. • Compare measures of dispersion. • Allows to present analysis graphically.	• Picture of the data which emerges from quantitative analysis lacks the richness of detail compared with data from qualitative analysis reduced to numerical form. • Quantitative implementation slow, and needs time compared with qualitative. • Can be expensive. • Low response rates. • Not simple to implement. • Quantitative often requires computer analysis.

Comparison of quantitative and qualitative methodologies   Table 5-2

Quanlitative	Quantitative
1. It is often an inductive process and the language is informal. 2. Can be faster and cheaper compared with quantitative. 3. Concepts are in the form of themes, motifs, and taxonomies. 4. The analysis proceeds by extracting themes or generalizations from evidence and organizing data to present a coherent picture. 5. Procedures are particular and replication is difficult.	1. It is a deductive process and the language is formal. 2. Can be relatively slow and more costly compared with qualitative. 3. Concepts are in the form of distinct variables. 4. The analysis proceeds by using statistics, tables, or charts. 5. Procedures are standard and replication is assumed.

4. Model

We have noted that an information system is a system that accepts data resources as input and processes them into information products as output. How does an information system accomplish this task? What system components and activities are involved?

Figure 5-2 illustrates an information system model that expresses a fundamental conceptual framework for the major components and activities of information systems. An information system depends on the resources of people (end users and IS specialists), hardware (machines and media), software (programs and procedures), data (data and knowledge bases), and networks (communications media and network support) to perform input, processing, output, storage, and control activities that transform data resources into information products.

This information system model highlights the relationships among the components and activities of information systems. It also provides a framework that emphasizes four major concepts that can be applied to all types of information systems:

- People, hardware, software, data, and networks are the five basic resources of information systems.

- People resources include end users and IS specialists, hardware resources consist of machines and media, software resources include both programs and procedures, data resources include data and knowledge bases, and network resources include communications media and networks.

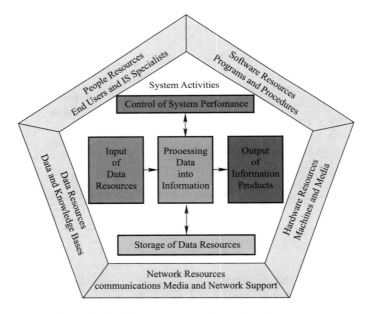

Figure 5-2 The components of an information system

All information systems us people, hardware, software, data, and network resources to perform input, processing, output, storage, and control activities that transform data resources into information products.

- Data resources are transformed by information processing activities into a variety of information products for end users.

- Information processing consists of the system activities of input, processing, output, storage, and control.

Review Questions and Problems:

1. What is the Information Systems?

2. Please elaborate the importance of the Information Systems.

5. 2　Big Data

5. 2 Professional Terms, Words and Phrases, Sentence Illustration

1.　Big Data

Big data is a term used to describe data collections that are so enormous and complex (from sensor data to social media data) that traditional data management software, hardware, and analysis processes are incapable of dealing with them. There are three characteristics about the big data:

(1) Volume

In 2014, it was estimated that the volume of data that exists in the digital universe was 4. 4 zettabytes (one zettabyte equals one trillion gigabytes). The digital universe is expected to grow to an amazing 44 zettabytes by 2020, with perhaps one-third of that data being of value to organizations.

The benefit gained from the ability to process large amounts of information is the main attraction of big data analytics. Having more data beats out having better models: simple bits of math can be unreasonably effective given large amounts of data. If you could run that forecast taking into account 300 factors rather than 6, could you predict demand better?

This volume presents the most immediate challenge to conventional IT structures. It calls for scalable storage, and a distributed approach to querying. Many companies already have large amounts of archived data, perhaps in the form of logs, but not the capacity to process it.

Assuming that the volumes of data are larger than those conventional relational database infrastructures can cope with, processing options break down broadly into a choice between massively parallel processing architectures—data warehouses or databases such as Greenplum and Apache Hadoop based solutions. This choice is often informed by the degree to which the one of the other "Vs" variety-comes into play. Typically, data warehousing approaches involve predetermined schemas, suiting a regular and slowly evolving dataset. Apache Hadoop, on the other hand, places no conditions on the structure of the data it can process.

At its core, Hadoop is a platform for distributing computing problems across a number of servers. First developed and released as open source by Yahoo, it implements the MapReduce approach pioneered by Google in compiling its search indexes. Hadoop's MapReduce involves distributing a dataset among multiple servers and operating on the data: the "map" stage. The partial results are then recombined: the "reduce" stage.

To store data, Hadoop utilizes its own distributed filesystem, HDFS, which makes data available to multiple computing nodes. A typical Hadoop usage pattern involves three stages:

- Loading data into HDFS.
- MapReduce operations.
- Retrieving results from HDFS.

127

This process is by nature a batch operation, suited for analytical or non-interactive computing tasks. Because of this, Hadoop is not itself a database or data warehouse solution, but can act as an analytical adjunct to one.

One of the most well-known Hadoop users is Facebook, whose model follows this pattern. A MySQL database stores the core data. This is then reflected into Hadoop, where computations occur, such as creating recommendations for you based on your friends' interests. Facebook then transfers the results back into MySQL, for use in pages served to users.

（2）Velocity

The velocity at which data is currently coming at us exceeds 5 trillion bits per second. This rate is accelerating rapidly, and the volume of digital data is expected to double every two years between now and 2020.

The importance of data's velocity—the increasing rate at which data flows into an organization—has followed a similar pattern to that of volume. Problems previously restricted to segments of industry are now presenting themselves in a much broader setting. Specialized companies such as financial traders have long turned systems that cope with fast moving data to their advantage. Now it's our turn.

Why is that so? The Internet and mobile era means that the way we deliver and consume products and services is increasingly instrumented, generating a data flow back to the provider. Online retailers are able to compile large histories of customers' every click and interaction: not just the final sales. Those who are able to quickly utilize that information, by recommending additional purchases, for instance, gain competitive advantage. The smartphone era increases again the rate of data inflow, as consumers carry with them a streaming source of geolocated imagery and audio data.

It's not just the velocity of the incoming data that's the issue: it's possible to stream fast-moving data into bulk storage for later batch processing, for example. The importance lies in the speed of the feedback loop, taking data from input through to decision. A commercial from IBM makes the point that you wouldn't cross the road if all you had was a five-minute old snapshot of traffic location. There are times when you simply won't be able to wait for a report to run or a Hadoop job to complete.

Industry terminology for such fast-moving data tends to be either "streaming data" or "complex event processing". This latter term was more established in product categories before streaming processing data gained more widespread relevance, and seems likely to diminish in favor of streaming.

There are two main reasons to consider streaming processing. The first is when the input data are too fast to store in their entirety: in order to keep storage requirements practical some level of analysis must occur as the data streams in. At the extreme end of the scale, the Large Hadron Collider at CERN generates so much data that scientists must discard the overwhelming majority of it—hoping hard they've not thrown away anything useful. The second reason to consider streaming is where the application mandates immediate response to the data. Thanks to the rise of mobile applications and online gaming this is an increasingly common situation.

Product categories for handling streaming data divide into established proprietary products such as IBM's InfoSphere Streams, and the less-polished and still emergent open source frameworks originating in the web industry: Twitter's Storm, and Yahoo S4.

As mentioned above, it's not just about input data. The velocity of a system's outputs can matter too. The tighter the feedback loop, the greater the competitive advantage. The results might go directly into a product, such as Facebook's recommendations, or into dashboards used to drive decision-making. It's this need for speed, particularly on the web, that has driven the development of key-value stores and columnar databases, optimized for the fast retrieval of precomputed information. These databases form part of an umbrella category known as NoSQL, used when relational models aren't the right fit.

(3) Variety

Data today comes in a variety of formats. Some of the data is what computer scientists call structured data—its format is known in advance, and it fits nicely into traditional databases. Sources of Big Data Organizations collect and use data from a variety of sources, including business applications, social media, sensors and controllers that are part of the manufacturing process, systems that manage the physical environment in factories and offices, media sources (including audio and video broadcasts), machine logs that record events and customer call data, public sources (such as government Web sites), and archives of historical records of transactions and communications (Figure 5-3). Much of this collected data is unstructured and does not fit neatly into traditional relational database management.

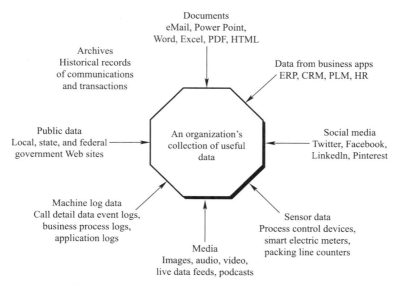

Figure 5-3　Sources of an organization's useful data

Rarely does data present itself in a form perfectly ordered and ready for processing. A common theme in big data systems is that the source data is diverse, and doesn't fall into neat relational structures. It could be text from social networks, image data, a raw feed directly from a sensor source. None of these things come ready for integration into an application.

Even on the web, where computer-to-computer communication ought to bring some guarantees, the reality of data is messy. Different browsers send different data, users withhold information, they may be using differing software versions or vendors to communicate with you. And you can bet that if part of the process involves a human, there will be error and inconsistency.

A common use of big data processing is to take unstructured data and extract ordered meaning, for consumption either by humans or as a structured input to an application. One such example is entity resolution, the process of determining exactly what a name refers to. Is this city London, England, or London, Texas? By the time your business logic gets to it, you don't want to be guessing. The process of moving from source data to processed application data involves the loss of information. When you tidy up, you end up throwing stuff away. This underlines a principle of big data: when you can, keep everything. There may well be useful signals in the bits you throw away. If you lose the source data, there's no going back.

Despite the popularity and well understood nature of relational databases, it is not the case that they should always be the destination for data, even when tidied up. Certain data types suit certain classes of database better. For instance, documents encoded as XML are most versatile when stored in a dedicated XML store such as MarkLogic. Social network relations are graphs by nature, and graph databases such as Neo4J make operations on them simpler and more efficient.

Even where there's not a radical data type mismatch, a disadvantage of the relational database is the static nature of its schemas. In an agile, exploratory environment, the results of computations will evolve with the detection and extraction of more signals. Semi-structured NoSQL databases meet this need for flexibility: They provide enough structure to organize data, but do not require the exact schema of the data before storing it.

2. Introduction

Big data is data exceeds the processing capacity of conventional database systems. The data is too big, moves too fast, or doesn't fit the strictures of your database architectures. To gain value from this data, you must choose an alternative way to process it.

The hot IT buzzword of 2012, big data has become viable as cost-effective approaches have emerged to tame the volume, velocity and variability of massive data. Within this data lie valuable patterns and information, previously hidden because of the amount of work required to extract them. To leading corporations, such as Walmart or Google, this power has been in reach for some time, but at fantastic cost. Today's commodity hardware, cloud architectures and open source software bring big data processing into the reach of the less well-resourced. Big data processing is eminently feasible for even the small garage startups, who can cheaply rent server time in the cloud.

The value of big data to an organization falls into two categories: analytical use, and enabling new products. Big data analytics can reveal insights hidden previously by data too costly to process, such as peer influence among customers, revealed by analyzing shoppers' transactions, social and geographical data. Being able to process every item of data in reasonable time removes the troublesome need for sampling and promotes an investigative approach to data, in contrast to the somewhat static nature of running predetermined reports.

The past decade's successful web startups are prime examples of big data used as an enabler of new products and services. For example, by combining a large number of signals from a user's actions and those of their friends, Facebook has been able to craft a highly personalized user experience and create a new kind of advertising business. It's no coincidence that the lion's share of ideas and tools underpinning big data have emerged from Google, Yahoo, Amazon and Facebook.

The emergence of big data into the enterprise brings with it a necessary counterpart agility. Successfully exploiting the value in big data requires experimentation and exploration. Whether creating new products or looking for ways to gain competitive advantage, the job calls for curiosity and an entrepreneurial outlook.

3. Hierarchy of Data

Data is generally organized in a hierarchy that begins with the smallest piece of data used by computers (a bit), progressing up through the hierarchy to a database. A bit is a binary digit (i. e. , 0 or 1) that represents a circuit that is either on or off. Bits can be organized into units called bytes. A byte is typically eight bits. Each byte represents a character, which is the basic building block of most information. A character can be an uppercase letter (A, B, C,..., Z), a lowercase letter (a, b, c,..., z), a numeric digit (0, 1, 2,..., 9), or a special symbol. Characters are put together to form a field. A field is typically a name, a number, or a combination of characters that describes an aspect of a business object (such as an employee, a location, or a plant) or activity (such as a sale). In addition to being entered into a database, fields can be computed from other fields. Computed fields include the total, average, maximum, and minimum value. A collection of data fields all related to one object, activity, or individual is called a record. By combining descriptions of the characteristics of an object, activity, or individual, a record can provide a complete description of it. For instance, an employee record is a collection of fields about one employee. One field includes the employee's name, another field contains the address, and still others the phone number, pay rate, earnings made to date, and so forth. A collection of related records is a file, for example, an employee file is a collection of all company employee records. Likewise, an inventory file is a collection of all inventory records for a particular company or organization.

At the highest level of the data hierarchy is a database, a collection of integrated and related files. Together, bits, characters, fields, records, files, and databases form the hierarchy of data (Figure 5-4). Characters are combined to make a field, fields are combined to make a record, records are combined to make a file, and files are combined to make a database. A database houses not only all these levels of data but also the relationships among them.

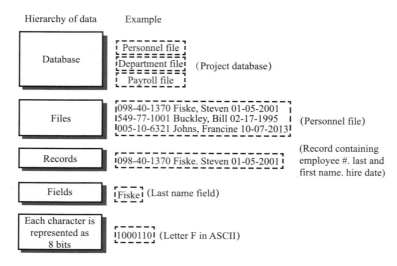

Figure 5-4　Hierarchy of data

4. Big Data Uses

Here are just a few examples of how organizations are employing big data to improve their day-to-day operations, planning, and decision making:

● Retail organizations monitor social networks such as Facebook, Google, LinkedIn, Twitter, and Yahoo to engage brand advocates, identify brand adversaries (and attempt to reverse their negative opinions), and even enable passionate customers to sell their products.

● Advertising and marketing agencies track comments on social media to understand consumers'responsiveness to ads, campaigns, and promotions.

● Hospitals analyze medical data and patient records to try to identify patients likely to need readmission within a few months of discharge, with the goal of engaging with those patients in the hope of preventing another expensive hospital stay.

● Consumer product companies monitor social networks to gain insight into customer behavior, likes and dislikes, and product perception to identify necessary changes to their products, services, and advertising.

● Financial services organizations use data from customer interactions to identify customers who are likely to be attracted to increasingly targeted and sophisticated offers.

● Manufacturers analyze minute vibration data from their equipment, which changes slightly as it wears down, to predict the optimal time to perform maintenance or replace the equipment to avoid expensive repairs or potentially catastrophic failure.

We have explored the nature of big data, and surveyed the landscape of big data from a high level. As usual, when it comes to deployment there are dimensions to consider over and above tool selection.

(1) Cloud or In-House

The majority of big data solutions are now provided in three forms: software-only, as an appliance or cloud-based. Decisions between which route to take will depend, among other things, on issues of data locality, privacy and regulation, human resources and project requirements. Many organizations opt for a hybrid solution: using on-demand cloud resources to supplement in-house deployments.

(2) Big Data Is Big

It is a fundamental fact that data that is too big to process conventionally is also too big to transport anywhere. IT is undergoing an inversion of priorities: It's the program that needs to move, not the data. If you want to analyze data from the U. S. Census, it's a lot easier to run your code on Amazon's web services platform, which hosts such data locally, and won't cost you time or money to transfer it.

Even if the data isn't too big to move, locality can still be an issue, especially with rapidly updating data. Financial trading systems crowd into data centers to get the fastest connection to source data, because that millisecond difference in processing time equates to competitive advantage.

(3) Big Data Is Messy

It's not all about infrastructure. Big data practitioners consistently report that 80% of the effort involved in dealing with data is cleaning it up in the firstplace, as Pete Warden observes in his Big Data Glossary: "I probably spend more time turning messy source data into something usable than I do on the rest of the data analysis process combined. "

Because of the high cost of data acquisition and cleaning, it's worth considering what you actually need to source yourself. Data marketplaces are a means of obtaining common data, and you are often able to contribute improvements back. Quality can of course be variable, but will increasingly be a benchmark on which data marketplaces compete.

(4) Culture

The phenomenon of big data is closely tied to the emergence of data science, a discipline that combines math, programming and scientific instinct. Benefiting from big data means investing in teams with this skill set, and surrounding them with an organizational willingness to understand and use data for advantage.

In his report, "*Building Data Science Teams*", J. Patil characterizes data scientists as having the following qualities:

• Technical expertise: the best data scientists typically have deep expertise in some scientific discipline.

• Curiosity: a desire to go beneath the surface and discover and distill a problem down into a very clear set of hypotheses that can be tested.

• Storytelling: the ability to use data to tell a story and to be able to communicate it effectively.

• Cleverness: the ability to look at a problem in different, creative ways.

The far-reaching nature of big data analytics projects can have uncomfortable aspects: data must be broken out of silos in order to be mined, and the organization must learn how to communicate and interpret the results of analysis.

Those skills of storytelling and cleverness are the gateway factors that ultimately dictate whether the benefits of analytical labors are absorbed by an organization. The art and practice of visualizing data is becoming ever more important in bridging the human-computer gap to mediate analytical insight in a meaningful way.

(5) Know Where You Want To Go

Finally, remember that big data is nopanacea. You can find patterns and clues in your data, but then what? Christer Johnson, IBM's leader for advanced analytics in North America, gives this advice to businesses starting out with big data: first, decide what problem you want to solve.

If you pick a real business problem, such as how you can change your advertising strategy to increase spend per customer, it will guide your implementation. While big data work benefits from an enterprising spirit, it also benefits strongly from a concrete goal.

5. Data Management

Data management is an integrated set of functions that defines the processes by which data is obtained, certified fit for use, stored, secured, and processed in such a way as to ensure that the accessibility, reliability, and timeliness of the data meet the needs of the data users within an organization. Data governance is the core component of data management; it defines the roles, responsibilities, and processes for ensuring that data can be trusted and used by the entire organization, with people identified and in place who are responsible for fixing and preventing issues with data. The Data Management Association (DAMA) International is a nonprofit, vendor-independent, international association whose members promote the understanding, development, and practice of managing data as an essential enterprise asset. This organization has identified 10 major functions of data management, as shown in Figure 5-5. The need for data management is driven by a variety of factors, including the need to meet external regulations designed to manage risk associated with financial misstatement, the need to avoid the inadvertent release of sensitive data, or the need to ensure that high data quality is available for key decisions. Haphazard or incomplete business processes and controls simply will not meet these requirements. Formal management processes are needed to govern data. Effective data governance requires business leadership and active participation—it cannot be an effort that is led by the information system organization. The data governance team should be a cross-functional, multilevel data governance team, consisting of executives, project managers, line-of-business managers, and data stewards. The team also develops a policy that specifies who is accountable for various portions or aspects of the data, including its accuracy, accessibility, consistency, completeness, updating, and archiving. The team defines processes for how the data is to be stored, archived, backed up, and protected from cyberattacks, inadvertent destruction or disclosure, or theft. It also develops standards and procedures that define who is authorized to update, access, and use the data. The team also puts in place a set of controls and audit procedures to ensure ongoing compliance with organizational data policies and government regulations. Data Lifecycle Management (DLM) is a policy-based approach to managing the flow of an enterprise's data, from its initial acquisition or creation and storage to the time when it becomes outdated and is deleted (Figure 5-6). Several vendors offer software products to support DLM such as IBM Information Lifecycle Governance suite of software products.

Figure 5-5   Data management

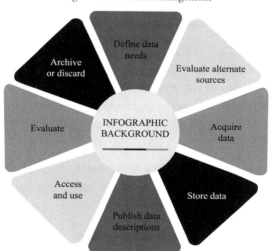

Figure 5-6   The big data life cycle

6. The Future of Big Data

2011 was the "coming out" ear for data science and big data. As the field matures in 2012, what can we expect over the course of the year?

(1) More Powerful and Expressive Tools for Analysis

This year has seen consolidation and engineering around improving the basic storage and data processing engines of NoSQL and Hadoop. That will doubtless continue, as we see the unruly menagerie of the Hadoop universe increasingly packaged into distributions, appliances and on-demand cloud services. Hopefully it won't be long before that's dull, yet necessary, infrastructure.

Looking up the stack, there's already an early cohort of tools directed at programmers and data scientists, as well as Hadoop connectors for established analytical tools such as Tableau and R. But there's a way to go in making big data more powerful: that is, to decrease the cost of creating experiments.

Here are two ways in which big data can be made more powerful.

① Better programming language support. As we consider data, rather than business logic, as the primary entity in a program, we must create or re-discover idiom that lets us focus on the data, rather than abstractions leaking up from the underlying Hadoop machinery. In other words: write shorter programs that make it clear what we're doing with the data. These abstractions will in turn lend themselves to the creation of better tools for non-programmers.

② We require better support for interactivity. If Hadoop has any weakness, it's in the batch-oriented nature of computation it fosters. The agile nature of data science will favor any tool that permits more interactivity.

(2) Streaming Data Processing

Hadoop's batch-oriented processing is sufficient for many use cases, especially where the frequency of data reporting doesn't need to be up-to-the-minute. However, batch processing isn't always adequate, particularly when serving online needs such as mobile and web clients, or markets with real-time changing conditions such as finance and advertising.

Over the next few years we'll see the adoption of scalable frameworks and platforms for handling streaming, or near real-time, analysis and processing. In the same way that Hadoop has been borne out of large-scale web applications, these platforms will be driven by the needs of large-scale location-aware mobile, social and sensor use.

For some applications, there just isn't enough storage in the world to store every piece of data your business might receive: at some point you need to make a decision to throw things away. Having streaming computation abilities enables you to analyze data or make decisions about discarding it without having to go through the store-compute loop of map/reduce.

Emerging contenders in the real-time framework category include Storm, from Twitter, and S4, from Yahoo.

(3) Rise of Data Marketplaces

Your own data can become that much more potent when mixed with other datasets. For instance, add in weather conditions to your customer data, and discover if there are weather related patterns to your customers' purchasing patterns. Acquiring these datasets can be a pain, especially if you want to do it outside of the IT department, and with some exactness. The value of data marketplaces is in providing a directory to this data, as well as streamlined, standardized methods of delivering it. Microsoft's direction of integrating its Azure marketplace right into analytical tools foreshadows the coming convenience of access to data.

(4) Development of Data Science Workflows and Tools

As data science teams become a recognized part of companies, we'll see a more regularized expectation of their roles and processes. One of the driving attributes of a successful data science team is its level of integration into a company's business operations, as opposed to being a sidecar analysis team.

Software developers already have a wealth of infrastructure that is both logistical and social, including wikis and source control, along with tools that expose their process and requirements to business owners. Integrated data science teams will need their own versions of these tools to collaborate effectively. One example of this is EMC Greenplum's Chorus, which provides a social software platform for data science. In turn, use of these tools will support the emergence of data science process within organizations.

(5) Everyone's Talking...

Data science teams will start to evolve repeatable processes, hopefully agile ones. They could do worse than to look at the ground-breaking work newspaper data teams are doing at news organizations such as the *Guardian* and *New York Times*: given short timescales these teams take data from raw form to a finished product, working hand-in-hand with the journalist.

(6) Increased Understanding of and Demand for Visualization

Visualization fulfills two purposes in a data workflow: explanation and exploration. While business people might think of a visualization as the end result, data scientists also use visualization as a way of looking for questions to ask and discovering new features of a data set.

If becoming a data-driven organization is about fostering a better feel for data among all employees, visualization plays a vital role in delivering data manipulation abilities to those without direct programming or statistical skills.

Throughout a year dominated by business' constant demand for data scientists, I've repeatedly heard from data scientists about what they want most: people who know how to create visualizations.

5.3   Data Mining

1. Introduction

5.3 Professional Terms, Words and Phrases, Sentence Illustration

Data mining is a BI analytics tool used to explore large amounts of data for hidden patterns to predict future trends and behaviors for use in decision making. Used appropriately, data mining tools enable organizations to make predictions about what will happen so that managers can be proactive in capitalizing on opportunities and avoiding potential problems. Among the three most commonly used data mining techniques are association analysis (a specialized set of algorithms sorts through data and forms statistical rules about relationships among the items), neural computing (historical data is examined for patterns that are then used to make predictions), and case-based reasoning (historical if-then-else cases are used to recognize patterns). The Cross-Industry Process for Data Mining (CRISP-DM) is a six-phase structured approach for the planning and execution of a data mining project (Figure 5−7). It is a robust and well-proven methodology, and although it was first conceived in 1999, it remains the most widely used methodology for data mining projects.

Here are a few examples showing how data mining can be used:

- Based on past responses to promotional mailings, identify those consumers most likely to take advantage of future mailings.

- Examine retail sales data to identify seemingly unrelated products that are frequently purchased together.

- Monitor credit card transactions to identify likely fraudulent requests for authorization.

- Use hotel booking data to adjust room rates so as to maximize revenue.

- Analyze demographic data and behavior data about potential customers to identify those who would be the most profitable customers to recruit.

- Study demographic data and the characteristics of an organization's most valuable employees to help focus future recruiting efforts.

- Recognize how changes in an individual's DNA sequence affect the risk of developing common diseases such as Alzheimer's or cancer.

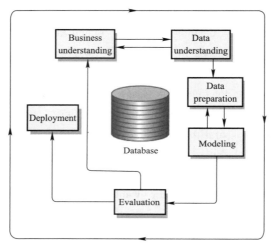

Figure 5-7　The Cross-Industry Process for Data Mining (CRISP-DM)

Data mining is the search for new, valuable, and nontrivial information in large volumes of data. It is a cooperative effort of humans and computers. In practice, the two primary goals of data mining tend to be prediction and description (Figure 5-8). Prediction involves using some variables or fields in the data set to predict unknown or future values of other variables of interest. Description, on the other hand, focuses on finding patterns describing the data that can be interpreted by humans. Therefore, it is possible to put data-mining activities into one of two categories:

(1) Predictive data mining, which produces the model of the system described by the given data set.

(2) Descriptive data mining, which produces new, nontrivial information based on the available data set.

On the predictive end of the spectrum, the goal of data mining is to produce a model, expressed as an executable code, which can be used to perform classification, prediction, estimation, or other similar tasks. On the other hand, descriptive end of the spectrum, the goal is to gain an understanding of the analyzed system by uncovering patterns and relationships in large data sets. The relative importance of prediction and description for particular data-mining applications can vary considerably.

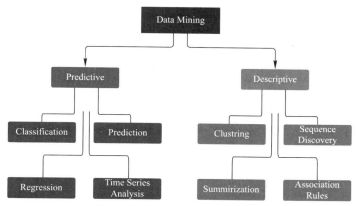
Figure 5-8　Data-mining activities

Data mining is one of the fastest growing fields in the computer industry. Once a small interest area within computer science and statistics, it has quickly expanded into a field of its own. One of the greatest strengths of data mining is reflected in its wide range of methodologies and techniques that can be applied to a host of problem sets. Since data mining is a natural activity to be performed on large data sets, one of the largest target markets is the entire data-warehousing, data-mart, and decision-support community, encompassing professionals from such industries as retail, manufacturing, telecommunications, healthcare, insurance, and transportation.

2. Reason of data mining

We live in a world where vast amounts of data are collected daily. Analyzing such data is an important need.

（1）Moving toward the Information Age

"We are living in the information age" is a popular saying; however, we are actually living in the data age. Terabytes or petabytes of data pour into our computer networks, the World Wide Web (WWW), and various data storage devices every day from business, society, science and engineering, medicine, and almost every other aspect of daily life. This explosive growth of available data volume is a result of the computerization of our society and the fast development of powerful data collection and storage tools. Businesses worldwide generate gigantic data sets, including sales transactions, stock trading records, product descriptions, sales promotions, company profiles and performance, and customer feedback. For example, large stores, such as Walmart, handle hundreds of millions of transactions per week at thousands of branches around the world. Scientific and engineering practices generate high orders of petabytes of data in a continuous manner, from remote sensing, process measuring, scientific experiments, system performance, engineering observations, and environment surveillance. Global backbone telecommunication networks carry tens of petabytes of data traffic every day. The medical and health industry generates tremendous amounts of data from medical records, patient monitoring, and medical imaging. Billions of Web searches supported by search engines process tens of petabytes of data daily. Communities and social media have become increasingly important data sources, producing digital pictures and videos, blogs, Web communities, and various kinds of social networks. The list of sources that generate huge amounts of data is endless. This explosively growing, widely available, and gigantic body of data makes our time truly the data age. Powerful and versatile tools are badly needed to automatically uncover valuable information from the tremendous amounts of data and to transform such data into organized knowledge. This necessity has led to the birth of data mining. The field is young, dynamic, and promising. Data mining has and will continue to make great strides in our journey from the data age toward the coming information age.

（2）Data Mining as the Evolution of Information Technology

Data mining can be viewed as a result of the natural evolution of information technology. The database and data management industry evolved in the development of several critical functionalities: data collection and database creation, data management (including data storage and retrieval and database transaction processing), and advanced data analysis (involving data warehousing and data mining). The early development of data collection and database creation mechanisms served as a prerequisite for the later development of effective mechanisms for data storage and retrieval, as well as query and transaction processing. Nowadays numerous database systems offer query and transaction processing as common practice. Advanced data analysis has naturally become the next step since the 1960s, database and information technology has evolved systematically from primitive file processing systems to sophisticated and powerful database systems. The research and development in database systems since the 1970s progressed from early hierarchical and network database systems to relational database systems (where data are stored in relational table structures), data modeling tools, and indexing and accessing methods. In addition, users gained convenient and flexible data access through query languages, user interfaces, query optimization, and transaction management. Efficient methods for Online Transaction Processing (OLTP), where a query is viewed as a read-only transaction, contributed substantially to the evolution and wide acceptance of relational technology as a major tool for efficient storage, retrieval, and management of large amounts of data. After the establishment of database management systems, database technology moved toward the development of advanced database systems, data warehousing, and data mining for advanced data analysis and web-based databases. Advanced database systems, for example, resulted from an upsurge of research from the mid-1980s onward. These systems incorporate new and powerful data models such as extended-relational, object-oriented, object-relational, and deductive models. Application-oriented database systems have flourished, including spatial, temporal, multimedia, active, stream and sensor, scientific and engineering databases, knowledge bases, and office information bases. Issues related to the distribution, diversification, and sharing of data have been studied extensively. Advanced data analysis sprang up from the late 1980s onward. The steady and dazzling progress of computer hardware technology in the past three decades led to large supplies of powerful and affordable computers, data collection equipment, and storage media. This technology provides a great boost to the database and information industry, and it enables a huge number of databases and information repositories to be available for transaction management, information retrieval, and data analysis. Data can now be stored in many different kinds of databases and information repositories. One emerging data repository architecture is the data warehouse. This is a repository of multiple heterogeneous data sources organized under a unified schema at a single site to facilitate management decision making. Data warehouse technology includes data cleaning, data integration, and Online Analytical Processing (OLAP)—that is, analysis techniques with functionalities such as summarization, consolidation, and aggregation, as well as the ability to view information from different angles. Although OLAP tools support multidimensional analysis and decision making, additional data analysis tools are required for in-depth analysis—for example, data mining tools that provide data classification, clustering, outlier anomaly detection, and the characterization of changes in data over time. Huge volumes of data have been accumulated beyond databases and data warehouses. During the 1990s, the World Wide Web and web-based databases (e. g. , XML databases) began to appear. Internet-based global information bases, such as the WWW and various kinds of interconnected, heterogeneous databases, have emerged and play a vital role in the information industry. The effective and efficient analysis of data from such different forms of data by integration of information retrieval, data mining, and information network analysis technologies is a challenging task.

In summary, the abundance of data, coupled with the need for powerful data analysis tools, has been described as a data rich but information poor situation (Figure 5-9). The fast-growing, tremendous amount of data, collected and stored in large and numerous data repositories, has far exceeded our human ability for comprehension without powerful tools. As a result, data collected in large data repositories become "data tombs"—data archives that are seldom visited. Consequently, important decisions are often made based not on the information-rich data stored in data repositories but rather on a decision maker's intuition, simply because the decision maker does not have the tools to extract the valuable knowledge embedded in the vast amounts of data. Efforts have been made to develop expert system and knowledge-based technologies, which typically rely on users or domain experts to manually input knowledge into knowledge bases. Unfortunately, however, the manual knowledge input procedure is prone to biases and errors and is extremely costly and time consuming. The widening gap between data and information calls for the systematic development of data mining tools that can turn data tombs into "golden nuggets" of knowledge.

3. Data Mining Process

Data Mining is a process of discovering various models, summaries, and derived values from a given collection of data. The word "process" is very important here. Even in some professional environments, there is a belief that data mining simply consists of picking and applying a computer-based tool to match the presented problem and automatically obtaining a solution. The general experimental procedure adapted to data-mining problems involves the following steps:

(1) State the Problem and Formulate the Hypothesis

Most data-based modeling studies are performed in a particular application domain. Hence, domain-specific knowledge and experience are usually necessary in order to come up with a meaningful problem statement. Unfortunately, many application studies tend to focus on the data-mining technique at the expense of a clear problem statement. In this step, a modeler usually specifies a set of variables for the unknown dependency and, if possible, a general form of this dependency as an initial hypothesis. There may be several hypotheses formulated for a single problem at this stage. The first step requires the combined expertise of an application domain and a data-mining model. In practice, it usually means a close interaction between the data-mining expert and the application expert. In successful data-mining applications, this cooperation does not stop in the initial phase; it continues during the entire data-mining process.

（2）Collect the Data

This step is concerned with how the data are generated and collected. In general, there are two distinct possibilities. The first is when the data-generation process is under the control of an expert (modeler): this approach is known as a designed experiment. The second possibility is when the expert cannot influence the data-generation process: this is known as the observational approach. An observational setting, namely, random data generation, is assumed in most data-mining applications. Typically, the sampling distribution is completely unknown after data are collected, or it is partially and implicitly given in the data-collection procedure. It is very important, however, to understand how data collection affects its theoretical distribution, since such a priori knowledge can be very useful for modeling and, later, for the final interpretation of results. Also, it is important to make sure that the data used for estimating a model and the data used later for testing and applying a model come from the same, unknown, sampling distribution. If this is not the case, the estimated model cannot be successfully used in a final application of the results.

（3）Preprocessing the Data

Data preprocessing usually includes at least two common tasks: ① Outlier detection (and removal). Outliers are unusual data values that are not consistent with most observations. Commonly, outliers result from measurement errors and coding and recording errors and, sometimes, are natural, abnormal values. Such nonrepresentative samples can seriously affect the model produced later. There are two strategies for dealing with outliers: (i) Detect and eventually remove outliers as a part of the preprocessing phase. (ii) Develop robust modeling methods that are insensitive to outliers. ② Scaling, encoding, and selecting features Data preprocessing includes several steps such as variable scaling and different types of encoding. Also, application-specific encoding methods usually achieve dimensionality reduction by providing a smaller number of informative features for subsequent data modeling. These two classes of preprocessing tasks are only illustrative examples of a large spectrum of preprocessing activities in a data-mining process. Data-preprocessing steps should not be considered completely independent from other data-mining phases. In every iteration of the data-mining process, all activities, together, could define new and improved data sets for subsequent iterations. Generally, a good preprocessing method provides an optimal representation for a data-mining technique by incorporating a priori knowledge in the form of application-specific scaling and encoding.

（4）Estimate the Model

The selection and implementation of the appropriate data-mining technique is the main task in this phase. This process is not straightforward; usually, in practice, the implementation is based on several models, and selecting the best one is an additional task.

（5）Interpret the Model and Draw Conclusions

In most cases, data-mining models should help in decision-making. Hence, such models need to be interpretable in order to be useful because humans are not likely to base their decisions on complex "black-box" models. Note that the goals of accuracy of the model and accuracy of its interpretation are somewhat contradictory. Usually, simple models are more interpretable, but they are also less accurate. Modern data-mining methods are expected to yield highly accurate results using high-dimensional models. The problem of interpreting these models, also very important, is considered a separate task, with specific techniques to validate the results. A user does not want hundreds of pages of numerical results. He does not understand them; he cannot summarize, interpret, and use them for successful decision making. Even though the focus is on steps 3 and 4 in the data-mining process, we have to understand that they are just two steps in a more complex process. A good understanding of the whole process is important for any successful application. No matter how powerful the data mining method used in step 4 is, the resulting model will not be valid if the data are not collected and preprocessed correctly or if the problem formulation is not meaningful. In practice, many of the tasks can be performed in a different order, and it will often be necessary to backtrack to previous activities and repeat certain actions. The model does not try to capture all possible routes through the data-mining process. The reader may recognize the connection and similarities between steps of data mining presented on Figure 5−9 and Figure 5−10.

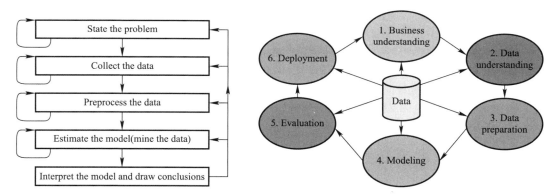

Figure 5−9　The data mining process　　　　Figure 5−10　CRISP-DM conceptual model

4. Data Mining Tools

Data mining tools are the software tools you use to query information in a data warehouse. These data-mining tools support the concept of OLAP—the manipulation of information to support decision-making tasks. Data mining tools include query and reporting tools, intelligent agents, multidimensional analysis tools, and statistical tools. Essentially, data-mining tools are to data warehouse users what data manipulation subsystem tools are to database users.

143

Query-and-reporting tools are similar to QBE tools, SQL, and report generators in the typical database environment. In fact, most data warehousing environments support simple and easy-to-use data manipulation sub system tools such as QBE, SQL, and report generators. Most often, data warehouse users use these types of tools to generate simple queries and reports.

Intelligent agents utilize various artificial intelligence tools such as neural networks and fuzzy logic to form the basis of "information discovery" and building business intelligence in OLAP. For example, Wall Street analyst Murray Riggiero uses OLAP software called Data Logic, which incorporates neural networks to generate rules for his highly successful stock and bond trading system. Other OLAP tools, such as Data Engine, incorporate fuzzy logic to analyze real-time technical processes. Intelligent agents represent the growing convergence of various IT tools for working with information. Previously, intelligent agents were considered only within the context of artificial intelligence and were seldom thought to be a part of the data organizing and managing functions in an organization. Today, you can find intelligent agents being used not only for OLAP in a data warehouse environment but also for searching for information on the Web.

Multidimensional Analysis (MDA) Tools are slice-and-dice techniques that allow you to view multidimensional information from different perspectives. Within the context of a data warehouse, we refer to this process as "turning the cube". That is, you're essentially turning the cube to view information from different perspectives.

This turning of the cube allows you to quickly see information in different sub cubes. If you refer back to the data warehouse, you'll notice that information by customer segment and timing of advertising is actually hidden. Using MDA tools, you can easily bring this to the front of the data warehouse for viewing. What you've essentially done is to slice the cube vertically by layer and bring some of the background layers to the front. As you do this, the values of the information are not affected.

Statistical tools help you apply various mathematical models to the information stored in a data warehouse to discover new information. For example, you can perform a time-series analysis to project future trends. You can also perform a regression analysis to determine the effect of one variable on another.

Sega of America, one of the largest publishers of video games, uses a data warehouse and statistical tools to effectively distribute its advertising budget of more than $50 million a year. With its data warehouse, product line specialists and marketing strategists "drill" into trends of each retail store chain. Their goal is to find buying trends that will help them better determine which advertising strategies are working best (and at what time of the year) and how to reallocate advertising resources by media, territory, and time. Sega definitely benefits from its data warehouse, and so do retailers such as Toys "R" Us, Walmart, and Sears—all good examples of customer relationship management through technology.

5. Data Mining Models

A Data mining model refers to a method that usually use to present the information and various ways in which they can apply information to specific questions and problems. Data mining uses raw data to extract information and present it uniquely. The data mining process is usually found in the most diverse range of applications, including business intelligence studies, political model forecasting, web ranking forecasting, weather pattern model forecasting, etc. In business operation intelligence studies, business experts mine huge data sets related to a business operation or a market and try to discover previously unrecognized trends and relationships. Data mining is also used in organizations that utilize big data as a raw data source to extract the required data.

(1) Predictive Data Mining Model

As per the specialists, the data mining regression model is the most commonly used data mining model. A predictive data mining model predicts the values of data using known results gathered from the different data sets. Predictive modeling cannot be classified as a separate discipline; it occurs in all organizations or industries across all disciplines. The main objective of predictive data mining models is to predict the future based on the past data, generally but not always on the statistical modeling. Predictive modeling is used in healthcare industries to identify high-risk patients with congestive heart failures, high blood pressure, diabetes, infection, cancer, etc. It is also used in the vehicle insurance company to assign the risk of accidents to the policyholder. A predictive model of a data mining task comprises classification, regression, prediction, and time series analysis. The predictive model of data mining is also called statistical regression. It refers to a monitoring learning technique that includes an explication of the dependency of a few attribute's values upon the other attribute's value in the same product and the growth of a model that can predict these attribute's values in previous cases.

(2) Descriptive Data Mining

A descriptive model differentiates the patterns and relationships in data. A descriptive model does not attempt to generalize to a statistical population or random process. A predictive model attempts to generalize to a population or random process. Predictive models should give prediction intervals and must be cross-validated; that is, they must prove that they can be used to make predictions with data that was not used in constructing the model. Descriptive analytics focuses on the summarization and conversion of the data into useful information for reporting and monitoring.

(3) Classification

In data mining, classification refers to a form of data analysis where a machine learning model assigns a specific category to a new observation. It is based on what the model has learned from the data sets. In other words, classification is the act of assigning objects to many predefined categories. One example of classification in the banking and financial services industry is identifying whether transactions are fraudulent or not. In the same way, machine learning can also be used to predict whether a loan application would be approved or not.

(4) Regression

Regression refers to a method that verifies the value of data for a function. Generally, it is used for appropriate data. A linear regression model in the context of machine learning or statistics is basically a linear approach for modeling the relationships between the dependent variable known as the result and your independent variable is known as features. If your model has only one independent variable, it is called simple linear regression, and else it is called multiple linear regression. There are two types of regression: Linear regression and Multi-linear regression. Linear regression is related to the search for the optimal line which fits the two attributes so that with the help of one attribute, we can predict the other. Multi-linear regression includes two or more than two attributes, and the data are fit to multi-dimensional space.

（5）Prediction

In data mining, prediction is used to identify data value based on the description of another corresponding data value. The prediction in data mining is known as Numeric Prediction. Generally, regression analysis is used for prediction. For example, in credit card fraud detection, data history for a particular person's credit card usage has to be analyzed. If any abnormal pattern was detected, it should be reported as "fraudulent action".

Data mining also involves time series analysis, clustering and association rules. Time series analysis refers to the data sets based on time. It serves as an independent variable to predict the dependent variable in time. Clustering is grouping a set of objects so that objects in the same group called a cluster are more similar than those in other groups clusters. Association rules determine a causal relationship between huge sets of data objects.

6. Major Issues in Data Mining

Data mining is a dynamic and fast-expanding field with great strengths. In this section, we briefly outline the major issues in data mining research, partitioning them into five groups: mining methodology, user interaction, efficiency and scalability, diversity of data types, and data mining and society. Many of these issues have been addressed in recent data mining research and development to a certain extent and are now considered data mining requirements; others are still at the research stage. The issues continue to stimulate further investigation and improvement in data mining.

（1）Mining Methodology

Researchers have been vigorously developing new data mining methodologies. This involves the investigation of new kinds of knowledge, mining in multidimensional space, integrating methods from other disciplines, and the consideration of semantic ties among data objects. In addition, mining methodologies should consider issues such as data uncertainty, noise, and incompleteness. Some mining methods explore how user-specified measures can be used to assess the interestingness of discovered patterns as well as guide the discovery process. Let's have a look at these various aspects of mining methodology.

Mining various and new kinds of knowledge: Data mining covers a wide spectrum of data analysis and knowledge discovery tasks, from data characterization and discrimination to association and correlation analysis, classification, regression, clustering, outlier analysis, sequence analysis, and trend and evolution analysis. These tasks may use the same database in different ways and require the development of numerous data mining techniques. Due to the diversity of applications, new mining tasks continue to emerge, making data mining a dynamic and fast-growing field. For example, for effective knowledge discovery in information networks, integrated clustering and ranking may lead to the discovery of high-quality clusters and object ranks in large networks.

Mining knowledge in multidimensional space: When searching for knowledge in large data sets, we can explore the data in multidimensional space. That is, we can search for interesting patterns among combinations of dimensions (attributes) at varying levels of abstraction. Such mining is known as (exploratory) multidimensional data mining. In many cases, data can be aggregated or viewed as a multidimensional data cube. Mining knowledge in cube space can substantially enhance the power and flexibility of data mining. Data mining—an interdisciplinary effort: The power of data mining can be substantially enhanced by integrating new methods from multiple disciplines. For example, to mine data with natural language text, it makes sense to fuse data mining methods with methods of information retrieval and natural language processing. As another example, consider the mining of software bugs in large programs. This form of mining, known as bug mining, benefits from the incorporation of software engineering knowledge into the data mining process.

Boosting the power of discovery in a networked environment: Most data objects reside in a linked or interconnected environment, whether it be the Web, database relations, files, or documents. Semantic links across multiple data objects can be used to advantage in data mining. Knowledge derived in one set of objects can be used to boost the discovery of knowledge in a "related" or semantically linked set of objects.

Handling uncertainty, noise, or incompleteness of data: Data often contain noise, errors, exceptions, or uncertainty, or are incomplete. Errors and noise may confuse the data mining process, leading to the derivation of erroneous patterns. Data cleaning, data preprocessing, outlier detection and removal, and uncertainty reasoning are examples of techniques that need to be integrated with the data mining process.

Pattern evaluation and pattern-or constraint-guided mining: Not all the patterns generated by data mining processes are interesting. What makes a pattern interesting may vary from user to user. Therefore, techniques are needed to assess the interestingness of discovered patterns based on subjective measures. These estimate the value of patterns with respect to a given user class, based on user beliefs or expectations. Moreover, by using interestingness measures or user-specified constraints to guide the discovery process, we may generate more interesting patterns and reduce the search space.

(2) User Interaction

The user plays an important role in the data mining process. Interesting areas of research include how to interact with a data mining system, how to incorporate a user's background knowledge in mining, and how to visualize and comprehend data mining results. We introduce each of these here.

Interactive mining: The data mining process should be highly interactive. Thus, it is important to build flexible user interfaces and an exploratory mining environment, facilitating the user's interaction with the system. A user may like to first sample a set of data, explore general characteristics of the data, and estimate potential mining results. Interactive mining should allow users to dynamically change the focus of a search, to refine mining requests based on returned results, and to drill, dice, and pivot through the data and knowledge space interactively, dynamically exploring "cube space" while mining.

Incorporation of background knowledge: Background knowledge, constraints, rules, and other information regarding the domain under study should be incorporated into the knowledge discovery process. Such knowledge can be used for pattern evaluation as well as to guide the search toward interesting patterns.

Ad hoc data mining and data mining query languages: Query languages (e. g. , SQL) have played an important role in flexible searching because they allow users to pose ad hoc queries. Similarly, high-level data mining query languages or other high-level flexible user interfaces will give users the freedom to define ad hoc data mining tasks. This should facilitate specification of the relevant sets of data for analysis, the domain knowledge, the kinds of knowledge to be mined, and the conditions and constraints to be enforced on the discovered patterns. Optimization of the processing of such flexible mining requests is another promising area of study.

Presentation and visualization of data mining results: How can a data mining system present data mining results, vividly and flexibly, so that the discovered knowledge can be easily understood and directly usable by humans? This is especially crucial if the data mining process is interactive. It requires the system to adopt expressive knowledge representations, user-friendly interfaces, and visualization techniques.

(3) Efficiency and Scalability

Efficiency and scalability are always considered when comparing data mining algorithms. As data amounts continue to multiply, these two factors are especially critical.

Efficiency and scalability of data mining algorithms: Data mining algorithms must be efficient and scalable in order to effectively extract information from huge amounts of data in many data repositories or in dynamic data streams. In other words, the running time of a data mining algorithm must be predictable, short, and acceptable by applications. Efficiency, scalability, performance, optimization, and the ability to execute in real time are key criteria that drive the development of many new data mining algorithms.

Parallel, distributed, and incremental mining algorithms: The humongous size of many data sets, the wide distribution of data, and the computational complexity of some data mining methods are factors that motivate the development of parallel and distributed data-intensive mining algorithms. Such algorithms first partition the data into "pieces". Each piece is processed, in parallel, by searching for patterns. The parallel processes may interact with one another. The patterns from each partition are eventually merged.

Cloud computing and cluster computing: Which use computers in a distributed and collaborative way to tackle very large-scale computational tasks, are also active research themes in parallel data mining. In addition, the high cost of some data mining processes and the incremental nature of input promote incremental data mining, which incorporates new data updates without having to mine the entire data "from scratch". Such methods perform knowledge modification incrementally to amend and strengthen what was previously discovered.

(4) Diversity of Database Types

The wide diversity of database types brings about challenges to data mining. These include:

Handling complex types of data: Diverse applications generate a wide spectrum of new data types, from structured data such as relational and data warehouse data to semi-structured and unstructured data; from stable data repositories to dynamic data streams; from simple data objects to temporal data, biological sequences, sensor data, spatial data, hypertext data, multimedia data, software program code, Web data, and social network data. It is unrealistic to expect one data mining system to mine all kinds of data, given the diversity of data types and the different goals of data mining. Domain-dedicated or application-dedicated data mining systems are being constructed for in-depth mining of specific kinds of data. The construction of effective and efficient data mining tools for diverse applications remains a challenging and active area of research.

Mining dynamic, networked, and global data repositories: Multiple sources of data are connected by the Internet and various kinds of networks, forming gigantic, distributed, and heterogeneous global information systems and networks. The discovery of knowledge from different sources of structured, semi-structured, or unstructured yet interconnected data with diverse data semantics poses great challenges to data mining. Mining such gigantic, interconnected information networks may help disclose many more patterns and knowledge in heterogeneous data sets than can be discovered from a small set of isolated data repositories. Web mining, multisource data mining, and information network mining have become challenging and fast-evolving data mining fields.

(5) Data Mining and Society

How does data mining impact society? What steps can data mining take to preserve the privacy of individuals? Do we use data mining in our daily lives without even knowing that we do? These questions raise the following issues:

Social impacts of data mining: With data mining penetrating our everyday lives, it is important to study the impact of data mining on society. How can we use data mining technology to benefit society? How can we guard against its misuse? The improper disclosure or use of data and the potential violation of individual privacy and data protection rights are areas of concern that need to be addressed.

Privacy-preserving data mining: Data mining will help scientific discovery, business management, economy recovery, and security protection (e. g. , the real-time discovery of intruders and cyberattacks). However, it poses the risk of disclosing an individual's personal information. Studies on privacy-preserving data publishing and data mining are ongoing. The philosophy is to observe data sensitivity and preserve people's privacy while performing successful data mining.

Invisible data mining: We cannot expect everyone in society to learn and master data mining techniques. More and more systems should have data mining functions built within so that people can perform data mining or use data mining results simply by mouse clicking, without any knowledge of data mining algorithms. Intelligent search engines and Internet-based stores perform such invisible data mining by incorporating data mining into their components to improve their functionality and performance. This is done often unbeknownst to the user. For example, when purchasing items online, users may be unaware that the store is likely collecting data on the buying patterns of its customers, which may be used to recommend other items for purchase in the future.

5.4 Artificial Intelligence

5.4 Professional Terms, Words and Phrases, Sentence Illustration

1. Introduction

Artificial (made by human) Intelligence (power of thinking) is the study of machines which can sense, make decision and act like human beings.

The meaning of intelligence is "the ability to acquire and apply knowledge and skills"; in Merriam-Webster intelligence is defined as "the ability to learn or understand or to deal with new or trying situations". So, an intelligent entity must be able to acquire knowledge through various ways like by observations, learning from experience, reading information (data) and processing text, by discussing with others. It should be able to reason this acquired knowledge to make decisions, summaries, setting and following goals, understand text and images etc.

Therefore, Artificial Intelligence (AI) is the study of science and engineering to build artifacts which can develop knowledge by learning from experience, reading and processing text written in natural languages, reason with the acquired knowledge (able to perform tasks such as explaining, planning, diagnosing, etc.) and acting rationally.

A machine is intelligent if it can learn, can do reasoning, and solve problems. In AI, the machines are not programmed to solve a single problem but they can learn and solve more complex problems. So, the machines are programs to be learned. In other word a machine can be called intelligent if it passes the Turing test. The test was named after its creator Alan Turing, the father of theoretical computer science, cryptanalyst and great mathematician (Figure 5-11).

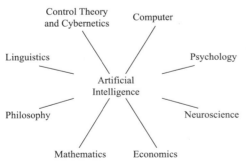

Figure 5-11 Foundation of AI

The foundation and development of AI is build based on an amalgamation of several subjects like Philosophy. The idea of knowledge acquisition, understanding and taking action based on the knowledge in the human mind which manifest from the physical brain. It gives the concept of "How some conclusion can be drawn by a machine from the formal rules".

● Mathematics: It involves computation, representation of logic, probability theory, and decision making. Mathematics is used to determine computability, forming model for knowledge representation and reasoning the knowledge.

● Economics: Is used for optimization and understanding of payoff quantity and duration.

● Neuroscience: How physical human brain works for logical reasoning. The working method in the brain for any particular action taken.

- Psychology: It gives the idea about how human mind thinks and takes action and intersects.

- Computer Engineering: How to build system to function like AI artifact. Improve their capacity and efficiency.

- Control Theory and Cybernetics: How can the AI artifacts can function or act itself. It involves adopt and feedback to adjust with the environment.

- Linguistics: The study of understanding natural languages by AI artifacts. The Natural Language Processing (NLP) is used widely.

The field of Artificial Intelligence has not yet seen an unifying theory that captures the fundamentals for the creation of intelligent machines. Since its conception at the Dartmouth conference in 1956, at least three paradigms have permeated its existence. The top-down paradigm was supposed to be for the creation of models of the mind and eventually led to different types of logic and reasoning and later also sub-symbolic processing. The second paradigm focused on the creation of intelligent machines (robots). Many scientists used introspection of their own mind as a tool for the creation of these machines which was challenged in 1969 using theories of biosemiotics, which is the interpretation of (sensory) signals in biological systems. This led to the bottom-up, behavior-based robotics. The third, but mostly forgotten, paradigm is the field of cybernetics, which was already being investigated when the Dartmouth conference was being held. Before the conference, in 1950, an article in the *Scientific American* showed two robots which consisted out of a few vacuum tubes, control loops and feedback mechanisms. The field of cybernetics could be defined as: the theoretical study of communication and control processes in biological, mechanical, and electronic systems, especially the comparison of these processes in biological and artificial systems. The division in the field of Artificial Intelligence cannot be accepted as the answer to the question of how to build intelligent machines. An integrated perspective is necessary. The field of neo-cybernetics tries to bridge the gaps in AI with an extra addition: the property of emergence. It is unknown whether neo-cybernetics is also sufficient. What is it to study Artificial Intelligence if there is not even a common denominator within the field? The entry chosen in this article toward the creation of intelligent machines is a post-structuralist approach based on the dynamical aspects of non-linear systems. It seems that neo-cybernetics and post-structuralism meet each other in nonlinear dynamical systems theory and can assist each other. Cybernetics requires the deeper underpinnings of post-structuralism, and post-structuralism can proof itself using intelligent machines based on neo-cybernetic mechanisms. This symbiosis is dubbed: Generative Artificial Intelligence. In Generative Artificial Intelligence (GAI), the possibility spaces of post-structuralism are actively being manipulated using neo-cybernetic mechanisms in order to scaffold the minds of intelligent machines.

2. Methods or Tools of Artificial Intelligence

Formal methods, tools, techniques, and applications in Artificial Intelligence are presented on Figure 5-12 and Figure 5-13.

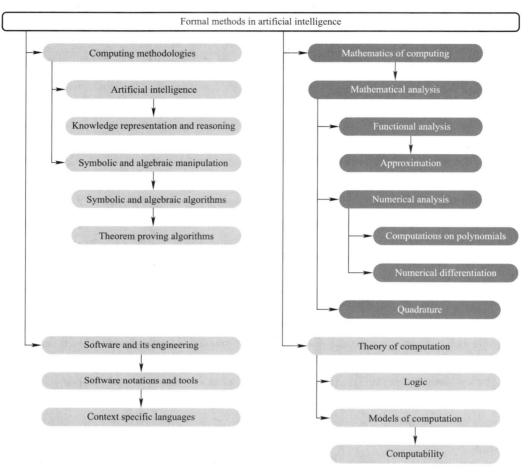

Figure 5-12　Formal methods in Artificial Intelligence

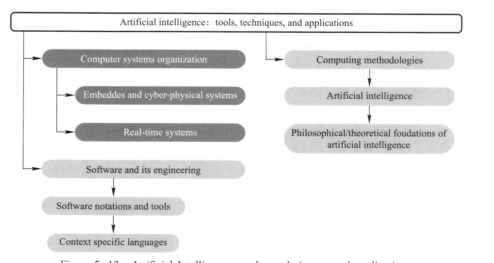

Figure 5-13　Artificial Intelligence：tools，techniques，and applications

3. Models

Artificial Intelligence (AI) has generated much excitement, but relatively little impact in how healthcare is delivered. While progress has accelerated in using Machine Learning (ML) to develop prediction and classification models that make up the bulk of current AI methods, efforts to use these models in the real world setting have not taken off at nearly the same pace and typically remain within the realm of "innovation" outside of the core processes that drive care delivery. To address how AI can be leveraged at scale, we need to both broaden and deepen our thinking around how AI fits into the complexities of healthcare delivery. As the data and computer sciences for developing AI based solutions have matured, we now need a delivery science to bring those solutions into use in healthcare.

Current efforts to use AI in healthcare often begin with "I have a ML model that can accurately predict or classify X.", but then get stuck at "how do I use it and for whom?" As a result, libraries of ML models remain on the shelf without finding appropriate use cases, or models are implemented but deemed to not be as valuable as initially imagined. A recently published ML model that predicts acute kidney injury with high accuracy was assumed by the authors to provide valuable information to clinicians, but when implemented in a real clinical environment, did not significantly improve patient care and in fact resulted in additional work for the physicians that was of unclear value. This example highlights the importance of understanding the complexities of care delivery associated with the clinical use case before building the ML model; just focusing on the capability to accurately perform a prediction task is not sufficient for improving care. This conundrum is not unique to AI; it frequently affects innovation pipelines for other biomedical technologies. For example, the lengthy and rigorous process required in drug development from preclinical experiments to observed health benefits in the real world illustrate the amount of work needed to translate scientific advances into useful therapies that actually improve care. Much of the in silico work around training and validating ML models can be compared to the preclinical testing of active ingredients in pharmaceutical research. Just as the active ingredient alone is not sufficient for creating a drug that works in humans, much less a clinical intervention that improves outcomes for a patient population, a ML model alone is unlikely to make significant improvements in healthcare outcomes.

It is time to move from model development in silico to design, implementation, and evaluation of AI enabled solutions in vivo where healthcare delivery happens. We propose a delivery science for AI in healthcare that rests on the following principles: (1) much of healthcare is delivered in complex adaptive systems, so AI must accommodate this complexity, (2) AI should be viewed as not the end product, but rather an enabling component of broader solutions, and (3) solutions enabled by AI are often complex systems of people, processes, and technologies. We need to take a more holistic view of what AI enabled solutions would look like beyond just a set of ML models. Rather, the human and technical components of the end product, such as the workflows, teams, and digital tools made possible by tasks that a ML model can perform, should be designed and implemented together as a system. The effects—beneficial or harmful—of AI enabled solutions on healthcare should also be evaluated at the system level as emergent properties that may be greater than the sum of its individual components. Identifying these emergent properties and characterizing their impact will require the system to be designed and implemented in its entirety in the healthcare environment where it is meant to operate. The task of implementing AI in healthcare, therefore, should not be about deploying a ML model; rather, it should be about how to design the best possible care delivery system for a given problem, using the ML model as a component in that delivery system.

Our initial experiences with the design, implementation, and evaluation of an AI enabled solution at an academic medical center has revealed the importance of marrying data science with disciplines, such as process improvement, design thinking, and implementation science (Figure 5-14). We had previously developed an all-cause mortality prediction model to act as a proxy for who may benefit from palliative care services such as advance care planning. Rather than jumping to a solution of simply showing the model output to physicians, we first leveraged methods from process improvement to derive the sources of process inefficiencies and breakdowns, and design thinking to observe how these processes affected the thoughts, feelings, and experiences of frontline stakeholders. These steps allowed us to first understand the complex system in which advance care planning is currently delivered before designing a solution enabled by our ML model that could improve on that delivery system.

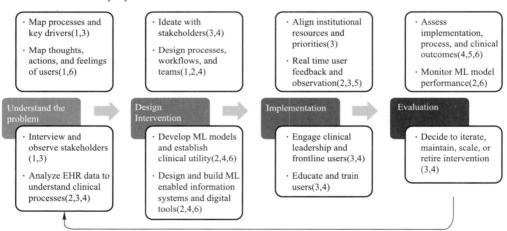

Figure 5-14   Multidisciplinary process for creating, implementing, and evaluating
an AI enabled system for healthcare

Methods from process improvement, design thinking, data science, information technology, and implementation science are combined into an iterative participatory process to build an AI enabled system for improving advance care planning. The expertise used across the different disciplines are as follows: (1) user experience design, (2) data science, (3) healthcare operations, (4) clinical informatics, (5) evaluation, and (6) ethical integrity assessment.

We made a key decision upfront to engage a multidisciplinary group of stakeholders, including front-line nurses, physicians, social workers, and occupational therapists—all who participate in the care of patients with serious illnesses who may benefit from advance care planning—from the beginning of the design process without any preconceived notions of how the

ML model would be used. Interviews and process analyses of the current state quickly revealed key barriers to advance care planning that would unlikely be solved by simply showing a model's output to any one group of clinicians. For example, clinical and logistical considerations around the appropriate timing of advance care planning, what should be discussed, and how should these discussions fit into the broader context of the hospitalization require coordinated, multidisciplinary efforts. Similarly, design thinking tools such as empathy mapping helped us more deeply understand how underlying feelings around role clarity and power structures between physician and non-physician members of the care team affected advance care planning workflow. These insights led us to identify key design goals that otherwise would not have surfaced, such as the need to empower non-physician care team members to identify candidate patients and lead the coordination of advance care planning—a task that was enabled by making transparent to the entire care team the list of candidate patients generated by the mortality prediction model each day and creating a workflow for the physician and non-physician team members to discuss these patients with each other about advance care planning needs. This objective identification of candidate patients by the prediction model allowed for the democratization of responsibility for deciding who needs advance care planning to the non-physician providers such as nurses, social workers, and occupational therapists—all who spend a lot of time with patients and are trained to engage in this topic. The design process also includes analyses to verify that our model's execution and runtime characteristics (such when in the day are predictions available) fit the logistical needs of these new workflows. This deeper understanding of current state gaps and improvement opportunities allowed us to build a system of workflows, teams, and digital tools enabled by the mortality prediction model to drive change in the complex environment of healthcare delivery. Other AI efforts that address the broader sociotechnical components of healthcare beyond just the ML model have offered similar lessons. For example, recent work around using AI to improve the treatment of sepsis committed months to assessing clinical processes and user experiences prior to even training a ML model, which yielded important insights for implementation, such as the need to focus on not just sepsis detection, but a method for standardizing followup care.

To be most useful, evaluations of AI enabled solutions should not simply ask whether it achieved the desired improvement in clinical process or outcome (e. g. , did the frequency or quality of advance care planning improve), but also how well or poorly was the solution implemented. Implementation science and systems engineering tell us that we can use rigorous scientific methods for both effectiveness and implementation questions. Such hybrid evaluations can assess the mechanism (s) by which AI enables the changes that lead to the desired clinical outcome (how did the mortality prediction tasks performed by the ML model mediate the improvement in advance care planning) and the properties of the overall AI enabled systems (what are the structures, patterns, and processes of the workflows, teams, and technologies that make up the new AI enabled system for delivering advance care planning). Frameworks such as RE-AIM13 (reach, effectiveness, adoption, implementation, and maintenance) can help identify the dimensions by which to assess implementation and subsequent dissemination efforts, and models for socio-technical systems such as SEIPS14 (Systems Engineering Initiative for Patient Safety) can help assess the complex interactions between people and technologies in a work system.

Naturally, questions about who is responsible for implementing such delivery systems, and quality control of the ML workflows will arise. Aside from existing processes in healthcare systems to design standard operating procedures, additional attention will be needed to implement quality controls on the models itself. Specifically, to monitor a model's calibration over time, it will be important to watch population drifts and ensure timely retraining so that the model's performance remains with in the execution and runtime characteristics required by the AI enabled system. Just as with clinical laboratory instruments, ML models in healthcare will need to be regularly re-calibrated and tuned. The characteristics of the ML models will also need to be appropriately communicated to clinical users. Fortunately, there is deep experience in the technology sector to draw upon. In-house informatics teams within health systems with expertise in data science, information technology, and clinical operations may be required to own this work. While the nature of these teams may vary across organizations, what is certain is that such a team will need to exist to ensure that AI will be used responsibly and deliver sustained value.

It is time to move AI research out from in silico model development into real world design, implementation, and evaluation for improving healthcare delivery. We will likely see that ML models will be necessary, but not sufficient components of broader AI enabled solutions. The delivery science of AI will need to address how such systems are designed, implemented, and evaluated, and how their emergent properties can be captured and utilized to transform healthcare.

Review Questions and Problems：

1. What is the essence of the AI?

2. Do you think there are any limitations to AI?

5.5 BIM

1. Introduction

Building Information Modeling (BIM) is a process supported by various tools, technologies and contracts involving the generation and management of digital representations of physical and functional characteristics of places. Building Information Models (BIMs) are computer files (often but not always in proprietary formats and containing proprietary data) which can be extracted, exchanged or

5.5 Professional Terms, Words and Phrases, Sentence Illustration

networked to support decision-making regarding a built asset. BIM software is used by individuals, businesses and government agencies who plan, design, construct, operate and maintain buildings and diverse physical infrastructures, such as water, refuse, electricity, gas, communication utilities, roads, railways, bridges, ports and tunnels. The concept of BIM has been in development since the 1970s, but it only became an agreed term in the early 2000s. Development of standards and adoption of BIM has progressed at different speeds in different countries; standards developed in the United Kingdom from 2007 onwards have formed the basis of international standard ISO 19650, launched in January 2019. The application of building information model to engineering cost management can effectively improve the effect of engineering cost, and the application of the provided data to the enterprise's engineering projects can effectively improve the final quality of engineering management. In the era of big data, the application of BIM technology in project cost management can realize the sharing of project cost data resources, facilitate the communication and cooperation between various parties, and promote the quality management of project cost with both quality and quantity guaranteed.

2. Methods or Tools of BIM

There are many methods, languages and tools for Information Modelling available (for instance EXPRESS, UML, OWL, etc.). Many building information models are developed using this information modelling languages, i. e. modelling languages with entities or objects as key elements, connected by relationships. An example is the EXPRESS language, the data modelling language of the ISO standard 10303, the STEP standard. 8 EXPRESS/G9 is also the default language in IAI IFCs.

An alternative is the Class Diagram of UML, which is widely known among software engineers and computer scientists, since it is the most popular object-oriented modelling language. An advantage of UML Class Diagrams is that it provides a useful syntax for behaviour of objects.

A recent alternative is OWL, the Ontology Web Language, developed by the World Wide Web Consortium (W3C). In OWL (so-called) ontologies are defined in which, a specific part of the Universe of Discourse is modelled. OWL is closely related to the Semantic Web vision as expressed by Berners-Lee (2001). OWL is currently applied in the EU-project SWOP (Semantic Web-based Ontology for Product Modelling).

Apart from the data modelling languages mentioned above, also process models can be very useful for BIM. Process models can be used for example for the identification of requirements of BIM data models. A rather old but still very useful example of a process modelling language is IDEF0. 10.

With the definition of BIM or building product model, the product model standards that are required for the B-C industry are, neither standards for the exchange of electronic versions of traditional technical drawings, nor standards for the exchange of geometric data form is only one of the relevant aspects. In fact, there is a need for standards that capture the project information semantically. From such a semantically rich Building Information Model, other models, such a geometrical model, or a Finite Element Model (FEM) can be derived automatically. Additionally, 2D-drawings or 3D models, and other documents could be generated from the same building product model. Since their debut in 1987, Graphisoft implemented this concept into their product ArchiCAD. This concept became known as the Virtual Building concept and has been followed by a number of other CAD vendors like Autodesk/Revit, Bentley and Nemetschek. Although these products do indeed provide the B-C industry some degree of interoperability, vendor-specific product models and supporting technologies are not the right solution (Figure 5 – 15). What is needed are standardized (preferable ISO) product models as technical basis for a future CIC. Due to the ad hoc nature of the B-C industry and the lack of rich and dedicated market leaders, it is extremely difficult to come up with something useful for B-C. In this regard, even ISO STEP AEC proved to be the wrong platform to accomplish this task.

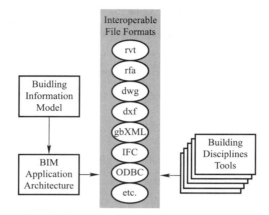

Figure 5-15　Interoperable file formats enabling communication of discipline tools in a dynamic
BIM environment (adapted from Kumar S., 2008)

3. Project Visualization

BIM facilitates interactive digital reproduction of interiors and exteriors of facilities in 3D, by enabling rich photo-realistic presentations. Figure 5-16 shows project visualization for facilities management using a digital building model. It enables stakeholders to visualise project details in a VR environment using very reliable (i. e. architecturally accurate) resources. Project visualization facilitates effective collaboration between parties and promotes constructive analysis of project designs and space provisions. In addition to this, it allows clients and end-users to review their intentions using multiple options in ways that optimise, value generation in investments and flexibility in (use and) management of facilities. Moreover, design conflicts and data inconsistencies can be detected early. Furthermore, BIM-enabled project visualization adds value to communication. With this technology, it is now possible to conduct off-site training on screen for purpose-made and general-need maintenance and operations, and at the same time simulate the functions of project components.

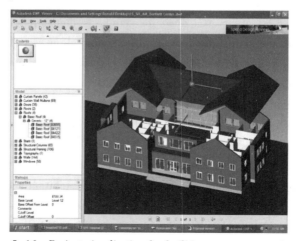

Figure 5-16　Project visualization for facilities management using BIM

Review Questions and Problems:

1. What is the BIM?

2. After reading the above analysis, please elaborate why BIM is important?

5.6   Database Management Systems

1. Introduction

A Database Management System (DBMS) is software that enables an organization to centralize data, manage them efficiently, and provide access to the stored data by application programs. The DBMS acts as an interface between application programs and the physical data files. The DBMS relieves the

5.6 Professional Terms, Words and Phrases, Sentence Illustration

programmer or end user from the task of understanding where and how the data are actually stored by separating the logical and physical views of the data. The logical view presents data, as they would be perceived by end users or business specialists, whereas the physical view shows how data are actually organized and structured on physical storage media. The database management software makes the physical database available for different logical views required by users.

2. Theory

The DBMS acronym is sometimes extended to indicate the underlying database model, with RDBMS for the relational, OODBMS for the object (oriented) and ORDBMS for the object-relational model. Other extensions can indicate some other characteristics, such as DDBMS for a distributed database management systems.

The functionality provided by a DBMS can vary enormously. The core functionality is the storage, retrieval and update of data. Codd proposed the following functions and services a fully-fledged general purpose DBMS should provide:

- Data storage, retrieval and update.
- User accessible catalog or data dictionary describing the metadata.
- Support for transactions and concurrency.
- Facilities for recovering the database should it become damaged.
- Support for authorization of access and update of data.
- Access support from remote locations.
- Enforcing constraints to ensure data in the database abides by certain rules.

It is also generally to be expected the DBMS will provide a set of utilities for such purposes as may be necessary to administer the database effectively, including import, export, monitoring, defragmentation and analysis utilities. The core part of the DBMS interacting between the database and the application interface sometimes referred to as the database engine.

Often DBMSs will have configuration parameters that can be statically and dynamically tuned, for example the maximum amount of main memory on a server the database can use. The trend is to minimize the amount of manual configuration, and for cases such as embedded databases the need to target zero-administration is paramount.

The large major enterprise DBMSs have tended to increase in size and functionality and can have involved thousands of human years of development effort throughout their lifetime.

Early multi-user DBMS typically only allowed for the application to reside on the same computer with access via terminals or terminal emulation software. The client-server architecture was a development where the application resided on a client desktop and the database on a server allowing the processing to be distributed. This evolved into a multitier architecture incorporating application servers and web servers with the end user interface via a web browser with the database only directly connected to the adjacent tier.

A general-purpose DBMS will provide public application programming interfaces (API) and optionally a processor for database languages such as SQL to allow applications to be written to interact with and manipulate the database. A special purpose DBMS may use a private API and be specifically customized and linked to a single application. For example, an email system performs many of the functions of a general-purpose DBMS such as message insertion, message deletion, attachment handling, blocklist lookup, associating messages an email address and so forth however these functions are limited to what is required to handle email.

3. Miscellaneous Features

Other DBMS features might include：

Database logs——This helps in keeping a history of the executed functions.

Graphics component for producing graphs and charts, especially in a data warehouse system.

Query optimizer——Performs query optimization on every query to choose an efficient query plan [a partial order (tree) of operations] to be executed to compute the query result. May be specific to a particular storage engine.

Tools or hooks for database design, application programming, application program maintenance, database performance analysis and monitoring, database configuration monitoring, DBMS hardware configuration (a DBMS and related database may span computers, networks, and storage units) and related database mapping (especially for a distributed DBMS), storage allocation and database layout monitoring, storage migration, etc.

Increasingly, there are calls for a single system that incorporates all of these core functionalities into the same build, test, and deployment framework for database management and source control. Borrowing from other developments in the software industry, some market such offerings as "DevOps for database".

4. Methods and Tools

(1) A system of the present invention includes a Relational Database Management System (RDBMS) having a hypertext report writing module. Methods are described for automatically recognizing relations between reports which are generated from the same or related database tables. The system automatically embeds (or assists the user in embedding) appropriate hypertext links so that information from one report may be cross-referenced immediately with information in another, related report. drill-down hypertext reports of increasing level of detail are illustrated. In addition

to drill-down reports, the system may create comprehensive hypertext reports for automatically tying together information which is related through underlying table relations but which ordinarily appears in different reports. By automatically placing hypertext links or cross-indexes between reports, the system ties together relatable information into a single, cross-indexed hypertext report.

(2) Systems and methods for managing data in relational database management system. A mechanism for managing data in Relational Database Management Systems (RDBMS). The method includes receiving a Structured Query Language (SQL) query to be executed on a Relational Database Management System (RDBMS). The RDBMS includes a schema of tables divided into a plurality of partitions and the SQL query includes an operation of data to be executed on the RDBMS. The method also includes determining whether the SQL query is a valid SQLT query. The SQL query is a valid SQLT query when the SQL query includes a join operation applied to data from tables in a same partition of the plurality of partitions. ... - (USPTO) -, the Patent Description & Claims data below is from USPTO Patent Application 20140280019, systems and methods for managing data in relational database management system. You can also monitor keywords and search for tracking patents relating to this systems and methods for managing data in relational database management system patent application.

(3) The Loyola Open-Heart Registry is a fully operational database that has hundreds of programs designed to input, modify, verify, maintain, update and analyze its raw data. It contains retrospectively collected data on approximately 4000 patients who underwent coronary bypass (CABG) or Cardiac Valve Replacement (CVR) from January 1970 to May 1981. Since 1981 we have collected detailed information on approximately 1300 patients per year. The system is described in clinical and technical terms. The means of data acquisition and input are described and a flow chart for the collection of data is provided. The system's hardware is described briefly, and the nature and limitations of the software are discussed. Specific datasheets are described, and examples of output retrievals are provided. A few comments are made regarding the administrative aspects of database management.

5. Models

The relational model is based on tables, of which Figure 5-17 is an example. This relation, or table, describes movies: their title, the year in which they were made, their length in minutes, and the genre of the movie. We show three particular movies, but you should imagine that there are many more rows to this table——one row for each movie ever made, perhaps.

The structure portion of the relational model might appear to resemble an array of structs in C, where the column headers are the field names, and each of the rows represent the values of one struct in the array. However, it must be emphasized that this physical implementation is only one possible way the table could be implemented in physical data structures. In fact, it is not the normal way to represent relations, and a large portion of the study of database systems addresses the right ways to implement such tables. Much of the distinction comes from the scale of relations——they are not normally implemented as main-memory structures, and their proper physical implementation must take into account the need to access relations of very large size that are resident on disk.

The operations normally associated with the relational model form the "relational algebra". These operations are table-oriented. As an example, we can ask for all those rows of a relation that have a certain value in a certain column. For example, we can ask of the table in Figure 5−17 for all the rows where the genre is "comedy".

title	year	length	genre
Gone With the Wind	1939	231	drama
Star Wars	1977	124	sciFi
Wayne's World	1992	95	comedy

Figure 5−17　An example relation

Review Questions and Problems：

1. What is the DBMS?

2. How do we use DBMS to solve problems?

5.7　ERP Systems

1. Introduction

Enterprise Resource Planning (ERP) is a set of integrated programs that manage a company's vital business operations for an entire organization, even a complex, multisite, global organization. At the core of the ERP system is a database that is shared by all users so that all business functions have access to current and consistent data for operational decision making and planning, as shown

5.7 Professional Terms, Words and Phrases, Sentence Illustration

in Figure 5−18. ERP systems evolved from Materials Requirement Planning (MRP) systems developed in the 1970s. These systems tied together the production planning, inventory control, and purchasing business functions for manufacturing organizations. During the late 1980s and early 1990s, many organizations recognized that their legacy TPSs lacked the integration needed to coordinate activities and share valuable information across all the business functions of the firm. As a result, costs were higher and customer service was poorer than desired. Large organizations, specifically members of the Fortune 1000, were the first to take on the challenge of implementing ERP. Businesses of all kinds have now implemented Enterprise Resource Planning (ERP) systems. ERP serves as a cross-functional enterprise backbone that integrates and automates many internal business processes and information systems within the manufacturing, logistics, distribution, accounting, finance, and human resource functions of a company. ERP also served as the vital software engine needed to integrate and accomplish the cross-functional processes that resulted. Now, ERP is recognized as a necessary ingredient that many companies need in order to gain the efficiency, agility, and responsiveness required to succeed in today's dynamic business environment. ERP gives a company an integrated real-time view of its core business processes, such as production, order processing, and inventory management, tied together by the ERP application software and a common database maintained by a database management system. ERP systems track business resources (such as cash, raw materials, and production capacity), and the status of commitments made by the business (such as customer orders, purchase orders, and employee payroll), no matter which department (manufacturing, purchasing, sales, accounting, and so on) has entered the data into the system. ERP software suites typically consist of integrated modules of manufacturing, distribution, sales, accounting, and human resource applications. Figure 5-19 presents the major application components of an ERP system. Figure 5-20 illustrates some of the key cross-functional business processes and customer and supplier information flows supported by ERP systems.

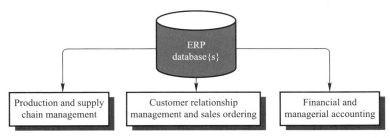

Figure 5-18   Enterprise resource planning system An ERP integrates business processes and the ERP database

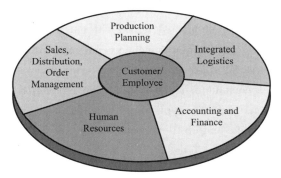

Figure 5-19   The major application components of enterprise resource planning demonstrate
the cross-functional approach of ERP systems.

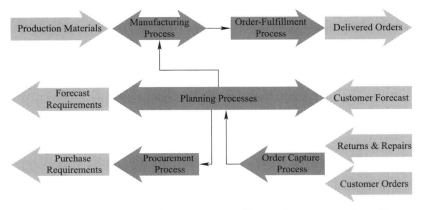

Figure 5-20   Some of the business process flows and customer and supplier
information flows supported by ERP systems.

2. Advantages of ERP Systems

ERP systems provide many advantages to companies. One of the main advantages is data integration. As mentioned earlier in the chapter, one result of the advent of desktop computing was that the same data was often housed in different departmental systems. The inability to keep information synchronized between systems often meant that multiple versions of data resided within the organization. In ERP systems, data is captured once and shared across the enterprise, reducing the risk of inaccuracies and redundancies in data and eliminating time wasted in checking, rechecking, and reconciling data. ERP systems even simplify the error correction process; if a mistake is made, it only has to be corrected once. Data integration gives stakeholders the ability to gain better visibility into business operations. The enterprise has a single version of "the truth", and all users benefit because they share access to—and responsibility for—information that is current, complete, and accurate.

Another advantage of ERP systems is real-time access to information, which improves collaboration and communication across the enterprise. With ERP systems, once data is entered, it is readily available online and in real time to all users in all departments (who have the authority to view or edit the data). The time lag that used to arise when documents sat in in-baskets waiting to be rekeyed into another system is eliminated, along with much of the paper documents involved. Information is available sooner, and interdepartmental communication improves. For example, in a company that has an ERP system, suppose a purchasing agent processes a purchase order for raw material. Once that event is committed in the system, the production department will know the material is coming, and thus production planning becomes more accurate. Customer service representatives will have complete and up-to-date information needed to provide intelligent support to customers on the status of their orders. This real-time, immediate access to enterprise information can help improve operations, corporate governance, and management of enterprise risk, creating a horizontally "joined up", process-centered company and ultimately improving productivity, insight, and optimized business processes.

An ERP system also requires that the company share a common process and data model covering broad and deep operational end-to-end processes such as those found in manufacturing and the supply chain. This standardization improves coordination within the organization and across the organization, making it easier to interact with internal and external stakeholders.

ERP vendors design their solutions around processes based on industry best practices. A best practice is a business process that is generally recognized as more effective and/or efficient than others in a particular industry. When managers of a company select an ERP package to implement, they are "buying into" a particular ERP vendor's view of best practices and relying on the system to support their efforts to embrace these practices. Matching best practices to organizational needs is what differentiates one ERP package from another and is a key contributor to the ultimate success of the implementation. Larger ERP vendors, such as SAP and Oracle, have thousands of best practices programmed into their software. These vendors support enormous research and development efforts to identify best practices in various industries and incorporate them into their solutions. As a result, the cycle of finding, codifying, and delivering best practices to customers allows the ERP vendor to increase its customer base by offering specific versions of their software called vertical solutions (or industry solutions). Figure 5−21 presents a complete list of vertical solutions offered by Oracle in its E-Business Suite.

Aerospace and Defense	Industrial Manufacturing
Automotive	Insurance
Chemicals	Media and Entertainment
Communications	Natural Resources
Consumer Goods	Oil and Gas
Education and Research	Professional Services
Engineering and Construction	Public Sector
Finance Services	Retail
Health Sciences	Travel and Transportation
High Technology	Utilities

Figure 5−21   Oracle's vertical solutions

Another advantage of ERP systems is that an ERP vendor's modules look and act the same. This similarity makes it easy for users to work in multiple modules. With a single interface and similar navigation, employees will encounter less friction and greater ease in using the ERP system versus working in multiple disparate systems.

Finally, ERP systems can reduce operational costs and increase revenue. Companies that implement ERP do so to gain efficiencies such as lower inventory costs, production costs, or purchasing costs. Similarly, companies implement ERP to transform parts (or all) of the business to improve revenue-generating processes, including time to market, marketing and sales, and customer service.

3. Methods and Tools

(1) Methodology

The basic methodology for ERP benefits realization simply involves taking baseline measurements (for example, inventory turnover or order-to-cash cycle time) early in the planning process, comparing them to projected measurements, and calculating the difference. These improvements in measurements are the benefits, and they should be able to be quantified. The culmination of all these benefits should become part of the business case for an ERP system. Quantifiable measurements are known as business metrics, and they are used to track and assess the efficacy of specific business processes. After the ERP system has been implemented, the organization needs to continue to track these metrics every few months to actually see if there is continued improvement toward the business case. Companies should also try to employ measurement methods that are not too difficult, time-consuming, or burdensome.

These benefits depend on the project scope and the amount of reengineering involved. For instance, if a company is implementing a module to help with purchasing and inventory management, then benefits such as improving the cycle time of the purchase to goods receipt process or reducing inventory levels will likely be part of a business case. If a production module is being implemented, benefits such as improved goods quality, lower manufacturing costs, increased throughput, less rework, and improved manufacturing schedule compliance may likely accrue. Key benefits for implementing financial accounting include integrated financial data across business units and locations, which helps in better business decisions and a faster period-end close. While some benefits are simple to quantify, others are more difficult, such as improved efficiency through better visibility of data; elimination of manual processes; better collaboration with partners, suppliers, and customers; and greater insight through business analytics.

(2) Information Management Tools

Data storage and information management with established workflow across different departments and functions are the backbones of any ERP system. Multiple solutions and tools are available for data storage, which include relational databases from companies like Oracle, Sybase, DB2, and open source free offerings like Microsoft MySQL, PostgreSQL, Apache Derby, etc. Other information management tools may include Content Management Systems (CMS) and repository applications.

Depending upon the industry and required functions, an appropriate one needs to be selected. A manufacturer may find a transactional database like Oracle or MySQL to be more relevant as transaction-based data moves through different statuses (from manufacturing to inventory to order capture to sale to supply status). On the other hand, an online content writing company may find a CMS repository system with version control a better fit for their needs.

The database or repository can be either a single centralized one, or multiple with automatic data flow from one database to the other. The defined workflow ensures seamless data movement. Databases can be hosted locally or remotely, or even in the cloud.

(3) Applications and Interfaces with Suitable Permission Control

Data storage and management require read-only or editing access to process the data. Once items are manufactured, they need to be marked as ready inventory. The stock management department then updates it as ready for sale. Following a purchase, the item should be updated to sold status and so on.

To accomplish this, easy-to-use applications and interfaces make an integral part of any ERP system that also has defined controls and permissions. For example, once an item is marked as sold, only logistics department operators should be able to update it further, while the ones from the manufacturing or inventory department should get view-only access.

Similarly, for a content writing ERP tool, once a writer submits the content to the editor for review, only the editor should be able to modify it, to avoid any duplication and content conflicts.

To enable such permission-based controls, applications, and interfaces to be built in, any ERP solution that may be browser based, desktop installations, or tablet/mobile apps. A manufacturing team at a stationary location will prefer a desktop-based interface, while a sales team constantly on the move will benefit from a browser-based interface or mobile app.

(4) Workflow Management Tool

An ERP system constitutes of multiple modules and data repositories where data updates and actions follow a logically defined sequence based on the business needs. This constitutes the workflow. Workflow can be thought of as the mind-controlling the various body functions (flow of blood, air, food and other supplies, body parts movement, etc.). A clearly defined workflow with appropriate access at various levels is a necessary part of any ERP solution.

Commonly used tools implemented within the ERP framework include Agiloft Workflow, WorkflowGen, Inceptico DMS, Intelex Business Management, SimpleECM, etc.

(5) Reporting Dashboard

Management level, department level, team level, or individual level report generation is another important requirement for an ERP system. It is usually available in either a dashboard form (with a real-time data view, showing such info as orders received but not yet shipped, failed payments of the last week, etc.) or customizable reports generated in common word-editing or data-editing applications like spreadsheets.

Most reporting tools and dashboards operate in real-time (or with a minimal time lag). Like the applications used by departments for data updates, these reporting tools/dashboard views are available as browser-based or desktop installations. They also include end-of-day reporting features offering to email reports with charts/graphs/tables as Microsoft Excel or Word attachments.

(6) Communication Tools

Within any system working across multiple departments, communication is mandatory. ERP systems facilitate this by offering tools for action-based automated mail generation, instant messaging, chat, or general broadcast features at individual and group levels.

Say once an order is marked as "Ready to Ship", an automated mailer should be triggered to the logistics department to initiate the dispatch process (or if a pizza shop kitchen has developed a problem); a general broadcast message can be sent to all other departments to stop taking further orders.

Further instant messaging functions (like those from Lync, Chatter, or Yammer) are incorporated to enable easy and instant communication.

In addition to the above tools that are an integral part of any ERP system, there are additional ones that can be integrated on an as-needed basis.

(7) Analytical Tools

A lot of analytical tools can be integrated within ERP system for business intelligence, predictive analysis, data mining and related analysis. These analytical tools are used to get valuable insights for creating strategic business decisions based on available data (like tracking consumer behavior around holiday shopping, comparative results for products in red colored shelf having more sales than those in blue colored shelf, etc.).

(8) Resource Allocation and Task Scheduling Tools

ERP systems can also integrate tools for allocating resources across departments and tasks (for labor-intensive industries). These tools work on the simple principle of defined time taken by a task/project against the resource availability schedule. On task completion, the resource is automatically assigned a new task matching his skills or is put in a pool for the next assignment.

Tools have functionality for manual intervention at the supervisor level in case a task is delayed. Benefits include clear visibility about current and future workload, optimum resource utilization, exploring possibilities for automation, etc.

(9) Other Add-On Features

ERP systems can integrate modules for human resource management, project management, time tracking systems, and document management, according to the business's needs. There are a large number of tools available specific to each industry and function type, and ERP vendors provide their assistance to interested clients on selecting the best fit. Internet is always available for self-help on getting required info.

(10) The Bottom Line

ERP is a complex framework to implement and usually needs a dedicated vendor for implementation. Two big bottlenecks identified with ERP implementations are high costs and the failure to adhere to best practices. While cost can be mitigated to a certain extent by careful valuation of different vendors and assessment of free open-source tools, the other challenge of failures due to lack of adherence to best practices can be mitigated by focused training to employees. Proper assessment at initial stages, partnering with vendors with right expertise and being clear on requirements from the start will help an efficient and successful implementation of ERP tools.

4. Models

ERP modeling, is the process of reverse engineering an Enterprise Resource Planning software package in order to align it to an organizational structure.

Although ERP modeling could possibly be performed by several methodologies, this entry deals with ERP modeling using Object Process Methodology, or OPM. OPM appears to be a usable methodology for modeling ERP systems, as the methodology focuses on optionality within objects and processes of an ERP system. ERP modeling is done by analyzing the optionality within an ERP system to identify the different functions of the system that the end-using company needs, regarding its organizational structure. Reverse engineering both ERP system and organizational structure to the same level of granularity makes both layers compatible for aligning the package in the organization.

ERP breaks down traditional functional barriers by facilitating data sharing, information flows, and the introduction of common business practices among all organizational users.

A Global Business Process Model is created which represents the whole ERP software product. This model is layered in 3 deeper levels.

The first level is the System Configuration Level, which scopes on high-level optionality on the entire system. Option definition is therefore static: once a high-level option of the ERP system is chosen to be used within the organization, the choice cannot be made undone.

One level deeper is the object level, which scopes on single data objects. The optionality on this level is more dynamic.

The deepest level is the occurrence level, which analyses single process occurrences.

Because this level elaborates on object parameters, the optionality is very dynamic, meaning that options can easily be altered.

The meta model below depicts the optionality levels of ERP modeling.

The optionality leveling is used to reverse engineer the ERP system and the organizational structure to its full extent. Once properly mapped, both aspects are fully alignable or at least compatible to be matched.

Review Questions and Problems:

1. What is the ERP System?

2. What are the benefits and advantages of the ERP?

5.8　Reading Material

1. Building Information Modeling: A New Frontier for Construction Engineering Education

Building Information Models are 3D parametric, virtual representations of the built environment. These models can contain the same amount of information as present in an actual building. They are also capable of representing specific details to facilitate extended analysis as needed ahead of construction. For example, all the performance parameters of specific materials such as concrete masonry units or fabricated structural steel are linked to particular installations within the BIM. This allows for the possibility of integrated engineering design such as finite element analysis. Consequently, as BIM technology progresses and improves, it has important implications for the practical and educational aspects of construction engineering.

For centuries, the roles of architect and constructor were intertwined as "master builder". The knowledge of building materials and methods was implicit in the process of design. Indeed, innovations in buildings stemmed as much from creating new means of construction as they did from new building forms. Invariably, this tradition continued until the renaissance when the use of perspective representation and orthographic drawing was introduced. With these new forms of communicating information about buildings, the processes of building became increasingly legalistic, codified, complex and adversarial. In fact, today's standard AIA contracts state that "the architect will not be responsible for construction means, methods, techniques or procedures." Fortunately, the introduction of Building Information Modeling (BIM) holds promise for ending the disassociation between constructing and designing, thereby paving the way for an increase in building innovations and the potential return of the "master builder" role.

Software that allows for thethree-dimensional (3D) construction of a virtual building (i. e. , BIM) will increasingly impact project delivery and the resulting interaction between architects, vendors, engineers and constructors. Due in part to redefined relationships between project stakeholders, BIM necessitates changes in education as well so that an integrated and consistent approach toward the built environment results as graduates enter the workforce. Yet, is BIM merely a tool to be taught and used to improve productivity while in school? Certainly, many schools of engineering, architecture, and construction are using BIM software already though questions remain regarding how it fits into curricula. Further, if students are to encounter the world of integrated design and construction once their course of study is complete, what are the components of an integrated construction education? Consequently, this paper addresses these questions through the lens of a case study which began in Fall 2006 at Texas State University and continues to the present. In addition, the authors demonstrate the importance of BIM as a new frontier for construction engineering education.

BIM requires an innovative approach to construction engineering education. In his 1985 book *Innovation and Entrepreneurship*, Peter Drucker outlined seven sources of opportunity for organizations in search of innovation. Four sources come from inside the organization and three stem from the outside world. Each is listed in order of increasing difficulty and uncertainty:

- The unexpected success that is gratefully received but rarely dissected to see why it occurred.

- The incongruity between what actually happens and what was supposed to happen.

- The inadequacy in an underlying process that is taken for granted.

- The changes in an industry or market structure that catch everyone by surprise.

- The demographic changes caused by wars, medical improvements and even superstition.

- The changes in perception, mood and fashion brought on by the ups and downs of the economy.

- The changes in awareness caused by new knowledge.

All are symptoms of change and, as such, serve as the template for this paper, its case study, and its projections regarding integrated practice. Accordingly, each source of innovation holds particular promise for the future of construction education.

2. Feasibility Analysis on the Application of BIM Technology in Project Cost Management in the Era of Big Data

(1) Realize the Project Cost Data Resource Sharing

In the project cost management, a large number of data will be generated. In the previous project cost management, data confusion or data loss is easy to occur. Through the application of BIM technology, data management and sharing can be easily realized, such as storing indicators, specific data and content of each project, establishing database and perfecting corresponding electronic database, so as to facilitate the future search and use. BIM technology can realize the sharing of data resources in the project cost management, significantly improve the work efficiency of the project cost management, avoid problems and loopholes in manual operation, ensure the accuracy of data, and effectively improve the effectiveness of the project cost management.

(2) Facilitate the Communication and Cooperation between the Parties

BIM technology can establish data information model according to the corresponding requirements, carry out rational analysis of human resources, carry out scientific and reasonable planning for the construction and design stage, accurately design and budget the entire project amount and all materials and engineering costs required by the project. The project plan tends to be perfect presentation, accurate budget of the project volume and cost, to ensure the smooth implementation of the project. The application of BIM technology is based on the Internet technology. With the help of the Internet platform, project parties can timely communicate with each other at the same time, and all departments can realize real-time consultation in all aspects of project planning, design, construction and decision-making. This kind of communication and cooperation between various parties can effectively improve the quality of the whole project and ensure the overall progress and efficiency of the project. BIM technology can realize the perfect communication between various departments of project cost management, realize the optimal allocation and reasonable arrangement of resources, accurately calculate the various human, financial and material resources needed in specific construction stages, and improve the utilization rate of funds and materials.

(3) Improve the Quality of All-dimensional Project Cost Management

BIM technology can include the design and construction stages of the whole project into the data information model and realize the cost management of the whole process. Through BIM technology, the leadership can clearly and intuitively understand the overall progress and specific situation of the whole project and provide timely feedback on the waste of resources and construction errors in the specific construction process. The management is familiar with the implementation of the whole project, and then accurately calculate the construction schedule of the whole project, to complete the project in time, quality and quantity. In addition, BIM technology can understand the cost of the whole project, ensure the economic benefits of the project, and conduct technical monitoring of the cost of the whole project.

(4) Change the Project Cost Management Mode

The application of BIM technology in project cost management can change the original passive mode of project cost management into active mode of management. By accurate analysis of information data, dynamic tracking analysis of project cost can be carried out. The resources used in the whole project can be displayed intelligently through data, and the cost management of the project can be effectively improved with the help of network data calculation method. At the same time, BIM technology can track the progress of the project in real time and give timely feedback. For example, the financial department can analyze the costs incurred by the construction project, compare the expected economic benefits, and analyze the deficiencies in the process of the construction project through economic difference. In addition, BIM technology realizes information verification before, during and after the implementation of engineering projects through whole-process management, to ensure the overall construction process and the final economic benefits.

3. Application of BIM Technology in Project Cost Management in the Era of Big Data

(1) Application of Project Investment Decision Stage

In the traditional engineering investment decision, there are more or less certain problems in the estimation of construction engineering, which leads to the deviation of the estimation of engineering price from the actual situation and the phenomenon of low economic benefit or zero economic benefit finally appears. There are some problems in the standard and set of investment estimation methods in the past, so it is difficult to ensure the accurate evaluation and prediction of engineering projects, and a series of problems occur in the estimation of engineering projects, which bring unnecessary troubles and serious economic losses to the development of construction enterprises. Therefore, in order to accurately estimate the whole project, a construction enterprise can apply BIM technology in the investment decision-making stage of the project, and summarize and integrate the information of the whole project through the data and information modeling of BIM technology. Accurate calculation of the relevant information of the project cost, and then by the project cost management personnel for a second accounting and appropriate adjustment, the project cost can be accurately estimated. In addition, if there are problems when the project cost management staff carries out the investment budget, they can also extract the data from the BIM database established to ensure the accuracy of the whole project investment budget and improve the efficiency of the project cost budget. BIM technology can also solve the problem that construction enterprises cannot accurately compare investment schemes, which is a difficult problem for construction enterprises in project investment estimation. Using computer, BIM technology can easily retrieve relevant data resources from the database, and then provide the most reasonable investment scheme and design and construction scheme for construction enterprises through data comparison and collation, which not only saves human resources, but also ensures the accuracy of investment scheme.

(2) Application in the Project Design Phase

The management of project design also belongs to the category of project cost management. Construction projects include the initial design stage of the whole project, the technical design stage of construction, and then the design stage of construction drawings. These stages also include budget estimates for project design, construction revisions and construction drawings. In the course of previous construction projects, project staff had to plan to determine the preliminary design and construction technical design, which was time-consuming and could not ensure the accuracy of the results. Therefore, BIM technology is used to change the working mode of construction enterprises, carry out reasonable modeling, calculate the amount of work and get the accurate project cost. When designing construction drawings, BIM technology is used to establish the model and design the construction drawings to ensure the consistency between the construction drawings and the actual construction effect. To solve the problem of discrepancy between the previous construction drawing and the actual construction, to ensure the effectiveness of project cost management. Therefore, the application of BIM technology in the project design stage can improve the rationality and accuracy of the project design, improve the overall project cost management efficiency, and avoid unnecessary problems caused by inaccurate project design.

(3) Application of Project Bidding Stage

In China, construction engineering projects are mostly selected through bidding. One of the problems is that the two parties differ greatly in project valuation. In the final process of project valuation, the bidding and tendering parties spend a lot of time, personnel and material force, and may not reach an agreement due to the inconsistency of information between the two parties. BIM technology can effectively solve this problem, so as to ensure the accuracy of project valuation information of both parties. Using BIM technology to extract corresponding data resources in the database, design a sound and reasonable project valuation data report according to the specific requirements of both parties. This not only saves the working time of both parties, but also improves the working efficiency, ensures the accuracy of project valuation of both parties, perfectly solves the problem of difference of project valuation between both parties, and improves the working efficiency of project cost management.

(4) Application in the Construction Stage of the Project

In the past, construction enterprises carried out construction according to the contract signed by both parties. After the completion of the construction task, they provided the tenderee with the specific construction situation and specific bill items. The tenderee shall entrust professionals to conduct final acceptance of the project, and only after the acceptance is passed will settlement be made to the construction enterprise. However, in this process, the project cost is often too high, or due to too many project cost management personnel, resulting in the inconsistency between the project cost and the actual fund, which will increase the time of acceptance and check, affecting the normal settlement of balance payment. The 5D modeling technology of BIM can perfectly solve these problems. 5D modeling is established based on 3D model, adding two dimensions of construction schedule and project cost to form a 5D model. This model enables enterprises to intuitively understand the specific situation of engineering construction, and adjust according to the actual situation, running through all links of the whole project. During the delivery with the tenderee, the funds of each stage will be directly displayed. Even if there is any inconsistency between the actual situation and the project cost, the tenderee can clearly see which link the project cost has increased and formulate a reasonable balance payment settlement method.

(5) Application at the Completion Stage of the Project

In the past, problems and mistakes were easy to occur in the completion stage of a project. The settlement of the completion of the project affects the project cost management, in the settlement, to check the project quantity. Project cost management personnel mostly check and compare every detail of the project construction through drawings and budget work books. This stage will spend a lot of time and energy, and there will be some deviations in labor more or less. BIM technology can perfectly solve this problem. Project cost management personnel can directly check the data in the BIM database, carry out completion settlement of construction projects, reduce the checking time, improve work efficiency, and ensure the accuracy of settlement data.

Chapter 6
Service System Operation and Management

6.1 Service Innovation and Management

1. Introduction of Service Innovation and Management

Service innovation management includes: decision management, process management, element management, mode management, output management. Decision management is the premise, process, mode, element management is the means of realization, and output management is the result.

6.1 Professional Terms, Words and Phrases, Sentence Illustration

(1) Classification by the Object of Innovation

① Product innovation: refers to the development and introduction of new service products for the market. For example, a new insurance type designed and developed by an insurance company is an example of product innovation.

② Process innovation: refers to the process innovation of service production and delivery, which can be divided into background innovation (production process innovation) and foreground innovation (delivery process innovation).

③ Organizational innovation refers to the increase or decrease of service organizational elements, the change of organizational form and structure, the introduction and renewal of management methods and means, etc.

④ Market innovation: refers to the new behavior of service enterprises in the market, including opening up new markets, developing new market segments in the original market, entering another industry and market, and changing the relationship with other actors in the market.

⑤ Technological innovation: refers to the introduction and application of existing or new technologies in service organizations.

(2) Classified by the Nature of Innovation

① Transmission innovation: refers to the innovation of the transmission system of service enterprises or the transmission media of service industries.

② Restructuring innovation: also known as "structural innovation", refers to the innovation generated by service enterprises by systematically restructuring or reusing existing service elements, including: the increase of new service elements; combination or reorganization of two or more existing service elements; decomposition of existing service elements.

③ Special innovation: refers to the innovative mode of proposing solutions to specific problems of customers in the process of interaction.

④ Formal innovation: the service elements in the above-mentioned innovations have changed in quality or quantity. "Formal innovation" does not change in quantity or quality, but changes in the "visibility" and standardization of various service elements.

Internal driving forces: enterprise strategy and management, employees, innovation departments. External driving forces: track, actor.

2. Methods and Tools of Service Innovation and Management

(1) Focus on customer expectations. In a market where competitors gather, enterprises do not need to easily change the product itself. As long as they pay attention to the grasp of the focus of customers' expectations, carefully listen to customers'reactions and modify suggestions in time, they can achieve satisfactory results. For example, when Toyota of Japan entered the Norwegian market, it found that Norwegians were more concerned about the convenience of car purchase, insurance and maintenance services. In response to this expectation of consumers, the company proposed a series of insurance incentives, and also provided free inspection services for customers. This marketing service strategy has made Toyota the best-selling automobile brand in Norway. It can be seen that understanding the needs of different customers, finding out their expectations, focusing on the most important customers, formulating strategies that exceed these expectations, and distinguishing from competitors in a unique way of service are the foundation of service innovation.

(2) Be kind to customers' complaints. Customer complaints indicate that the service is defective or the service method needs to be improved, which is the opportunity for service innovation. If you ignore customers' complaints, you will lose these customers. At the same time, due to oral communication, enterprises will lose more potential customers. If necessary and timely remedial measures are taken for customers' complaints, it will enhance the reputation of the enterprise and win customers' loyalty.

(3) The service should be flexible. The objects of service are very wide, and different objects have different expectations and needs. Therefore, good service needs to maintain a certain degree of flexibility to meet the consumption needs of different customers. At the same time, there are many things that are difficult to measure in service. If we pursue accuracy, it will not only be difficult to achieve, but also cause trouble to employees. Customers' expectations are flexible, and enterprises must change services according to customers' expectations. But flexibility is not an excuse for failing to fulfill service commitments. Flexibility can be used to balance consumer dissatisfaction, and consumer commitments must be 100% fulfilled.

(4) Hypothetical innovation. Service is driven by customers. When people's living standard is not high, the demand mode is relatively unified; with the improvement of living standards, people's consumption needs have also changed, which changes with people's values. But sometimes customers themselves may not be able to understand their changed desires and needs. At this time, operators in the service industry are required to speculate boldly and guide a new consumption trend.

(5) Service starts with product design. That is to say, in the early stage of product design,

we should consider the factors of service and take design as the beginning of service. When all enterprises in the industry provide the same service, this service item may become a subsidiary part of the product, and consumers will not consider it as a part of additional benefits. So the process of service is that with the improvement of service quality, the original part of the service is absorbed by the product, which forces the service manager to constantly provide new services. If there is no innovation, enterprises will not provide services.

（6）Change "responding to every request" active service. Different enterprises have different service definitions. Many enterprises have a narrow understanding of services. For example, commodity retailers may think that services are sufficient inventory and free delivery. This understanding only limits the service to the scope of "responding to every request" and passively adapts to the requirements of customers. In order to win in the competition, an enterprise must also change its passivity into initiative, actively explore the expectations of customers, and achieve them before customers put forward them. In this way, it can be one step ahead of its competitors in the service market and be in an advantageous position.

（7）Reasonably restrict customer expectations. Enterprises strive to meet the needs of customers and serve customers unconditionally, which is the basic principle to achieve first-class service level. However, it must be flexible in strategy, and it is necessary to reasonably restrict customers' expectations. Customers' evaluation of service quality is easily affected by preconceived expectations. When their expectations exceed the service level provided by the enterprise, they will feel dissatisfied; when the service level of enterprises exceeds their expectations, they will be satisfied. Enterprises must strictly control the promises of advertising and salesmen to customers to avoid customers' high expectations. In the actual provision of services, we should try our best to exceed the expectations of customers.

（8）Innovative services through corporate culture. Nowadays, the service industry uses advanced high technology to assist service activities, such as ATM machines used by banks. However, it is worth noting that the adoption of high-tech means does not mean service innovation. Service is an act of mutual assistance between people. Most customers appreciate the service of high-level interpersonal contact. However, it is difficult to control the service process by relying on certain operating standards. It is necessary to form a set of internal code of conduct so that service personnel can flexibly use it in the face of customers to achieve satisfactory results. Therefore, building a strong corporate culture is the source of improving service level and promoting service innovation.

3. Models of Service Innovation and Management

（1）The downstream service innovation mode refers to that manufacturing enterprises intervene in the downstream service links of the industrial chain and obtain more income by enhancing the innovation of enterprises in marketing, brand and other links. Enterprises that adopt the downstream service innovation model often believe that the income from selling services is far greater than that from selling products themselves, so such enterprises will integrate products and services in different forms and to different degrees. The services they provide usually fall into three categories: embedded services, companion services, and integrated solutions.

Embedded service refers to a service that simply packs products and services to play specific functions. For example, while selling aircraft, aircraft manufacturers provide information management service software to aviation service operators to realize self-diagnosis and analysis of aircraft equipment, which were previously done by airline mechanics.

Incidental services refer to additional services that facilitate customers to purchase products. For example, GM's auto financial services company provides financing and credit services for customers to buy cars and other products.

The integrated solution refers to an innovative mode that closely combines products and services into an organic whole to meet the specific needs of customers. For example, when selling household appliances, home appliance manufacturers will provide a package solution including consultation, transportation, installation, design, maintenance, maintenance, etc. Haier's "star service" for customers has won it a strong control position in the industrial chain; Nokia not only provides operators with switches and transmission equipment, but also provides after-sales technical support, equipment maintenance, network system planning services and other integrated "product service packages"; in the early stage of entering the communication equipment market, Huawei provided a series of after-sales service solutions for customers through a large number of manual services, thus winning the trust of customers and occupying a place in the market.

(2) The upstream service innovation mode refers to a mode in which enterprises compete and make profits through the innovation of upstream service links based on the professional knowledge and ability accumulated in research and development, design, planning and other links. This mode requires manufacturing enterprises to have strong R&D capabilities, such as reserves of professional knowledge and talents, sufficient funds, the ability to resist risks, and the ability to transform R&D and design experience and knowledge into the ability to provide services to third parties.

Logistics equipment system integration industry is a knowledge intensive industry that integrates products and services, namely "hardware + software (control system)". Even a single physical product and equipment must form a final systematic "product service package" that meets the specific needs of customers through advanced design, installation and service integration means. The industry has three characteristics: knowledge and technology intensity, accumulation of knowledge and technology, and "overall solution" for customer needs. The competitiveness of enterprises in this industry depends on two factors, namely, core component technology and system integration technology.

In the early stage of entering the logistics industry, the company only has basic convey or production and manufacturing capacity. Subsequently, it adopted the imitation innovation strategy and independent research and development strategy based on introduction, digestion and absorption, as well as effective intellectual property protection strategies, continuously cultivated and enhanced technology research and development and service capabilities, and developed core products with industry-leading levels. It is precisely because the technology, capabilities and experience accumulated in core products have gradually changed to the role of system integrator, providing customers with high-end system design, consulting and general contracting services, and outsourcing the production of hardware that initially achieved their own products.

（3）Completely de-manufacturing innovation mode. This service innovation mode is an innovation mode in which manufacturing enterprises completely withdraw from low value manufacturing links and only engage in high value-added upstream and downstream service links. Enterprises that implement this model have accumulated rich experience and strong capabilities in the upstream and downstream service links, and have control over the entire industrial chain. Therefore, they can separate manufacturing outsourcing and carry out high-end competition through research and development, design, brand management, sales, extended services and other activities with high added value. This mode requires a complete transformation of enterprise strategy, organizational structure, business model and human resources, and has a high threshold for entry. Nike doesn't have a factory of its own, but it has mastered the key upstream research and development, design, downstream brand management and sales, and achieved "complete de-manufacturing". The withdrawal of blue giant IBM from PC manufacturing to provide high value-added solution based IT services is also a manifestation of the "complete de-manufacturing" innovation model.

6.2 Service Finance

1. Introduction

Service economy refers to an economic state in which the relative proportion of the output value of the service economy in GDP exceeds 60%. In other words, service economy refers to an economic situation in which the relative proportion of the employment in the service economy in the employment of the whole national economy exceeds 60%. Modern service economy came into being in the stage of high development of industrialization, and it has developed relying on information

6.2 Professional Terms, Words and Phrases, Sentence Illustration

technology and modern management concepts. The degree of development of modern service economy has become one of the important symbols to measure regional modernization, national defense and competitiveness, and it is a new growth point with great potential for regional economy.

Service economy is a new economic form rising in recent 50 years. It plays an extremely important role in the composition of the national economy. It covers a wide range of market economy categories and forms of service industry and evenforeign service trade. In foreign countries, the service economy has basically formed a relatively mature system and has its own mode of operation. In China, with the development of market economy, the service economy has begun to receive great attention from the competent government departments, and gradually increase its proportion in the national economy. It is the main way for China to adjust and upgrade the industrial structure. It is related to the trend and innovation of future economic development, and has very important strategic significance.

Since the 1950s, the global economy has experienced a structural change, which was called "service economy" by Victor R. Fuchs, an American economist, in 1968. Fuchs believes that the United States is the first in western countries to enter the service economy and society. Fuchs' declaration indicates the arrival of the service economy that began in the United States on a global scale. With the rapid development of information revolution and technology, service economy also shows a new development trend.

2. Methods (Grouping Services by Delivery Process)

Concepts of service management should be applicable to all service organizations. For example, hospital administrators could learn something about their own business from the restaurant and hotel trade. Professional services such as consulting, law, and medicine have special problems because the professional is trained to provide a specific clinical service (to use a medical example) but is not knowledgeable in business management. Thus, managing professional service firms offers attractive career opportunities for business school graduates.

A service classification scheme can help to organize our discussion of service management and break down the industry barriers to shared learning. As suggested, hospitals can learn about housekeeping from hotels. Less obviously, dry-cleaning establishments can learn from banks—cleaners can adapt the convenience of night deposits enjoyed by banking customers by providing laundry bags and after-hours drop off boxes. For professional firms, scheduling a consulting engagement is similar to planning a legal defense or preparing a medical team for open-heart surgery.

To demonstrate that management problems are common across service industries, Roger Schmenner proposed the service process matrix in Table 6 – 1. In this matrix, services are classified across two dimensions that significantly affect the character of the service delivery process. The vertical dimension measures the degree of labor intensity, which is defined as the ratio of labor cost to capital cost. Thus, capital-intensive services such as airlines and hospitals are found in the upper row because of their considerable investment in plant and equipment relative to labor costs. Labor-intensive services such as schools and legal assistance are found in the bottom row because their labor costs are high relative to their capital requirements.

Criteria for evaluating the service package   **Table 6−1**

Supporting Facility 1. *Location*: Is it accessible by public transportation? Is it centrally located? 2. *Interior decorating*: Is the proper mood established? Quality and coordination of furniture. 3. *Supporting equipment*: Does the dentist use a mechanical or air drill? What type and age of aircraft does the charter airline use?	4. *Architectural appropriateness*: Renaissance architecture for university campus. Unique recognizable feature of a blue tile roof. Massive granite facade of downtown bank. 5. *Facility layout*: Is there a natural flow of traffic? Are adequate waiting areas provided? Is there unnecessary travel or backtracking?

continued

Facilitating Goods	
1. *Consistency*:	3. *Selection*:
Crispness of french fries.	Variety of replacement mufflers.
Portion control.	Number of menu items.
2. *Quantity*:	Rental skis available.
Small, medium, or large drink.	
Information	
1. *Consistency*:	3. *Useful*:
Up-to-date customer addresses.	X-ray to identify a broken bone.
Correct credit report.	Inventory status.
2. *Timely*:	
Severe storm warning.	
Explicit Services	
1. *Training of service personnel*:	3. *Consistency*:
Is the auto mechanic certified by the National Institute for Automotive Service Excellence (NIASE)?	Airline's on-time record.
	Professional Standards Review Organization (PSRO) for doctors.
To what extent are paraprofessionals used?	4. *Availability*:
Are the physicians board certified?	Twenty-four-hour ATM service.
2. *Comprehensiveness*:	Is there a website?
Discount broker compared with full service.	Is there a toll-free number?
General hospital compared with clinic.	
Implicit Services	
1. *Attitude of service*:	4. *Status*:
Cheerful flight attendant.	Flying first-class.
Police officer issuing traffic citation with tact.	Box seats at sports event.
Surly service person in restaurant.	5. *Sense of well-being*:
2. *Atmosphere*:	Large commercial aircraft.
Restaurant decor.	Well-lighted parking lot.
Music in a bar.	6. *Privacy and security*:
Sense of confusion rather than order.	Attomey advising client in private office.
3. *Waiting*:	Magnetic key card for hotel room.
Joining a drive-in banking queue.	7. *Convenience*:
Being placed on hold.	Use of appointments.
Enjoying a martini in the restaurant bar.	Free parking.

The horizontal dimension measures the degree of customer interaction and customization, which is a marketing variable that describes the ability of the customer to affect personally the nature of the service being delivered. Little interaction between customer and service provider is needed when the service is standardized rather than customized. For example, a meal at McDonald's, which is assembled from prepared items, is low in customization and served with little interaction occurring between the customer and the service providers. In contrast, a doctor and patient must interact fully in the diagnostic and treatment phases to achieve satisfactory results. Patients also expect to be treated as individuals and wish to receive medical care that is customized to their particular needs.

The four quadrants of the service process matrix have been given names, as defined by the two dimensions, to describe the nature of the services illustrated. Service factories provide a standardized service with high capital investment, much like a line-flow manufacturing plant. Service shops permit more service customization, but they do so in a high-capital environment. Customers of a mass service will receive an undifferentiated service in a labor-intensive environment, but those seeking a professional service will be given individual attention by highly trained specialists.

Managers of services in any category, whether service factory, service shop, mass service, or professional service, share similar challenges. Services with high capital requirements (i. e. , low labor intensity), such as airlines and hospitals, require close monitoring of technological advances to remain competitive. This high capital investment also requires managers to schedule demand to maintain utilization of the equipment. Alternatively, managers of highly labor-intensive services, such as medical or legal professionals, must concentrate on personnel matters. The degree of customization affects the ability to control the quality of the service being delivered and the perception of the service by the customer.

3. Models

It is apparent that the true service component of the economy continues to grow in significance, especially through business opportunities associated with the application of new information technology. Although limitations of data availability and industry classification cloud the overall phenomena, it also seems clear that R&D and innovation in services also continues to grow, often in ways quite unlike the precedents of manufacturing and other sectors. In this paper, to explore the nature of service innovation we question whether or not this sector is truly poised for significant new growth through a unique innovation process or if its innovation is due to ongoing incremental changes—perpetual beta testing—typical of the history of this sector of the economy. Although Martin, Horne, and Chan70 focus on the inseparable production and consumption process in services, we also recognize a secondary or indirect process of innovation as well. This distinction is akin to the direct service impact of doctors giving advice to patients in consultations and indirectly over time; due to patients' behavioral change their state of health improves, whereas over longer periods of time learning from patterns of such clinical interventions indirectly impacts the practice of medicine.

To appreciate the nature of service innovation as an engine of growth, we need to understand this phenomenon in as thorough a manner as possible for traditional manufacturing contexts. Our approach is to concentrate on essential differences between services and manufacturing as a basis for thinking about the domain of service innovation. Because the term service encompasses such a diffuse range of economic activity, we narrow the scope of our exploration to the growing and dynamic class of services characterized by information mediated advice and support.

Although there has been relatively littleempirical evidence on innovation in services, there are some reports of substantial differences between service and nonservice (e. g. , manufacturing) innovation processes. For example, Martin and Horne found little or no planning evident in service innovation development; strong influence by customers and competitors (i. e. , the need for information from the business environment) and the majority of service firms surveyed do not use a service champion in development of new offerings. We seek to identify other substantial differences, and associated relationships, that merit further research.

As a basis for this pursuit we first review existing comparisons between manufacturing and services seeking to identify distinctions that would suggest underlying differences in the innovation process. Our sense of the growing importance and special uniqueness of service innovation—their products are always coproduced with customers—leads us to identify new targets for systematic managerially relevant research. We consider several important classes of service enterprise that appear to bring their own special service innovation requirements, and we develop propositions for research based on critical review of literature. In particular, we argue that incumbent service organizations typically lack the formal R&D function of manufacturing companies as a structure for their innovation and their preferred form of innovation is via the gradual coevolution process with customers. We call this the perpetual beta transition, after the familiar beta testing that typically precedes new product launch to signify that the service is inconstant motion when customers are involved. By contrast, the challenge for the other two enterprise contexts (i. e. , service extensions of manufacturing and service start-ups) is to deal with radical service innovation at the divide after Piore and Sable, when the path of technological innovation is the issue.

The model that emerges for this literature review appears in Figure 6−1. The asterisk in each cell marks the predictions supported by the literature about the type of innovation likely to emerge from three types of service firms.

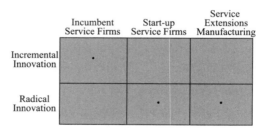

Figure 6−1   Service sector typology

Unfortunately, little, if any, systematic research in the service sector specially directed at innovation has been published. Outstanding exceptions include the following examples. Walter R. Nord and Sharon Tucker conducted an in-depth study of a variety of financial institutions and the introduction of NOW accounts (interest-bearing checking accounts—which became legal outside of New England on January 1, 1981) during this period and their results are quite consistent with the notion of understanding technology as either radical or incremental (which they call routine). Radical shifts in the banking industry were taking place about the same time. Not only do commercial banks invest billions of dollars in financial systems every year ($ 30 billion, to be exact, from 1981—1985), financial institutions have become quite innovative in introducing new service products.

No one outside New England had to design the product from scratch, so the innovation presented some interesting opportunities for a controlled comparison. And, every firm adopting NOW accounts essentially started at thesame time—when they became legal at the beginning of 1981. Banks as well as savings & loans offered the product, but their histories were significantly different, as everyone knows (see Table 6-2).

The authors divide financial institution cases into four categories of degree of success in implementing NOW accounts. At the top are the very successful cases, such as First Commercial Bank. Next are themoderately successful cases, such as First National S&L; then moderately unsuccessful cases, such as First Regional Bank; and finally, the unsuccessful cases, such as First National S&L.

This is a limited number of cases, but do you see the pattern in these success/failure categories? Look carefully at the designations for each institution and count the frequencies of S&Ls versus banks in each category. Now do you see the pattern?

Now accounts were a "radical departure from past practices for S&Ls, but a rather routine one for Banks". Given this context, it is not surprising to see the patterns of success and failure in Table 6-2. Banks, with checking experience—a high transaction business—generally did much better with NOW accounts than S&Ls. Radical and incremental are relative terms.

Classification of firms on the basis of success in implementation of NOW accounts

Table 6-2

Very Successful
First Commercial Bank
Second Commercial Bank
Third Commercial Bank
Second Capital S & L
First City Bank
Moderately Successful
First National S & L (after consultants)
Second City Bank
First Neighborhood S & L
Second Neighborhood S & L
Moderately Unsuccessful
First Regional Bank
First Capital S & L
Unsuccessful
First National S & L (before consultants)
Second National S & L

Note: The ordering within classes is not intended to reflect a ranking of success.
Source: Walter R. Nord and Sharon Tucker, *Implementing Routine and Radical Innovations*, Lexington, MA,
    D. C.
Heath and Company, 1987, Table 12-1, p. 307.

Hunter and Timme tested the Galbraith-Schumpeter hypothesis of scale bias: larger firms with larger R&D budgets innovate at a faster rate than smaller firms that are resource constrained. The hypothesis assumes that product mix is constant and that technological advancement affects all factors equally. They used a sample from the Federal Reserve end-of-year reports of income and dividends for the seven years from 1980 to 1986. This is nearly identical to the period studied by Nord and Tucker. Technological change was defined as the unexplained residual in the estimating equations for a sample of 219 banks. As a result of innovation, real costs were reduced by approximately an average of 1 percent per year, holding other factors constant. However, larger banks did not innovate faster than smaller banks, and the Galbraith-Schumpeter hypothesis is, therefore, not supported by these results. It is worth noting that larger banks did enjoy a larger percentage of cost savings than smaller banks. A subgroup of the largest banks averaged cost reductions of about 1.5 percent and a subgroup of the smallest banks in the sample averaged a cost savings of about 0.25 percent, suggesting scale economies of these effects. Apparently, there is a need to expand the scale of output in order to become more cost efficient.

We recently compared manufacturing and service new offerings in a sample of 67 cases of which 30 (45%) were service firms and 37 (55%) were manufacturing firms. We found, significantly, that sector (manufacturing) is directly related to new offering success. Length of participation in market has an inverse, significant impact on new offering success, which supports disruptive technology effects and shows sector differences—here manufacturing is disadvantaged. We also support the hypothesis of coincidence of new strategy adoption with novelty of new offering having sector differences. As predicted, manufacturing firms are more likely than service firms to formalize their strategic efforts for new products. Our results on beta testing show significant sector effects but only for services demonstrating shorter beta testing before launch. There were no significant sector differences in initiation of beta testing. Finally, we found significantly that when services (not manufacturers) invest in R&D they are likely to enjoy increased levels of product novelty. The discussion focuses on sector differences in the innovation process as they relate to management of this challenging process, the general theory of innovation and future research in this area.

At the risk of overstating the obvious and overemphasizing best practices as a concept, the results of recent work by Robert Cooper and his colleagues is summarized here as a capstone to this chapter. Bob has worked for years on predicting and helping companies achieve success in the complex process. A summary chart appears in Figure 6 − 2, which captures much of the best practices research he has done recently, to distinguish best "not so best" practices in new product development. Note that the first two of these best practices involve senior management (commitment) and management (annual objectives).

The PDMA (Product Development Management Association) has benchmarking data from two successive survey attempts and trends are quite stable over time.

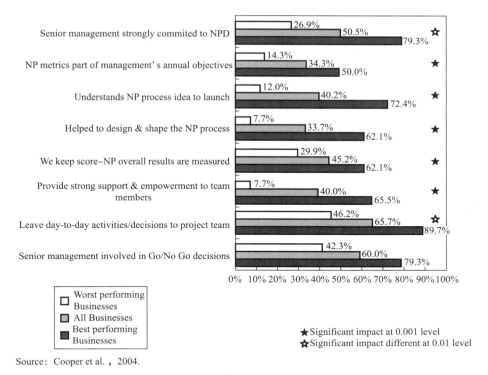

★Significant impact at 0.001 level
☆Significant impact different at 0.01 level

Source: Cooper et al. , 2004.

Figure 6-2   Percentage of business where senior management
demonstrates commitment to NPD

6.3   Service System

1. Definitions

Many definitions of service are available but all contain a common theme of intangibility and simultaneous consumption. The following represent a sample of service definitions:

6.3 Professional Terms, Words and Phrases, Sentence Illustration

Services are deeds, processes, and performances.

Services are economic activities offered by one party to another, most commonly employing time-based performances to bring about desired results in recipients themselves or in objects or other assets for which purchasers have responsibility. In exchange for their money, time, and effort, service customers expect to obtain value from access to goods, labor, professional skills, facilities, networks, and systems; but they do not normally take ownership of any of the physical elements involved.

A service system is a value-coproduction configuration of people, technology, other internal and external service systems, and shared information (such as language, processes, metrics, prices, policies, and laws).

2. Main Functions of Service System

(1) Improve Service Operation Capability

As a key role of the organization, managers'responsibilities involve strategic planning, resource allocation, decision-making, writing reports, participating in meetings, etc. they need to take advantage of the modern service system with special functions to take a comprehensive view of the overall operation of the organization and effectively improve the service operation ability. For example, Lockheed Martin Aerospace Co. has continuously improved its existing service system. In order to complete the design and supply services of supersonic stealth fighter parts required by the U. S. Department of Defense, it has formed a network interactive service system with more than 80 suppliers scattered in 187 regions. As a result, the drawing time of design drawings has been reduced from 400 hours to 125 hours, the project managers of the Ministry of Defense and Lockheed can track the daily work progress in a timely manner.

(2) Strengthen Knowledge Service Management

More and more service enterprises regard knowledge as core competitive resources and important strategic assets. More success depends on the ability of knowledge generation, collection, storage and dissemination, as well as the more effective expansion and application of scarce resources. Operating profits come more from the contribution of knowledge to the creation, production and transmission process of service products, and these knowledge has the characteristics of difficult imitation and long-term profits. Modern service enterprises can continuously strengthen knowledge service management through continuous investment and improvement of the construction of knowledge repository in the service system. This is because the knowledge base can record knowledge from different sources in the form of memos, reports, briefings, articles, etc. through digital storage and retrieval, it is convenient for relevant members of the system to mine and sort out knowledge, share and spread knowledge, and create and integrate knowledge. At the same time, many service enterprises have also set up Chief Knowledge Officers (CKOS), who, as senior managers, are mainly responsible for strengthening knowledge management, including knowledge management plan design, new knowledge search, and efficient use of existing knowledge.

(3) Provide Intelligent Technology Services

With the progress of science and technology, modern service systems make more use of intelligent technologies such as neural networks, fuzzy logic, genetic calculation, intelligent tools, and strive to improve service quality and customer satisfaction. Among them, neural network refers to a technical tool that simulates the biological brain processing mode to solve real problems. It continuously interacts with a large number of sensory and processing nodes to identify the true and false. For example, the financial service system uses neural network tools to analyze and process a large amount of input data. Investment companies can rely on the information output from the system to predict the future trend of stocks and funds, bond grades, the possibility of corporate bankruptcy, etc. Fuzzy logic refers to a technical tool that solves practical problems in an imprecise range according to rules or technical requirements. It expresses logic through imprecise concept description, or solves problems by imprecise, uncertain and unreliable inference. In specific applications, the hardware implements fuzzy logic rules (such as when the room temperature is low and the humidity is high, and when the outdoor wind force is high and the temperature is low, the temperature should be increased and the humidity should be reduced). The programmer imprecisely describes various influencing factors (such as temperature, humidity, outdoor wind force, etc.) and compiles application software to convert language expressions (such as warmth) into computer operable numbers, so as to achieve the goal of the service system. Genetic algorithms, also known as adaptive computing, refers to a technical tool that solves practical problems according to the appropriate survival mode or evolution principle of species. It controls the generation, variation, adaptation and selection of solutions through derivative programs or methods such as replication, mutation, natural selection, change or recombination (like genetic process). Intelligent agent refers to a technical tool that can perform specific, repetitive and predictable tasks without human intervention. Users can make decisions according to their personal preferences, such as deleting spam, arranging appointments, seeking the cheapest tickets, etc. Users can cooperate with others in the same environment with the help of intelligent tools. Users can query the completion of tasks, training or education progress in time, and can also hide difficult or complex tasks, monitoring events and their development.

3. Methods and Tools of Service System

We defined the service package as a bundle of attributes that a customer experiences. This bundle consists of five features: supporting facility, facilitating goods, information, explicit services, and implicit services. With a well-designed service system, these features are coordinated harmoniously in light of the desired service package. Consequently, the definition of the service package is key to designing the service system itself. This design can be approached in several ways.

Routine services can be delivered through a production-line approach. With this approach, services are provided in a controlled environment to ensure consistent quality and efficiency of operation. Another approach is to encourage active customer participation in the process. Allowing the customer to take an active role in the service process can result in many benefits to both the consumer and the provider. An intermediate approach divides the service into high and low-customer-contact operations. This allows the low contact operations to be designed as a technical core that is isolated from the customer. Advances in information technology have driven the information empowerment approach.

We note that combinations of these approaches also can be used. For example, banks isolate their check-processing operation, use self-serve automated tellers, and provide personalized loan service.

(1) Production-Line Approach

We tend to see service as something personal—it is performed by individuals directly for other individuals. This humanistic perception can be overly constraining, however, and therefore can impede development of an innovative service system design. For example, we sometimes might benefit from a more technocratic service delivery system. Manufacturing systems are designed with control of the process in mind. The output often is machine-paced, and jobs are designed with explicit tasks to be performed. Special tools and machines are supplied to increase worker productivity. A service taking this production-line approach could gain a competitive advantage with a cost leadership strategy.

McDonald's provides the quintessential example of this manufacturing-in-the-field approach to service. Raw materials (e. g. , hamburger patties) are measured and prepackaged off-site, leaving the employees with no discretion as to size, quality, or consistency. In addition, storage facilities are designed expressly for the predetermined mix of products. No extra space is available for foods and beverages that are not called for in the service.

The production of french fries illustrates attention to design detail. The fries come precut, partially cooked, and frozen. The fryer is sized to cook a correct quantity of fries. This is an amount that will be not so large as to create an inventory of soggy fries or so small as to require making new batches very frequently. The fryer is emptied into a wide, flat tray near the service counter. This setup prevents fries from an overfilled bag from dropping to the floor, which would result in wasted food and an unclean environment. A special wide-mouthed scoop with a funnel in the handle is used to ensure a consistent measure of french fries. The thoughtful design ensures that employees never soil their hands or the fries, that the floor remains clean, and that the quantity is controlled. Further, a generous-looking portion of fries is delivered to the customer by a speedy, efficient, and cheerful employee.

This entire system is engineered from beginning to end, from prepackaged hamburgers to highly visible trash cans that encourage customers to clear their table. Every detail is accounted for through careful planning and design. The production-line approach to service system design attempts to translate a successful manufacturing concept into the service sector, and several features contribute to its success.

(2) Limited Discretionary Action of Personnel

A worker on an automobile assembly line is given well-defined tasks to perform along with the tools to accomplish them. Employees with discretion and latitude might produce a more personalized car, but uniformity from one car to the next would be lost. Standardization and quality (defined as consistency in meeting specifications) are the hallmarks of a production line. For standardized routine services, consistency in service performance is valued by customers. For example, specialized services like muffler replacement and pest control are advertised as having the same high-quality service at any franchised outlet. Thus, the customer can expect identical service at any location of a particular franchise operation (e. g. , one Big Mac is as desirable as another), just as one product from a manufacturer is indistinguishable from another. If more personalized service is desired, however, the concept of employee empowerment becomes appropriate.

(3) Division of Labor

The production-line approach suggests that the total job be broken down into groups of simple tasks. Task grouping permits the specialization of labor skills (e. g. , not everyone at McDonald's needs to be a cook). Further, the division of labor allows one to pay only for the skill that is required to perform the task. Of course, this raises the criticism of many service jobs as being minimum-wage, dead-end, and low-skill employment. Consider, for example, a concept in health care where patients are processed through a fixed sequence of medical tests, which are part of the diagnostic work-up. Tests are performed by medical technicians using sophisticated equipment. Because the entire process is divided into routine tasks, the examination can be accomplished without an expensive physician.

(4) Substitution of Technology for People

The systematic substitution of equipment for people has been the source of progress in manufacturing. This approach also can be used in services, as seen by the acceptance of automated teller machines in lieu of bank tellers. A great deal can be accomplished by means of the "soft" technology of systems, however. Consider, for example, the use of mirrors placed in an airplane galley. This benign device provides a reminder and an opportunity for flight attendants to maintain a pleasant appearance in an unobtrusive manner. Another example is the greeting card display that has a built-in inventory replenishment and reordering feature; when the stock gets low, a colored card appears to signal a reorder. Using a laptop computer, insurance agents can personalize their recommendations and illustrate the accumulation of cash values.

(5) Service Standardization

The limited menu at McDonald's guarantees a fast hamburger. Limiting service options creates opportunities for predictability and preplanning; the service becomes a routine process with well-defined tasks and an orderly flow of customers. Standardization also helps to provide uniformity in service quality, because the process is easier to control. Franchise services take advantage of standardization to build national organizations and thus overcome the problem of demand being limited only to the immediate region around a service location.

4. Models of Service System

Figure 6-3 illustrates the models of service system.

Operation system: The task of the service operating system is production and processing, that is, dealing with customer input. The system is similar to a factory. The main problems to be solved in operation management include: how to improve the standardization and mechanization of products; how to control costs; how to improve efficiency and quality. This part is produced according to the customized needs of customers.

Delivery system: Deliver service products to customers. This part includes: visible part of the operating system + customer contact area. A service product is a service package containing intangible and tangible elements. All the constituent elements of the service delivery system, including service personnel, delivery methods and processes, other customers, production and processing activities extending at the front desk, other visible factors in the service area, etc. The time, place and way of service delivery are the three key elements of designing the service delivery process. Key elements of evaluation: speed, accuracy and enthusiasm. At present, the mode of delivery is undergoing a profound revolution with the electronization. Consider the impact of internal employees on service quality: workplace design, post design, employee selection and employee development, employee motivation, appropriate authorization, customer service tools.

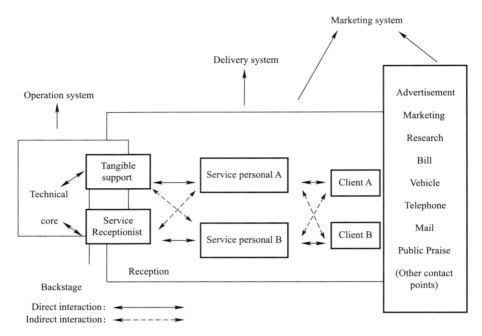

Figure 6-3　Models of service system

Marketing system: Communicate with customers, convey the product information of the service enterprise and the commitment of the service enterprise to customers to customers. It affects customers' evaluation and selection of service enterprises, customer satisfaction and loyalty, and enterprise brand image. All factors that affect customers' views on service enterprises constitute a service marketing system. For high contact service enterprises, the vast majority of marketing work is carried out in stores. Therefore, customer contact is the core of the operation of service marketing system.

Service operating system, service delivery system and service marketing system have the relationship of mutual intersection and overlap. Generally speaking, the main function of the service operating system is production, but its visible part is also included in the service delivery system. The main function of service delivery system is delivery. However, since the main perception, experience and evaluation of customers are formed here, the tangible elements and delivery process of the service delivery system have also become the main elements of the service marketing system. In addition to the elements of the service delivery system, the service marketing system also includes some other customer contact elements.

6.4　Service Operations

1. Introduction of Service Operations

The word service means many different things to different people, and even within the Service Operations Community there is no commonly agreed definition. This is due in no small way to the many different industries that perceive themselves as providers of services in one form or other. However, in the context

6.4 Professional Terms, Words and Phrases, Sentence Illustration

of this chapter it is important to have a framework around which we can work with the term "service operations management". Therefore, when we talk about service in the context of this chapter, and the wider operations management community, the following definition will be applied: Service Operations Management: the implementation of the organizations strategy through the operational control of the organization by focusing on not only product or service development, but also the delivery of products and services to the end customer in a way that drives co-creation of value between customer and business.

When we look at the term "service" in this context it takes on a very important "primary" role for the organization. This is indeed as it should be. Many organizations still relegate "service" led activity to a support role such as customer care, complaint management, or some other "cost-centric" role. In doing so, organizations are missing a clear opportunity to use their service capabilities to drive revenue.

Customers participate in the service process. When customers appear in the service process as participants, service managers must pay attention to the design of facilities. Customers' knowledge, experience, motivation and even honesty will directly affect the efficiency of the service system. First, the participation of customers reduces the number of people who need to be managed, such as welfare expenditure. Secondly, because customers pay labor when they need it, the service ability changes directly with the demand, rather than completely subject to the number of employees. This strategy is generally accepted in countries with strong autonomy.

The production and consumption of services occur at the same time. The fact that the production and consumption of services occur at the same time, but services cannot be stored is a remarkable feature of service management. Services cannot be stored, which makes the service industry unable to rely on storage or to buffer or adapt to demand changes like manufacturing. Service open system is fully affected by the demand changes in the delivery system. The simultaneous production and consumption of services also makes it impossible to detect products in advance, so we must rely on other indicators to ensure service quality.

Services are perishable goods. For example, an empty seat on a plane, an empty room in a hospital or hotel. In this case, a loss of opportunity occurred. The service cannot be stored. If it is not used, it will be lost forever. The full use of service capacity has become a management challenge, because customer demand changes greatly, and it is not feasible to use inventory to adapt to demand fluctuations. The choice of location depends on the customer. In the service industry, customers and providers must meet in person. The customer may go to the service place, or the service personnel may go to the customer's place (such as ambulance). Travel time and cost are reflected in the economics of place selection. As a result, many small service centers are located close to potential customers. Of course, we have to weigh the fixed cost of facilities and the cost of customers' journey. Due to the widespread use of the Internet, the service industry has also undergone some changes.

Labor intensive. In most service organizations, labor force is the key resource to determine organizational efficiency. In an expanding organization, recruitment is an important way to acquire new knowledge. In an organization with slow or stagnant development, the only feasible strategy is continuous recultivation. The interaction between customers and employees in service makes it possible for employees to gain more comprehensive work experience. The formulation of standards and the training of employees in an appropriate way are the key to ensure the consistency of services.

2. Methods and Tools of Service Operations

First, develop and maintain a good and lasting customer relationship. Not only the importance of service elements in customer relations is increasing, but also customers' requirements for flexible services from service providers are increasing. If the employees of a service enterprise master the necessary knowledge, have a service-oriented attitude towards work and customers, and the enterprise is also competitive in other aspects, then market success is natural. We must develop and maintain a good and lasting customer relationship.

Secondly, effectively manage services. Demand service refers to providing help directly to people (or organizations), or providing services to equipment owned by people (or organizations). In the production and trading services, front-line employees and customers are in direct face-to-face contact, and no one else can respond to sudden changes in customer needs and aspirations. In this case, front-line employees must immediately make decisions and take necessary actions; or according to the information revealed by the customer's behavior, change their working methods. Of course, the standard method of market research can measure and calculate the market demand in advance, which still needs to be continued. Therefore, employees who contact customers and produce services must analyze customers' needs and wishes at the moment of service production and consumption.

Thirdly, do a good job in service. In the service competition, the nature of marketing is also changing. Although traditional marketing activities, such as market research, advertising, marketing and promotional activities carried out by professional sales teams, are still as important as before, they are not the only activities carried out by marketing. The marketing function is more extensive than before and runs through the whole organization. When maintaining or strengthening lasting customer relationships, the conventional means of competition is mainly to establish new customer relationships. In order to further develop the existing customer relationship, the exchange of goods, services and information, as well as the exchange of financial interests and social relations are of great importance.

Finally, build organizational, technical and management support. It often happens that the organizational structure of many enterprises does not support the operation of customer orientation and high-quality service, but the front-line employees or departments that must cooperate with each other to create services do their own things in the organization. In order to develop service into a powerful means of competition, enterprises must adjust the organizational structure so that the organization, whether formal or informal, supports employees to provide high-quality services. It should be pointed out that the importance of technology in the service economy is not lower than before, on the contrary, it is even more important. If a technical measure or material resource meets the needs and aspirations of users, or is suitable for the environment used, it will greatly improve the service quality. Regular technical support can enable employees to create better services. In addition, strong management support is also a necessary condition for employees to provide quality services.

3. Models of Service Operations

(1) Service Outsourcing

In the process of development, service outsourcing has experienced three generations. The first-generation outsourcing is limited to the procurement contract arrangement of non-core competence, which is mainly driven by cost reduction or layoffs. Enterprises contract simple background functions or peripheral activities, such as salary processing, safety and cleaning, catering services, etc., to more efficient service providers. The second generation of new outsourcing has developed since the mid-1980s, and enterprises began to outsource near core activities, namely, major supply chain activities. In the manufacturing sector, the development of offshore outsourcing is conducive to the use of low-cost, professional skills and technical know-how, free from geographical, spatial and resource constraints. At the same time, the field of information technology outsourcing has also developed greatly. The third generation outsourcing shows that enterprises begin to outsource tradition. In essence, enterprises operate virtual value chains, and their suppliers are regarded as partners in their value-added activities. Each industry in the primary and secondary industries can be divided into production and producer services. Producer services in the primary industry and producer services in the secondary industry have the same attributes as producer services in the tertiary industry.

(2) Self-support Services of Manufacturers

The manufacturing enterprises set up functional departments of producer services to meet their own demand for producer services. Self-service does not need to consider the cooperation between enterprises and external service providers, and it completely depends on the internal coordination of enterprises to promote the integration of productive services and production processes. Enterprises must have sufficient resources and skills (including manpower, capital, equipment, technology, etc.) to attract producer services to the manufacturing sector to serve the production and sales of manufacturing products. The typical mode of self-supporting service is self-production and self-sale. In self production, the production enterprise has its own research team, equipped with corresponding researchers, production equipment and production personnel. In self-sale, it is required to have a product marketing team, be able to conduct market research, and have a sales location. Its main form is direct selling. Direct selling is a marketing method that products are not distributed through traditional public sales channels such as shopping malls and supermarkets, but directly organized by manufacturers or distributors. Direct selling is actually a business form that transfers part of the profits of products from agents, distributors and advertisers to direct sellers. Direct selling can effectively shorten the channel, get close to customers, quickly deliver products to customers, speed up capital operation, and better feedback customers' opinions and needs to the enterprise quickly, which is conducive to the adjustment of enterprise strategy and the transformation of tactics. Therefore, direct selling can quickly rise and become a cutting-edge of modern marketing.

（3）Industrial Clusters

Industrial clusters are the result of social division of labor and cooperation. Enterprises extend or decompose the product value chain, increase the processing depth and breadth of products, and improve the output value of resources. From the perspective of the composition of the global value chain, productive service activities such as commodity logistics, technology development, brand marketing and human resource management occupy the core link in the whole value chain. The important driving force for the dynamic development of modern industrial value chain comes from the change of industrial knowledge scale and structure. The rapidly updated knowledge structure mainly promotes the adjustment of modern industrial value chain in the following two aspects: institutions and enterprises that master new professional knowledge continue to join the industrial chain, the industrial value chain becomes thicker and longer, the value-added links of the value chain increase, and the decomposability is improved. Second, the addition of new knowledge has changed the nature of some links in the value chain and their position in the value chain. Enterprises must increase technology investment, accelerate information construction, promote the decomposition of resource value chain by the change of knowledge in the extractive industry, and promote the formation and large-scale operation of productive service projects. Enterprise groups with enterprise companies as the core, including enterprise product research institutes, domestic and foreign trade companies, engineering companies and production bases, have formed a complete industrial chain with technology research and development, marketing, manufacturing and engineering business as the main functions, improving the influence and competitiveness in the industry.

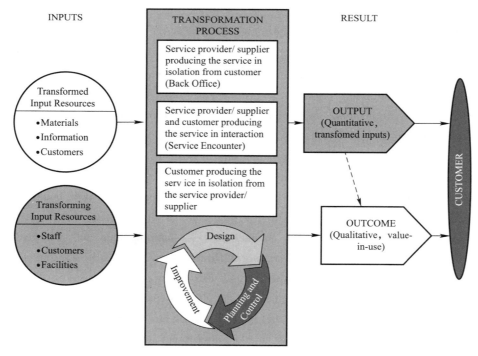

Figure 6-4　Service operations

6.5　Reading Material

Changing EMS Business Models

OEMs are now dictating margins to EMS companies, and margins are going down. This may make OEM shareholders happy, but in time, this trend could significantly weaken their own supply chain. What Ralph Kenton (of Ralph Kenton and Associates) refers to as the hollowing-out of the OEM is their increasing urge to outsource everything in order to focus on their core competencies (Lyell, 2000).

This trend is expected to result in OEMs' complete dependence on their suppliers—the same ones whose margins they are driving down. The disparity in perceived value for the design and marketing functions (OEM) versus the manufacturing and logistics functions (EMS), creates potential conflict between the two. This is because the margin equation is weighted heavily in OEMs' favor, due not only to inherently high margins (55% ~ 65%) dictated by their business models, but also because they control their suppliers' margins (in the 4% ~ 7% range for the typical EMS focused on PCB assembly).

The only force that offsets a potential collision between OEMs and EMS is industry growth, and the single greatest source of EMS growth is OEM divestitures. 65% of all EMS growth, as reported by Technology Forecasters, is through the acquisition of OEM facilities. As long as this growth-by-acquisition trend continues, the two independent industries will continue to prosper, albeit in delicate balance.

The current rate of growth will eventually lead to a saturation of the total available market. There are currently many debates regarding the amount of time this process will take. However, if the trend stays constant, major penetration will be noticed in five years and complete in less than ten. Should this happen, it could have a profound impact on the delicate balance between OEM and EMS.

Consolidation has been an effective way to keep the shareholders of the declining margin electronics distribution business temporarily satisfied. Yet consolidation in distribution is a mixed-bag for mid-tier OEM/EMS customers. Procurement of many component lines from a single supplier helps enormously to lower material logistics costs, but service is much worse than from smaller suppliers competing for the business. A significant part of distributor consolidation success—never easy—is due to a business model that allows the convergence of customer bases, and the ability to support thousands of purchasers.

Recent moves by semiconductor manufacturers indicate that they will not participate in the eroding margin game.

What was once two separate supply chains (EMS/electronic distribution) with margins for both has now collapsed into one. EMS suppliers currently have an upper hand because of lower transaction costs and higher return on assets, but this advantage could change with the commitment to a demand creation model by the component manufacturers.

Yet, there are several reasons an EMS might think of acquiring a distributor. Distributors understand material logistics far better than an EMS. Owning a distributor and eliminating double mark-up could increase EMS margins. The problem is that there are probably very few worthwhile distribution acquisitions left and a lot of competition for them.

More recently, with the increased emphasis on globalization, the practice of shedding functions previously thought to be integral to the company's success is becoming widespread, with companies switching all, or a substantial proportion, of their manufacturing from in house to external contract manufacturers. Such developments have caused the growth of contract manufacturers such as Flextronics and Solectron, who run large offshore manufacturing operations.

This is particularly true in the electronics field where recent years have seen spectacular growth in the electronics manufacturing services (EMS) industry. In 1998, the estimated value of EMS was $90 billion. One forecaster projected this value to grow 26% a year, which means, if this projection is correct, that the value of EMS will exceed $2880 billion by the year 2013.

Clearly, there are efficiencies to be realized in terms of lower labour costs and knowledge of basic production techniques and processes applicable across the products of several manufacturers. The result, at least in the short term, is lower costs, higher profits, an enhanced competitive position, and perhaps lower prices to the consumer.

Yet from the point of view of new product development and product improvement, it seems that there is an important hidden cost here. For years, spurred on by Japanese practice, it has been heard about product improvements having their roots in the factory floor.

Then there is the impact on designers and engineers responsible for product development. While the lack of factory floor suggestions is likely to have its greatest effect on incremental improvements in the product, it may also have an influence on the development of new products.

It is not only production that is at issue. Large contractors such as Solectron, Celestica, and Flextronics undertake to provide expanded functions such as new product design and development, and even new product launch services. Product innovation and improvement are skills that are honed by use and used as key elements in product differentiation and as points of competitive advantage.

One will never know exactly how the large-scale contracting out of manufacturing and other functions has affected the development of new products and the improvement of existing products. It is well to bear in mind, however, that with disuse, abilities decay and functions atrophy. It pays to bear that in mind when evaluating decisions on large-scale outsourcing.

Chapter 7
Logistics System Design, Optimization and Supply Chain Management

7.1　Logistics System Design

1. Introduction

7.1 Professional Terms, Words and Phrases, Sentence Illustration

Logistics deals with the planning and control of material flows and related information in organizations, both in the public and private sectors. Broadly speaking, its mission is to get the right materials to the right place at the right time, while optimizing a given performance measure (e. g. minimizing total operating costs) and satisfying a given set of constraints (e. g. a budget constraint). In the military context, logistics is concerned with the supply of troops with food, armaments, ammunitions and spare parts, as well as the transport of troops themselves. In civil organizations, logistics issues are encountered in firms producing and distributing physical goods. The key issue is to decide how and when raw materials, semi-finished and finished goods should be acquired, moved and stored. Logistics problems also arise in firms and public organizations producing services. This is the case of garbage collection, mail delivery, public utilities and after-sales service.

(1) Significance of Logistics

Logistics is one of the most important activities in modern societies. A few figures can be used to illustrate this assertion. It has been estimated that the total logistics cost incurred by USA organizations in 1997 was 862 billion dollars, corresponding to approximately 11% of the USA Gross Domestic Product (GDP). This cost is higher than the combined annual USA government expenditure in social security, health services and defence. These figures are similar to those observed for the other North America Free Trade Agreement (NAFTA) countries and for the European Union (EU) countries. Furthermore, logistics costs represent a significant part of a company's sales, as shown in Table 7-1 for EU firms in 1993.

(2) Logistics Systems.

A logistics system is made up of a set of facilities linked by transportation services. Facilities are sites where materials are processed, e. g. , manufactured, stored, sorted, sold or consumed. They include manufacturing and assembly centres, warehouses, distribution centres (DCs), transshipment points, transportation terminals, retail outlets, mail sorting centres, garbage incinerators, dump sites, etc.

Logistics costs（as a percentage of GDP）in EU countries

（T, transportation；W, warehousing；I, inventory；A, administration） Table 7-1

Sector	T	W	I	A	Total
Food/beverage	3.7	2.2	2.8	1.7	10.4
Electronics	2.0	2.0	3.8	2.5	10.3
Chemical	3.8	2.3	2.6	1.5	10.2
Automotive	2.7	2.3	2.7	1.2	8.9
Pharmaceutical	2.2	2.0	2.5	2.1	8.8
Newspapers	4.7	3.0	3.6	2.1	13.4

Transportation services move materials between facilities using vehicles and equipment such as trucks, tractors, trailers, crews, pallets, containers, cars and trains. A few examples will help clarify these concepts.

（3）Logistics Goals

Some important logistics goals/objectives include：

① Quick response to change in the market and customer orders.

② Minimize variances in logistics service.

③ Minimize inventory to reduce expense.

④ Combine product movement by grouping shipments.

⑤ Uphold high quality and engage in constant enhancement.

⑥ Support the entire product life cycle and the reverse logistics supply chain.

（4）Logistics Strategies

① Coordinating and managing functions：Physical inventory can be reduced by improving communication with suppliers by communicating with them regularly and keep them on the same page about logistics plans. If possible, team up with suppliers and share knowledge about the demand trend. Design the routing in such a way so that the inventory is kept in transit most of the time；this strategy reduces inventory cost. Also clear the freight while it is still in transit on the road, on water, or in the air so it does not have to spend much time in customs, which reduces costs.

② Integrating the supply chain：As logistics management is a vital part of the supply chain, for uninterrupted flow of goods and information, requires logistics internal process integration between its layers as well as alignment between various functions along the supply chain are required. Layers of transportation management include intermodal, equipment, infrastructure, networks, modes, and basics. Transportation managers find the best ways to align the strengths and weaknesses of these various layers to provide high-quality, low-cost service to customers. Supply chain functions include purchasing, logistics, production control, research and development, marketing and sales, and distribution.

③ Substituting information for inventory：In order to construct the logistics network, substituting information is crucial and requires taking key steps. The first step is to locate in the right locations/countries. Once all geographical locations are identified, then analyze the forward and reverse chains of supply and compare which locations that makes the logistics function efficient and cost effective. The next step is to develop an export import strategy. Estimate the volume of the product being exported and imported, how many freights are needed, and then select the location at which to place the inventory for strategic advantage. Step three is selecting the warehouse location. Evaluate the number of warehouses needed, determine the distance of the warehouses from markets, and then build the warehouses around the world in an efficient way to minimize cost and delivery time. Step four is to selecting the mix of transportation modes and carriers to supply the deliveries in an efficient manner. Selecting the right number of partners also plays a significant role in constructing the logistics network. This requires developing robust information systems to quickly track accurate demand information and locate inventory using GPS systems and barcoding technology.

④ Reducing supply chain partners to an effective minimum number: More partners in the system makes it difficult and expensive to manage the supply chain. Fewer partners in the system reduces cycle time, operational costs, and inventory-holding costs.

⑤ Pooling risks: Both manufacturers and suppliers should stock the common inventory components associated with the broad family of products in a centralized warehouse to avoid storage cost and stock outs risk. This strategy is especially helpful when high variability in demand is associated with a product.

2. Methodology

(1) Qualitative Methods

Qualitative methods are mainly based on expert judgement or on experimental approaches, although they can also make use of simple mathematical tools to combine different forecasts. Qualitative methods are usually employed for long and medium-term forecasts when there are not enough data to use a quantitative approach. This is the case, for example, when a new product or service is launched on the market, when a product packaging is changed or when the forecasts are expected to be affected by political changeovers or technological advances. The most widely used qualitative methods are management judgement, the Delphi method and market research.

In management judgement, a forecast is developed by the workforce, for example the company's management or sales force. As a rule, the workforce can provide accurate estimates since it knows a lot about the company's business, including shifts in customers' behaviour and the profile ofprospective customers. China currently has a share of about 30% of world sales of luxury articles. Experts of McKinsey estimate an annual growth of the Chinese market for these articles equal to about $15 billion for the next five years. In the Delphi method, a series of questionnaires is submitted to a panel of experts. Every time a group of questions is answered, new sets of information become available. Then a new questionnaire is prepared by a coordinator in such a way that every expert is faced with the new findings. This procedure eliminates the bandwagon effect of majority opinion. The Delphi method terminates as soon as all experts share the same viewpoint. This technique is mainly used to estimate the influence of political or macro-economical changes on data patterns.

The Delphi method has been used recently to estimate the tourist flows in the Lazio coastal region in Italy. The group of experts involved was made up of 800 hotel managers and tour operators, coordinated by a team of 10 employees of the Lazio regional authority.

Market research is based on interviews with potential consumers or users. It is time consuming and requires a deep knowledge of sampling theory. For these reasons, it is used only occasionally, for example when deciding whether a new product should be launched.

Tienda is a Spanish company manufacturing and marketing aromatic oils. Its lemon-scented oil, obtained from citrus fruits and olives, has recently been introduced. To forecast its demand, the company has asked a market research company to carry out a survey. For this purpose, a sample of 1455 customers were selected in 32 Spanish supermarkets in the area of Seville. Each questionnaire allowed researchers to estimate the probability that the customer would buy the new product. On the basis of these data, a forecast of the new product's sales was generated. Table 7-2 summarizes the features of the main qualitative forecasting methods.

Features of the main qualitative methods   Table 7-2

Feature	Forecasting method		
	Management judgement	Delphi method	Market survey
Time horizon	Medium or short	Medium or long	Medium
Effort	Moderate, if based on the companys'experts	Large	Large
Costs	Low, if based on the companys'experts	High	High
Data required	No	No	No
Accuracy	Low	High	Moderate

（2）Quantitative Methods

Quantitative methods can be used every time there is sufficient demand history. Such techniques belong to two main groups: causal methods and time series extrapolation. Causal methods are based on the hypothesis that future demand depends on the past or current values of some variables. They include regression, econometric models, input-output models, life-cycle analysis, computer simulation models and neural networks. Most of these approaches are difficult to implement, even for larger companies. In practice, only single or multiple regression is used for logistics planning and control. Time series extrapolation presupposes that some features of the past demand time pattern will remain the same. The demand pattern is then projected in the future. This can be done in a number of ways, including the elementary technique, moving averages, exponential smoothing techniques, the decomposition approach and the Box-Jenkins method. The choice of the most suitable quantitative forecasting technique depends on the kind of historical data available and the type of product (or service). However, as a rule, it is best to select the simplest possible approach. This principle is based on the following observations.

- Forecasts obtained by using simple techniques are easier to understand and explain. This is a fundamental aspect when large sums of money are involved in the decision-making process.

- In a business context, complex forecasting procedures seldom yield better results than simple ones.

This rule is often kept in mind by logisticians, as confirmed by several surveys carried out in North America and in the EU (see Table 7-3). The usage frequencies reported in columns 2 and 3 of Table 7-3 should be adjusted in order to take into account the variable levels of familiarity of the decision makers with different forecasting methods (column 4). For example, when comparing the decomposition technique and the more complex Box-Jenkins method in the medium term, one should consider the different level of familiarity that the decision makers have (57% and 37%, respectively) with such approaches. This can be done by computing the values that the quotas of use would likely have if all the decision makers knew both techniques ($12/0.57 = 21\%$ and $5/0.37 = 13.5\%$, respectively).

Quota of use of the main quantitative forecasting methods in USA (1994) Table 7-3

Forecasting method	Use (%) in short term	Use(%) in medium term	Level (%) of familiarity
Decomposition	7	12	57
Elementary technique	19	14	84
Moving average	33	28	96
Exponential smoothing	20	17	83
Regression	25	26	83
Box-Jenkins	2	5	37

Source: Interfaces 24(2),92-100, Sanders N. R. and Manrodt K. B. (1994).

3. Models

Relevant logistics issues have to be tackled when planning a number of public services (firefighting, transport of the disabled, ambulance dispatching, to name a few). In such contexts, it is often of primary importance to ensure not only a low logistics cost, but also an adequate service level to all users. As a result, specific models have to be applied when locating public facilities. For example, in the P-centre model described below, the service time of the most disadvantaged user is to be minimized, whereas in the location-covering model one has to determine the least-cost set of facilities such that each user can be reached within a given maximum travel time.

(1) P-Centre Models

In the P-Centre model, the aim is to locate p facilities on a graph in such a way that the maximum travel time from a user to the closest facility is minimized. The P-Centre model finds its application when it is necessary to ensure equity in servicing users spread on a wide geographical area.

The problem can be modelled on a directed, undirected or mixed graph $G(V, A, E)$, where

V is a set of vertices representing both user sites and road intersections, while A and E (the set of arcs and edges, respectively) describe the road connections among the sites. Exactly p facilities have to be located either on a vertex or on an arc or edge. For p2, the P-Centre model is NP-hard.

If G is a directed graph, there exists an optimal solution of the P-Centre problem such that every facility location is a vertex (vertex location property). If G is undirected or mixed, the optimal location of a facility could be on an internal point of an edge. In what follows, a solution methodology is described for the 1-centre problem. The reader should consult specialized books for a discussion of the other cases. If G is directed, the 1-centre is simply the vertex associated with the minimum value of the maximum travel time to all the other vertices. In the case of an undirected or mixed graph, the 1-centre can correspond to a vertex or an internal edge point. To simplify the discussion, we will refer only to the case of the undirected graph [A, the procedure can be easily applied in the case of mixed graph. For each $= \phi(i, j)$], although $\in E$, let a_{ij} be the traversal time of edge (i, j). Furthermore, for each pair of vertices $i, j \in V$, denote by t_{ij} the shortest travel time between i and j, corresponding to the sum of the travel times of the edges of the shortest path between i and j. Note that, on the basis of the definition of travel time, the result is

$$t_i^j \leqslant a_{ij}, (i, j) \in E \tag{7-1}$$

Finally, denote by $\tau_h(p_{hk})$ the travel time along edge $(h, k) \in E$ between vertex $h \in V$ and a point p_{hk} of the edge. In this way, the travel time $\tau_h(p_{hk})$ along the edge (h, k) between the vertex $k \in V$ and p_{hk} results as (Figure 7-1):

$$\tau_k(p_{hk}) = a_{hk} - \tau_h(p_{hk}) \tag{7-2}$$

The 1-centre problem can be solved by the following algorithm proposed by Hakimi.

Step 1. Computation of the travel time. For each edge $(h, k) \in E$ and for each vertex $\in V$, determine the travel time $T_i(p_{hk})$ from $i \in V$ to a point p_{hk} of the edge (h, k) (Figure 7-2):

$$T_i(p_{hk}) = \min[t_i^h + \tau_h(p_{hk}), t_i^k + \tau_k(p_{hk})] \tag{7-3}$$

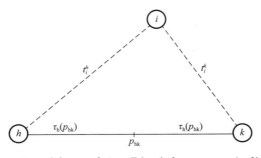

Figure 7-1　Computation of the travel time $T_i(p_{hk})$ from an user $i \in V$ to a facility in p_{hk}

Step 2. Finding the local centre. For each edge $(h, k) \in E$, determine the local centre p_{hk}^* as the point on (h, k) minimizing the travel time from the most disadvantaged vertex:

$$p_{hk}^* = \operatorname*{argmin}_{} \max_{i \in V} \{T_i(p_{hk})\} \tag{7-4}$$

where $\max_{i \in V}\{T_i(p_{hk})\}$ corresponds to the superior envelope of the functions $T_i(p_{hk})$, $i \in V$ (Figure 7-3).

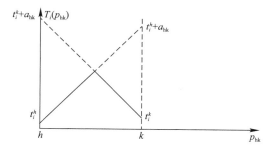

Figure 7-2   Travel time $T_i(p_{hk})$ versus the position of point p_{hk} along edge (h, k)

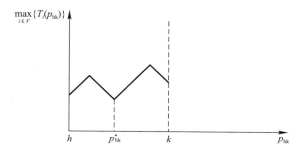

Figure 7-3   Determination of the local centre of edge $(h, k) \in E$.

Step 3. Determination of the 1-centre. The 1-centre p is the best local centre p_{hk}^*, $(h, k) \in E$, i. e.

$$p^* = \arg \min_{(h, k) \in E} \left\{ \min \max_{i \in V} \left[T_i(p_{hk}) \right] \right\} \tag{7-5}$$

In the LaMancha region of Spain (Figure 7-4) a consortium of town councils, located in an underpopulated rural area, decided to locate a parking place for ambulances. A preliminary examination of the problem revealed that the probability of receiving a request for service during the completion of a previous call was extremely low because of the small number of the inhabitants of the zone. For this reason the team responsible for the service decided to use only one vehicle. In the light of this observation, the problem was modelled as a 1-centre problem on a road network G where all the connections are two-way streets (Table 7-4). Travel times were calculated assuming a vehicle average speed of 90 km/h (Table 7-5).

Travel times t_i^j, $i, j \in V$, are reported in Table 7-6. For each edge $(h, k) \in E$ and for each vertex $i \in V$ the travel time $T_i(p_{hk})$ from vertex i to a point p_{hk} of the edge (h, k) can be defined through Equation (7-1). This enables the construction, for each edge $(h, k) \in E$ of the function $\max_{i \in V}\{T_i(p_{hk})\}$, whose minimum corresponds to the local centre p_{hk}^*. For example, Figure 7-5 depicts the function $\max_{i \in V}\{T_i(p_{23})\}$, and Table 7-7 gives, for each edge $(h, k) \in E$, both the position of p_{hk}^* and the value $\max_{i \in V}\{T_i(p_{hk}^*)\}$.

Consequently the 1-centre corresponds to the point p^* on the edge $(8, 10)$. Therefore, the optimal positioning of the parking place for the ambulance should be located on the road between Montiel and Almedina, at 2.25 km from the centre of Montiel. The villages least advantaged by this location decision are Villanueva de la Fuente and Torre de JuanAbad, since the ambulance would take an average time of 11.5 min to reach them.

Vertices of La Mancha 1-centre problem　　　　　　　　Table 7-4

Vertex	Locality
1	Torre de Juan Abad
2	Infantes
3	Villahermosa
4	Villanueva de la Fuente
5	Albaladejo
6	Terrinches
7	Santa Cruz de los Canamos
8	Montiel
9	Infantes-Montiel crossing
10	Almedina
11	Puebla del Principe

(2) The Location-Covering Model

In the location-covering model, the aim is to locate aleast-cost set of facilities in such a way that each user can be reached within a maximum travel time from the closest facility. The problem can be modelled on a complete graph G ($V_1 \cup V_2$, E), where vertices in V_1 and in V_2 represent potential facilities and customers, respectively, and each edge $(i, j) \in E = V_1 \times V_2$ corresponds to a least-cost path between i and j.

Travel time (in minutes) on the road network edges in the La Mancha problem

Table 7-5

(i, j)	a_{ij}	(i, j)	a_{ij}
(1,2)	12	(1,11)	8
(2,3)	9	(2,9)	8
(3,4)	11	(2,10)	9
(4,5)	9	(3,9)	4
(5,6)	2	(4,8)	10
(6,7)	3	(5,8)	6
(7,8)	4	(6,11)	5
(8,9)	1	(7,10)	5
(8,10)	7	(1,10)	6
(10,11)	4		

Travel times (in minutes) t_i^j, i, $j \in V$, in the La Mancha problem   Table 7-6

j	i										
	1	2	3	4	5	6	7	8	9	10	11
1	0	12	18	23	15	13	11	13	14	6	8
2	12	0	9	19	15	16	13	9	8	9	13
3	18	9	0	11	11	12	9	5	4	12	16
4	23	19	11	0	9	11	14	10	11	17	16
5	15	15	11	9	0	2	5	6	7	10	7
6	13	16	12	11	2	0	3	7	8	8	5
7	11	13	9	14	5	3	0	4	5	5	8
8	13	9	5	10	6	7	4	0	1	7	11
9	14	8	4	11	7	8	5	1	0	8	12
10	6	9	12	17	10	8	5	7	8	0	4
11	8	13	16	16	7	5	8	11	12	4	0

Let f_i, $i \in V_1$, be the fixed cost of potential facility i; p_j, $j \in V_2$, the penalty incurred if customer j is unserviced; t_{ij}, $i \in V_1$, $j \in V_2$, the least-cost travel time between potential facility i and customer j; a_{ij}, $i \in V_1$, $j \in V_2$, a binary constant equal to 1 if potential facility i is able to serve customer j, 0 otherwise (given a user defined maximum time T, $a_{ij} = 1$, if $t_{ij} \leqslant T$, $i \in V_1$, $j \in V_2$, otherwise $a_{ij} = 0$). The decision variables are binary: y_i, $i \in V_1$, is equal to 1 if facility i is opened, 0 otherwise; z_j, $j \in V_2$, is equal to 1 if customer j is not served, otherwise it is 0.

The location-covering problem is modelled as follows:

Minimize
$$\sum_{i \in V_1} f_i y_i + \sum_{j \in V_2} p_j z_j \tag{7-6}$$

Distances of the local centres p_{hk}^* from vertices h (in kilometres) and

$\max_{i \in V} \{ T_i(p_{hk}^*) \}$ (in minutes) in the La Mancha problem   Table 7-7

(h, k)	$\gamma_h(p_{hk}^*)$	$\max_{i \in V} \{ T_i(p_{hk}^*) \}$	(h, k)	$\gamma_h(p_{hk}^*)$	$\max_{i \in V} \{ T_i(p_{hk}^*) \}$
(1,2)	18.00	19.0	(1,11)	12.00	16.0
(2,3)	6.00	17.0	(2,9)	12.00	14.0
(3,4)	0.00	18.0	(2,10)	13.50	17.0
(4,5)	13.50	15.0	(3,9)	6.00	14.0
(5,6)	0.00	15.0	(4,8)	15.00	13.0
(6,7)	3.75	13.5	(5,8)	9.00	13.0
(7,8)	2.25	12.5	(6,11)	4.50	15.0
(8,9)	0.00	13.0	(7,10)	0.00	14.0
(8,10)	2.25	11.5	(1,10)	9.00	17.0
(10,11)	6.00	16.0			

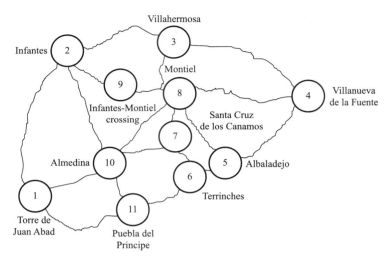

Figure 7-4　Location problem in La Mancha region

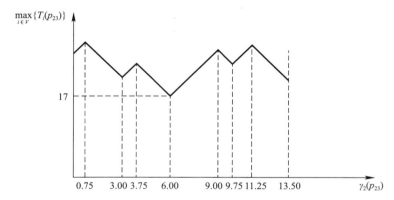

Figure 7-5　Time $\max\limits_{i \in V}\{T_i(p_{23})\}$ versus position $\gamma_2(p_{23})$ of p_{23} in the La Mancha problem

$$\text{Subject to} \quad \sum_{i \in V_1} a_{ij}y_i + z_j \geq 1, j \in V_2 \quad\quad (7-7)$$

$$y_i \in \{0,1\}, i \in V_1$$

$$z_j \in \{0,1\}, j \in V_2$$

The objective function $(7-6)$ is the sum of the fixed costs of the open facilities and the penalties corresponding to the unserviced customers. Constraints $(7-7)$ impose that, for each $j \in V_2$, z_j is equal to 1 if the facilities opened do not cover customer j (i. e. if $\sum_{i \in V_1} a_{ij}y_i = 0$).

If all customers must be served (i. e. if the penalties p_j are sufficiently high for each $j \in V_2$), variables z_j, $j \in V_2$, can be assumed equal to 0. Hence, the location covering problem is a generalization of the well-known set covering problem and is therefore NP-hard.

Several variants of the location-covering model can be used in practice. For example, iffixed costs f_i are equal for all potential sites $i \in V_1$, it can be convenient to discriminate among all the solutions with the least number of open facilities the one corresponding to the least total travelling time, or to the most equitable demand distribution among the facilities. In the former case, let x_{ij},

$i \in V_1$, $j \in V_2$, be a binary decision variable equal to 1 if customer j is served by facility i, 0 otherwise. The problem can be modelled as follows:

Minimize
$$\sum_{i \in V_1} My_i + \sum_{i \in V_1} \sum_{j \in V_2} t_{ij} x_{ij} \tag{7-8}$$

Subject to

$$\sum_{i \in V_1} a_{ij} x_{ij} \geqslant 1, \ j \in V_2 \tag{7-9}$$

$$\sum_{j \in V_2} x_{ij} \leqslant |V_2| y_i, \ i \in V_1 \tag{7-10}$$

$$y_i \in \{0,1\}, \ i \in V_1 \tag{7-11}$$

$$x_{ij} \in \{0,1\}, \ i \in V_1, j \in V_2 \tag{7-12}$$

where M is a large positive constant. Constraints (7-9) guarantee that all the customers $j \in V_2$ are serviced, while constraints (7-10) ensure that if facility $i \in V_1$ is not set up ($y_i = 0$), then no customer $j \in V_2$ can be served by it.

Another interesting variant of the location-covering model arises when one must locate facilities to ensure double coverage of demand points. A classic case is ambulance location when users are better protected if two ambulances are located within their vicinity. If one of the two ambulances has to answer a call, there will remain one ambulance to provide coverage.

7.2 Logistics System Optimization

1. Introduction

7.2 Professional Terms, Words and Phrases, Sentence Illustration

With the development of science and technology and the accelerating urbanization process, the urban economy develops rapidly. However, many negative problems in urban development have gradually become prominent, such as the urban deterioration and the shortage of resources. Among them, traffic congestion is a relatively serious problem. The quality of urban traffic not only affects the travel of citizens, but also has a great impact on the efficiency of urban logistics. In order to efficiently meet the logistics needs of cities, it is urgently necessary to build a smooth and reliable urban logistics system.

In reality, there are many random factors that affect the efficiency of the urban transportation network. On the one hand, the customers' needs are usually based on the prediction, there are errors in the value, and the customers' needs usually fluctuate. On the other hand, due to the impact of some emergencies, such as bad weather, natural disasters will lead to the failure of the logistics center. Therefore, customer needs may not necessarily be met. If considered from the perspective of improving prediction accuracy, it have limitations and cannot fundamentally address the impact of demand uncertainty. Reliability is an important measure of the serviceability of the network under the influence of random factors. The normal service capacity of the city can meet the needs of production and life. However, due to the impact of emergencies, urban traffic flow will change randomly. If the unblocked reliability of the network is too low, it may cause goods to reach the customer point in time.

Based on the theory of unblocked reliability, we study the optimization of urban logistics system distribution, improving the traffic efficiency of the network, and reducing the negative impact on logistics in the case of line failure.

Unblocked reliability refers to the probability that the road traffic operation state can meet the unblocked state within the specified time and the road network is under normal use conditions. In the road network system, the road unit capacity reliability can be defined as the probability that a vehicle on a road section or intersection unit can drive at a smooth service level within a certain period (generally peak time). Set unblocked reliability of road unit is W_i, then:

$$W_i = \frac{\text{Number of road section } i \text{ unblocked during rush hours}}{\text{Total observations of road section } i \text{ during rush hours}} \qquad (7-13)$$

The logistics distribution transportation network is a collection of all possible paths connected between the distribution nodes based on the existing transportation network. The logistics distribution transportation network is composed of multiple distribution paths, while each distribution route is composed of multiple distribution nodes. Distribution node is the most basic component unit in the network, which shows that the determination of the unblocked reliability between the distribution nodes is the basis for the unblocked reliability analysis of the logistics distribution and transportation network. From the perspective of traffic accessibility, the vehicle operation between the two connected distribution nodes can be regarded as a traffic between an OD pair, and there are multiple paths to choose. Therefore, based on the basic theory of unblocked reliability, we can believe that the unblocked reliability between the two distribution nodes is equivalent to an OD pair in the road network, thus using the OD pair unblocked reliability formula for smooth reliability calculation between two distribution nodes. According to the characteristics of logistics distribution, each distribution line is a series system composed of multiple distribution nodes. Using the probability theory, we can conclude that the unblocked reliability of each distribution line is the product of the unblocked reliability between all the distribution nodes on the line. If the unblocked reliability of a distribution line is W_n, then:

$$W_n = \prod W_{ij} \qquad (7-14)$$

where W_{ij} is the smooth reliability of node i to node j in this distribution line.

In the logistics distribution network system, because the scale and quantity of each distribution line will be different according to the actual arrangement, so the importance of each distribution line is different. Importance is determined based on the proportion of distribution points owned by each distribution line in the number of customers throughout the system. On the basis of the unblocked reliability evaluation of each line, the unblocked reliability of the distribution and transportation network can be obtained through the weighted sum. Assuming that the unblocked reliability of the distribution network is W, there is:

$$W = \sum \xi_n W_n \qquad (7-15)$$

where W_n is the smooth reliability of n distribution line in the distribution network; ξ_n is the importance of n line in this distribution transportation network, and $\sum \xi_n = 1$, n is the total number of distribution lines in this distribution network.

2. Methodology

The proposed methodology includes mainly three steps: first one is the collection of relevant data for logistics provider selection in last-mile delivery systems from final customers. The main critical points in data collection part are to assess criteria for logistics provider selection of final customers in cargo deliveries. Key performance indicators of the delivery operations affecting customer decisions and used in the proposed model are indicated in Table 7-10.

The defined indicators given in Table 7-8 are obtained by using semi-structured interview method. The surveys are conducted in both verbal and written forms in a group of 250 customers and collected scores of different cargo delivery companies for different performance indicators. Final customers filled up the surveys and questionnaires in a range of $1 \sim 10$. Score 1 indicates the decision of "not relevant" and Score 10 indicates "major" impact in supplier selection processes. After collecting scores for different logistics providers, final scores of different performance indicators in supplier selection are taken as an average of all scores obtained from all surveys under the same criteria. This means that let us assume that set of α indicates the set of performance indicators, set of k shows the set of logistics providers and i indicates the set of final customers. Therefore, parameter of ψ_{kai} shows the score of logistics provider k for performance indicator α given by customer i. $\dfrac{\sum\limits_{i \in I} \psi_{kai}}{|I|}$ gives the score table of each provider per performance indicator, and this table will be the main input of the TOPSIS system.

List of key performance indicators of last-mile delivery operations in customer decisions

Table 7-8

Criteria 1	Unit price per kg cargo
Criteria 2	Compliance with time windows
Criteria 3	Lead times of the deliveries
Criteria 4	Traceability of cargo
Criteria 5	Safety of cargo
Criteria 6	Accessibility to the company via mobile/web channels
Criteria 7	Air pollution policies
Criteria 8	Noise pollution policies
Criteria 9	Technological infrastructure
Criteria 10	Proximity of regional office
Criteria 11	Availability of pick-up services
Criteria 12	Standardized services
Criteria 13	Geographical range for delivery
Criteria 14	Policies over security of private data

Stage 2 is Discrete Optimization. In the second step of proposed model, a complex decision problem is structured at hierarchical levels and decision alternatives are generated to decrease complexity in multi-criteria problems by using TOPSIS. Decision makers predefine associated weights, and alternative solution sets are performed by using different weights. Algorithm 1 given below gets final scores of different last-mile delivery companies under defined performance indicators

Algorithm 1:

0: Identification of alternative logistics providers(k) and performance indicators (α)

1: Compute $N_{k\alpha} = \left\{ \dfrac{\sum\limits_{ia} \Psi_{kai}}{|I|} \right\}^2$, $\quad \forall k \in K$, $\quad \forall \alpha \in A$

2: Compute $N_{k\alpha}^* = \dfrac{N_{k\alpha}}{\sqrt[2]{\sum\limits_{\alpha \in A} N_{k\alpha}}}$, $\quad \forall k \in K$, $\quad \forall \alpha \in A$

3: Calculate variance of weights $V_\alpha = \dfrac{1}{|A|} \sum\limits_{k \in K} (N_{k\alpha}^* - N_{k\alpha})^2$, $\quad \forall \alpha \in A$

4: for $\alpha \in A$ do

5: Obtain weights $\chi_\alpha = \dfrac{V_\alpha}{\sum\limits_{\alpha \in A} V_\alpha}$, such that $\sum\limits_{\alpha \in A} \chi_\alpha = 1$, $\forall \alpha \in A$

6: Compute $\chi_\alpha \cdot N_{k\alpha}^*$, $\forall k \in K$, $\forall \alpha \in A$

7: Determine $\max\{\chi_\alpha \cdot N_{k\alpha}^*\}$ and $\min\{\chi_\alpha \cdot N_{k\alpha}^*\}$, $\forall \alpha \in A$

8: Compute $\pi_k = \dfrac{\sum\limits_{\alpha \in A}\{\chi_\alpha \cdot N_{k\alpha}^* - \min\{\chi_\alpha \cdot N_{k\alpha}^*\}\}^2}{\sum\limits_{\alpha \in A}\{\chi_\alpha \cdot N_{k\alpha}^* - \min\{\chi_\alpha \cdot N_{k\alpha}^*\}\}^2 + \sum\limits_{\alpha \in A}\{\chi_\alpha \cdot N_{k\alpha}^* - \max\{\chi_\alpha \cdot N_{k\alpha}^*\}\}^2}$,

$\forall k \in K$

After collecting final performance scores of different companies (π_k), final scores of companies are given into mathematical model as parameter. Pareto frontier for sustainable distribution channels in city centres is tried to be obtained.

As indicated in the study of Resat, green zones should be created within the city centres in order to achieve more environmental cases. In this study, major assumption is that only drone deliveries are allowed to operate in these regions and that carbon emissions caused by high transportation activities will decrease in these highly crowded and carbon-dense areas. Logistics operations start from the Distribution Centres (DCs) located outside of the city centres, and single type of product (a standard parcel) is considered. It is only allowed that a single type of medium truck from distribution centres to transfer points carries the cargo. The capacities of these trucks are considered as constant and their capacities are just a ton. When trucks come to Transfer Points (TPs), there will be transfer from conventional vehicles to the drones. The capacities of drones are also assumed as constant. The degree of extra warehousing requirement for drone delivery dominates the comparison of drone and truck-based scenarios, because non-operating drones should also be stored in some specific warehouses. For servicing an urban area with on-demand delivery, two main approaches have been proposed. The first is to locate distribution centres such that all of the service area is within delivery range of a distribution centre. The second is to establish way stations such that drones can fly from one to another and exchange batteries in a series of hops from distribution centre to customer destination. In this study, way stations (transfer points) are considered and drones are stored at these places, and delivery operations start from these stations. After the transfer points, last-mile deliveries are made by using only drones. However, due to lower the battery lives of drones and flight ranges, there will be some options to recharge these drones during the routing. In our problem, it is assumed that each drone can be recharged at only recharging stations. In addition, there is no limitation in the recharging ratios that means that drones can be recharged less than the maximum level. Drone batteries are recharged with constant ratios, and each battery has a constant capacity.

Assumptions:

● All of the customers have to be visited once during a day.

● All the routes are started in the transfer points and ended again in the transfer points (not exactly the same one).

● Different logistics providers can use and store their drones at different transfer points.

● The total demands of the customers in the green zones should not exceed the truck capacities (back order option is eliminated).

● Transportation times are directly depending on Euclidean distances between nodes.

● The distances between the routes are taken as symmetric ($d_{ij} = d_{ji}$).

● Demands of the customers are known beforehand.

3. Construction of the Model

Since there is a relatively abstract concept between reliability and cost, the cost including human resources, material resources, and financial resources to increase the reliability of the unit, it is difficult to obtain the statistics between cost and reliability. In order to overcome this problem, Dale proposes a generalized cost function. The function is built on a model of considering feasible f_i, unit minimum reliability $R_{i, \min}$ and unit maximum reliability $R_{i, \max}$

$$C_i(R_i, f_i, R_{i,\min}, R_{i,\max}) = e^{(1-f_i)\left(\frac{R_i - R_{i,\min}}{R_{i,\max} R_i}\right)} \tag{7-16}$$

where the f_i values range between 0 and 1, the greater the value indicates the greater the feasibility of improving the unit. The generalized cost function is a nonlinear growth function for cost about units, and achieving maximum reliability theoretically means a considerable cost, but rather a low reliability. This coincides with the actual characteristics of cost growth with reliability. The characteristics of the generalized cost function provide the basis for the integration of the influencing factors in the system reliability distribution. Therefore, this book constructs the reliability distribution model of fresh agricultural products electricity business based on the importance and complexity of the system.

$$\min z = \sum_{i=1}^{n} \frac{1}{\omega_i} e^{u_i\left(\frac{R_i - R_{i,\min}}{R_{i,\max} - R_i}\right)} \qquad (7-17)$$

$$\text{s.t.} \prod_{i=1}^{n} R_i \geqslant R^* \qquad (7-18)$$

$$R_{i,\min} < R_i < R_{i,\max}, \quad i = 1, 2, \ldots, n \qquad (7-19)$$

where R_i is the reliability of unit i;

$R_{i,\min}$ is the minimum reliability of the R_i;

$R_{i,\max}$ is the maximum reliability of the R_i;

R^* is the reliability of the system to reach;

ω_i is the unit importance factor;

u_i is the unit complexity improvement factor;

z is the cost target function.

The objective function (7-17) of the model is based on the generalized cost function, increasing the importance and complexity improvement factors. First, the importance degree coefficient is introduced by restricting the amplification and reduction of the generalized cost function to the cost of different units. The higher the importance with smaller reciprocal, the more units of higher importance achieve higher reliability. Secondly, by replacing the feasibility parameter through the unit complexity improvement coefficient, the proportion of the total units of the system represents the complexity of the unit. The higher the complexity of the unit, the lower feasibility of the improvement is, and the cost of the actual input increases.

The model constraint Equation (7-18) indicates that the reliability after the optimal allocation is greater than or equal to the system. Formula (7-19) indicates that the reliability of each unit allocation must be greater than its respective minimum reliability and less than its maximum reliability.

7.3 Supply Chain

1. Introduction

Supply chain management is a vital process for the competitiveness and profitability of companies. Supply chain consists of a large and complex network of components such as suppliers, warehouses, customers, etc. which are connected in almost every possible way. Companies' main aim is to optimize the components

7.3 Professional Terms, Words and Phrases, Sentence Illustration

of these complex networks to their benefit. This constitutes a challenging optimization problem and often, traditional mathematical approaches fail to overcome complexity and to converge to the optimum solution. More robust methods are required sometimes in order to yield to the optimal. The field of artificial intelligence offers a great variety of meta-heuristic techniques which specialize in solving such complex optimization problems, either accurately, or by obtaining a practically useful approximation, even if real time constraints are imposed. Nature-inspired intelligence is a specific branch of artificial intelligence. Its unique characteristic is the algorithmic imitation of real life systems such as ant colonies, flock of birds etc. in order to solve complex problems.

2. Methodology

Nowadays, most firms face difficulties in obtaining a competitive advantage over other companies due to the fact that most of their underlying processes have become complex. A remedy to this issue is to adopt the organizational scheme of supply-chains: an international network of external partners such as suppliers, warehouses, distribution centres. A starting point of this functional chain can be considered the collection of raw materials and an ending point the preparation of the final product and the delivery to its final destination (customer or any other terminal) (Silva et al. 2002). Logistics is a particular part of this process and deals with the planning, handling and control of the storage of goods between the manufacturing and the consumption point. One crucial challenge for decision makers is to satisfy all customers, using the available transportation fleet, while at the same time minimizing any intermediate costs (storage costs, transportation costs, delivery time etc.). The above problem can get very complex, especially in the case where various real life constraints regarding time, cost, availability etc. are imposed. A general term that characterizes these kinds of problems is the term "scheduling problems" (Silva et al. 2002). A wide range of methodologies has been used to solve this optimization problem. However, traditional mathematical methods have proven insufficient in tackling the requirements rising from the development of market competition. Nature-inspired intelligent techniques are considered to be quite efficient in handling NP-hard problems (i. e. , optimization problems in which the optimum cannot be found in polynomial time). The main characteristic of these methods is the imitation of the way natural systems function and evolve in order to deal with real-world situations. For example, natural ant colonies cooperate so as to find high-quality food source, a flock of birds implements a scheme of indirect communication with the aim of finding the optimal direction, etc. Some examples of nature-inspired algorithms are the following:

Ant Colony Optimization (ACO).

Particle Swarm Optimization (PSO).

Genetic Algorithms.

Genetic Programming.

Memetic Algorithms.

Artificial Immune Systems.

DNA Computing.

All of the above methods have been applied tohard optimization problems. However, literature indicates that only some of them have been applied to the optimization of logistic processes. Specifically, the focus is on certain parts of the supply chain, where certain processes need to be optimized such as finding the optimal route for a fleet. Academic research indicates that the use of NI methods is beneficial in dealing with this kind of problems. The contribution of this study is to collect the majority of academic work regarding the application of NI algorithms in logistic processes and to give a clear presentation of the usefulness and applicability of these techniques for future research projects.

3. Models (Inventory Control Models)

There is a variety of research methodological approaches on risk and disruption management. These research papers can be classified in two major categories. The first one addresses inventory and production systems where the supply or production rate varies. In these systems the quantities delivered or produced differ from the replenishment or production orders (random yield). A second category includes methodologies that model the disruption mechanisms. We refer to this research area as disruption modeling. In both categories we can distinguish methodologies for single sourcing or for dual/multiple sources. Table 7-9 depicts a classification of the research papers that we have included in this review. The reader can find comprehensive literature reviews on quantitatively-oriented approaches for determining lot sizes when the production or supply yields are random in Yano and Lee (1995), Khouja (1999), Tang (2006), and Minner (2003).

Production random yield problems with a single supplier or production facility have been studied by several authors in various forms. Comprehensive literature reviews on stochastic manufacturing flow control and lot sizing with random yields or unreliable manufacturers can be found in Haurie (1995), as well as Yano and Lee (1995). In addition, Wang and Gerchak (2000) consider make-to-order batch manufacturing with random yield. In this paper it is proven that the optimal policy is of the threshold control type—stop if and only if the stock is larger than some critical value. This critical value is studied for different production cases. Moreover, Henig and Gerchak (1990) developed a periodic review production/inventory model with random supply yield.

Classification of inventory control models Table 7-9

Methodology	Single sourcing	Dual/multiple sourcing
Random Yield	(Haurie, 1995), (Yano and Lee, 1995), (Wang and Gerchak, 2000), (Henig and Gerchak, 1990)	(Agrawal and Nahmias. 1998), (Tomlin and Wang, 2005), (Tomlin, 2006), (Federgruen and Yang, 2009), (Dada et al. , 2007)
Disruption Management	(Moinzadch and Aggarwal, 1997), (Parlar, 1997), (Arreola-Risa and DeCroix, 1998), (Xia et al. , 2004), (Xiao and Qi, 2008), (Iakovou et al. , 2007)	(Parlar and Perry, 1996), (Gurler and Parlar, 1997), (Golany et al. 2002), (Snyder et al. , 2006), (Wu et al. , 2007), (Wilson, 2007), (Tang, 2006)

Agrawal and Nahmias (1998) developed a multiple-sourcing deterministic demand model to determine the optimal lot sizes and number of suppliers, when the supply yield from each supplier is random. The authors consider also the fixed costs associated with each supplier. Later on, Tomlin and Wang (2005) developed a single period dual-sourcing model with yield uncertainty (i. e. uncertainty at the time of order placement as to the fraction of the order that will be delivered). By considering one unreliable and one reliable (and thus more expensive) supplier the focus of this paper is on inventory and sourcing mitigation. In the same context, Tomlin

(2006) developed a Markov chain single-product model by considering capacity constraints for both suppliers and order quantity flexibility for the reliable vendor (extra capacity is available in case of a disruption). It is shown that contingent rerouting may constitute a basic element of the optimal disruption management strategy by reducing a firm's system-wide costs. Furthermore, Federgruen and Yang (2009) and Dada et al. (2007) examined the multiple sourcing random yield problem and proposed interesting analytical and heuristic solutions based on type I service level-related constraints.

As far as supply chain disruptions modeling in a single-sourcing setting is concerned, Moinzadeh and Aggarwal (1997) considered the an (s, S) inventory policy for a constant production and demand rate system with random disruptions in a bottleneck production facility, in which supply could be randomly disrupted and the disruption lasts a random period. Near optimal production policies are derived via a heuristic procedure. Parlar (1997) considered random supply disruptions with stochastic demand and lead-time in a continuous review inventory system, while supplier availability is modeled as a semi-Markov process. Next, Arreola-Risa and DeCroix (1998) considered a stochastic (s, S) inventory system in which supply could be randomly disrupted for a random period. This paper considers partial backorders—that is scenarios in which some customer orders may wait as backorders, while others lead to lost sales. Xia et al. (2004) developed a deterministic EOQ-type inventory model for a two-stage supply chain that is susceptible to several types of production-related and demand-related disruptions. In this work, two classes of problems are defined: one with fixed setup epochs and another with flexible setup epochs. More recently, Xiao and Qi (2008) investigated a supply chain with one supplier and two competing retailers that experiences a disruption in production cost during a single period. Appropriate quantitative conditions are derived that indicate when the maximum profit can be achieved once a disruption in the original production plan occurs. Finally, Iakovou et al. (2007) present a risk management policy for a single period supply chain with known disruption probabilities.

Two significant research works in the field of joint disruption inventory management and dual sourcing are those of Parlar and Perry (1996) and Gurler and Parlar (1997). Both papers consider a firm that faces constant demand and sources from two identical-cost infinite-capacity suppliers. The firm faces a fixed cost of ordering, which is only incurred once even if the order is split between suppliers. Inter failure and repair times are exponentially distributed for both suppliers in Parlar and Perry. The authors propose a suboptimal ordering policy that is solved numerically. Gurler and Parlar extended the work of Parlar and Perry by considering the case of Erlang inter failure times and general repair times.

7.4　Reading Material

1. Emerging Trends in Logistics

In recent years, several strategic and technological changes have had a marked impact on logistics. Among these, there are worthy of mention: globalization, new information technologies and e-commerce.

2. Globalization

An increasing number of companies operate at the world level in order to take advantage of lower manufacturing costs or cheap raw materials available in some countries. This is sometimes achieved through acquisitions or strategic alliances with other firms. As a result of globalization, transportation needs have increased. More parts and semi-finished products have to be moved between production sites, and transportation to markets tends to be more complex and costly. The increase in multimodal container transportation is a direct consequence of globalization. Also, as a result of globalization, more emphasis must be put on the efficient design and management of supply chains, sometimes at the world level.

3. Information Technologies

Suppliers and manufacturers make use of EDI. This enables them to share data on stock levels, timing of deliveries, positioning ofin-transit goods in the supply chain, etc. At the operational level, geographic information systems (GISs), global positioning systems (GPSs) and on-board computers allow dispatchers to keep track of the current position of vehicles and to communicate with drivers. Such technologies are essential to firms engaged in express pick-up and delivery operations, and to long-haul trucking companies.

4. E-commerce

An increasing number of companies make commercial transactions through the internet. It is common to distinguish between business-to-business (B2B) and business-to-consumers (B2C) transactions. The growth of e-commerce parallels that of globalization and information technologies. As a result of e-commerce, the volume of goods between producers and retailers should go down while more direct deliveries should be expected between manufacturers and end-users.

E-commerce leads to a more complex organization of the entire logistics system (e-logistics), which should be able to manage small-size and medium-size shipments to a large number of customers, sometimes scattered around the world. Furthermore, the returnflow of defective (or rejected) goods becomes a major issue (reverse logistics). Table 7-10 reports the main differences between traditional logistics and e-logistics.

In an e-logistics system different approaches for operating warehouses and distribution are generally adopted. The virtual warehouse and the Points Of Presence In The Territory (POPITT) are just a few examples. A virtual warehouse is a facility where suppliers and distributors keep their goods in stock in such a way that the e-commerce company can fulfil its orders. A POPITT is a company-owned facility where customers may go either for purchasing and fetching the ordered goods, or for returning defective products. Unlike traditional shops, a POPITT only stores already sold goods waiting to be picked up by customers and defective products waiting to be returned to the manufacturers. This solution simplifies distribution management but reduces customer service level since it does not allow for home deliveries.

Main differences between traditional logistics and e-logistics   Table 7-10

Item	Traditional logistics	E-logistics
Type of load	High volumes	Parcels
Customer	Known	Unknown
Average order value	> $ 1000	< $ 100
Destinations	Concentrated	Highly scattered
Demand trend	Regular	Lumpy

Chapter 8
Safety Engineering and Management

8.1 Human Factors Engineering

8.1 Professional Terms, Words and Phrases, Sentence Illustration

1. Introduction

We may define the goal of human factors as making the human interaction with systems one that:

- Enhances performance.
- Increases safety.
- Increases user satisfaction.

Human factors involves the study of factors and development of tools that facilitate the achievement of these goals.

In considering these goals, it is useful to realize that there may be trade-offs between them. For example, performance is an all-encompassing term that may involve the reduction of errors or an increase in productivity (i. e. , the speed of production). Hence, enhanced productivity may sometimes cause more operator errors, potentially compromising safety. As another example, some companies may decide to cut corners on time-consuming safety procedures in order to meet productivity goals. Fortunately, however, these trade-offs are not inevitable. Human factors interventions often can satisfy both goals at once. For example, one company that improved its workstation design reduced worker's compensation losses in the first year after the improvement from \$400,000 to \$94,000. Workers were more able to continue work (increasing productivity), while greatly reducing the risk of injury (increasing safety).

In the most general sense, the three goals of human factors are accomplished through several procedures in the human factors cycle, illustrated in Figure 8 – 1, which depicts the human operator (brain and body) and the system with which he or she is interacting. At point A, it is necessary to diagnose or identify the problems and deficiencies in the human-system interaction of an existing system. To do this effectively, core knowledge of the nature of the physical body (its size, shape, and strength) and of the mind (its information-processing characteristics and limitations) must be coupled with a good understanding of the physical or information systems involved, and the appropriate analysis tools must be applied to clearly define the cause of breakdowns. For example, why did the worker in our first story suffer the back injury? Was it the amount of the load or the awkward position required to lift it? Was this worker representative of others who also might suffer injury? Task analysis, statistical analysis, and incident/accident analysis are critical tools for gaining such an understanding.

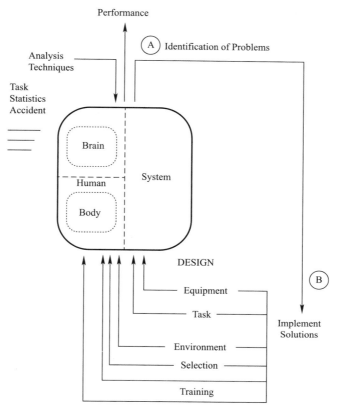

Point A identifies a cycle when human factors solutions are sought because a problem (e. g. , accident or incident) has been observed in the human-system interaction. Point B identifies a point where good human factors are applied at the beginning of a design cycle.

Figure 8-1   The cycle of human factors

2. Methodology

(1) Archival Data

One source of data for human factors researchers is archival data, that is, preexisting data that have been collected for some other purpose.

Archival data may be useful for developing hypotheses to test experimentally and to obtain important information about an operational system. In addition, they can be used to look for evidence that a phenomenon established primarily in laboratory research generalizes to the real world.

(2) Naturalistic Observation and Ethnographic Methods

In human factors, one role of observational research is to characterize the way that people perform their work in real-world, functioning systems. Observation can be casual or formal. Observational measurement methods also vary in several other ways:

① The observations can be recorded at the time the observation is made or later.

② The content and amount of detail in the observations can vary.

③ The length of time during which observations are made can be short or long.

④ Observations can vary in terms of the amount of inference, or degree of interpretation, that is required to classify events into the measurement categories.

An ethnographic study is a type of observational method that comes from the discipline of anthropology. With respect to human factors, the method is used to understand the users' culture and their work environments, and to identify the artifacts they use to accomplish goals.

Within human factors, ethnographic methods may be used in product development, where the ultimate goal is to bring the group of potential users to life so that engineers have a sense of who the users of a product or system are, develop empathy for them, and ultimately develop products to fit their needs.

(3) Surveys and Questionnaires

Questionnaires or surveys are particularly useful when you want to elicit information from a large group of users and the issues of concern are relatively simple. By using a carefully designed set of questions, you can obtain a succinct summary of the issues, and determine probable relations among variables. The benefits of questionnaires include being able to obtain information from different user populations and getting information that is relatively easy to code.

(4) Between-Subject Designs

In between-subject designs, two or more groups of people are tested, and each group receives only one of the treatment conditions of theindependent variable. Subjects in such experiments are usually assigned to each condition randomly. Because subjects are randomly assigned, the groups are equivalent (within chance limits) on the basis of preexisting variables. Thus, any reliable performance difference should be a function of the independent variable.

(5) Within-Subject Designs

Random assignment, stratified sampling, and matching are ways by which we try to make groups equivalent. Another way to equate different groups is to use the same subjects in each one. That is, each person is tested in all conditions, and serves as his or her own control. This increases the sensitivity of the design, making it more likely that small differences in the treatment conditions will be detected. It also substantially reduces the number of people who must be tested.

3. Models

(1) Helson's Hypothesis

Harry Helson developed what he called hypotheses, which are really generic models of human behavior and its performance implications. His U-Hypothesis deals principally with performance. The quest to identify the optimum is exceedingly important in ergonomic design even though it is not important that the exact optimum is specified.

The Par Hypothesis is another important idea developed by Helson. This hypothesis states that people monitor their own performance and modify it as a result of what they observe.

Helson's third hypothesis concerned anticipation and averaging. People learn intricate movement patterns over time. At first, people tend to perform movements as a series of discrete steps. With practice, more complex sequences of movements, or movement patterns, are learned. Learning these patterns allows people to anticipate future movements within the pattern. People still follow the general outline of the pattern, when they are under time pressure, but start to leave out some of the details.

(2) Other Models

People are often modeled as having three general capacities: People can obtain information from the environment using sensory organs, such as eyes or ears, process it with their brain, and then make physical responses using output devices, such as the hands and voice. Developing a basic understanding of these capabilities, as well as the interrelationships among them, is the primary focus of most introductory human factors or ergonomics courses.

This modeling perspective is particularly applicable to communication processes. Communication between people requires one person to use an output device, such as the voice, which is compatible with another person's input device, such as the ear. Commands may be communicated or questions may be asked by one person of another, who responds by following the command or giving an answer. Every element in the communications sequence takes time and introduces the possibility of error.

The Signal Detection Theory (SDT) is another model used in ergonomics that is based on probability theory. SDT has been used to describe decision making by both humans and machines in a wide variety of applications. Visual inspection is one of the more common applications of SDT.

Learning curves provide another, often mathematical, model of how performance improves with experience. The different models have advantages and disadvantages, and distinguishing the better fitting model empirically is not always easy.

8.2　Safety Engineering

1. Introduction

8.2 Professional Terms, Words and Phrases, Sentence Illustration

Safety engineering is a field that focuses on preventing accidents and lessening opportunities for human error in engineered environments or in engineering design. The goal of the safety engineering is to prevent/mitigate failures (Risk Management) in a system that might be harmful to its users.

Safety engineers usually work on the Risk Management Integrated Product Team (IPT) of an acquisition program. Safety engineers often make use of computer models, prototypes, or recreations of a situations to assess the hazards and risks. Safety engineers consider a number of factors that may affect the safety of a situation or product, including design, technical safety, material reliability, legislation, and human factors.

Herbert W. Heinrich was a pioneering occupational health and safety researcher, whose 1931 publication *Industrial Accident Prevention: A Scientific Approach* was based on the analysis of workplace injuries and accident data collected by his employer, a large insurance company. This work, which continued for more than thirty years, identified causal factors of industrial accidents including "unsafe acts of people" and "unsafe mechanical or physical conditions". Heinrich also put forward the domino model of accident causation, a simple linear accident model.

The most famous result is the incident/accident pyramid, also known as the "safety pyramid", the "accident triangle" and "Heinrich's law". The pyramid, as illustrated by Heinrich in the 1941 edition of his book, is shown in Figure 8-2.

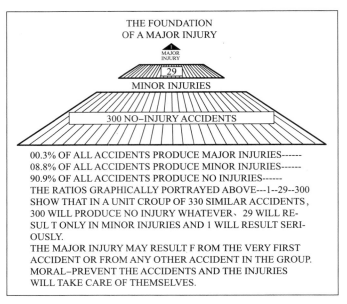

THE FOUNDATION
OF A MAJOR INJURY

MAJOR
INJURY

29

MINOR INJURIES

300 NO-INJURY ACCIDENTS

00.3% OF ALL ACCIDENTS PRODUCE MAJOR INJURIES------
08.8% OF ALL ACCIDENTS PRODUCE MINOR INJURIES------
90.9% OF ALL ACCIDENTS PRODUCE NO INJURIES------
THE RATIOS GRAPHICALLY PORTRAYED ABOVE---1--29--300
SHOW THAT IN A UNIT CROUP OF 330 SIMILAR ACCIDENTS,
300 WILL PRODUCE NO INJURY WHATEVER、29 WILL RE-
SUL T ONLY IN MINOR INJURIES AND 1 WILL RESULT SERI-
OUSLY.
THE MAJOR INJURY MAY RESULT F ROM THE VERY FIRST
ACCIDENT OR FROM ANY OTHER ACCIDENT IN THE GROUP.
MORAL–PREVENT THE ACCIDENTS AND THE INJURIES
WILL TAKE CARE OF THEMSELVES.

Figure 8-2　The foundation of a major injury

The "accident pyramid", as depicted by Herbert W. Heinrich in the second edition of his book *Industrial Accident Prevention: A Scientific Approach*, page 27. Note the last sentence: "Moral—prevent the accidents and the injuries will take care of themselves".

This work suggested that the ratio between fatal accidents, accidents, injuries and minor incidents (often reported as 1-10-30-600, and sometimes called "Heinrich's Law" or the "Heinrich ratio") is relatively constant, over time and across companies. Note that these numbers refer to accidents and occupational injuries that were reported to the insurance company and incidents discussed with the researchers, which may be rather different from the real number of accidents and incidents.

"Accident-proneness" theory: During the period 1920—1960, a number of industrial psychologists put forward a theory that certain workers are more "accident-prone" than others (they are more likely than others to sustain accidents, even though exposed to equal risk). Some people working in high-hazard industries still hold this belief. However, research since the 1960s shows that this theory has little validity.

2. Methodology

Analysis techniques can besplit into two categories: qualitative and quantitative methods. Both approaches share the goal of finding causal dependencies between a hazard on system level and failures of individual components. Qualitative approaches focus on the question "What must go wrong, such that a system hazard may occur?", while quantitative methods aim at providing estimations about probabilities, rates and/or severity of consequences.

Safety engineers conduct design analysis to identify risk and safety hazards. The most common analysis techniques include:

(1) Failure Modes & Effects Analysis (FMEA) is an analytical tool used for identifying all possible failures in a design, a manufacturing process in a product. FMEA is used in Risk Management to identify various ways in which systems elements can fail and what's their overall impact (consequence) to other elements and/or the overall system. The purpose of the FMEA is to prevent, reduce or eliminate potential product failures by starting with the top risks with the greatest consequences.

(2) Fault Tree Analysis (FTA) is a graphical tool to explore the causes of system-level failures. FTA is a Risk Management tool that assesses the safety-critical functions within a system's architecture and design. It analyzes high-level failures and identifies all lower-level (sub-system) failures that cause them. FTA is useful during the initial product design phase as a tool for driving the design through an evaluation of both reliability and fault probability perspectives. It can be used to estimate and develop a system's performance reliability requirements to reduce the likelihood of undesired events occurring.

FTA analysis involves five steps:

- Step 1: Define the undesired event to study.
- Step 2: Obtain an understanding of the system.
- Step 3: Construct the fault tree.
- Step 4: Evaluate the fault tree.
- Step 5: Control the hazards identified.

(3) Damage Mode and Effects Analysis (DMEA) is an analysis of a system or piece of equipment to determine the extent of damage sustained from a given level of hostile weapon damage. It examines the effect of that damage on the continued controlled operation and mission completion capabilities of the system or equipment.

DMEA is the ability of a system to survive an enemy attack that directly impacts its wartime sustainability. The DMEA (part of the FMEA process) serves to influence the system and component design and to identify the additional logistic support resources required to achieve the wartime readiness objectives. The frequency and severity of combat damage occurrences are estimated through combat simulations and tests.

3. Models

(1) Heinrich's Domino Model of Accident Causation

Herbert W. Heinrich was a pioneering occupational safety researcher. He is most famous for originating the concept of the "safety pyramid". He also developed the "five domino model" of accident causation, a sequential accident model which has been influential in the development of occupational safety thinking. His "domino theory" represents an accident sequence as a causal chain of events, represented as dominos that topple in a chain reaction. The fall of the first domino leads to the fall of the second, followed by the third, etc. , as illustrated below (Figure 8-3).

Figure 8-3　The injury is caused by the action of preceding factors

The domino model of accident causation, as depicted by Herbert W. Heinrich in the 1950 edition of his book *Industrial Accident Prevention: A Scientific Approach*.

This theory of accident causation was later further developed by Frank Bird, who improved the description of managerial "dominos", and who generalized the last "accident" domino to cover any loss (lost production, damage to equipment or other assets, and not only injuries). This linear accident model is simple and easy to understand.

(2) Rasmussen's Migration Model

Pioneering safety researcher Jens Rasmussen represented the competing priorities and constraints that affect sociotechnical systems in his "migration model". Any large system is subjected to multiple pressures: operations must be profitable, they must be safe, and workers' workload must be feasible.

All organizations are affected by different pressures and adaptive processes, which compete for attention, and lead to migration or drift, often towards situations with higher levels of risk.

Rasmussen's migration model illustrates that small optimizations and adaptations can accumulate over time, taking the system far from its initial design parameters. If there is no counterweight to this "practical drift" from operations staff who are alert to the possibility and the dangers of the normalization of deviance, from the safety function, or from an effective regulator, systems are likely to drift towards catastrophe.

8.3　Safety in Design

1. Introduction

Safety in design is the integration of hazard identification and risk assessment methods early in the design process to eliminate or minimise the risks of injury throughout the life of the building or structure being designed, including construction, use, maintenance and demolition. In the USA, this concept is called

8.3 Professional Terms, Words and Phrases, Sentence Illustration

the Prevention through Design (PtD), which is defined as the practice of anticipating and "designing out" potential occupational safety and health hazards and risks associated with new processes, structures, equipment or tools, and organising work, taking into consideration the construction, maintenance, decommissioning and disposal/recycling of waste material, and recognising the business and social benefits of so doing. In Australia, instead of using the term "safety in design", an alternative term of "safe design" and a broader definition was given by Safe

Work Australia in its *Safe Design of Structures Code of Practice*. The Code states that safe design means the integration of control measures early in the design process to eliminate or, if this is not reasonably practicable, minimise risks to health and safety throughout the life of the structure being designed. The safe design of a structure will always be part of a wider set of design objectives, including practicability, aesthetics, cost and functionality. These sometimes competing objectives need to be balanced in a manner that does not compromise the health and safety of those who work on or use the structure over its life. Safe design begins at the concept development phase of a structure when making decisions about: the design and its intended purpose; materials to be used; possible methods of construction, maintenance, operation, demolition or dismantling and disposal; and what legislation, codes of practice and standards need to be considered and complied with.

As indicated by the definitions given above, there are two key principles of safety in design. First, the concept aims to identify and eliminate or mitigate safety risks early in the design stage. Eliminating hazards at the design stage is often easier and cheaper to achieve than making changes later, when the hazards become real risks in the workplace. The concept is based on the popular premise in project management, which argues that it is easier and cheaper to influence a project early in the project life cycle rather than in later stages. Second, the concept encourages relevant stakeholders to identify potential safety risks not only in the construction stage, but also during the operation and maintenance of the facility or structure and during the dismantling process at the end of the lifetime of the facility or structure.

Schulte et al. provide a brief description of the historical development of the safety-in-design concept, particularly in the US context. The link between design and safety has actually been recognised since the beginning of 1800s, involving inherently safer design and the widespread implementation of guards for machinery, controls for elevators and boiler safety practices. Following this, there was enhanced design for ventilation, enclosures, system monitors, lockout controls and hearing protectors. More recently, there has been the development of chemical process safety, ergonomically engineered tools, chairs, work stations, lifting devices, and many others. Since the 1970s, the safety in design concept has been manifested in various management efforts. One of those efforts was the Safety and Health Awareness for Preventive Engineering (SHAPE), a collaborative programme between the US National Institute for Occupational Safety and Health (NIOSH), engineering professional societies and engineering schools to enhance the education of engineering students in health and safety, in which a series of nine instructional modules has been produced. The Accreditation Board for Engineering and Technology also voiced the need to adopt new evaluation criteria, calling for health and safety curricular objectives and specific requirements in design, laboratory and professional practice instruction. The US Occupational Safety and Health Administration (OSHA) established the Alliance Program Construction Round table to bring construction-related alliance programme participants together to discuss and share information on Workplace Safety and Health (WSH), in which one of the topics is about designing for construction safety. Other efforts include the issuance of the *Process Safety*

Management of Highly Hazardous Chemical Standards, the National Safety Council's Integrating Safety through Design Symposium, the establishment of the Institute for Safety through Design and the Whole Building Design approach.

2. Safety in Design Policies and Guidelines

Several countries have developed and implemented policies and guidelines on safety in design and four of such countries are chosen for discussion: the UK, Australia, the USA and Singapore.

(1) In the UK

In the UK, the government hasrecognised the importance of safety in design by introducing the CDM Regulations 1994, which came into force in 1995. This has since been replaced by CDM Regulations 2007, which also bring the Construction (Health Safety and Welfare) Regulations 1996 into a single set of regulations. The CDM Regulations are about focusing attention on effective planning and management of construction projects from the design stage onwards. Its aim is for health and safety considerations to be treated as a normal part of a project's development, not an afterthought. The objective of the CDM Regulations is to reduce the risk of harm to those who build, use, maintain and demolish structures.

Section 11 of the CDM2007 states the duties of designers in maintaining and improving health and safety in the construction industry. It requires all project designers, so far as is reasonably practicable, to eliminate hazards and risks during design and provide information about remaining risks. CDM2007 defines a designer as anyone who prepares designs for construction work, including variations. The designer includes anyone who arranges for their employees or other persons under their control to prepare designs.

Part 4 of the CDM2007 also spells out in detail each party's duty and responsibility in relation to safety during the design stage, including safe places of work, good order and site security, stability of structures, demolition or dismantling, explosives, excavations, fire, lighting, fresh air, temperature, weather protection and emergency procedures. In principle, when hazards cannot be removed by designers, design solutions should reduce the overall risk to an acceptable level. In practice, this means that when a potential hazard in the design is identified and cannot be removed, designers must reduce the likelihood of a harmful occurrence, reduce the potential severity of harm resulting from an occurrence, reduce the number of people exposed to the harm and reduce the exposure to harm in terms of duration or frequency. CDM2007 also requires designers to provide information to assist other stakeholders to identify and manage any significant remaining risks that have not been designed out.

(2) In the US

In the US, currently there is no regulation on safety in design, although initiatives and standards exist. The US NIOSH is leading a national PtD initiative to promote the concept and highlight its importance in all business decisions. The national PtD initiative requires input from key industries including agriculture, forestry and fishing; mining; construction; manufacturing; wholesale and retail trade; transportation, warehousing and utilities; services and healthcare and social assistance. The PtD initiative is framed within four functional areas:

research, practice, education and policy. Research focuses on questioning current practices to generate improvement. Practice focuses on encouraging businesses to demand safer designs and motivating design professionals to increase their awareness of those design features that can impact worker health and safety. Education focuses on promoting PtD through the augmentation of curricula and by stimulating professional accreditation programmes to value PtD issues and to include them in competency assessments. Policy focuses on supporting the other functional areas and providing incentives for the incorporation of health and safety considerations in design decisions.

In 2011, the American Society of Safety Engineers (ASSE) announced the approval of the American National Standards Institute (ANSI)/ASSE Z590. 3 standard, *Prevention through Design: Guidelines for Addressing Occupational Risks in Design and Redesign Processes*. The standard provides guidance on including PtD concept within an occupational safety and health management system. It further provides guidance for a life cycle assessment and design model that balances environmental and occupational safety and health goals over the life span of a facility, process, or product. Another PtD initiative is the Design for Construction Safety which is the process of addressing construction site safety and health in the design of a construction project. This initiative is the product of the US OSHA Alliance Program's Construction Round Table, a platform which allows OSHA participants who share a common interest in construction related topics and issues to discuss and share experiences on workplace health and safety.

3. Building Information Modelling (BIM) for Safety in Design

BIM, including a range of digital tools, such as online databases, virtual reality, Geographic Information Systems (GIS), 4D (or nD) CAD, and location-based sensing and warning technologies have a potential to change the way safety can be approached by automatically detecting and eliminating hazards. As discussed in the previous sections, safety in design is mainly about the identification of potential hazards and the decision of choosing corresponding safety measures in the design stage. As such, accurate and precise identification of potential safety hazards is critical to the safety in design process. In practice, failures in identifying hazard are often due to limited experience, poor training and oversight of construction staff. Another issue is the separation between safety and design processes which may involve different actors who do not communicate sufficiently with one another. This issue creates difficulties for safety personnel to analyse what, when, why, and where safety measures are needed has a potential to change the way safety can be approached by automatically detecting and eliminating hazards, either at the design or construction stage. For example, BIM allows greater details to be developed earlier in a project. This may enhance designers' awareness of construction safety issues. A range of digital tools, as listed earlier, has been developed and used to help contractors manage safety in the design and construction stages. However, in comparison, digital tools for managing safety in design are less mature and relatively limited in their application, and in the following sections, we discuss several BIM-based examples that are directly or indirectly related to safety in design.

One example of using BIM for safety in design is the ToolSHed™, which is an information and decision support tool to help designers integrate the management of safety risks into the design process. ToolSHed™ is a web-based tool developed to provide designers with specialist safety knowledge and guidance. Knowledge was acquired from Australian Occupational Health and Safety guidance material, industry standards and codes, and an expert panel. The knowledge was modelled in a series of logic diagrams which represent a template for reasoning in complex situations. At present, ToolSHed™ only deals with the design-related risks of falling from heights during maintenance work on building roofs. The risk assessment prompts designers to enter information about relevant design features that could impact upon the risk of falling from a height. A risk report is generated to advise the designers about the level of risk of falling from heights, and an explanation of the design factors contributing to the inferred level of risk.

The second example is Zhang et al. (2013) who developed an automated rule-based safety checking system for fall prevention due to openings in slabs, edges on floor, and openings in walls. An initial set of rules was generated using a set of fall-prevention rules for the three conditions. Once the rules were established, the system was able to detect various locations requiring fall protection, based on design drawings; for example, exterior walls are examined to determine where edge protection is needed; openings in slabs are examined to prevent fall through openings; openings in exterior walls are examined to determine where additional wall opening protection is required and interior walls around slab openings are examined for fall protection from wall openings. This tool can be used in the design stage to identify fall hazards during different stages of construction.

As the third example, BIM is also valuable during constructability reviews, in which many argue that they are able to improve construction safety. For example, in a project, designers may have design BIM models, the contractor has a BIM model for use in sequencing the work and major supplier shave prefabrication BIM models of building elements. An integrated BIM model with information derived from these different disciplines will help decision-makers to identify, visualise and resolve conflicts among various building systems when conducting constructability reviews. As discussed earlier, projects with high levels of constructability facilitate ease of construction which promotes better safety performance.

Sulankivi et al. (2014) use BIM to promote constructability which has positive impacts on construction site safety. A basic prerequisite of good constructability is the integration of various elements in correct and accurate design drawings. BIM can assist in this integration process by combining drawings from various design disciplines into one file and performing semi-automatic clash detection. This way, design conflicts, for example, between structural elements and mechanical components, can be identified and eliminated. Fewer design conflicts and errors lead to fewer disruptions on site and less ad hoc decisions, which are known to increase safety hazards. BIM also can become a useful tool for cooperation between designers and contractors to improve constructability and safety. Detailed BIM models have been found to improve the visualisation of constructability issues, thus becoming a useful tool during constructability assessment meetings.

8.4　Reading Material

1. Emotional Task Analysis

In the Human Factors 1.0 framework, one standard technique or method was Behavioral Task Analysis (BTA). To do a BTA the practitioner would look at a complex task (e.g. performing maintenance on a washing machine) and would analyze all the steps/tasks involved—breaking everything down to a fine-grained level that could inform the question at hand. A BTA could be used to help create training programs, identify opportunities for improvement, and a wide range of other design goals. The cognitive revolution spurred the mutation of BTA into Cognitive Task Analysis (CTA). No longer were the practitioners of Human Factors 2.0 satisfied with a behavioral task analysis—now they began to map-out the cognitive aspects of task performance. Such cognitive task analysis could uncover a whole new class of cognitive design constraints: decision points, dependencies, categorizations, and information needs. Both BTA and CTA are essential tools in the HFE toolkit. As we move into Human Factors 3.0, I here introduce the method of Emotional Task Analysis (ETA). When designing a system, Human Factors 3.0 practitioners must perform: a behavioral task analysis (to understand physical limitations), a cognitive task analysis (to understand cognitive limitations), and an emotional task analysis (to understand emotional limitations/aspirations). It's not rocket science; it is just another way of thinking about any compound task.

To perform an emotional task analysis you break down the task into steps (as small as required) and then you identify any emotions that might beevoked during (or before/after) each step. For example, for a software APP to onboard a new user, there will be several steps where the user might feel uncertain, or confused, or untrusting, or happily surprised. Once these emotions are understood (and explicitly mapped) the designer can then begin to design around them. The artful designer might want to add features (information, icons, sounds, or other mechanisms) to either alleviate these emotions (such as the various trust icons used on websites) or to accentuate them (such as text alerts that congratulate you for creating an account). The world of behavioral economics and nudge-theory has a whole raft of potential design solutions that can then come into play. But, it is important to note, it is the role of the human factors engineer to uncover these requirements or constraints for the designer.

While this approach is clearly important for designing tools and systems like websites, it plays an even bigger rolein the realm of social robotics. For example, imagine we are helping design a "social" robot to perform home healthcare. When the robot attempts to wake the patient for a doctor's visit, the emotional task analysis tells us that the patient might be confused or upset. So a designer might have the robot say or do something to increase calm and trust. Or, if the robot is working with a dementia patient, the designer might need to acknowledge the near constant confusion and add requirements to design features that moderate every action. Perhaps the robot should play music? Or perhaps the robot should have a face that can be used to immediately convey various emotional states.

Performing BTA, CTA, and ETA are all essential steps in helping to inform the design of a social robot. Themechanical and electrical engineers clearly have vital contributions to make (to ensure the machine can move, sense, and interact). And computer scientists also have vital contributions to make (to write the software that orchestrates everything). But, the human factors engineer also has vital contributions to make in designing the behavioral, cognitive, and emotional repertoires of the robot.

2. Human Factors X. 0

If these iterations of Human Factors Engineering are additive—i. e. , Human Factors 3. 0 includes all the aspects of 1. 0 and 2. 0—where will we go next?

As we move into the future, we begin to see a Human Factors field that strives to include all the other aspects of human experience in the design process. For example, a designer might consider the experiential, environmental, social, technological, or political implications of a design choice. These additionaldimensions can add new constraints to the designer's toolkit. And, each of these different dimensions will have new methods and tools to help uncover relevant constraints. One approach that we have found useful is to do a task-analysis around different dimensions of interest. We call this approach Multidimensional Task Analysis (MTA). MTA can encompass a wide range of task analyses. Some of the task analyses that we have found useful include:

(1) Informational task analysis (where, when, what info is needed?)

(2) Decisional task analysis (where, when, what decisions must be made?)

(3) Attentional task analysis (where, when, how should attention be focused?)

(4) Social task analysis (what social interactions are happening?)

(5) Teamwork task analysis (where, how, when, and what cooperative actions?)

Of course, there are many relevant methods beyond task analysis, but this approach demonstrates the broader theme around expanding our constraint spaces. As we move into the future of Human Factors Engineering there is no way to know what new sets of constraints might emerge to help inform design. Currently "emotional constraints" and "emotional design" are areas of needed focus. Of course, ecological, environmental, and sustainability constraints are also vitally important and are now being used to inform design. As we move into future iterations of Human Factors Engineering we must be ready to identify, consider, examine, measure, and use whatever dimensions are seen as relevant to the design challenges at hand. "Human Factors X. 0" is this future, ever-evolving, multidimensional approach to human factors engineering. We must be ready to move transversally through design constraint space: acknowledging and (re) defining dimensions as we navigate the ever-shifting seas of user-needs and internal/ external constraints.

With new legal and regulatory requirements being introduced by safety organizations andgovernment agencies almost daily, safety engineering is evolving continuously. Safety engineering requires interpretation of new information and innovative technologies, adapting programs and policies, and implementing procedures and products to meet the social and industrial needs of changing business environments.

The most recenttrends in safety engineering include increased emphasis on prevention by the anticipation of hazard potentials; changing legal concepts with regard to product liability and negligent design or manufacture, as well as the developing emphasis on consumer protection; and the development of national and international legislation and controls, not only in the areas of transportation safety, product safety, and consumer protection but also in occupational health and environmental control.

Chapter 9
Reliability and Quality Engineering

9.1 Reliability

9.1 Professional Terms, Words and Phrases, Sentence Illustration

1. Definition

"Reliability" refers to the ability of a product to perform without failure over a given period of time. Thus, reliability is a function of time. It is related to the length of time a product performs before a failure occurs. This length of time to failure is referred to as "life". This life is a random variable in the sense that in a given population, although the units may all have been built by the same process, the life of one unit for the first failure, for example, will be different from another's. Even for the same unit, the time to first failure will be different from that of the second failure, and so on. Those life values can be viewed as values of a random variable usually denoted as T.

In the above definition of "life" of a product, the term "failure" is an important component. In fact, the life is defined with respect to a particular failure under consideration. The life for a product may be one value for a cosmetic failure, another for a minor failure and yet another value for a major failure. So, we should first define the failure that is of interest and then define the reliability with respect to that failure.

The variability in the life-variable can be described by a frequency distribution, and this frequency distribution can be obtained from data collected on lives of sample units if the product already exists. The frequency distribution of a future product can be projected based on similar past models. An example of a frequency distribution is shown in Figure 9−1. This frequency distribution can also be represented by a mathematical function, which we call the Probability Density Function (PDF) of the random variable T (We will assume that T, which generally represents life in hours, days, or months, is a continuous variable) The frequency distribution of the life variable is the basic information necessary to assess the reliability of a product. The cumulative distribution function of the life variable is called its "life distribution".

Reliability is expressed as a function of time (Reliability for a product at 1000 hrs will be different from reliability at 5000 hrs) The reliability of a product at time t, denoted as $R(t)$, is defined as the probability that the product will not fail before the time t, under a stated set of conditions. In notations,

$$R(t) = P(T > t) \tag{9-1}$$

This probability can be seen in Figure 9−1, where the curve represents the probability distribution of the life of the product. This probability is the area under the curve above t. It can be seen this probability also represents the proportion of the population that survives beyond time t. If $f(t)$ is the pdf of T, the function form of the curve, then

$$R(t) = \int_t^\infty f(x)\ dx \qquad (9-2)$$

Also, it can be seen that $R(t) = 1 - F(t)$, where $F(t)$ is the cumulative distribution function (CDF) of T.

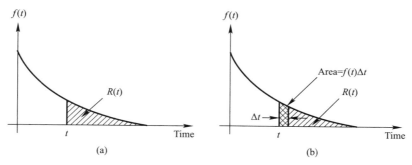

Figure 9-1   Frequency distribution of life and definition of reliability

2. Theory

In most organizations, the quality assurance function is designed to continually improve the ability to produce products and services that meet or exceed customer requirements. Narrowly construed, this means, in the manufacturing industries, producing parts with dimensions that are within tolerance. Quality engineering must expand this narrow construction to include reliability considerations, and all quality engineers should have a working knowledge of reliability engineering. What, then, is the distinction between these two fields?

● Once an item has been successfully manufactured, the traditional quality assurance function has done its job (although the search for ways to improve is continuous). The reliability function's principal focus is on what happens next. Answers are sought to questions such as:

    - Are components failing prematurely?

    - Was burn-in time sufficient?

    - Is the constant failure rate acceptable?

    - What changes in design, manufacturing, installation, operation, or maintenance would improve reliability?

Another way to delineate the difference between quality and reliability is to note how data are collected. In the case of manufacturing, data for quality engineering are generally collected during the manufacturing process. Inputs such as voltages, pressures, temperatures, and raw material parameters are measured. Outputs such as dimensions, acidity, weight, and contamination levels are measured. The data for reliability engineering generally are collected after a component or product is manufactured. For example, a switch might be toggled repeatedly until it fails, and the number of successful cycles noted. A pump might be run until its output in gallons per minute falls below a defined value, and the number of hours recorded.

- Quality and reliability engineers provide different inputs into the design process. Quality engineers suggest changes that permit the item to be produced within tolerance at a reasonable cost. Reliability engineers make recommendations that permit the item to function correctly for a longer period of time.

The preceding paragraphs show that although the roles of quality and reliability are different, they do interrelate. For example, in the product design phase both quality and reliability functions have the goal of proposing cost-effective ways to satisfy and exceed customer expectations. This often mandates that the two functions work together to produce a design that both works correctly and performs for an acceptable period of time. When processes are designed and operated, the quality and reliability engineers work together to determine the process parameters that impact the performance and longevity of the product so that those parameters can be appropriately controlled. A similar interrelationship holds as specifications are developed for packaging, shipment, installation, operation, and maintenance.

Reliability will be impacted by product design and by the processes used in the product's manufacture. Therefore, the designers of products and processes must understand and use reliability data as design decisions are made. Generally, the earlier reliability data are considered in the design process the more efficient and effective their impact will be.

Once a reliable product is designed, quality engineering techniques are used to make sure that the processes produce that product.

3. Role of the Reliability Function in the Organization

The study of reliability engineering is usually undertaken primarily to determine and improve the useful lifetime of products. Data are collected on the failure rates of components and products, including those produced by suppliers. Competitors' products may also be subjected to reliability testing and analysis.

Reliability techniques can also help other facets of an organization:

- Reliability analysis can be used to improve product design. Reliability predictions provide guidance as components are selected. Derating techniques aid in increasing a product's useful lifetime. Reliability improvements can be effected through component redundancy.

- Marketing and advertising can be assisted as warranty and other documents that inform customer expectations are prepared. Warranties that are not supported by reliability data can cause extra costs and inflame customer ire.

- It is increasingly important to detect and prevent or mitigate product liability issues. Warnings and alarms should be incorporated into the design when hazards can't be eliminated. Products whose failure can introduce safety and health hazards need to be analyzed for reliability so that procedures can be put in place to reduce the probability that they will be used beyond their useful lifetime. Failure rates typically escalate in the final phase of a product's life. Components whose useful lifetime is shorter than the product's should be replaced on a schedule that can be determined through reliability engineering techniques.

- Manufacturing processes can use reliability tools in the following ways:

- The impact of process parameters on product failure rates can be studied.

- Alternative processes can be compared for their effect on reliability.

- Reliability data for process equipment can be used to determine preventive maintenance schedules and spare parts inventories.

- The use of parallel process streams to improve process reliability can be evaluated.

- Safety can be enhanced through the understanding of equipment failure rates.

- Vendors can be evaluated more effectively.

• Every facet of an organization, including purchasing, quality assurance, packaging, field service, logistics, and so on, can benefit from a knowledge of reliability engineering. An understanding of the lifecycles of the products and equipment they use and handle can improve the effectiveness and efficiency of their function.

4. Methodology

Reliability engineering techniques help quantify the "pay me now or pay me later" concept. The goal is to determine the reliability level that will minimize the total lifecycle cost of the product. The lifecycle cost of a product includes the cost to purchase, operate, and maintain the product during its useful lifetime. In some cases, such as automotive products, where the customer seldom keeps the product for its entire useful lifetime, costs associated with depreciation may be factored into lifecycle costs.

The real cost of failures is frequently underestimated. If a 90-cent natural gas valve component fails to function, the cost may far exceed the 90-cent replacement cost.

Reliability engineers take the long-term view and develop cost-effective ways to reduce lifecycle costs. These may range from design techniques such as redundancy and derating to specification of manufacturing parameters such as burn-in time.

Increased reliability sometimes means increased manufacturing cost and selling price. Properly implemented, however, the result will be a decrease in lifecycle cost. Consider, for instance, a national truck line who discovered that its most frequent cause of vehicle downtime was loss of a headlight bulb. This entailed stopping the truck at the side of the road and summoning a repair vehicle from the nearest company depot. The resultant delay caused late deliveries and dissatisfied customers. The trucking company determined that a much more reliable bulb reduced lifecycle costs even though the new bulb had a considerably higher initial purchase price and required retrofitting a step-up transformer to obtain the required voltage. The company now specifies the more reliable bulb for new truck purchases. In this case the truck manufacturer can be faulted for producing a product that didn't have the lowest lifecycle cost.

As component and product design decisions are made, the reliability engineer can aid in calculating the cost-benefit relationships by providing life expectancies for various design options.

Quality Function Deployment (QFD) provides a process for planning new or redesigned products and services. The input to the process is the voice of the customer. The QFD process requires that a team discover the needs and desires of their customer and study the organization's response to these needs and desires. The QFD matrix aids in illustrating the linkage between the VOC and the resulting technical requirements. A quality function deployment matrix consists of several parts. There is no standard format matrix or key for the symbols, but the example shown in Figure 9-2 is typical. A map of the various parts of Figure 9-2 is shown in Figure 9-3. The matrix is formed by first filling in the customer requirements ① which are developed from analysis of the VOC. This section often includes a scale reflecting the importance of the individual entries. The technical requirements are established in response to the customer requirements and placed in area ②. The symbols on the top line in this section indicate whether lower (↓) or higher (↑) is better. A circle indicates that target is better. The relationship area ③ displays the connection between the technical requirements and the customer requirements. Various symbols can be used here. The most common are shown in Figure 9-2 Area ④ is not shown on all QFD matrices. It

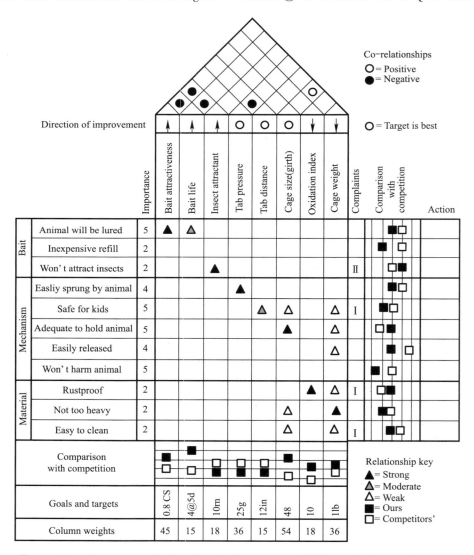

Figure 9-2　Example of a Quality Function Deployment (QFD) matrix for an animal trap

236

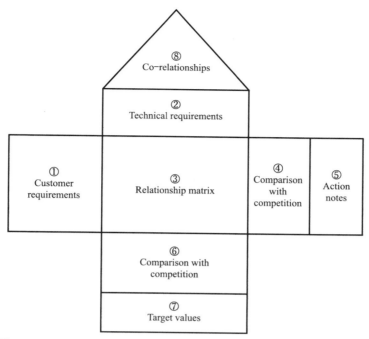

Figure 9-3   Map to the entries for the QFD matrix illustrated in Figure 9-2

plots comparison with competition for the customer requirements. Area ⑤ provides an index to documentation concerning improvement activities. Area ⑥ is not shown on all QFD matrices. It plots comparison with competition for the technical requirements. Area ⑦ lists the target values for the technical requirements. Area ⑧ shows the co-relationships between the technical requirements. A positive co-relationship indicates that both technical requirements can be improved at the same time. A negative co-relationship indicates that improving one of the technical requirements will make the other one worse. The "column weights" shown at the bottom of the figure are optional. They indicate the importance of the technical requirements in meeting customer requirements. The values in the column weights row are obtained by multiplying the value in the "Importance" column in the customer requirements section by values assigned to the symbols in the relationship matrix. These assigned values are arbitrary, and in the example a strong relationship was assigned a 9, moderate 3, and weak 1.

The completed matrix can provide a database for product development, serve as a basis for planning product or process improvements, and suggest opportunities for new or revised product or process introductions.

The customer requirements section is sometimes called the "what" information while the technical requirements section is referred to as the "how" area. The basic QFD product planning matrix can be followed with similar matrices for planning the parts that make up the product and for planning the processes that will produce the parts (Figure 9-4).

If a matrix has more than 25 customer voice lines it tends to become unmanageable.

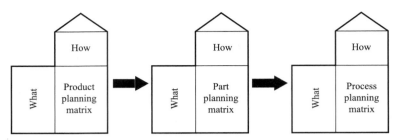

Figure 9-4　Sequence of QFD matrices for product, part, and process planning

The release of a preliminary version of a product to a restricted set of users has come to be known as beta testing. A principal advantage of this technique is the exposure of the product to a larger audience with varied needs and levels of expertise who might detect flaws that inhouse (alpha) testing missed. The customers entrusted with the early designs are expected to report good and bad features and recommendations to the development team. This frequently results in the identification of potential corrections and improvements that can be factored into the final version. Beta testing tends to be more important with complex products for which unusual combinations of usage circumstances may not be envisioned by designers.

5. Model

(1) Static System Reliability Models

① Series System

A system block diagram reduces the system to its subsystems and provides a tool for understanding the effect on the system of a subsystem failure. The most basic of the static block diagrams is the series model. A reliability series model block diagram shows that the successful operation of the system depends on the successful operation of each of the subsystems. The failure of any subsystem will result in the failure of the system. This is a natural way to design and build systems. Consequently, most systems are series unless some effort is made to incorporate redundancy into the design.

In the series system block diagram each block represents a subsystem, as shown in Figure 9-5. There is only one path for system success. If any subsystem fails, the system will fail. It is important not to overlook the subsystem interfaces as they may be a source of failure.

To analyze the system reliability using a series block diagram it is necessary to assume that the probabilities of failure for the individual subsystems are independent. The assumption of independence is

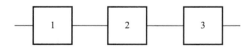

Figure 9-5　The series system

reasonable, and need only apply until the time of first failure. Any secondary failure, although it may be a safety consideration, does not affect the reliability analysis. The system has already failed. This is not true of all models. Other models require the user to assume that the probabilities of subsystem failure are completely independent for the entire mission.

It is necessary that all subsystems survive the mission if the system is to survive the mission. This is the joint occurrence of the success of the subsystems, and the product law for the joint occurrence of independent events is used to calculate system reliability.

The reliability of the system $[R_{\text{System}}(t)]$ is the probability of success of the system for the mission time t. The reliability of a subsystem i $[R_i(t)]$ is the probability of the success of that subsystem for a mission of time t. If there are n subsystems and the reliability of each subsystem is known, the system reliability can be found as

$$R_{\text{System}}(t) = [R_1(t)] \times [R_2(t)] \times \cdots \times [R_n(t)] \tag{9-3}$$

The reliability of each subsystem is less than one. The reliability of the system will be less than the reliability of any subsystem:

$$R_{\text{System}}(t) < R_i(t) \tag{9-4}$$

Example 9-1:

A system consists of three subsystems connected in series.

The reliability for each subsystem for a mission time of t is:

$$\begin{cases} R_1(t) = 0.99 \\ R_2(t) = 0.98 \\ R_3(t) = 0.94 \end{cases} \tag{9-5}$$

The system reliability for mission time t:

$$R_{\text{System}}(t) = (0.99)(0.98)(0.94) = 0.91 \tag{9-6}$$

System modeling will assist in identifying reliability problems and the implementation of a reliability improvement effort. If significant reliability improvement is to be made to a series system, the subsystem with the minimum reliability must be improved. Maximum improvement in system reliability will be achieved by increasing the reliability of the subsystem with the minimum reliability.

If the reliability of subsystem 1 in the above example is improved to 0.999, the improvement in system reliability is marginal.

$$R_{\text{System}}(t) = (0.999)(0.98)(0.94) = 0.92 \tag{9-7}$$

Regardless of the amount of improvement in subsystems 1 and 2, the system reliability can not exceed 0.94. The focus for system reliability improvement should be on subsystem 3.

There are other block diagram models that could result in higher system reliability. These models will be considered. However, it should be noted that there are many highly reliable series systems in use. The series design has some advantages over other designs. A series system will require a minimum number of parts, consume minimum power and therefore dissipate less heat, take less room, add less weight, and be cheaper to build than other system configurations.

② Parallel System

Redundancy can be designed into a system to increase system reliability. A parallel system provides more than one path for system success, as shown in Figure 9-6. An active redundancy system has subsystems on line that can individually perform the functions required for system success. If a subsystem fails, system success can be accomplished with the successful operation of a remaining subsystem. The system fails only when all the redundant subsystems fail.

To analyze a parallel system, it is necessary to assume that the probabilities of failure for the various subsystems are totally independent for the entire mission time. This requires that the redundant system design be engineered to ensure that this assumption is valid. If a single event can cause more than one subsystem to fail, or if the failure of one subsystem can cause a secondary failure of a redundant subsystem, the desired improvement in system reliability due to the redundancy is lost. For example, a single power supply failure might cause the failure of redundant navigational systems. This situation is referred to as a single point failure. Also, particular attention must be given to the interconnection points of the redundant subsystems. Many times these are the source of single-point failures.

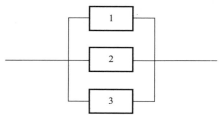

Figure 9-6　The parallel system

A redundant system will fail only if all subsystems fail. If a redundant system consists of n independent subsystems, and if the reliability of each subsystem is known, then system reliability can be calculated as:

Example 9-2:

An active parallel system has three independent subsystems.

The reliability for each subsystem for a mission time of t is:

$$\begin{cases} R_1(t) = 0.99 \\ R_2(t) = 0.98 \\ R_3(t) = 0.94 \end{cases} \tag{9-8}$$

The reliability of the system for mission time t is equal to

$$R_{\text{System}}(t) = 1-(1-0.99)(1-0.98)(1-0.94) = 0.99998 \tag{9-9}$$

It should be noted that the reliability of the system is greater than the reliability of any of the redundant subsystems.

$$\begin{cases} R_{\text{System}}(t) > R_i \text{ for all } i=1 \text{ to } n \\ R_{\text{System}}(t) = 1-[1-R_1(t)] \times [1-R_2(t)] \times \cdots \times [1-R_n(t)] \end{cases} \tag{9-10}$$

Active redundancy is an important reliability tool available to the system designer. It should not, however, be used to improve the reliability of a poor design. It is much more efficient to engineer the design for the highest possible reliability and then use active redundancy if the desired reliability is still not achieved.

(2) Series-Parallel Model

A system may be modeled as a combination of series and parallel subsystems. For this model the same assumptions apply as for individual series or parallel systems. The combined system reliability can be found by converting the system to an equivalent series or Equivalent Parallel Model.

Example 9-3:

Figure 9-7 shows a series-parallel system. The reliabilities for each subsystem are shown on the diagram. Find the reliability for the system.

The reliability for the two parallel subsystems is:

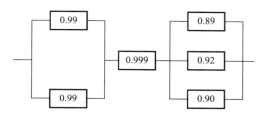

Figure 9-7   A series-parallel model

$$\begin{cases} R_1 = 1-(1-0.99)(1-0.99) = 1-(1-0.99)^2 \\ R_1 = 0.9999 \end{cases} \qquad (9-11)$$

The reliability for the three parallel subsystems is:

$$\begin{cases} R_3 = 1-(1-0.89)(1-0.92)(1-0.90) \\ R_3 = 0.99912 \end{cases} \qquad (9-12)$$

The system is now an equivalent series system with R_1 and R_3 and $R_2 = 0.999$.

The system reliability can be found as:

$$\begin{cases} R_{\text{System}} = R_1 \times R_2 \times R_3 = (0.9999)(0.999)(0.99912) \\ R_{\text{System}} = 0.998 \end{cases} \qquad (9-13)$$

9.2   Quality Engineering

9.2 Professional Terms, Words and Phrases, Sentence Illustration

1. Definition

The experience of the past few decades has shown that quality is achievable through a well-defined set of methods used during the design, production, and delivery of products. The collection of these methods and the theoretical concepts behind them can be viewed as falling into an engineering discipline, which some have already called "quality engineering". The American Society for Quality, a premier organization of quality professionals, uses this name to signify the body of knowledge contributing to the creation of quality in products and services that leads to customer satisfaction. They even offer training programs in quality engineering and certify those who pass a written examination and acquire a certain level of experience in the quality field.

The term "quality engineering" has been used in quality literature to denote many things. Some authors have used the term to refer to the process of improving product quality using improvement tools. Many have used it to signify the process of selecting targets and tolerances for process parameters through designed experiments. Some have used it to mean the selection of product characteristics that will satisfy customer needs. The term is used here, however, with a much broader meaning.

The body of knowledge needed to make quality products has assumed different names at different times based mainly on the available set of tools at those times. It was called "quality control" when final inspection before the product was shipped to the customer was the only tool employed to achieve product quality. When statistical principles were used to create control charts and sampling plans, it assumed the name "statistical quality control". It also took the name "quality assurance" at this time because the control charts were used to control the process upstream of final inspection and prevent defectives from being produced so as to assure defect-free shipments to customer. "Statistical Process Control" (SPC) was another term used at this time because of the control charts used for process control which were designed using statistical principles. Then came the addition of elements such as drawing control, procurement control, instrument control, and other components of a total quality system when people recognized that a system was necessary to achieve quality. When a new management philosophy became necessary to deal with the quality system, the body of knowledge was called "Total Quality Management" (TQM). It was also known as "Company-Wide Quality Control" (CWQC). Quality engineering has come to mean that the body of knowledge needed for making quality products includes the science, mathematics, systems thinking, psychology, human relations, organization theory, and the numerous methods created from them that are used during the design, production, and delivery of the product. It may be worth mentioning that the Six Sigma methodology that has become so popular in recent years, as a means of improving quality and reducing waste, encompasses almost the same set of knowledge that we refer to here as "quality engineering".

2. Methods (Methods of Enumeration)

Enumeration involves counting techniques for very large numbers of possible outcomes. This occurs for even surprisingly small sample sizes. In quality engineering, these methods are commonly used in a wide variety of statistical procedures.

The basis for all of the enumerative methods described here is the multiplication principle. The multiplication principle states that the number of possible outcomes of a series of experiments is equal to the product of the number of outcomes of each experiment. For example, consider flipping a coin twice. On the first flip, there are two possible outcomes (heads/tails) and on the second flip there are also two possible outcomes. Thus, the series of two flips can result in $2 \times 2 = 4$ outcomes. Figure 9-8 illustrates this example.

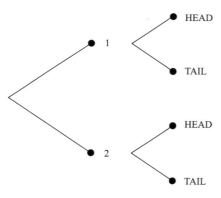

Figure 9-8   Multiplication principle
applied to coin flips

An ordered arrangement of elements is called a permutation. Suppose that you have four objects and four empty boxes, one for each object. Consider how many different ways the objects can be placed into the boxes. The first object can be placed in any of the four boxes. Once this is done there are three boxes to choose from for the second object, then two boxes for the third object and finally one box left for the last object. Using the multiplication principle you find that the total number of arrangements of the four objects into the four boxes is $4 \times 3 \times 2 \times 1 = 24$. In general, if there are n positions to be filled with n objects there are possible arrangements. The symbol $n!$ is read n factorial. By definition, $0! = 1$.

$$n\ (n-1)...(2)(1)=n!\qquad(9-14)$$

In applying probability theory to discrete variables in quality control we frequently encounter the need for efficient methods of counting. One counting technique that is especially useful is combinations. The combination formula is shown in Equation (9-15).

$$C_r^n = \frac{n!}{r!\ (n-r)!}\qquad(9-15)$$

Combinations tell how many unique ways you can arrange n objects taking them in groups of r objects at a time, where r is a positive integer less than or equal to n. For example, to determine the number of combinations we can make with the letters X, Y, and Z in groups of 2 letters at a time, we note that $n=3$ letters, $r=2$ letters at a time and use the above formula to find

$$C_2^3 = \frac{3!}{2!\ (3-2)!} = \frac{3\times2\times1}{(2\times1)(1)} = \frac{6}{2} = 3\qquad(9-16)$$

The 3 combinations are XY, XZ, and YZ. Notice that this method does not count reversing the letters as separate combinations, i. e. , XY and YX are considered to be the same.

3. Model (Kano Model)

Although customers seldom spark true innovation (for example, they are usually unaware of state-of-the-art developments), their input is extremely valuable. Obtaining valid customer input is a science itself. Market research firms use scientific methods such as critical incident analysis, focus groups, content analysis and surveys to identify the "voice of the customer". Noritaki Kano developed the following model of the relationship between customer satisfaction and quality (Figure 9-9).

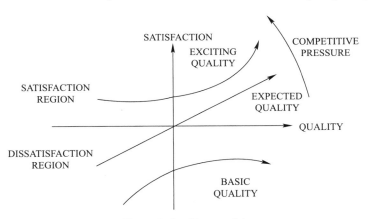

Figure 9-9　Kano model

The Kano model shows that there is a basic level of quality that customers assume the product will have. For example, all automobiles have windows and tires. If asked, customers don't even mention the basic quality items, they take them for granted. However, if this quality level isn't met the customer will be dissatisfied; note that the entire "Basic Quality" curve lies in the lower half of the chart, representing dissatisfaction. However, providing basic quality isn't enough to create a satisfied customer.

The expected quality line represents those expectations which customers explicitly consider. For example, the length of time spent waiting in line at a checkout counter. The model shows that customers will be dissatisfied if their quality expectations are not met; satisfaction increases as more expectations are met.

The exciting quality curve lies entirely in the satisfaction region. This is the effect of innovation. Exciting quality represents unexpected quality items. The customer receives more than they expected. For example, Cadillac pioneered a system where the headlights stay on long enough for the owner to walk safely to the door.

Competitive pressure will constantly raise customer expectations. Today's exciting quality is tomorrow's basic quality. Firms that seek to lead the market must innovate constantly. Conversely, firms that seek to offer standard quality must constantly research customer expectations to determine the currently accepted quality levels. It is not enough to track competitors since expectations are influenced by outside factors as well. For example, the quality revolution in manufacturing has raised expectations for service quality as well.

9.3 Risk Analysis

9.3 Professional Terms, Words and Phrases, Sentence Illustration

1. Definition

Risk analysis is an emerging science, and it is a decision-making paradigm. Terje Aven (2018) makes a powerful argument for risk analysis as a new emerging science (Figure 9-10). Although it is rapidly developing it is not yet widely regarded as a science unto itself. As a paradigm, it is capable of producing knowledge about risks and risky activities in the real world. As a science, it also produces knowledge about concepts, theories, frameworks, methods, and the like to understand, assess, communicate, and manage risks. This latter knowledge set makes risk analysis as much a science as statistics is, for example. The risk analysis paradigm presented in this text is frequently referred to as risk management, especially by those who practice enterprise risk management.

> 1. The Scientific Basis
> 2. Concepts
> 3. Risk Assessment
> 4. Risk Perception and Communication
> 5. Risk Management
> 6. Solving Real Risk Problems and Issues
> Source: Aven (2018).

Figure 9-10　Pillars of risk analysis science

The traditional scientific method is often not applicable for decision making, especially when uncertainties are large and social values are prominent. Risk analysis is a process for decision making under uncertainty that consists of three tasks: risk management, risk assessment, and risk communication, as shown in Figure 9-11. We can think of it as the process of examining the whole of a risk by assessing the risk and its related relevant uncertainties for the purpose of efficacious management of the risk, facilitated by effective communication about the risk. It is a systematic way of gathering, recording, and evaluating information that can lead to recommendations for a decision or action in response to an identified hazard or opportunity for gain.

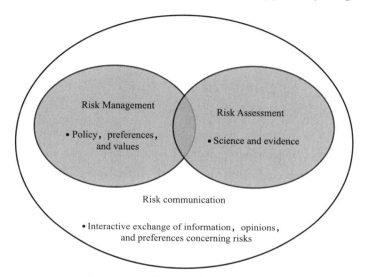

Figure 9-11   Three tasks of risk analysis

Risk analysis for real world problems is not pure science; it is not certain; it is not a solution; it is not static. We may be uncertain about one or more aspects of the consequence of the risk (s) of concern to us or its likelihood of occurring.

(1) Risk Management

Risk management is a process of problem identification, requesting information, evaluating risks, and initiating action to identify, evaluate, select, implement, monitor, and modify actions taken to alter levels of unacceptable risk to acceptable or tolerable levels. The goals of risk management are often said to include scientifically sound, cost-effective, integrated actions that reduce risks while taking into account economic, environmental, social, cultural, ethical, political, and legal considerations. More informally, risk management is the work one has to do to pose and then answer the following kinds of questions:

① What's the problem?

② What information do we need to solve it, that is, what questions do we want risk assessment to answer?

③ What can be done to reduce the impact of the risk described?

④ What can be done to reduce the likelihood of the risk described?

⑤ What are the trade-offs of the available options?

⑥ What is the best way to address the described risk?

⑦ Is it working? (Once implemented)

（2）Risk Assessment

Risk assessment is a systematic process for describing the nature, likelihood, and magnitude of risk associated with some substance, situation, action, or event that includes consideration of relevant uncertainties. Risk assessment can be qualitative, quantitative, or a blend (semiquantitative) of both. It can be informally described by posing and answering the following questions that build on the Kaplan and Garrick triplet (1981):

① What can go wrong?

② How can it happen?

③ What are the consequences?

④ How likely is it to happen?

（3）Risk Communication

Risk communication is the open, two-way exchange of information and opinion about risks intended to lead to a better understanding of the risks and better risk management decisions. It provides a forum for the interchange of information with all concerned about the nature of the risks, the risk assessment, and how risks should be managed. Risk communication may be informally characterized by its own set of questions:

① Why are we communicating?

② Who are our audiences?

③ What do our audiences want to know?

④ How will we communicate?

⑤ How will we listen?

⑥ How will we respond?

⑦ Who will carry out the plans? When?

⑧ What problems or barriers have we planned for?

⑨ Have we succeeded?

2. Methodology（Risk Assessment Methods）

Any self-contained systematic procedure conducted as part of a risk assessment is a risk assessment method. These methods are conveniently divided into qualitative and quantitative methods. There has been a misperception on the parts of some and a bias on the parts of others who have suggested that qualitative risk assessment is not a valid form of risk assessment. I think it fair to say that quantitative risk assessment is preferred whenever there are data adequate to support it. It is equally fair to say that qualitative risk assessment is a valid and valuable form of risk assessment. Quantitative assessments use numerical expressions to characterize the risks, qualitative assessments do not.

（1）Qualitative Risk Assessment

The fundamental need is to manage risk intentionally and to do that better than has been done in the past. Quantitative risk assessment is not always possible or necessary, so qualitative risk assessment is often a viable and valuable option. It is especially useful:

- For routine noncontroversial tasks.

- When consistency and transparency in handling risk are desired.

- When theory, data, time, or expertise are limited.

- When dealing with broadly defined problems where quantitative risk assessment is impractical.

A qualitative risk assessment process compiles, combines, and presents evidence to support a nonnumerical estimate and description of a risk. Numerical data and analysis may be part of the input to a qualitative risk assessment, but they are not part of the risk characterization output. Qualitative assessment produces a descriptive or categorical treatment of risk information. It is a formal, organized, reproducible, and flexible method based on science and sound evidence that produces consistent descriptions of risk that are easy to explain to others. Its value stems from its ability to support risk management decision making. If you can answer the risk manager's questions adequately and describe the risk in a narrative or categorically, then a qualitative assessment is sufficient. Uncertainty in qualitative assessments is generally addressed through descriptive narratives.

(2) Quantitative Risk Assessment

Quantitative risk assessment relies on numerical expressions of risk in the risk characterization. Numerical measures of risk are generally more informative than qualitative estimates. When the data and resources are sufficient, a quantitative assessment is preferred, except where the risk manager's questions can be adequately answered in a narrative or categorical fashion.

Quantitative assessments can be deterministic or probabilistic. Deterministic assessments produce point estimates of risks. Probabilistic assessments rely on probability distributions and probability statements to estimate risks. The choice depends on the risk manager's questions, available data, the nature of the uncertainties, the skills of the assessors, the effectiveness of outputs in informing and supporting decision makers, and the number and robustness of the assumptions made in the assessment.

Generally, quantitative risk characterizations address risk management questions at a finer level of detail and resolution than a qualitative risk assessment. This greater detail usually introduces a more sophisticated treatment of the uncertainty in the risk characterization than is found with qualitative assessment.

3. Model (Risk Assessment Modes)

The generic risk assessment tasks you've been reading about have been standardized for a variety of applications and Communities of Practice (CoP). The food-safety community, for example, has been aggressive in trying to harmonize risk assessment methods in part to facilitate international trade. They, like other CoPs, have promulgated models for use by their constituents. A few of these models are presented in this section to illustrate the diverse range of ways in which these rather generic risk assessment activities are being formalized for specific applications. The details of the model are less important than the overarching point that risk assessors exercise a great deal of latitude in the specific ways they do risk assessments.

The Codex Alimentarius represents the international food-safety community. They employ a familiar risk assessment model, shown in Figure 9-12. Within or alongside of this framework, CoPs have developed distinctive models and methodologies for different hazards like food-additive chemicals, pesticides, microbiological hazards, food nutrients, antimicrobial resistance, and genetically modified organisms.

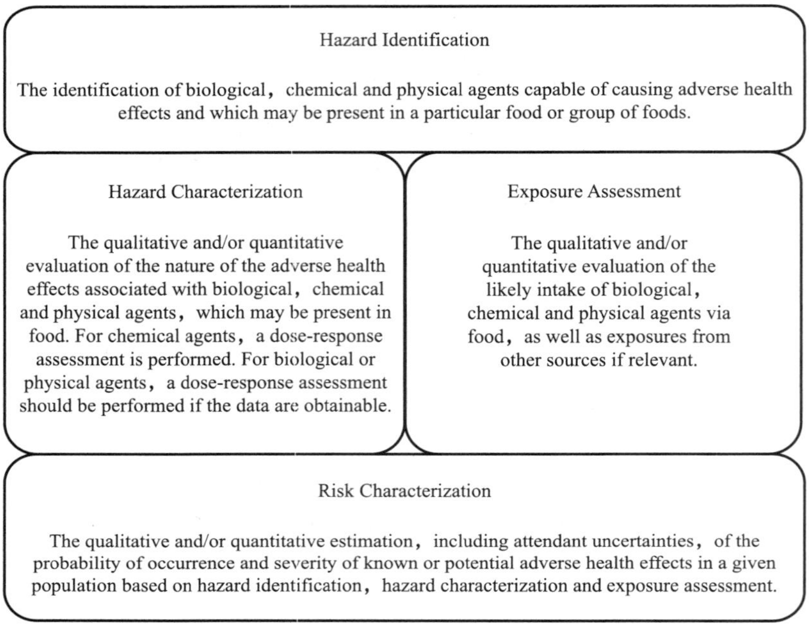

Figure 9-12   Generic Codex description of the risk assessment components

Chemical food additives are evaluated using a safety assessment, which on the surface looks quite different from the generic model of this chapter. Its six steps comprise the following: test toxicity, identify NOAEL, choose a safety factor, calculate the ADI, calculate the EDI, and characterize the risk with the ratio EDI/ADI.

A conceptual application of the model is presented in Figure 9-13. Toxicity studies, most often based on animal data, are used to identify a level of exposure to a chemical, usually measured in a lifetime dose that causes no adverse effects. This is equivalent to a hazard characterization. In the example in Figure 9-13, this level is 5 mg per kg of body weight daily for a lifetime.

To extrapolate from animal studies and their typically high doses to humans and their typically low doses, an uncertainty factor (in the example, 100) is used to identify an ADI. Thus, a NOAEL of 5 mg/kg/day/lifetime divided by 100 yields an ADI of 0.05 mg/kg/day/lifetime.

A survey of consumption behavior yields the daily consumption of the additive for a high-end consumer, say the 90th percentile consumer of this additive, and this is used as the EDI. This constitutes the exposure assessment. The risk characterization is completed by simply comparing the EDI to the ADI. There is no effort to explicitly identify the likelihood of an adverse outcome in

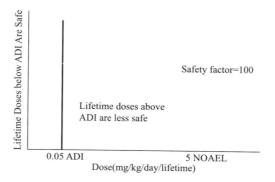

Figure 9-13   Representation of the food-additive safety assessment model

this assessment model.

Pesticide chemical risks are somewhat similar, although the language changes a little:

• Identify pesticide residue of interest.

• Undertake toxicity studies of substance if needed.

• Determine the NOAEL.

• Select a safety factor or uncertainty factor to extrapolate results from animals to humans.

• Calculate the ADI.

• Identify a suitable index of residue levels to predict residue intake—usually the Maximum Residue Limit (MRL).

• Estimate the dietary intake of the residue (exposure assessment).

• Compare exposure to ADI (when exposure exceeds ADI, some sort of risk mitigation is required).

Note that although the language differs in each, they all exhibit elements of the previously described generic process. The hazard is identified; the consequences and likelihoods (or exposures) are assessed; and it is all pulled together in some sort of characterization of the risk.

Antimicrobial-resistant risk assessment is used to evaluate the safety of new animal drugs with respect to concerns for human health. Exposing bacteria in animals to antimicrobial drugs could increase the number of resistant bacteria to the point where it reduces the efficacy of antimicrobial drugs prescribed for human health. This model, shown in Figure 9-14 and taken from FDA Guidance Document 152 (FDA, 2003), suggests a qualitative approach for identifying new drugs as potentially high, medium, or low risks for human health.

Food safety is not the only COP to have developed standardized mental models to guide thinking about risk assessment. The U.S. EPA (1998) developed the model shown in Figure 9-15 for ecological risk assessment. Note that it differs from the four-step definition of the "Red Book" but has clear roots in that model as well. The "Red Book" model was developed principally for assessing human health risks due to chemicals in the environment. The ecological model expands the notion of hazards to include a broad class of stressors and it includes adverse effects on ecosystems. It has three main steps: problem formulation, analysis, and risk characterization.

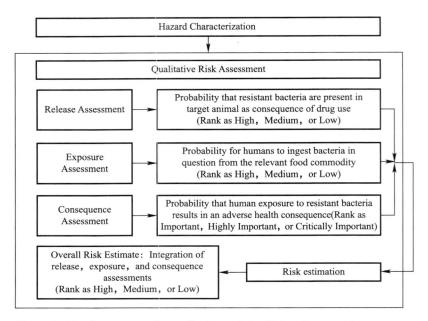

Figure 9-14   Components of a qualitative antimicrobial-resistance risk assessment

Hazards are identified as stressors in problem formulation. The analysis step is divided into characterizations of exposure and ecological effects, the latter of which is evocative of the hazard characterization step. The risk characterization step serves the familiar purpose. The point here is that although the models vary in their language and details, they remain firmly committed to the principles articulated in the tasks identified earlier in this chapter.

If you search Internet images using the phrase"risk assessment model", you'll see thousands of different models in millions of hits. Many risk assessment problems are so unique that they cannot be usefully fit to any of the existing mental models for risk assessment. It is always wise to familiarize yourself with any standardized assessment models used by your CoP. More importantly, you should always feel free to adapt these models or to develop your own mental model when it suits your decision-making needs to do so. If you flounder at times, keep coming back to the four informal questions: What can go wrong? How can it happen? What are the consequences? How likely is it? Find a way to ask and answer these questions and you will be doing risk assessment, formal model or not.

Very often an organization has a model with a well-established structure. Consider the model in Table 9-1, which is used to estimate the costs of a dredging project that includes marsh creation for disposal of the dredged material. It is not difficult to imagine that risk managers may be concerned with the risk of a cost overrun. There is no need here to develop a conceptual model. In this instance, the structure of the model is well established and we need only reach into the risk assessor's toolbox for the appropriate techniques for assessing this risk using our four informal questions. For now it is sufficient to understand that there is a large class of problems that require no specific risk assessment model. Often it is sufficient to pay appropriate attention to the uncertainty that has always been present in our work. In many instances, risk assessment can

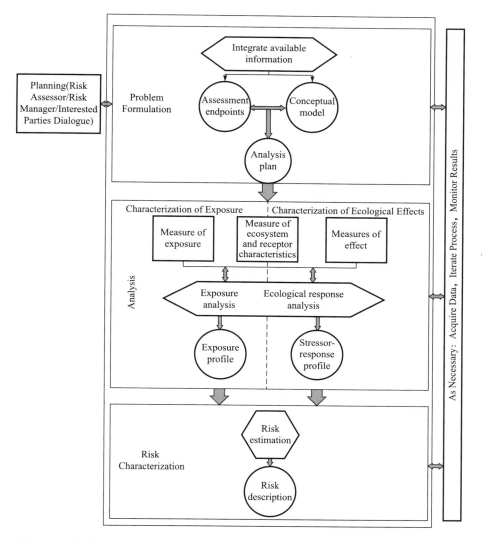

Figure 9-15   Ecological risk assessment framework, with an expanded view of each phase

mean doing what you have always done, with the exception of paying close attention to the things you do not know. Using the generic risk assessment activities described here should provide you with a serviceable model when a formal one is not available.

	Channel modification dredging cost estimate				Table 9-1
Account Code	Description	Quantity	Unit	Unit Price	Amount
01	Lands and damages	0	LS	—	—
	Relocations				
02	Lower 20 pipeline, 653+00	427	LF	$ 843,66	$ 359,979
	Remove 8″ pipeline, 678+00	986	LF	$ 47,85	$ 47,197
02	*Total-relocations*				$ 407,176

continued

Account Code	Description	Quantity	Unit	Unit Price	Amount
06	Fish and wildlife facilities (mitigation) Oyster reef creation	0	ACR	—	—
06	*Total-fish and wildlife facilities (mitigation)*				—
12	Navigation, ports, and harbors Mobe and demobe	1	LS	$ 500,000	$ 500,000
	Pipeline dredging, Reach 1	576,107,00	CY	$ 2,43	$ 1,398,788
	Pipeline dredging, Reach 2	1,161,626,68	CY	$ 2,76	$ 3,209,691
	Pipeline dredging, Reach 3A	1,532,227,12	CY	$ 3,72	$ 5,693,450
	Pipeline dredging, Reach 3B	708,252,02	CY	$ 2,89	$ 2,049,398
	Scour pad, Reach 1	16,484	SY	$ 16,62	$ 273,906
	Geotubes, 30', Reach 1	1,345	LF	$ 221,03	$ 297,192
	Geotubes, 45', Reach 1	4,601	LF	$ 291,00	$ 1,338,995
	Scour pad, Reach 3	39,059	SY	$ 16,62	$ 649,029
	Geotubes, 45', Reach 3	13,848	LF	$ 291,00	$ 4,029,879
12	*Total-navigation, ports, and barbors Sabtotal*				$ 19,440,328
30	Engineering and design	8%			$ 1,587,800
31	Construction management	6%			$ 1,190,850
	Total project cost				$ 22,626,154

Abbreviations: LF = linear feet; LS = lump sum; CY = cubic yards; SY = square yards; ACR = acres.

9.4 Reading Material

The Seven Quality Management Principles

1. QMP 1 Customer Focus

Organizations should know who their customers are and understand the current and future needs of those customers and strive to meet and exceed the customers' needs and expectations. Align organization's objectives with the needs of the customers, communicate customer needs throughout the organization, design, produce and deliver products to meet customer needs, measure and monitor customer satisfaction, and manage relationship with customers to sustain a successful relationship.

2. QMP 2 Leadership

Leaders should establish the mission, vision, and strategy to achieve them, and communicate them throughout the organization. They should create a set of guiding values of fairness, ethical behavior, trust, and integrity in the organization. They should commit themselves to quality goals and encourage such commitment organization-wide. They should make sure they provide required resources and training to the people, and allow them authority to act with accountability. They should inspire, encourage, and recognize people's contribution.

3. QMP 3 Engagement of People

People at all levels should be involved in the pursuit of the chosen quality goals so that all their abilities are fully utilized for the benefit of the organization. This needs communication to people on the importance of their individual contribution, collaborative effort among people, open discussion and sharing of knowledge, and empowering people to take initiatives without fear. Peoples' contribution should be acknowledged and rewarded. Surveys should be conducted to assess people's satisfaction and results should be shared with them and acted upon where improvements are necessary.

4. QMP 4 Process Approach

A productive organization is a collection of interrelated and interacting processes, with each process transforming some inputs into outputs through the use of some resources. Figure 9-16 has been drawn to show that an enterprise is a process made up of several sub-processes, which are interrelated. If the organization and its activities are analyzed as processes, it helps in gaining a good understanding of the individual processes and their interdependencies. This improves the chances of discovering opportunities for making improvements to the processes and making them both effective and efficient (Effectiveness refers to choosing the right objectives and achieving them fully; efficiency refers to achieving the objectives with economic use of resources).

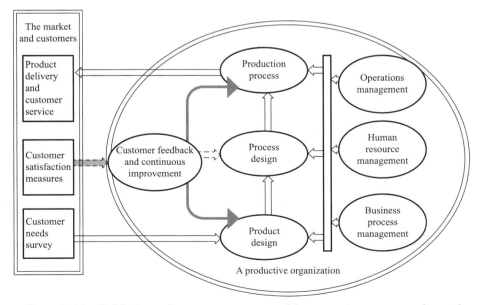

Figure 9-16   Model of a quality management system (the system is a process made up of several interconnected sub-processes)

Organizations should view their entire system as made-up processes and assign authority, responsibility, and accountability to the individual processes. They should make sure resources and capabilities are available to operate the processes, and manage the processes and their interrelationships so as to maximize organization's quality objective. They should make sure necessary information is available to operate and improve processes. They should evaluate the individual processes and the overall system and manage risks that can affect the output of processes and output of the overall system.

5. QMP 5 Improvement

Organizations should continually look for opportunities to improve their processes in order to improve customer satisfaction and efficiency of internal processes. They should establish improvement objectives and train people at all levels on how to apply basic tools and methods to achieve improvements. They should encourage and facilitate improvement projects throughout the organization; evaluate improvement projects for planning, implementation, and results; and publicize successes. They should provide suitable rewards to recognize successful projects.

6. QMP 6 Evidence-Based Decision Making

Organizations should encourage decision making based on evidence from data, or information gathered from processes, rather than on the feelings and beliefs of people. They should measure and monitor key indicators of performance of processes and the system and make the data available to relevant people. They should ensure that the data is accurate, reliable, and secure. They should make sure that the data are analyzed using proper methods by people who have the expertise in these methods, and that the results of analysis are used in making improvements—properly moderated by experience and intuition.

7. QMP 7 Relationship Management

Organizations should enter into interdependent, mutually beneficial relationships with interested parties in order to enhance the abilities and create value for all. They should first identify their interested parties—suppliers, partners, investors, customers, employees, and the society as a whole—and prioritize the relationships that need to be managed. They should share information, expertise, and resources with interested partners so as to benefit all. They should measure the performance of the entire system and provide feedback to all to enhance improvement initiatives. They should recognize and reward improvements and successes of suppliers and partners.

What follows is a summary of the 10 requirements in the ISO 9001:2015 standard. Although there are 10 "requirements" listed in the standard, the first three are simply preliminaries and definitions leaving only seven, starting from the fourth, as the requirements of the quality management system.

This summary is provided more to give the reader (a "student") a bird's-eye view of the standard's requirements than provide an exhaustive recounting of the requirements. The legalese in the standard has been paraphrased in simpler English, keeping the essence of the requirement in focus and making the text easy to follow. In this attempt, however, some of the nuances of the original standard might have been lost. Some of the language that is in the standard to make it applicable to a wide range of organizations has been mostly avoided to keep the summary simple. Where there is a term whose meaning is not readily understandable, a certain explanation is added in parentheses. Any reader will benefit from this summary as a preliminary study before studying the requirements in fuller detail in the original standard.

Again, to reinforce a point, the summary below does not constitute the requirements of the ISO 9001 International Standard; it is presented here for a student to be able to make a comparative study of various models for a quality management system presented in this chapter. The reader is advised to refer to the standard published by ISO if he or she plans to implement the standard in an organization.

Chapter 10
Software Engineering and Applications

10. 1　Software Engineering

10. 1 Professional Terms, Words and Phrases, Sentence Illustration

1. Definition

Software engineering is an engineering that is concerned with all aspects of software production from the early stages of system specification through to maintaining the system after it has gone into use.

（1）Engineering Discipline

Engineering make things work. They apply theories, methods, and tools where these are appropriate. However, they use them selectively and always try to discover solutions to problems even when there are non-applicable theories and methods. Engineering also recognize that they must work within organizational and financial constraints, and they must look for solutions within these constraints.

（2）All Aspects of Software Production

Software engineering are not just concerned with the technical processes of software development. It also includes activities such as software projects management and the development of tools, methods, and theories to support software development.

（3）Internet Software Engineering

The development of the Internet and the World Wide Web has had a profound effect on all of our lives. Initially, the web was primarily a universally accessible information store, and it had little effect on software systems. These systems ran on local computers and were only accessible from within an organization. Around 2000, the web started to evolve, and more and more functionality was added to browsers. This meant that web-based systems could be developed where, instead of a special-purpose user interface, these systems could be accessed using a web browser. This led to the development of a vast range of new system products that delivered innovative services, accessed over the web. These are often funded by adverts that are displayed on the user's screen and do not involve direct payment from users.

As well as these system products, the development of web browsers that could run small programs and do some local processing led to an evolution in business and organizational software. Instead of writing software and deploying it on users' PCs, the software was deployed on a web server. This made it much cheaper to change and upgrade the software, as there was no need to install the software on every PC. It also reduced costs, as user interface development is particularly expensive. Wherever it has been possible to do so, businesses have moved to web-based interaction with company software systems.

The notion of software as a service was proposed early in the 21 st century. This has now become the standard approach to the delivery of web-based system products such as Google Apps, Microsoft Office 365, and Adobe Creative Suite. More and more software run on remote "clouds" instead of local servers and is accessed over the Internet. A computing cloud is a huge number of linked computer systems that is shared by many users. Users do not buy software but pay according to how much the software is used or are given free access in return for watching adverts that are displayed on their screen. If you use services such as web-based mail, storage, or video, you are using a cloud-based system.

The advent of the web has led to adramatic change in the way that business software is organized. Before the web, business applications were mostly monolithic, single programs running on single computers or computer clusters. Communications were local, within an organization. Now, software is highly distributed, sometimes across the world. Business applications are not programmed from scratch but involve extensive reuse of components and programs.

This change in software organization has had a major effect on software engineering for web-based systems. For example:

① Software reuse has become the dominant approach for constructing web-based systems. When building these systems, you think about how you can assemble them from preexisting software components and systems, often bundled together in a framework.

② It is now generally recognized that it is impractical to specify all the requirements for such systems in advance. Web-based systems are always developed and delivered incrementally.

③ Software may be implemented using service-oriented software engineering, where the software components are stand-alone web services.

④ Interface development technology such as AJAX and HTML5 have emerged that support the creation of rich interfaces within a web browser.

2. Diversity of Software Engineering

Software engineering is a systematic approach to the production of software that takes into account practical cost, schedule, and dependability issues, as well as the needs of software customers and producers. The specific methods, tools, and techniques used depend on the organization developing the software, the type of software, and the people involved in the development process. There are no universal software engineering methods that are suitable for all systems and all companies. Rather, a diverse set of software engineering methods and tools has evolved over the past 50 years.

Perhaps the most significant factor in determining which software engineering methods and techniques are most important is the type of application being developed. There are many different types of application, including:

(1) Stand-Alone Applications

These are application systems that run on a personal computer or apps that run on a mobile device. They include all necessary functionality and may not need to be connected to a network.

Examples of such applications are office applications on a PC, CAD programs, photo manipulation software, travel apps, productivity apps, and so on.

(2) Interactive Transaction-Based Applications

These are applications that execute on a remote computer and that are accessed by users from their own computers, phones, or tablets. Obviously, these include web applications such as e-commerce applications where you interact with a remote system to buy goods and services. This class of application also includes business systems, where a business provides access to its systems through a web browser or special-purpose client program and cloud-based services, such as mail and photo sharing. Interactive applications often incorporate a large data store that is accessed and updated in each transaction.

(3) Embedded Control Systems

These are software control systems that control and manage hardware devices. Numerically, there are probably more embedded systems than any other type of system. Examples of embedded systems include the software in a mobile (cell) phone, software that controls antilock braking in a car, and software in a microwave oven to control the cooking process.

(4) Batch Processing Systems

These are business systems that are designed to process data in large batches. They process large numbers of individual inputs to create corresponding outputs. Examples of batch systems are periodic billing systems, such as phone billing systems, and salary payment systems.

(5) Entertainment Systems

These are systems for personal use that are intended to entertain the user. Most of these systems are games of one kind or another, which may run on special-purpose console hardware. The quality of the user interaction offered is the most important distinguishing characteristic of entertainment systems.

(6) Systems for Modeling and Simulation

These are systems that are developed by scientists and engineers to model physical processes or situations, which include many separate, interacting objects. These are often computationally intensive and require high-performance parallel systems for execution.

(7) Data Collection and Analysis Systems

Data collection systems are systems that collect data from their environment and send that data to other systems for processing. The software may have to interact with sensors and often is installed in a hostile environment such as inside an engine or in a remote location. "Big data" analysis may involve cloud-based systems carrying out statistical analysis and looking for relationships in the collected data.

(8) Systems of Systems

These are systems, used in enterprises and other large organizations, that are composed of a number of other software systems. Some of these may be generic software products, such as an ERP system. Other systems in the assembly may be specially written for that environment.

3. The Software Process and Software Development Life Cycle

A process is a collection of activities, actions, and tasks that are performed when some work product is to be created. An activity strives to achieve a broad objective (e. g. , communication with stakeholders) and is applied regardless of the application domain, size of the project, complexity of the effort, or degree of rigor with which software engineering is to be applied.

In the context of software engineering, a process is not a rigid prescription for how to build computer software. Rather, it is an adaptable approach that enables the people doing the work (the software team) to pick and choose the appropriate set of work actions and tasks. The intent is always to deliver software in a timely manner and with sufficient quality to satisfy those who have sponsored its creation and those who will use it.

A process framework establishes the foundation for a complete software engineering process by identifying a small number of framework activities that are applicable to all software projects, regardless of their size or complexity. In addition, the process framework encompasses a set of umbrella activities that are applicable across the entire software process. A generic process framework for software engineering encompasses five activities:

(1) Communication

Before any technical work can commence, it is critically important to communicate and collaborate with the customer (and other stakeholders). The intent is to understand stakeholders' objectives for the project and to gather requirements that help define software features and functions.

(2) Planning

Any complicated journey can be simplified if a map exists. A software project is a complicated journey, and the planning activity creates a "map" that helps guide the team as it makes the journey. The map—called a software project plan—defines the software engineering work by describing the technical tasks to be conducted, the risks that are likely, the resources that will be required, the work products to be produced, and a work schedule.

(3) Modeling

Whether you're a landscaper, a bridge builder, an aeronautical engineer, a carpenter, or an architect, you work with models every day. You create a "sketch" of the thing so that you'll understand the big picture—what it will look like architecturally, how the constituent parts fit together, and many other characteristics. If required, you refine the sketch into greater and greater detail in an effort to better understand the problem and how you're going to solve it. A software engineer does the same thing by creating models to better understand software requirements and the design that will achieve those requirements.

(4) Construction

What you design must be built. This activity combines code generation (either manual or automated) and the testing that is required to uncover errors in the code.

(5) Deployment

The software (as a complete entity or as a partially completed increment) is delivered to the

259

customer who evaluates the delivered product and provides feedback based on the evaluation.

These five generic framework activities can be used during the development of small, simple programs; the creation of Web applications; and for the engineering of large, complex computer-based systems. The details of the software process will be quite different in each case, but the framework activities remain the same.

Software Development Life Cycle, SDLC for short, is a well-defined, structured sequence of stages in software engineering to develop the intended software product. It is a team of engineers must incorporate a development strategy that encompasses the process, method and tools layers. Each phase has various activities to develop the software product. It also specifies the order in which each phase must be executed. A software life cycle model is either a descriptive or prescriptive characterization of how software is or should be developed. A descriptive model describes the history of how a particular software system was developed. The software development paradigm helps developer to select a strategy to develop the software. A software development paradigm has its own set of tools, methods and procedures, which are expressed clearly and defines software development life cycle.

The SDLC aims to produce a high-quality software that meets or exceeds customer expectations, reaches completion within times and cost estimates. SDLC is a process followed for a software project, within a software organization. It consists of a detailed plan describing how to develop, maintain, replace and alter or enhance specific software. The life cycle defines a methodology for improving the quality of software and the overall development process.

4. Methodology

(1) Model-Driven Software Development

Software engineers grapple with abstraction at virtually every step in the software engineering process. As design commences, architectural and component-level abstractions are represented and assessed. They must then be translated into a programming language representation that transforms the design (a relatively high level of abstraction) into an operable system with a specific computing environment (a low level of abstraction). Model-driven software development couples domain-specific modeling languages with transformation engines and generators in a way that facilitates the representation of abstraction at high levels and then transforms it into lower level. Model-driven approaches address a continuing challenge for all software developers—how to represent software at a higher level of abstraction than code. Domain-specific modeling languages (DSMLs) represent "application structure, behavior and requirements within particular application domains" and are described with meta-models that "define the relationships among concepts in the domain and precisely specify the key semantics and constraints associated with these domain concepts". The key difference between a DSML and a general-purpose modeling language such as UML is that the DSML is tuned to design concepts inherent in the application domain and can therefore represent relationships and constraints among design elements in an efficient manner.

（2）Search-Based Software Engineering

Many activities in software engineering can be stated as optimization problems. Search-Based Software Engineering (SBSE) applies meta-heuristic search techniques such as genetic algorithms to software engineering problems. Lionel Briand believes that evolutionary and other search techniques are more easily scaled to industrial-size problems than model-driven techniques and that there are opportunities for synergy between the two. Search-based software engineering was devised on the premise that it is often easier to check that a candidate solution solves a problem than it is to construct a solution from scratch.

Search-based software engineering techniques can be used as the basis for genetic improvement to grow software products by grafting on new functional and nonfunctional features to existing software product line. Genetic improvement of software has already resulted in dramatic performance improvements (e. g. , execution time, energy usage, and memory consumption) in existing software products. Successful software products evolve continually; however, evolution, if not properly managed, may weaken the software quality and may need to be refactored to remain viable.

（3）Test-Driven Development

In Test-Driven Development (TDD), requirements for a software component serve as the basis for the creation of a series of test cases that exercise the interface and attempt to find errors in the data structures and functionality delivered by the component. TDD is not really a new technology but rather a trend that emphasizes the design of test cases before the creation of source code.

Before the first small segment of code is created, a software engineer creates a test to exercise the code (to try to make the code fail). The code is then written to satisfy the test. If it passes, a new test is created for the next segment of code to be developed. The process continues until the component is fully coded and all tests execute without error. However, if any test succeeds in finding an error, the existing code is refactored (corrected) and all tests created to that point are executed again. This iterative flow continues until there are no tests left to be created, implying that the component meets all requirements defined for it.

During TDD, code is developed in very smallincrements (one sub-function at a time), and no code is written until a test exists to exercise it. You should note that each iteration results in one or more new tests that are added to a regression test suite that is run with every change. This is done to ensure that the new code has not generated side effects that cause errors in the older code.

5. Software Process Model

（1）The Waterfall Model

The first published model of the software development process wasderived from engineering process models used in large military systems engineering. It presents the software development process as a number of stages. Because of the cascade from one phase to another, this model is known as the waterfall model or software life cycle. The waterfall model is an example of a plan-driven process. In principle at least, you plan and schedule all of the process activities before starting software development. The stages of the waterfall model directly reflect the fundamental software development activities:

① Requirements Analysis and Definition

The system's services, constraints, and goals are established by consultation with system users. They are then defined in detail and serve as a system specification.

② System and Software Design

The systems design process allocates the requirements to either hardware or software systems. It establishes an overall system architecture. Software design involves identifying and describing the fundamental software system abstractions and their relationships.

③ Implementation and Unit Testing

During this stage, the software design is realized as a set of programs or program units. Unit testing involves verifying that each unit meets its specification.

④ Integration and System Testing

The individual program units or programs are integrated and tested as a complete system to ensure that the software requirements have been met. After testing, the software system is delivered to the customer.

⑤ Operation and Maintenance

Normally, this is the longest life-cycle phase. The system is installed and put into practical use. Maintenance involves correcting errors that were not discovered in earlier stages of the life cycle, improving the implementation of system units, and enhancing the system's services as new requirements are discovered.

(2) The Prototype Model

A prototype is an early version of a software system that is used to demonstrate concepts, try out design options, and find out more about the problem and its possible solutions. Rapid, iterative development of the prototype is essential so that costs are controlled and system stakeholders can experiment with the prototype early in the software process.

System prototypes allow potential users to see how well the system supports their work. They may get new ideas for requirements and find areas of strength and weakness in the software. They may then propose new system requirements. Furthermore, as the prototype is developed, it may reveal errors and omissions in the system requirements. A feature described in a specification may seem to be clear and useful. However, when that function is combined with other functions, users often find that their initial view was incorrect or incomplete. The system specification can then be modified to reflect the changed understanding of the requirements.

Both stakeholders and software engineers like the prototyping paradigm. Users get a feel for the actual system, and developers get to build something immediately. Yet, prototyping can be problematic for the following reasons:

① Stakeholders see what appears to be a working version of the software. They may be unaware that the prototype architecture (program structure) is also evolving. This means that the developers may not have considered the overall software quality or long-term maintainability.

② As a software engineer, you may be tempted to make implementation compromises to get a prototype working quickly. If you are not careful, these less-than-ideal choices have now become an integral part of the evolving system.

Although problems can occur, prototyping can be an effective paradigm for software engineering. The key is to define the rules of the game at the beginning; that is, all stakeholders should agree that the prototype is built in part to serve as a mechanism for defining requirements. It is often desirable to design a prototype so it can be evolved into the final product. The reality is developers may need to discard (at least in part) a prototype to better meet the customer's evolving needs.

(3) The Spiral Model (Evolutionary Process Model)

The spiral model, originally proposed by Boehm, is an evolutionary software process model that couples the iterative nature of prototyping with the controlled and systematic aspects of the linear sequential model. It provides the potential for rapid development of incremental versions of the software. Using the spiral model, software is developed in a series of incremental releases. During early iterations, the incremental release might be a paper model or prototype. During later iterations, increasingly more complete versions of the engineered system are produced.

A spiral model is divided into a number of framework activities, also called task regions. Project entry point axis is defined this axis represents starting point for different types of projects. Every framework activities represent one section of the spiral path. As the development process starts, the software team perform activities that are indirect by a path around the spiral model in a clockwise direction. It begins at the center of spiral model. Typically, there are between three and six task regions. In blow figure depicts a spiral model that contains six task regions:

• Customer communication: tasks required to establish effective communication between developer and customer.

• Planning: tasks required to define resources, time lines, and other project related information.

• Risk analysis: tasks required to assess both technical and management risks.

• Engineering: tasks required to build one or more representations of the application.

• Construction and release: tasks required to construct, test, install, and provide user support (e. g. , documentation and training).

• Customer evaluation: tasks required to obtain customer feedback based on evaluation of the software representations created during the engineering stage and implemented during the installation stage.

Advantages of Spiral model:

• High amount of risk analysis hence, avoidance of risk is enhanced.

• Good for large and mission-critical projects.

• Strong approval and documentation control.

• Additional Functionality can be added at a later date.

- Software is produced early in the software life cycle.

Disadvantages of Spiral model:

- Can be a costly model to use.
- Risk analysis requires highly specific expertise.
- Project's success is highly dependent on the risk analysis phase.
- Doesn't work well for smaller projects.

When to use Spiral model:

- When costs and risk evaluation is important.
- For medium to high-risk projects.
- Long-term project commitment unwise because of potential changes to economic priorities.
- Users are unsure of their needs.
- Requirements are complex.
- New product line.
- Significant changes are expected (research and exploration).

(4) The Fountain Model

The fountain model is primarily used to describe the object-oriented development process, and the term "fountain" captures the iterative and gapless nature of the object-oriented development process. Iteration means that the development activities in the model often need to be repeated several times, each time adding or clarifying some properties of the target system, but not essentially changing the results of previous work. Gapless means that there are no distinct boundaries between development activities (e. g. , analysis, design, programming), but rather allow the various development activities to proceed in an intersecting, iterative fashion.

Advantages of Fountain Model:

- Seamless and can be synchronizable developed.
- Improve development efficiency and save development time.
- Suitable for object-oriented software development.

Disadvantages of Fountain Model:

Various information, requirements and materials may be added at any time during the software development process, requiring strict management of the documentation, which causes a gradual increase in the difficulty of auditing.

(5) Component Assembly Model

The problem is a Software Development Life Cycle (SDLC) plan called Component Assembly Model. Instead of starting over with different codes and languages, developers who use this model tap on the available components and put them together to build a program. Component Assembly Model is an iterative development model. It works like the Prototype model, constantly creating a prototype until software that will cater the need of businesses and consumers is realized.

Component Assembly Model has a close resemblance with the Rapid Application Development (RAD) model. This SDLC model uses the available tools and GUIs to build software. With the number of SDKs released today, developers will find it easier to build programs using lesser codes with the help of SDK. Since it has enough time to concentrate on other parts of the programs aside from coding language; RAD concentrates or user inputs and graphical interaction of the user and program.

Component Assembly Model on the other hand uses a lot of previously made components. CAM doesn't need to use SDKs to develop programs but it will be putting together powerful components. All the developers have to do is to know what the customer wants, look for the components to answer the need and put together the components to create the program.

Component Assembly Model is just like the Prototype model, in which first a prototype is reacted according to the requirements of the customer. Thus, this is one of the most beneficial advantages of component assembly model as it saves lots of time during the software development program.

Component Assembly Model has been developed to answer the problems faced during the Software Development Life Cycle (SDLC). Instead of searching for different codes and languages, the developers using this model opt for the available components and use them to make an efficient program. Component Assembly Model is an iterative development model that works like the Prototype model and keeps developing a prototype on the basis of the user feedback until the prototype resembles the specifications provided by the customer and the business.

(6) Unified Process Model

In some ways the Unified Process (UP) is an attempt to draw on the best features and characteristics of traditional software process models but characterize them in a way that implements many of the best principles of agile software development. The Unified Process recognizes the importance of customer communication and streamlined methods for describing the customer's view of a system (the use case). It emphasizes the important role of software architecture and "helps the architect focus on the right goals, such as understandability, reliance to future changes, and reuse". It suggests a process flow that is iterative and incremental, providing the evolutionary feel that is essential in modern software development.

UML, the unified modeling language, was developed to support their work. UML contains a robust notation for the modeling and development of object-oriented systems and has became a de-facto industry standard for modeling software of all types.

10.2   Requirement Analysis

1. Introduction

Requirements analysis, or deciding what information you as a user need from a computer-based information system, is one of the most important aspects of choosing and implementing a Management Information System (MIS). Yet it is also one of the most difficult. Conventional design methods say very little about it

10.2 Professional Terms, Words and Phrases, Sentence Illustration

and seem to assume that information needs are easy to identify and will emerge spontaneously once the manager recognizes that he or she has a problem. These' hit or miss' approaches are causing users to spend large sums of money on information systems that provide a poor fit. They have little relevance to real needs and may soon fall into disuse.

Managers need to undertake a requirements analysis for a number of different reasons. Their company may be carrying out a comprehensive review of its information needs prior to introducing a portfolio of new MIS applications. In this case the requirements analysis procedure will be complex and time consuming. They may be developing a system which incorporates a number of shared databases. This too can be complex and account will now have to betaken of a variety of different user needs.

Or they may be focusing on the easier problem of designing and introducing a single application such as an MIS for the chief administrator. Even this simpler task will have its own complications. Any new system must fit with the needs of the organization using it. It must provide the information that is required without forcing new, unfamiliar and unwanted modes of working on users. It must be simple to learn and easy to use and it must work well technically.

It can be seen that for all of these applications, requirements analysis is not an easy process. The things that contribute most to its difficulty are the following. First, the size and complexity of the new system. Large integrated systems and shared databases will be far more difficult to handle than the single application because of the numbers of users and organizational units involved. Second, the ability of users to specify their information requirements. Some users when asked "What information do you need?" will describe only the information they required to address their most recent problems. Others will go to the other extreme and ask for every item of information they have needed in the last twelve months.

Skill in providing a set of information requirements that can guide the development or choice of software will depend on a number of things. These include the user's experience with a similar system, their knowledge of the business area where the system is to be located, and most importantly, their ability to think analytically.

While much is required of users if information requirements are to be identified and prioritized, a parallel range of skills is required in the systems analysts. They must be able to elicit information from the user, evaluate the importance of this, and create an information system that improves greatly on the existing system.

Many of the problems impeding effective requirements analysis are difficult to handle because they are related to our psychological make-up. For example, unless we are very old we tend to have short-term memories. We remember recent events but forget the past. We are also poor at selecting and prioritizing. We think of what we might want, not what we do want. Our selection of information needs is also greatly influenced by our training, prejudices and attitudes. For example, in a nuclear plant managers with degrees in physics tended to look at problems from a physics viewpoint and wanted information related to their discipline. Chemists, although they were addressing the same problems, wanted information related to chemistry.

Again, most senior staff are doers rather than thinkers and when asked to spend time reviewing their information needs they are not always very receptive. A final problem is the "forgotten" user. The person who has a considerable interest in the proposed information system but nobody thinks to ask what his or her needs are.

Turning from difficulties to opportunities, an interest in carrying out effective requirements analysis can be stimulated if individuals are helped to understand how information technology can benefit their work and the work of the company as a whole. This understanding can often be realized through creative discussion in which groups of users take part. These groups should contain representatives of all the different users of the new system. Knowledge of this kind is not readily achieved through the traditional approach of systems analysts interviewing individual members of staff.

Good requirements analysis can be greatly helped by methods which assist the user to think systematically and analytically about his or her information needs. Methods of this kind help users to structure information needs, to assist an efficient search process to ensure that all relevant needs are known, and to provide an understanding of the needs of other users. They also help to create an information model which the group can accept as a reasonably accurate picture of priority information needs.

Over the years a variety of approaches have been used to assist the identification of information needs. Most prevalent has been the traditional systems analyst technique of individual interviewing. Unfortunately, this approach has many of the problems discussed earlier and has been proved not to work well. It also has the major disadvantage of leaving the systems analysts with the task of integrating a number of different sets of needs. An alternative approach is "brainstorming", in which people are brought together and encouraged to discuss with few restrictions on the nature of their contributions. Guided brainstorming is similar, but places some boundaries around the discussion and directs attention to certain issues. Lastly, there are group methods, such as QUICKethics, the one described in this book, in which a theoretical model of the individual's job and of the organization's mission is used to guide and structure the discussion. QUICKethics uses a cybernetic model developed by Professor Stafford Beer for this purpose.

Requirements analysis, like many aspects of systems design, implementation and use, is, and has to be, a social process. Group discussion enables old ideas to be questioned and new ideas to be developed. It enables users to understand better the roles, responsibilities, problems and information needs of their colleagues. The design of a new information system then becomes a participative process that reinforces positive norms and attitudes, as well as producing a core information system that all involved are happy to accept.

2. Requirement Modeling Principles

Over the past four decades, several requirements modeling methods have been developed. Investigators have identified requirements analysis problems and their causes and have developed a variety of modeling notations and corresponding sets of heuristics to overcome them. Each analysis method has a unique point of view. A set of operational principles relates analysis methods:

Principle 1. The information domain of a problem must be represented and understood. The information domain encompasses the data that flow into the system (from end users, other systems, or external devices), the data that flow out of the system (via the user interface, network interfaces, reports, graphics, and other means), and the data stores that collect and organize the data that are maintained permanently.

Principle 2. The functions that the software performs must be defined. Software functions provide direct benefit to end users and those that provide internal support for those features that are user visible. Some functions transform data that flow into the system. In other cases, functions effect some level of control over internal software processing or external system elements.

Principle 3. The behavior of the software (as a consequence of external events) must be represented. The behavior of computer software is driven by its interaction with the external environment. Input provided by end users, control data provided by an external system, or monitoring data collected over a network all cause the software to behave in a specific way.

Principle 4. The models that depict information, function, and behavior must be partitioned in a manner that uncovers detail in a layered (or hierarchical) fashion. Requirements modeling is the first step in software engineering problem solving. It allows you to better understand the problem and establishes a basis for the solution (design). Complex problems are difficult to solve in their entirety. For this reason, you should use a divide-and-conquer strategy. A large, complex problem is divided into subproblems until each subproblem is relatively easy to understand. This concept is called partitioning or separation of concerns, and it is a key strategy in requirements modeling.

Principle 5. The analysis task should move from essential information toward implementation detail. Analysis modeling begins by describing the problem from the end-user's perspective. The "essence" of the problem is described without any consideration of how a solution will be implemented. For example, a video game requires that the player "instruct" its protagonist on what direction to proceed as she moves into a dangerous maze. That is the essence of the problem. Implementation detail (normally described as part of the design model) indicates how the essence will be implemented. For the video game, voice input might be used. Alternatively, a keyboard command might be typed, a game pad joystick (or mouse) might be pointed in a specific direction, a motion-sensitive device might be waved in the air, or a device that reads the player's body or eye movements directly can be used.

The requirements engineering phase is the first major step towards the solution of a data processing problem. During this phase, the user's requirements with respect to the future system are carefully identified and documented. These requirements concern both the functions to be provided and a number of additional requirements, such as those regarding performance, reliability, user documentation, user training, cost, and so on. During the requirements engineering phase we do not yet address the question of how to achieve these user requirements in terms of system components and their interaction. This is postponed until the design phase.

3. Methodology

(1) Requirement Engineering

Requirements engineering is a broad domain that focuses on being the connector between modeling, analysis, design, and construction. It is the process that defines, identifies, manages, and develops requirements in a software engineering design process. This process uses tools, methods, and principles to describe the system's behavior and the constraints that come along with it. Requirements engineering is the most important part every business must follow, in order to build and release a project successfully, as it is the foundation to key planning and implementation.

(2) Requirements Engineering Tasks

The software requirements engineering process includes the following steps of activities:

Inception: This is the first phase of the requirements analysis process. This phase gives an outline of how to get started on a project. In the inception phase, all the basic questions are asked on how to go about a task or the steps required to accomplish a task. A basic understanding of the problem is gained and the nature of the solution is addressed. Effective communication is very important in this stage, as this phase is the foundation as to what has to be done further. Overall in the inception phase, the following criteria have to be addressed by the software engineers:

- Understanding of the problem.
- The people who want a solution.
- Nature of the solution.

Communication and collaboration between the customer and developer.

Elicitation: This is the second phase of the requirements analysis process. This phase focuses on gathering the requirements from the stakeholders. One should be careful in this phase, as the requirements are what establishes the key purpose of a project. Understanding the kind of requirements needed from the customer is very crucial for a developer. In this process, mistakes can happen in regard to, not implementing the right requirements or forgetting a part. The right people must be involved in this phase. The following problems can occur in the elicitation phase:

- Problem of Scope: The requirements given are of unnecessary detail, ill-defined, or not possible to implement.

- Problem of Understanding: Not having a clear-cut understanding between the developer and customer when putting out the requirements needed. Sometimes the customer might not know what they want or the developer might misunderstand one requirement for another.

- Problem of Volatility: Requirements changing over time can cause difficulty in leading a project. It can lead to loss and wastage of resources and time.

Elaboration: This is the third phase of the requirements analysis process. This phase is the result of the inception and elicitation phase. In the elaboration process, it takes the requirements that have been stated and gathered in the first two phases and refines them. Expansion and looking into it further are done as well. The main task in this phase is to indulge in modeling activities and develop a prototype that elaborates on the features and constraints using the necessary tools and functions.

Negotiation: This is the fourth phase of the requirements analysis process. This phase emphasizes discussion and exchanging conversation on what is needed and what is to be eliminated. In the negotiation phase, negotiation is between the developer and the customer and they dwell on how to go about the project with limited business resources. Customers are asked to prioritize the requirements and make guesstimates on the conflicts that may arise along with it. Risks of all the requirements are taken into consideration and negotiated in a way where the customer and developer are both satisfied with reference to the further implementation. The following are discussed in the negotiation phase:

- Availability of resources.
- Delivery time.
- Scope of requirements.
- Project cost.
- Estimations on development.

Specification: This is the fifth phase of the requirements analysis process. This phase specifies the following:

- Written document.
- A set of models.
- A collection of use cases.
- A prototype.

In the specification phase, the requirements engineer gathers all the requirements and develops a working model. This final working product will be the basis of any functions, features or constraints to be observed. The models used in this phase include ER (Entity Relationship) diagrams, DFD (Data Flow Diagram), FDD (Function Decomposition Diagrams), and Data Dictionaries.

Validation: This is the sixth phase of the requirements analysis process. This phase focuses on checking for errors and debugging. In the validation phase, the developer scans the specification document and checks for the following:

- All the requirements have been stated and met correctly.
- Errors have been debugged and corrected.
- Work product is built according to the standards.

This requirements validation mechanism is known as the formal technical review. The review team that works together and validates the requirements include software engineers, customers, users, and other stakeholders. Everyone in this team takes part in checking the specification by examining for any errors, missing information, or anything that has to be added or checking for any unrealistic and problematic errors.

Requirements Management: This is the last phase of the requirements analysis process. Requirements management is a set of activities where the entire team takes part in identifying, controlling, tracking, and establishing the requirements for the successful and smooth implementation of the project.

In this phase, the team is responsible for managing any changes that may occur during the project. New requirements emerge, and it is in this phase, responsibility should be taken to manage and prioritize as to where its position is in the project and how this new change will affect the overall system, and how to address and deal with the change. Based on this phase, the working model will be analyzed carefully and ready to be delivered to the customer.

(3) Activities Involved in Software Requirement Analysis

Software requirements means requirement that is needed by software to increase quality of software product. These requirements are generally a type of expectation of user from software product that is important and need to be fulfilled by software. Analysis means to examine something in an organized and specific manner to know complete details about it.

Therefore, Software requirement analysis simply means complete study, analyzing, describing software requirements so that requirements that are genuine and needed can be fulfilled to solve problem. There are several activities involved in analyzing software requirements. Some of them are given below:

- Problem recognition.
- Evaluation and synthesis.
- Modeling.
- Specification.
- Review.

4. Models

The requirements modeling action results in one or more of the following types of models:

- Scenario-based models of requirements from the point of view of various system "actors".
- Class-oriented models that represent object-oriented classes (attributes and operations) and how classes collaborate to achieve system requirements.
- Behavioral models that depict how the software reacts to internal or external "events".
- Data models that depict the information domain for the problem.
- Flow-oriented models that represent the functional elements of the system and how they transform data as they move through the system.

These models provide a software designer with information that can be translated to architectural-level, interface-level, and component-level designs. Finally, the requirements model (and the software requirements specification) provides the developer and the customer with the means to assess quality once software is built.

10. 3 Internet Application and Internet of Things

1. Definition

The Internet of Things (IoT) encapsulates a vision of a world in which billions of objects with embedded intelligence, communication means, and sensing and actuation capabilities will connect over IP (Internet Protocol) networks. With the rapid development of Internet of Things (IoT), it has now become a buzzword

10. 3 Professional Terms, Words and Phrases, Sentence Illustration

for everyone who works in this area of research. Further, it is seen that with the rapid development of sensors and devices with their connection to IoT become a treasure trove for big data analytics.

It has found numerous applications in developing smart cities where predictions of accidents and traffic flow in the cities can be effectively monitored; smart health care where the doctor is able to get useful information from the implant sensor chip in the patient's body; industrial production can also be enhanced manifolds by efficient prediction of the working of machinery and smart metering in helping the electric distribution company to understand the individual household energy expenses and making smart homes with connected appliances to name a few. The 21st century is for IoT, where it is viewed as a network of physical devices coming together from electronics, sensors, and software. It is envisioned that the network of approximately 27 billion of physical devices on IoT are presently available and the list grows. These devices can be uniquely identifiable through embedded computing system and can be connected from anywhere through suitable information and communication technology, to achieve greater service and value. The "THING" in IoT means everything and anything around us that includes machines, buildings, devices, animals, human beings, etc. Today's smart health care, smart homes, smart traffic, and smart household devices use this technology for a better digital world.

2. IoT Challenges and Capabilities

As IoT is gaining everybody's attention, there is an emergent need to understand the role of AI methods to gain insights into the market scenario and the readiness of the competitors to address the situation by then. In an article published by Harvard Business Review, it has been well said that IoT should be capable of addressing the following four basic issues such as monitoring, control, optimization, and autonomy for making it more sensible for the use of the customer in a smart connected environment. While monitoring is needed for the effective operation of sensor nodes in the working environment with utmost control, optimization is needed for improving the performance based on the feedback received from first two steps. Finally, autonomy makes the IoT work independently with self-diagnosis and repair.

3. IoT-Enabled Applications

(1) Home and Building Automation

As the smart home market has seen growing investment and has continued to mature, ever more home automation applications have appeared, each designed for a specific audience. The result has been the creation of several disconnected vertical market segments. Typical examples of increasingly mainstream applications are related to home security and energy efficiency and energy saving. Pushed by the innovations in light and room control, the IoT will foster the development of endless applications for home automation. In general, building automation solutions are starting to converge and are also moving, from the current applications in luxury, security and comfort, to a wider range of applications and connected solutions; this will create market opportunities. While today's smart home solutions are fragmented, the IoT is expected to lead to a new level of interoperability between commercial home and building automation solutions.

(2) Smart Cities

Cities are complex ecosystems, where quality of life is an important concern. In such urban environments, people, companies and public authorities experience specific needs and demands in domains such as healthcare, media, energy and the environment, safety, and public services. A city is perceived more and more as being like a single "organism", which needs to be efficiently monitored to provide citizens with accurate information. IoT technologies are fundamental to collecting data on the city status and disseminating them to citizens. In this context, cities and urban areas represent a critical mass when it comes to shaping the demand for advanced IoT-based services.

（3）Smart Grids

A smart grid is an electrical grid that includes a variety of operational systems, including smart meters, smart appliances, renewable energy resources, and energy-efficient resources. Power Line Communications (PLC) relate to the use of existing electrical cables to transport data and have been investigated for a long time. Power utilities have been using this technology for many years to send or receive (limited amounts of) data on the existing power grid.

（4）Industrial IoT

The Industrial Internet of Things (IIoT) describes the IoT as used in industries such as manufacturing, logistics, oil and gas, transportation, energy/utilities, mining and metals, aviation and others. These industries represent the majority of gross domestic product among the G20 nations.

（5）Smart Farming

Modern agriculture is facing tremendous challenges as it attempts to build a sustainable future across different regions of the globe. Examples of such challenges include population increase, urbanization, an increasingly degraded environment, an increasing trend towards consumption of animal proteins, changes in food preferences as a result of aging populations and migration, and of course climate change. A modern agriculture needs to be developed, characterized by the adoption of production processes, technologies and tools derived from scientific advances, and results from research and development activities.

Precision farming or smart agriculture is an area with the greatest opportunities for digital development but with the lowest penetration, to date, of digitized solutions. The farming industry will become arguably more important than ever before in the next few decades. It could derive huge benefits from the use of environmental and terrestrial sensors, applications for monitoring the weather, automation for more precise application of fertilizers and pesticides (thus reducing waste of natural resources), and the adoption of planning strategies for maintenance.

4. Methodologies

Derived from real-world IoT projects, the Ignite | IoT Methodology (Slama et al. , 2016) is aimed at various IoT stakeholders, including product managers, project managers, and solution architects. The methodology has two major groups of activities: IoT Strategy Execution and IoT Solution Delivery. IoT Strategy Execution aims to define an IoT strategy and a project portfolio supporting this strategy. IoT Solution Delivery supports IoT solution design and IoT project management, along with some artifacts, such as project templates, checklists, and solution architecture blueprints. These two groups of activities should be synchronized to keep the project portfolio in line with the strategy and revise the strategy according to the outcomes of the project portfolio. Figure 10-1 illustrates the process flow of Ignite.

IoT Strategy Execution is about business perspective and involves identifying an opportunity, developing a business model, and making decisions on how to manage these opportunities (such as internal project, external acquisition, and spin-off).

IoT Solution Delivery is about delivering a solution, which is conceptually defined during the IoT Strategy Execution phase, and has a life cycle consisting of the planning, building, and running of the system. Planning starts with project initiation, in which an initial solution design and a project organization chart are delivered. Moreover, stakeholder, environment, requirements, risk, and resource analysis should be conducted. After the initiation, the tasks are managed under seven work streams: (1) project management, (2) crosscutting tasks, (3) solution infrastructure and operations, (4) back-end services, (5) communication services, (6) on-asset components, and (7) asset preparation. Project management encompasses the activities for initiating, planning, executing, monitoring, controlling, and closing a project. Crosscutting tasks address the dependencies among subsequent work streams, such as security and testing. Solution infrastructure and operations include the installation and management of hardware and software infrastructure, on which an IoT system will be developed and operated. Back-end services refer to the IoT services typically hosted on a private or public cloud and interacting with IoT devices. Communication services encompass the installation and management of communication infrastructure. On-asset components refer to the development or procurement of software and the manufacturing or procurement of hardware and network components to be integrated with a thing in an IoT system. Asset preparation addresses the manufacturing and procurement of a thing in an IoT system.

5. Fog Deployment Models

Based on the ownership of Fog computing infrastructure and underlying resources, Fog models can be described as:

Private Fog: Created, owned, managed, and operated by a private organization and/or third party. The Fog resources are exclusively deployed within the premises of that organization to be used by the different business units in that organization.

Public Fog: Created, owned, managed, and operated by a government organization and/or academic institutes to be used by the general public.

Community Fog: Created, managed, and operated by community organizations and/or third party and resources are exclusively deployed to be used by the members of specific communities having shared concerns.

Hybrid Fog: Combines the use of private/public/community fog with public/private clouds. Hybrid Fog scales the resources (computing, storage) of Fog platforms and is suitable for real-life use cases, which demand resources other than those available in Fog infrastructure.

Similar to cloud computing, Fog computing provides virtualized resources to its users in three ways, i. e. :

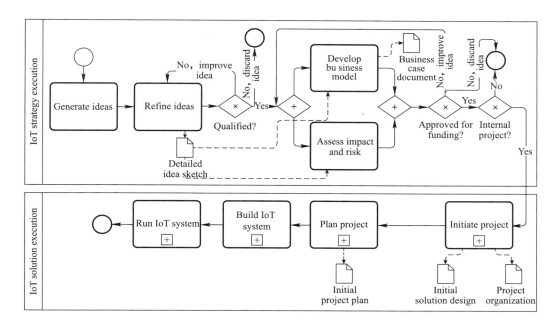

Figure 10-1　Ignite process flow

FogIaaS (Fog-infrastructure-as-a-service) offers hardware (i. e. computing, storage, communication, etc.) resources without revealing the details of physical hardware. End users are able to deploy utilities on the available pool of virtualized resources.

FogPaaS (Fog-platform-as-a-service) built on the top of FogIaaS and offers operating software and/or development environment. It provides a quick and cost-effective solution for software development, testing, and deployment.

FogSaaS (Fog-software-as-a-service) offers software applications without installing them on their personal computer. The services are accessed from the web browser remotely through a network.

10. 4　Application of Digital Twin in Manufacturing and Construction

1. Definition of Digital Twin

The term "digital twin" refers to a digital replica of a physical entity—a product, a service, a process, or even a living being—which is continuously informed by live data collected from sensors within the real structure it replicates, thus pairing the virtual and physical worlds with the two-way dynamic mapping between the physical object and its digital model.

10. 4 Professional Terms, Words and Phrases, Sentence Illustration

The "twin" concept itself can be traced back to NASA in the 1960s during the first trips to the moon, when NASA built exact replicas of everything that was launched into space. During production, these replicas were prototypes of the actual objects, and after the objects were on their way to remote destinations, they became a living, analog twin of the equipment in use: all modifications made by the astronauts on their way into space were also made to the twin. For instance, during the ill-fated Apollo 13 mission where there was a serious malfunction in the service module 2 days into the journey, simulations were made and validated on the analog twin on earth before mission control sent instructions to the astronauts.

The concept of DT is not new, as product and process engineering teams have used 3D CAD models, asset models and process simulations to ensure and validate manufacturability for more than 30 years. In particular, DTs have primarily been used in the manufacturing sector, allowing for the product to be tested at all stages of the design process to ensure the design is feasible, safe, efficient and reliable.

2. Application of Digital Twin in Manufacturing and Construction

Digital twins have seen extensive application in industrial design, manufacturing, maintenance, and operation, where a real-world object is linked to its digital representation that is continuously using data from sensors located on a physical object to establish the representation of the virtual object. This truthful digital representation can be used for visualization, modeling, analysis, simulation, and further planning, triggering the feedback loop of decisions and changes in workflows that influence the control processes of the real object system.

In the manufacturing field, for example, SAP and Dassault relied on DT to reduce the deviation between functional requirement and actual performance. For civil engineering, Dassault used its 3D Experience Platform to build a "DT Singapore" to support urban planning, construction, and services. Intellect soft is exploring the DT applications on construction site to detect potential problems and prevent dangerous operations. Concerning renewable energy facilities, Doosan partnered with Microsoft and Bentley Systems to develop DTs of its wind farms, allowing operators to remotely monitor equipment performance and predict energy generation based on weather conditions. This solution uses Azure DTs to combine real-time and historical IoT, weather, and other operational data with physics and ML-based models to accurately predict production output for each turbine in the farm, allowing to proactively adjust the pitch and performance of individual turbines, maximize energy production, and generate insights that will improve the future designs. Similarly, General Electric (GE) built a digital wind farm based on its Predix platform by creating a DT for every wind turbine, to optimize maintenance strategy, improve reliability, and increase energy production. These cloud-based virtual representations use data captured from their real counterparts to let engineers digitally play out different scenarios, such as running an aircraft engine longer and in a hotter or wetter environment than its current conditions, obtaining insights to maximize output and spot problems before they lead to an unplanned outage. In addition to using physical sensors on the machines, DTs can employ virtual sensors which have ability to guess fairly precisely a value (such as temperature or pressure) by using other data from sensors and smart algorithms based on historical data or models.

3. Digital Twin Driven Product Design Methods

In order to realize effective interaction and integration between the virtual space and the physical space, Grieves proposed the notion of DT in 2014. The rapid advancement of information technologies, which are increasingly being applied in PLC, has paved the way for DT R&D. In light of the great potential of the DT in adapting to the changing market, accelerating product development speed, and saving product development costs, more efforts have been devoted to the application of DT at the product design stage.

The DT is mostly used for simulation, optimization, and validation in the virtual space for product design. Tuegel et al. discussed how the DT can be used for predicting the life of aircraft structure and detailed the technical challenges in developing and applying the DT technologies. Tao et al. discussed the application of DT in design, manufacturing, and service stages and proposed a DT-driven product design framework. Zheng et al. summarized the related research of DT technology and proposed an application framework for product life cycle management. Zhang et al. proposed a DT-based approach for the rapid customization of a hollow glass production line. Guo et al. proposed a modular approach to help in building a flexible DT to quickly evaluate different designs and identify design flaws in an easy way.

In addition to product design, studies of DT technology are also widely conducted in the design and optimization of manufacturing workshops. Tao et al. proposed a novel concept of DT shop-floor and discussed four key components, including physical shop-floor, virtual shop-floor, shop-floor service system, and shop-floor DT data. Liu et al. proposed a DT-driven methodology for rapid individualized design of the automated flow-shop manufacturing system. Uhlemann et al. introduced a DT-based learning factory to demonstrate the potentials and advantages of real-time data acquisition and subsequent simulation. Leng et al. proposed a DT-driven manufacturing cyber-physical system for the parallel control of smart workshops. In order to make CNCMT more intelligent, Luo et al. put forward a DT-driven multidomain unified modeling method and explored a mapping strategy between the physical space and the digital space Zhuang et al. proposed a framework of DT-based smart production management and control approach for complex product assembly shop floors.

At present, research on DT technologies mainly focuses on several aspects: building the mirror model in the virtual space, implementing the mapping from the physical space to the virtual space, and optimizing product design effects according to the virtual model or data. Comparatively, the research of DT technologies in product evaluation is still lacking. When the model of the virtual space can be well mapped to the physical space, the PDE model in the virtual space can better guide each stage of PLC.

In consideration of the four objectives (cost, quality, environment, and service), this chapter describes a DT-driven PDE method. The method not only considers those factors of PLC but can also be applied in the big data context to improve accuracy and dynamism of the evaluation. As a result, designers are enabled to evaluate product design prior to production and service; hence, they can make timely adjustment and optimization at the early stage.

4. Models

The digital twin technology allows the physical and virtual world to communicate, as shown in Figure 10-2. The concept behind it is that it provides a platform where the non-living objects can

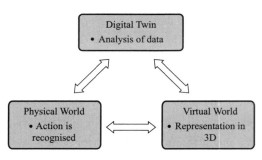

Figure 10-2　Digital twin model

show a living behavior. For example, if we build a twin of a city, then the working will be the same as at the original site. It will monitor by taking all the necessary data and analyze its future necessities or capabilities. If any kind of problem is there, it will be able to predict for the coming future. The digital twin layer will inform beforehand and will also suggest the best way to solve it. Right now, it asks for suggestions from humans but in the coming future, it might be able to make its decision without human implication. The first step for this goal is to be able to find the activity performed in its surrounding.

Human Action Recognition is categorized into various steps. Figure10-3 shows the architecture of human action recognition.

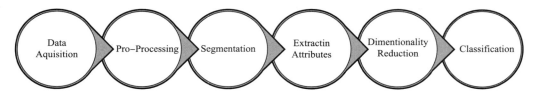

Figure 10-3　Architecture of human action recognition

The first step is data acquisition, in which data is first captured and then pre-processed. After pre-processing, the data is segmented. The required features are extracted from segmented data. Then dimension reduction takes place and at last, the data is classified and we get the desired information.

Construction of workload digital twin model:

In order to integrate the workloads with the CNCMTs DT for simulation in LD, a workload-DT model should be established based on the analysis of workload earlier, as shown in Figure 10-4. The workload-DT model is a hierarchical representation of the working conditions of CNCMTs with clear classification. For example, to meet the target performance indicators of spindle vibration, structural mechanics simulation for the spindle should be carried out.

This type of simulation can obtain corresponding workload data efficiently according to the structural mechanics workload-DT model.

After the workload-DT model is constructed, it can be stored in an XML file, which is machine readable, well organized, reusable, and capable of transmission.

There are two advantages of introducing the workload-DT model into LD as follows:

The workload-DT model can be reused to avoid repeated domain knowledge modeling. The ambiguity caused by different definitions and expressions for design concepts and terms can be eliminated by building a unified model with well-organized structure. Therefore data interaction will become more convenient and efficient based on this workload-DT model.

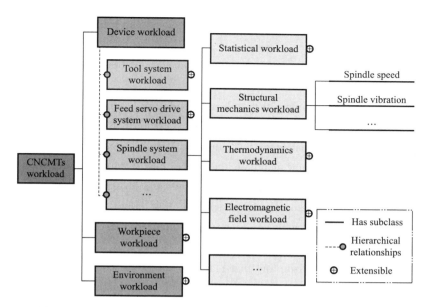

Figure 10-4   Workload-DT model of CNCMTS, computerized numerical control machine tools; DT, ditital twin

As a result of the clear hierarchical presentation of the workload-DT model, data collection and utilization during LD process become more efficient. Furthermore, simulation based on the instance of the workload-DT model will generate more precise and realistic results to guide design of CNCMTs.

10. 5   Reading Material

Emerging Trends in Software Engineering

Throughout the relatively brief history of software engineering, practitioners and researchers have developed an array of process models, technical methods, and automated tools in an effort to foster fundamental change in the way we build computer software. Even though past experience indicates otherwise, there is a tacit desire to find the "silver bullet"—the magic process or transcendent technology that will allow us to build large, complex, software-based systems easily, without confusion, without mistakes, without delay—without the many problems that continue to plague software work.

1. Software Engineering as a Discipline

For almost 50 years, many academic researchers and industry professionals have clamored for a true engineering discipline for software. In an important follow-on to her classic 1990 paper on the subject, Mary Shaw comments on this continuing quest:

Engineering disciplines typically evolve from craft practices of a technology, sufficient for local or ad hoc use. When the technology becomes economically significant, it requires stable production techniques and management control. The resulting commercial market is based on experience, rather than a deep understanding of the technology ... an engineering profession emerges when ... science becomes sufficiently mature to support purposeful practice and design evolution with predictable outcomes.

We would argue that the industry has achieved "purposeful practice", but that "predictable outcomes" have remained elusive.

As mobility begins to dominate the software landscape, Shaw identifies challenges that "emerge from the deep interdependencies between very complex systems and their users". She argues that the knowledge base that leads to "purposeful practice" has been democratized by the specialized social networks that now populate the Web. For example, rather than referencing a centrally controlled software engineering handbook, a software developer can pose a problem on an appropriate forum and obtain a crowd-sourced solution that draws from the experience of many other developers. The proposed solution if often critiqued in real time, with alternatives and adaptations offered as options.

But this is not the level of discipline that many demand. As Shaw states: "Problems facing software engineers are increasingly situated in complex social contexts and delineating the problem's boundaries is increasingly difficult". As a consequence, isolating the scientific underpinnings of a discipline remains a challenge. At this point in the history of our field, it is reasonable to state that "the discovery of new software engineering ideas is, by now, naturally incremental and evolutionary".

2. Open-World Software

Concepts such as ambient intelligence, 6context-aware applications, and pervasive ubiquitous computing all focus on integrating software-based systems into an environment far broader than a laptop, a mobile computing device, or any other digital device. These separate visions of the near-term future of computing collectively suggest "open-world software"—software that is designed to adapt to a continually changing environment "by self-organizing its structure and self-adapting its behavior".

To help illustrate the challenges that software engineers will face in the near future, consider the notion of ambient intelligence (AmI), defines AmI in the following way: "People are surrounded by intelligent, intuitive interfaces that are embedded in all kinds of objects. The ambient intelligence environment is capable of recognizing and responding to the presence of different individuals in a seamless, unobtrusive way."

With the widespread use of low-cost, yet increasingly powerful smartphones, we are well on our way to ubiquitous AmI systems. The challenge for software engineers is to develop apps that provide ever-increasing functionality in products of all types—functionality that adapts to user needs while at the same time protecting privacy and providing security. The rise of digital assistants and intelligent chat bots are indicative of the types of applications ahead.

The engineering of variability intensive systems focuses on software that needs to accommodate different usage and deployment scenarios, as well as intentional and unintentional variability in functionality or quality attributes (e.g., performance). This includes meeting the challenges posed by context-aware apps, autonomous agents, and pervasive computing as well as creating product-line software. These systems can be highly variable during all software engineering activities (e. g. , dynamic run-time conditions, rapidly changing requirements, configuration management), and we need to improve our understanding of how to design and manage them in a cost-effective manner.

3. The Grand Challenge

There is one trend that is undeniable—software-based systems will undoubtedly become bigger and more complex as time passes. It is the engineering of these large, complex systems, regardless of delivery platform or application domain, that poses the " grand challenge" for software engineers. Manfred Broy suggests that software engineers can meet " the daunting challenge of complex software systems development" by creating new approaches to understanding system models and using those models as a basis for the construction of high-quality next-generation software. Techniques currently being studied for variability intensive systems (continuous delivery, self-adaptive software, value-based software engineering, content aware computing) may benefit the developers of all types of software products.

Chapter 11
Standardized Engineering

11. 1 Standardization

1. Standardization

11. 1 Professional Terms, Words and Phrases, Sentence Illustration

Standardization is simplification. Standardization is characterized as the sum of inter-conditional actions and measures that lead to a rational unification of recurring solutions. It is the act of finding the mean or average of competing ideas and consolidating them into one to simplify two things or several things. It is the way in which businesses can reduce their costs (whether financial or time) and the way an organization which aims to ensure clear, visualized and safe working environment. With proper implementation of standards prevents defects in production and at the same time constitute procedures to prevent the occurrence of other errors that could have an impact on production. It is therefore desirable to standardize all processes carried out in the manufacturing sector.

De facto standards are different in this sense because they are established by rolling all competing ideas into the most dominant idea instead of finding the middle way. Aside from de facto standards, however, the so-called consensus standards are established through discussions aimed at finding the middle way. This process realizes the largest aggregate cost savings for the market.

The foundation of standardization is simplifying certain things that would otherwise grow complex if left alone, thereby raising the degree of interoperability among things. Simplification brings about cost efficiencies and increased convenience. Standardization is a key element of lean manufacturing and its process is considered the basis for continuous improvement. Improving standardized work is a never-ending process.

Every improvement and change in the manufacturing process is completed the development of standards. The standards define best practices for the implementation of the work. The aim is to do the job right the first time without error, without negative effects on humans and the surroundings. If you improve the standard, the new standard becomes the basis for further improvements etc. The standards are used to:
- the reduction of variation and error correction.
- improved safety.
- facilitate communication.
- visibility problems.
- assistance in training and education.

- increasing labor discipline.
- facilitating the response to the challenges.
- clarification of the working procedures.

The intention of the standard is to carry out actions without mistakes, the first time around, efficiently and without waste. In the standards are a precisely described how it is necessary to perform the job, i. e. , it describes each step sequence.

The standard must have the following characteristics:

(1) Maximum brevity-only contains the necessary instructions to the operator process.

(2) Simplicity and visualization, the worker immediately easily found and understood the necessary instructions.

(3) The possibility of rapid changes in process parameters.

(4) Clarity which ensures that every worker has all relevant activities in the process as well.

(5) The ability to monitor the implementation of standards and their impact on the process parameters.

There are two types of standards:

(1) Management standards—that are necessary for the management of staff and administrative purposes—come here, for example, administrative regulations.

(2) Operating standards—which looks at how employees carry out their work.

Operating standards are structured, visual process standards in the workplace with the definition of potential process risks and predefined solutions for the worker.

Standards in the company have a role to minimize the three main areas of weaknesses including:

(1) Overloading, exertion (MURI).

(2) Imbalances, deviations (MURA).

(3) Losses and wastage (MUDA).

Within the framework of these areas are using different methods and tools. The basic methods using standardization include:

(1) 5S.

(2) Standardization of processes.

(3) Visual management.

2. Eight Main Principles of Standardization

(1) Voluntary Nature

Participation in standards work and the use of standards are both voluntary.

(2) Openness and Transparency

All standards proposals and draft standards are made public for comments before the final version is published. Those having comments or objections are asked to join in the negotiations, and every objection is to be discussed with the person making it.

(3) Broad and Balanced Participation

Standards are developed in Technical Committees composed by experts representing all stakeholders. Anyone interested can participate in this process. Balanced participation of all stakeholders' groups is intended.

Thus, standards are not only accepted by industry, but also by users, including consumers and trade unions, and public administrations as well as non-governmental organizations, e. g. , environmental NGOs.

Standardization internal rules encourage the agreement of all working decisions by consensus, while voting is to be used in exceptional cases.

(4) Consensus

The content of standards is thus laid down on the basis of mutual understanding and general agreement. Strategic decisions requiring balloting are approved only with the support of large majorities. This is highly valued by users, especially in terms of consumer protection, environmental protection and occupational health and safety.

(5) Consistency

The collection of standards covers all technical disciplines. The rules of procedure in standards work ensure the coherence and consistency of these standards.

(6) Market Relevance

Standardization takes account of current technical knowledge and ensures the rapid implementation of new findings. A standard is developed only where there is a need, technically acceptable, expressed by the market, because standardization is not an end in itself.

(7) Beneficial for Society

Standards always take the needs of society as a whole into consideration. The benefits to the general public take priority over the benefits of individuals.

(8) Wide Geographical Relevance

International and European standards help eliminate technical barriers, being a strong basis for free global trade and the European Single Market.

3. Benefits and Limits of Standardization

There are many secondary benefits of standardization, two of which are efficiency gains and economic advancement. More specifically, standardization is expected to deliver benefits including the following:

(1) Faster information communications and greater precision.

(2) Development of understanding among retailers and consumers at an earlier stage.

(3) Mitigation of conflicts between manufacturers and consumers.

(4) Enhancement of maintenance and repair efficiencies.

(5) Effective prevention of the recurrence of problems or accidents. When standardization costs outweigh the standardization benefits, however, the result is neither efficiency gains nor economic advancement. In such case, standardization should be avoided.

Furthermore, people will obviously not accept standards for products wherein personal taste, choice, preference, or usability is involved, e. g. , clothing designs, which are subject to personal taste and preferences. Products like these should not be standardized. The same applies to matters of national secrecy (e. g. , defense). In other words, standardization is not for everything; it has definite boundaries.

4. Other Standardization Concerns

In addition to the limits to standardization as discussed above, and in view of the objectives and benefits of standardization, standardization in general should only cover the major provisions related to the standard's target; it should not attempt to regulate every side issue. For instance, a national standard trying to ensure the interoperability of a part should define only the minimum required dimensions for safety and interoperability and refrain from placing restrictions on any other dimension.

For standards for finished goods or raw materials, the ordinary standardization of only the material quality and testing methods will suffice. Defining the manufacturing methods, for example, is not appropriate because this will impede the progress of the manufacturing technology. When product quality or safety cannot be guaranteed without a regulated manufacturing method, however, defining manufacturing methods and related particulars is appropriate.

For the sake of not hindering technical progress, the provisions of standards should usually focus on performance whenever possible and eschew provisions on design such as appearance or shape and provisions on specifications including dimensions or materials. Moreover, when drafting a national standard, the standardizing body must work to ensure that the standard will be internationally acceptable so as to eliminate unnecessary trade barriers.

Caution must be exercised with company rules on matters such as work procedures. If the rules are unnecessarily detailed or strict, observing them may be impossible, or they may impose excessive burden on enforcement and management.

Another important consideration is maintaining consistency between the provisions of all standards and avoiding contradictions whenever possible. Remember, contradictions between various standards not only run counter to the objectives and benefits of standardization but often lead to misuse as well.

Before embarking on a standardization project, clearly defining the objectives and end purpose of the project and subsequently proceeding with these in mind are essential. Standardization is a very human activity. In light of standardization's purpose, i. e. , to promote community benefits, it goes without saying that the standardization benefits will not be manifested if rules and criteria are established but people and organizations do not observe them. If standardization is not bearing fruit because of problems in the rules or agreements, then rethinking the rules may be necessary.

5. Case Study

China Goes Smart:

China ranked second behind the United States in smart grid investment in 2012, spending $3. 2 billion, a 14% increase over 2011, and continues to boost its investment in its electrical infrastructure. China's transmission upgrades are expected to reach more than $72 billion in revenue by 2020 on a cumulative basis. China also plans to install 300 million smart meters by 2015. According to the 12th Five-Year Plan for Grid Intelligence Construction of Smart Grid Corporation of China (SGCC), smart meter bid invitations occupied 97.18% of the total meter bidding for smart grid-related equipment in 2012, reaching a bid invitation volume of 78,043,000 units. "Overall," Bob Lockhart, senior research analyst with Navigant Research, says, "smart grid development in China will generate $127 billion in cumulative revenue from 2012 to 2020." China's home electronics and IT industries, such as IGRS and ITop Home, have gradually developed a comprehensive set of national standards for home networking, while telecom operators, including China Telecom and China Unicom, are promoting smart home services targeting high-income households.

For India, having experienced two major blackouts in 2012, one of which left 600 million people without electricity, the smart grid is a priority. The India Smart Grid Forum, which has the support of the Indian government's Ministry of Power, says India's power system has roughly doubled in the past decade and grew similarly in the previous decade. The forum's membership is global in scope; its American members include IBM, Texas Instruments, Oracle, Cisco Systems, and Honeywell. India operates the world's largest synchronous grids with 250 gigawatts connected capacity and about 200 million consumers. However, 40% of the population has no access to electricity and per capita consumption of electricity in India is one-fourth of the world average. The potential demand by 2032 is estimated to be as high as 900 gigawatts. The forum held regular workshops through 2013 to finalize a program that fits into the country's 12th Five-Year Plan (2010—2015). "The Ministry of Power wanted to start work on the Smart Grid Road map after the Five-Year Plan allocations were final." said Reji Kumar Pillai, managing director of Magnetar Venture, an India-focused clean tech venture capital fund, and president of the India Smart Grid Forum. As for the development and adaption of appropriate standards, the forum expected its first set of smart grid standards "relevant to the Indian context" to be in place by 2014. Based on the outcome of its pilot programs, full roll out of smart grids in pilot project areas are expected to be in place by 2017—in major urban areas by 2022, and nationwide in India by 2027.

The Indian government created the Restructured Accelerated Power Development and Reforms Program (R-APDRP) in 2008 to essentially transform the power distribution sector in India. Through this program, utilities plan on building an IT infrastructure with applications and automation systems. India's government has put together about 14 demo/pilot smart grid projects that are under implementation by different state distribution utilities and cover a range of issues and programs that are scheduled to be completed by 2015—from advanced metering and outage management to distributed generation, peak load management, and power quality. The boom in this sector has also attracted several IT majors who have formed partnerships to develop smart grid solutions in India. The Indian government has also created the India Smart Grid Task Force to accelerate the deployment of smart grids across the country.

Demand response is a key. Another big step by the India Smart Grid Forum is to form a strategic relationship with the Open ADR Alliance whose focus is to promote the development and adoption of the Open Automated Demand Response (Open ADR) standard. The plan is to help India's utilities improve and maintain their grid reliability and provide their customers with demand response-enabled products and services.

In Japan, the Ministry of Economy, Trade, and Industry (METI) already had working relationships with international standards groups, including the IEEE, the IEC, and CEN/CENELEC. METI sets the country's energy policy, and operates Japan's grids; Japan has two separate grids that operate at different frequencies. Each service area is owned and operated by a different electrical power company. Japan also formed the Japan Smart Communities Alliance that represents a cross-section of views from industry, the public sector, and academia to formulate plans for smart grid standards and technology. Japan's smart grid plans are complicated by the phase out of its nearly 50 gigawatts of nuclear capacity over the next few decades. Nuclear power had produced about 30% of Japan's electricity prior to the 2011 Fukushima crisis. Rather than overhaul its entire grid infrastructure, Japan plans to invest in renewable energy and integrate it into the grid, using alternative power sources such as solar, wind, and nuclear for homes and commercial buildings—without any major disruptions of its energy supply. One possible solution promoted by Japanese consortia is to create a decentralized system that would subdivide the existing grid into interconnected cells of varying sizes and assign the equivalent of Internet Protocol addresses to generators, wind farms, and other grid sources within the cells to power the country's needs.

South Korea's smart grid policies and development are being driven to a large extent by a perceived requirement for national security and economic growth and a series of extreme weather events over the past several years. The country's electricity network is largely state controlled, but its historical interest in green technologies has helped create an environment of aggressive smart grid programming in the country. In 2011, South Korea's legislature approved the Smart Grid Promotion Act, which provides a framework for sustainable smart grid projects and a plan for smart grid development and commercialization. The Korea Smart Grid Association, made up of both government and private sector interests, and the Korea Smart Grid Institute, are leading ambitious national programs that emphasize a smart power grid and smart transportation. All of the country's programs emphasize coordination between the government and industry. The country hopes to complete the final planned phase of its smart grid program between 2020 and 2030.

The Middle East and North Africa (MENA) region is among the leaders in smart grid development among emerging markets. Smart grid activity is largely a state-driven process in MENA with the strongest potential in the Gulf States, where high electricity consumption is expected to drive smart meter deployments.

11.2   Corporate Standardization

1. Introduction to Corporate Standards

Most large corporations have internal standards used for daily operations.

11.2 Professional Terms, Words and Phrases, Sentence Illustration

These standards are typically categorized proprietary. They often have another set of standards that, while not reviewed by the public, are made available to them.

(1) Corporate Public Standards

Public standards are used by corporations to inform the public and their customer base of information related to their product. There are literally millions of such standards in both printed and electronic formats. These standards range in topics from computers and computer chips to pipes and fittings. Many of these company public standards become national standards as time goes on or are incorporated into existing standards. The standards are developed over some time and they may start with one product or service and then slowly increase in volume to cover a wider range of needs. Many of these standards, while not created or maintained using the process, are intended to provide information to assist the public in using or specifying company products, so they are made publicly available and can often be accessed over the internet. A few private organizations, such as UL, follow the rigorous ANS process to produce standards that are used in much of their work and as standards for the public safety as well.

(2) Corporate Proprietary Standards

All corporations have proprietary standards used for their operation. Their development is necessitated by the need to operate consistently or deal with products in a systematic manner. These standards are typically kept proprietary in order to give the corporation an advantage over competitors, although it is sometimes a matter of simply not wanting them to be open to question by outside entities. In many cases these standards are purposely not patented for competitive reasons. This is because once a product is patented, that patent is public record, and at the end of the term of the patent others can use information in the patent to produce a competitive product. The development and fine-tuning of these standards can take a long time and, in many cases, proprietary standards are considered intellectual property of the corporation. The development of these standards is done at various levels of the corporation and access to them is sometimes limited to an as-needed basis.

2. Corporate Standardization Management

As demonstrated in the discussions above, standards and standardization might incorporate important implications for strategic management, since they have been expressed by a number of scholars as playing a potentially vital role in strategy realization.

Management of standardization originated in the late 1800s, when the first attempts of managerial theorization sprang from engineers' endeavors to codify and systematize manufacturing practices, primarily within railroad operations. Nowadays, standardization is progressively employed in a plethora of business activities, such as product design, software engineering, and other types of tangible and intangible work. However, existing research has been highly limited to conversations on the anticipated and realized effects through standards, while scarcely considering how standardization should be managed.

Betancourt and Walsh (1995) were the first to introduce the concept of (strategic) standardization management. They stated that they set out to write about the concept of standardization management "because of its importance as a management discipline and methodology in today's dynamic business environment" (referring to the business environment of more than two decades ago). In particular, aspects such as globalization of markets, increasing competition (both domestic and international), rapidly developing technologies, and complex manufacturing facilities are among the principal areas that Betancourt and Walsh detected a need for firms to leverage the various aspects of standardization in an attempt to enhance, or even safeguard, their global competitiveness. The authors claimed that their article is based on the experiences of "many best-in-class companies" whose competitive position has been strongly enhanced by properly applied strategic standardization management, although the authors neither named any of these companies nor explicated in detail how the companies conducted their standardization management.

De Casanove and Lambert (2015), similarly to Betancourt and Walsh (although 20 years later), elaborated on how critical it remains for corporations (probably even more critical than it was two decades ago) to embrace and leverage standardization in order to enhance, or even preserve, their competitive positions in an increasingly competitive and globalized business environment. What Betancourt and Walsh (1995) depicted as " strategic standardization management", de Casanove & Lambert (2015) discussed as "standardization strategy"—yet both publications bring forward the coordinative aspects of standardization (throughout the overall corporation), and the importance of the standardization strategy (or strategic standardization management) being well aligned with the global strategy of the corporation. That is, corporations should very carefully select the kind of standards to develop (or, in other words, the type of standardization to be involved in), making sure " to capture the ins and outs of corporate standardization" (that is, the highest benefits possible).

In that sense, for efficient standardization management, de Casanove and Lambert stressed attention towards the prominence of the "community" (that is subsequently supposed to use the newly developed standard); if the standard does not meet the needs of the community efficiently, it will soon be forgotten, hence wasting the time and resources that were devoted to its development. In order to make sure that this risk is eliminated to the greatest degree possible, the relevant stakeholders need to be involved in the process. Otherwise, merely "assembling a set of high-level experts around the table is not a guarantee of success".

In addition, since standards require a number of resources to be developed, as de Casanove and Lambert also added, an organization ought to carefully consider its standardization strategy and intentions in advance, before becoming involved in a (probably long and costly) standardization process that might lead nowhere (in particular if the necessary assessments were not cautiously made beforehand).

Of course, making meticulous assessments and reaching appropriate decisions is easier said than done. In practice, the standardization scenery has become "some kind of a jungle", which "creates risks for a company to miss new business opportunities emerging from standards (think USB stack taking over most traditional communication buses), or updates that would impact performances of new products (e. g. , certification authorities changing regulation, for instance the

FAA allowing twin-jets for long haul flight across oceans), or disrupt an established market".

Hence, it might be too challenging for firms to detect where (and how) their efforts and resources (fees, delegated personnel, etc.) should be dedicated (meaning in what standardization fields, since deploying every one of them is simply not possible). It is a matter of standardization management (as well as of strategic management) to select those standardization fields of primary importance, as well as to coordinate and optimize the company's involvement and strategies (that is, standardization strategies), although in practice little is known about the specific intraorganizational processes and activities taking place.

3. Model

As we want to determine the best practice, we need to define success: When is it possible to say that company standardization has been successful? In the case of dominant players such as Microsoft, company standards set the requirements for products and systems available on the market. In most other cases, company standards primarily serve the internal functioning of organizations and contribute to effectiveness and efficiency. Benefits of such company standards include the interoperability of systems, quality, reliability and safety of products, services and systems, efficiency in production, less maintenance and stock, and savings in procurement. These differences in possible benefits hindered a common perception of best practice. Therefore, we looked for a more general indicator. In line with ISO 9001 (International Organization for Standardization, 2000b), we can define success as user satisfaction. We will use the term direct user for people that read the standard. Other users use products, services, systems, and so forth in which the standard has been implemented. Again, however, because of the diversity of standards and user categories, it is difficult to measure this satisfaction and subsequently relate it to best practices in the way of preparing the standards.

A third method appeared to be more feasible. The success of company standardization results from the processes that constitute it (Figure 11-1). Therefore, we relate success to these processes. The definition of success per process resulted from the interviews carried out within the six companies and from discussions with people who work with, or are professionally engaged with, standardization. These findings were completed with insights from literature. We have distinguished three steps for measuring the success of a standard.

(1) Step 1: The standard should be there.

The demand for a (company) standard starts either within the organization or arises from external obligations, for example, legislation. Then, this demand should be assessed and it should be decided whether or not to develop the standard. Such a decision should be based on standardization policy, and the possible development of the proposed standard should be balanced against other requests for standards development (prioritizing).

The development of the standards is the next process; this process consists of the composition of a draft version of the standard, commentary rounds, the writing of the final version of the standard, and the approval of this standard. The output is an approved company standard (or normative document). To develop the standard, there is a need for competent personnel (human resource management), the standard has to be paid for (funding process), and IT tools should be in place to support standards development (facility management).

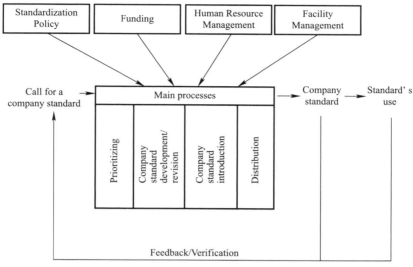

Figure 11-1   Company standardization model

(2) Step 2: The standard is known and available.

When a standard has been developed (and accorded for), the next step toward success is that the standard becomes available to the intended users and that they are aware of its existence. This is a second prerequisite for success.

During this introduction process the potential direct users should get informed about the standard's existence and its potential fitness for use. The benefits of the standard and the reasons for certain choices in the standard can be explained. The more and the better the standard is known, the higher the chance that users will actually implement it and do so in the way intended by the standard's developers. In our model, the output of a process forms the input of the following process. However, practice can be less rigid. For instance, it can be important to start with the introduction (promotion) of the standard already during its development. Also, after the introduction period, the promotion of the standard can continue.

For the standard's availability to the direct users (physically), a distribution process should be in place. This process should assure that the standards reach the direct user in a fast and easy way. This can be done by, for instance, subscription, ordering on demand, or in the form of publishing on demand using an intranet. An extra success factor is that the direct user always works with the right version of the standard. After a period of time, the standard may be revised, so the distribution process has to be defined in such a way as to make sure that the right version of the standard is always being used.

(3) Step 3: The standard is used.

Company standardization can only be a success when the standard is used in practice (in the right way). A standard that is of a high quality but that is not used in practice has no value; there has to be a market for the standard. So, the potential direct users must be willing to use the standard and be capable of understanding and using it. We can even define success one step further when we look at our standardization definition. The product of the company standardization, the company standard, has to solve the matching problem. The standard has to be the answer to the demand out of the organization, which was the starting point of the process.

Evaluation of the standard's use may form the basis for withdrawing, maintaining, or changing the standard. The developed standard should be an answer to the question for which it was produced: Are the (potential) users of the standard satisfied? Therefore, user feedback to those who have decided to make the standard as well as to the people who have developed it is essential. The picture shows one feedback loop, but this is a simplification; more might be drawn because the (quality) management of each process needs a form of feedback as in the Deming circle: plan, do, check, act. A process approach that uses feedback and aims at enhancing customer satisfaction by meeting their needs is characteristic for the ISO 9000:2000 quality management approach (ISO, 2000a, 2000b).

4. Case Study of Corporate Standards

Strictly Business:

In January 2013, the SGIP transitioned from a strictly government funded organization to a self-sustaining, tax exempt entity with the majority of funding coming from industry stakeholders. The organization became a non-profit 501(c)(3) legal entity, with a new identity, SGIP 2. 0 Inc., but still dedicated to advancing the original mission of coordinating standards development and encouraging global harmonization. The SGIP 2. 0 board has one member from each of the 22 specific stakeholder categories, plus an "at-large" category made up of three members. The at-large members were selected for their broad and lengthy standards development experience. The change to a member-funded organization created a membership issue. As a result, the SGIP had to put a membership campaign together, "a value proposition story, and also continue to run the government funded NIST organization", says McDonald. The SGIP got $750,000 from NIST near the end of 2012, and expected to receive an additional $1million from NIST in 2014 and in 2015. Still, the pay-to-play scheme created certain challenges. "In 2010, 2011, and 2012, we had approximately 800 organizations on the books", says McDonald. "Figure 200 to 300 of those are active, and the rest are monitoring what's going on. Of that number, 200 are from outside the United States. Each /member representative/is an expert in their own company and they're used to getting their own way. And I have 25 of them. " As of July 2013, SGIP 2. 0 had about 200 dues paying members. It was at about that point that the SGIP put out a formal call for a director of marketing and membership, anew position within the organization, tasked to attract new members and retain existing members. Patrick Gannon, formerly an executive with OASIS, was hired to fill the slot. The dues-paying member list climbed to about 230 by early 2014.

McDonald has spent much of his time on international outreach, signing MoUs with several countries through 2013 and into 2014. Among the countries that have begun investing in substantial smart grid infrastructure are Canada, Mexico, Brazil, India, Japan, Korea, Australia, China, and many EU member states. In addition, NIST and the International Trade

Administration (ITA) have partnered with the USDoE to establish the ISGAN, a multinational collaboration of 17 countries. ISGAN complements the GSGF, a global stakeholder organization that serves as an "association of associations" to bring together leaders from smart grid stakeholder organizations from around the world. Several of these countries have gone beyond the MoU stage to full due spaying members, giving them voting status. "Their goal is to harmonize their standards globally," McDonald said. "This is extremely important. Without harmonization, you have trade barriers and that's the goal of these MoU." Several US federal agencies are focusing on the trade aspect of harmonization, including the US Department of Commerce, which has its own smart grid department.

5. Methods

Policy making—strategic level:

To make company standardization work, there has to be a (organizational) framework and a policy within which the standardization activities are executed. There has to be enough engagement to the policy by the people that have to carry out the standardization activities and their management (and the higher levels of management). In our best practice, top management is represented in company standardization or at least supports it. The most effective way to make this work is by means of a steering group in which the standardization department, (technical) managers from business units, and a member of a top-level management (e.g., technical director) are represented.

Figure 11-2 presents a possible organizational structure. For making a good standard, the technical expertise of one or more technical experts (who, in general, work within the business units) should be combined with the standardization expertise of a standards engineer (who may work within a standardization department). A networking structure, in one way or another, is expected to be the best way to do this.

All the companies have filled in the score presented in Table 11-1, and the score has been discussed. In the following section, we will present a few of the graphs that can be constructed out of the answers of the six companies.

Scorecard for the policy making process at the strategic Level   Table 11-1

\multicolumn{3}{c}{Scorecard Policy Making-Strategic Level}		
No.	Description	Score
1	There is a clear strategic policy on company standardization.	
2	At the corporate level a clear framework has been for operating company standardization.	
3	At the corporate level tasks, competencies and responsibilities for company standardization have been defined.	
4	Standardization expertise has sufficient influence on the company's strategic policy.	
5	At the corporate level, management is aware of the importance and benefits of having (company) standards and standardization.	

continued

No.	Description	Score
6	The maintenance of the existing system of company standards is a part of the strategic policy on company standardization.	
7	The business units have sufficient influence on the strategic policy on company standardization (to make sure that their needs in this area are met).	
8	The business units commit to the strategic policy on company standardization.	
9	The strategic policy on company standardization is derived from the general strategic policy of the company (it sup-ports the general policy and it does not conflict with it).	
10	In this strategic policy on company standardization the goals are clearly defined.	
11	The management is willing to steer company standardization at a high (top) level in the organization in order to mini-mize the danger of sub-optimization.	
12	The management is aware that by using (company) standards company-wide the company can achieve cost-benefits for the purchasing of materials.	
13	The management is aware that by using (company) standards company-wide the company can reduce cost of engi-ncering and maintenance.	
14	The managerment is aware that (company) standards use is needed to assure a specified quality-level of the company.	
15	The management recognizes company standardization as an essential activity and steers this activity at a corporate-level.	
16	Corporate management has authorized the strategic level company standardization.	
17	The strategic policy on company standardization has enough status and is being pursued by the total company.	

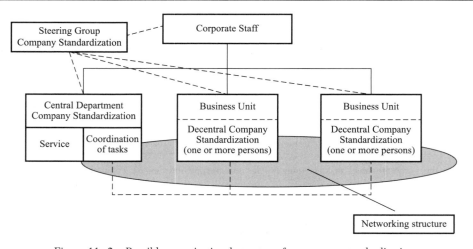

Figure 11-2　Possible organizational structure for company standardization

Statement 17: The strategic policy on company standardization has enough status and is being pursued by the total company.

Statement 17 is one of the statements in which there is a variation between the scores of the different companies. These are the more interesting statements. It can mean three things: either this part of the best practice does not fit within the culture of this company; this is not best practice; or it is a focus point for the company to improve its process. These statements have been the focus points in the discussions with the companies. All companies saw Statement 17 as best practice and, therefore, as an important focus point when they scored low.

It is important that company standardization has enough status in order to make sure that standards are being developed and used. It helps a lot when company standardization is supported at a corporate level within the organization, because frequently, the company focus is on short-term moneymaking. The graph in Figure 11-3 shows that most companies do not score high on this statement. To give company standardization enough status, it is helpful when, at a corporate level in the organization, the importance of standardization and the benefits that it can bring are recognized and formalized. Subsequently, when this policy is communicated in the right way, it is more likely that company standardization becomes a success.

Companies that scored low on the status also scored low in the participation of the business units in the definition of a strategic policy on company standardization (Figure 11-4). Although recognition of the importance of standardization at a high level within the organization is an essential factor, this is not enough. In order to make it work also on the other levels, these levels must be involved in the formulation of the strategic policy. In practice, the importance of this fact was recognized, but not many of the companies did, in fact, involve the BUs in strategic policy development.

Now we will address in short the tactical and operational level in policy making. The best practice statements related to these levels can be found in Appendix 1.

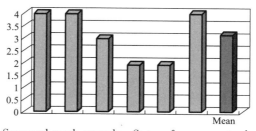

Figure 11-3   Scorecard graph example—Status of company standardization policy

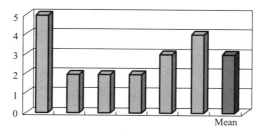

Figure 11-4   Scorecard graph example—The influence of business unites on the strategic policy concerning company standardization

11.3　Engineering Standards

11.3 Professional Terms, Words and Phrases, Sentence Illustration

1. Introduction

Engineering standards are sets of rules and procedures developed, documented, approved by general consensus, and configuration managed to assure the adequacy of a given product, methodology, or operation. Standards are normally developed in committees by people who have experience in a particular field of endeavor and who have an interest in the outcome that the standard is intended to ensure.

There are many ways of looking at and classifying standards. These include performance versus design (descriptive, or prescriptive), mandatory versus voluntary, purpose, intended user group, the way they were developed.

The International Organization for Standardization (ISO) and the International Electrotechnical Commission (IEC) Guide 2, *Standardization and Related Activities-General Vocabulary*, offers a number of ways of looking at standards in addition to providing vocabulary such as the following:

- Level of standardization, which is a generally geopolitical classification based on the coverage of the standard.

- Aims of standardization, addressing issues from fitness for purpose and safety, through protection of the environment.

- Category of the standard, such as technical specifications (e.g., ASME B16.5), codes of practice (e.g., ASME Boiler and Pressure Vessel Code), and regulations (e.g., OSHA and DOT regulations).

- Type of standard, from terminology to testing, product, process, service, interface, and data to be provided.

With many possible approaches, we will first look at standards as they fit into the following three categories:

- Limited consensus.

- General consensus (also referred to as Voluntary Consensus Standards).

- Governmental action.

(1) Limited Consensus Standards

Limited consensus standards, by their nature, are developed by experts in a given organization and then made available to the organization for its guidance. Prime examples are some internal company standards for work hardened, heavy wall, stainless steel tubing for ultrahigh pressure applications, and a number of company standards for compression fittings. Trade groups such as the Heat Exchange Institute (HEI) and the TEMA have developed standards specific to their lines of work. While keeping a greater level of control than would be allowed them if their standards were subject to the American National Standards Institute (ANSI) process and requirements, these organizations reap for the company or trade group as well as for society many of the same benefits that they would achieve by following that more public process.

（2）Voluntary Consensus Standards（VCS）

There is a great difference between the procedures involved in writing limited consensus and voluntary consensus standards. Voluntary consensus standards are developed by experts to serve the need of a given industry with substantial input from other interested parties, and potentially from the public. An example of such standard is the ASME's BPVC. The BPVC contains numerous standards（referred to in the BPVC as sections, divisions, and parts）as will be explained later. The development of each of these standards follows a unique process by which experts from differing interest groups（designers, fabricators, users, and insurers of pressure vessels, and perhaps others）collaborate in writing the rules in order to arrive through a balanced consensus process at a product that is not dominated by any one particular interest group. The resulting standard becomes acceptable to a wide range of interested parties within the industry since all entities were involved in developing it. These standards have been so successful and have garnered such a high level of respect that they are often cited in laws and regulations（a process referred to as "Incorporation by Reference" or "IBR"）.

Typically, in the United States, the organizations developing such standards follow a process certified by the ANSI and note that fact by including "ANSI" in the document name, identifying number, or on their cover or title page. International standards typically follow a similar process. Because of the integrity of the process and the quality of the resulting product, the standards from many US standards developers are commonly accepted, or even demanded, overseas, and many of the international standards are likewise accepted or required in the United States, both by industry and by jurisdictions.

（3）Governmental Standards

Both jurisdictional and non-jurisdictional standards are produced by a wide range of governmental organizations. Jurisdictional standards are those promulgated by governmental agencies to implement laws, ordinances, and other legal documents, and carrying with them legal enforceability by fines, injunctions, imprisonment, or other sanctions. Nonjurisdictional governmental standards are developed by governmental entities for their own use, whether for internal purposes or for contracted or other outside work.

2. A Few Examples of Standards throughout the Ages

One of the first known, and very rudimentary, standards, known as the Code of Hammurabi, was developed approximately 4000 years ago, apparently to ensure fairness in the kingdom of Babylonia. In this case, the standard was promulgated by the king and enshrined in laws. Many of the laws included in this document related to crimes, torts, marriage, and general legal obligations. The Code of Hammurabi may be most well-known for its "an eye for an eye and a tooth for a tooth" approach to justice, but portions of this document also provide very basic performance standards for construction of buildings and boats. That is, the document specified what must be achieved. Walls must not fall down, and boats must be tight.

It appears that there was a problem with the quality of workmanship in the kingdom of Babylonia, but the solution had no specific criteria for how things were to be constructed. Rather, the standard that was put in place simply required that the construction be good, and if it failed, specified the penalty. This approach, using what are referred to as performance standards, typically provides little or no guidance as to how the requirements are to be met, simply specifying the required result. A performance standard is in some cases the easiest to write, and it allows the maximum level of flexibility to the implementer, since any means of accomplishing the end is sufficient. This particular standard promoted a fair and just—if somewhat brutal—society. It should also be noted that this standard dealt with very limited aspects of the products, and including in a performance standard all the details that are needed to ensure a successful product can be challenging.

Another step on the way to modern standards came about as a result of a massive fire that burned most of the city of London in 1666. *The Rebuilding London Acts*, promulgated by the Parliament of England over the following several years, are precursors of current building and safety codes. The specific motivation of these acts was first to ensure safety and stability in society, and they did so by widening streets and by specifying brick construction, so as to prevent recurrence of the disastrous fire.

Compared to the Code of Hammurabi, these Acts are quite prescriptive, specifying street widths, brick construction, thickness of walls (in terms of bricks), story heights and maximum heights of houses, and requirements for roof drainage. The effect of these and other associated requirements was to improve access, provide fire breaks in case another fire got started, and reduce the probability of its spread by replacing what was previously almost entirely wooden construction largely with bricks. Safety was enhanced, and it is to be expected that quality of life may also have been improved.

With the advent of the industrial revolution, other benefits of standards became obvious. As society developed the ability to produce products in quantity, and as machine tools were developed, the interchangeability of components became desirable. In the mid-1800s, for example, the British Standard Whitworth thread system was developed to allow for interchangeability of threaded parts.

Throughout the 1800s, there were many boiler explosions. While mourned, these seemed to be somewhat accepted as a cost of having boilers, which were providing benefits to society in the forms of more efficient transportation, working efficiency, and heating. The explosion of the boiler in a shoe factory in Brockton, MA, in 1905, which resulted in close to 60 deaths, and another shoe factory boiler explosion in Lynn, MA, the following year led to a greater concern with industrial safety. In 1907, the Massachusetts legislature passed the Massachusetts Boiler Law. This was followed by the first ASME Boiler Code in 1914.

The years between then and now have seen a proliferation of standards. These include the further development of the ASME Boiler Code [later to become the Boiler and Pressure Vessel Code (BPVC)] with sections on various types of pressure vessels, materials, welding, inspection, etc., and piping codes, lifting devices standards, electrical codes, and more. More recent work includes standards in the fields of energy efficiency, electronic components, software development, assessment of risk, and conformity assessment, and every time a new technology arises, it seems that standards for its application are not far off.

3. Tool Support

The tool support for our approach has to fulfill the following key requirements:

- Allow the creation of UML class diagrams which we use as a notation for representing our conceptual model.
- Allow the creation of a custom UML profile.
- Support the creation of OCL constraints at the level of the profile.
- Support the validation of OCL constraints.
- Provide customization of the messages given to the user when a constraint is violated.
- Provide the ability to create instances of the elaborated models.
- Provide the ability to create customized reports by querying the constructed models.

Any tool that fulfills the above requirements can be used as a platform for applying our approach. Amongst the existing alternatives, we have chosen Rational Software Architect (RSA) by IBM to provide tool support for our approach. In addition to meeting all the above requirements, RSA is a mature and industry strength tool with good usability, thus making it easier to apply our approach in an industrial setting and making it more likely for the approach to be adopted by practitioners.

Specifically, we used RSA to create the UML class diagrams for the conceptual model of the standard as well as the domain models for elaboration. We then used RSA to create the UML profile of the IEC61508 standard. RSA supports adding OCL constraints at the level of the profile. More importantly, it has a built-in OCL validation engine that we could utilize to provide the guidance for elaborating the domain models according to the IEC61508 profile. The messages given to the user when a constraint is violated can be customized. RSA also includes a report designer based on Business Intelligence Reporting Tool (BIRT) /8/, that can be used to publish reports in user-defined layouts based on the data in the models. While we have not yet customized this report designer for generating safety certification reports, the existence of such a flexible report generation framework was an important consideration that we had to account for.

The domain models can be created in a hierarchy. This allows one to start with a high-level view and then create more detailed models as and when necessary. Large diagrams can also be split into a number of smaller diagrams, but if an overall view of a particular element is required, then a "browse" diagram can be automatically generated. A "browse" diagram shows all the elements that a chosen element is related to and helps in understanding how that element fits into the overall system depicted in the model providing a snapshot of the overall context of an element. These diagrams are not permanent diagrams: they are generated from the most current information in the models and hence a browse diagram can be refreshed to show the latest state of the model elements. It is also possible to convert a browse diagram to an editable diagram. This provides a means to both get an overall context of an element and proceed to edit it if necessary.

SA further allows for custom documentation to be added to the stereotypes. When the mouse cursor hovers over a stereotype, a pop-up window displays the associated documentation. All stereotypes can be documented in this way to provide further assistance to the user while applying the stereotypes.

To help in the creation of the instance models, there is a properties view that shows the slots for the selected instance. Each slot is a mapping to an attribute of the classifier that has been instantiated and every time a value is created for a particular attribute, the properties view is updated to reflect the change. The creator of the instance model can thus see which slots have values already and which ones still need values. In this way, RSA can guide the user in creating a complete instance model.

4. Conceptual Model of a Safety Standard

A conceptual model is a formal description of some aspect of the physical and social world around us for the purpose of understanding and communicating amongst humans. It employs some formal notation which is a combination of diagrammatic and linguistic constructs and serves as a point of common agreement amongst a team of people and can also be used as a means of forwarding this understanding to newcomers joining the team.

A conceptual model of a safety standard should thus capture the main concepts and relationships in the evidence information required for showing compliance to the standard. We use UML class diagrams for conceptual modeling of safety standards. In UML class diagrams, concepts are represented as classes and concept attributes as class attributes. Relationships are represented by associations. Generalization associations are used to derive more specific concepts from abstract ones. When an attribute assumes a value from a predefined set of possible values, we use enumerations. Finally, the package notation is used to make groupings of concepts and thus better manage complexity.

Our choice of UML is based on the fact that it is a well-recognized and standardized notation and that the UML class diagram notation adequately fulfills our needs. From a practical standpoint, it is in general useful to ensure that the notation being employed is already accepted in industry and at the same time easy to learn for practitioners.

Creating a conceptual model of a standard requires a careful analysis of the standard's text to identify the salient concepts and relationships mentioned in the text. To record the concepts and relationships in a systematic way, we follow a process as we read through the standard: we label each concept with a name and create a definition for it in a glossary when it is first encountered. As we proceed through the text, we either create new labels or reuse previous ones based on the definitions we have. As we create the labels, we also identify the connections between them and represent all this within a UML class diagram. This process is in line with how qualitative data analysis /19,6/is performed in general, whereby text is analyzed to describe, classify and connect the information presented in it.

We exemplify the above process over a small excerpt of the IEC61508 standard that concerns software safety life cycle requirements. The excerpt is shown in Figure 11-5. In the figure, we highlight the key concepts and relationships by enclosing the relevant text in a box and numbering it.

Box 1 shows that the concepts phase and activity are of importance during the software development life cycle. Box 2 identifies some important relationships between phases and activities. An activity is performed during a phase and has specified inputs and outputs. Box 3 indicates that a generic life cycle is prescribed by the standard, though deviations in terms of phases and activities are not precluded. Box 4 includes the concepts: Technique, Safety Integrity Level and Technique Recommendation—indicating that activities should utilize certain techniques based on the safety integrity level. The same concepts and relationships can be found in several places in the standard and thus a glossary is created to ensure that consistent terms are used to refer to the same concepts and relationships.

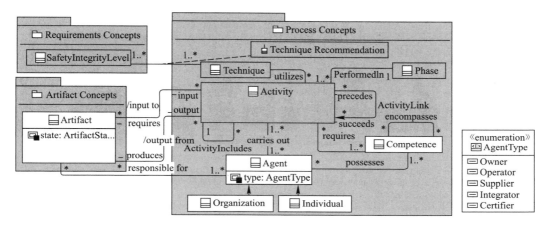

Figure 11-5   IEC61508 process concepts and their relationships

A graphical representation of the concepts and relationships from the excerpt is given in Figure 11-6. In the figure, we show some additional concepts (covered by the standard but not present in the excerpt) to aid the discussion about the process concepts in the rest of the article. We further note that the model in Figure 11-6 is still a partial representation of the concepts and relationships relevant to the development process. A full treatment can be found in Appendix A.

In Figure 11-6, we can see that an activity can include sub activities or it can be linked to another activity by either preceding or succeeding it; these relationships are modeled by the elements activity includes and activity link, along with the properties precedes and succeeds. Activities are to be performed by competent agents using techniques that are acceptable for the safety integrity level assigned to a component. All these aspects are modeled using the concepts agent, competence and technique and the relationships requires, carries out, possesses and technique recommendation. An activity may require certain artifacts as input and upon completion produce certain artifacts as output. These are modeled by the elements Artifact, Input To, Output From, Requires, Produces, Input and Output.

Sometimes a concept appears again, not in the same form as encountered previously, but rather as a specific case. In such instances, we use the generalization association from UML to indicate the relationship between the general and the more specific concepts. As an example, we show in Figure 11−7 a specific activity called SW Module Design Development during which the design for software modules and their corresponding test specifications are created. It has specific input and output artifacts of different types. In Figure 11−7, we can see two types of artifacts-Specification and Instruction, which are specialization of Artifact. Subsequently, we have specializations of instruction as Programming Guidelines and Development Tools Instruction; and specializations of Specification as SW Module Design, SW Module Test and SW System Design.

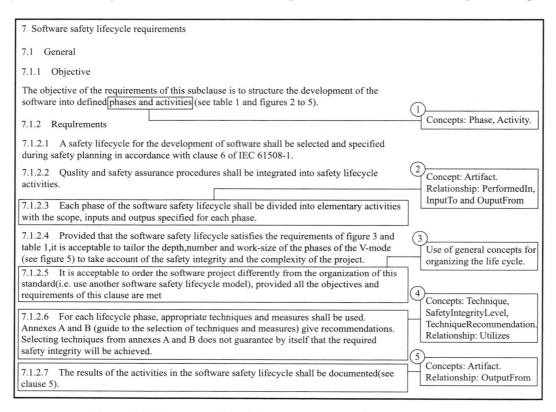

Figure 11−6 An excerpt from IEC61508 showing the textual source of some of the concepts and relationships

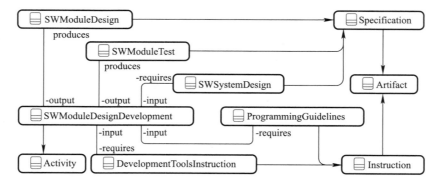

Figure 11−7 Software module design activity

The model resulting from the first step of our approach provides an explicit and precise interpretation of the evidence requirements in the underlying standard and is used in step 2 for creating a UML profile for the standard.

5. Case Study of Engineering Standards

The ZigBee Story:

ZigBee has its own history, but represents no less of a success story than Bluetooth. ZigBee's early supporters took it a little slower in the development of the technology and in pitching the wireless sensor network technology for the markets ZigBee was specifically designed for—remote monitoring and control, wireless sensing and monitoring (including medical apps), indoor wireless lighting controls, location sensing, home control, building automation, and advertising on mobile devices.

Initially designated as IEEE standard 802. 15. 4, ZigBee is part of a system of protocols that also serve Wireless HART, a wireless version of the Highway Addressable Remote Transducer (HART) used mainly in automation and industrial control apps, and the Internet Engineering Task Force (IETF)-developed 6LoWPAN (RFC5933 and RFC4919) that's part of Internet Protocol IPv6. Built around a network capable of transmitting data over long distances by passing data between intermediate devices, the technology was developed to fill holes in applications not addressed by Bluetooth and Wi-Fi. The standard covers Layer 1[the Physical Layer (PHY)]and Layer 2 [the Media Access Controller (MAC)] of the network. The ZigBee stack software provides network and applications layers.

A short-range, multichannel system for low-data-rate mesh networks that serve the fast-growing home automation device market, analysts are projecting annual shipments of ZigBee-enabled devices to grow more than five times from 2012 to 2018 with a Compound Annual Growth Rate (CAGR) of more than 30%. ZigBee chip set producers are expected to be key beneficiaries.

Market analysts see a particularly big opportunity for ZigBee in the home energy sector. Greg Potter of the Multimedia Research Group says, "ZigBee has been recognized as the connected and smart home technology of choice, due to its worldwide standardization and acceptance via the cable TV and service provider industries. Once the cable companies have taken the first step of providing ZigBee networks in the majority of new set-top boxes, it helps create a thriving industry of ZigBee add——on devices for the home." Potter expects revenues from services derived from ZigBee backbones to "skyrocket" within the home into 2017. Peter Cooney, practice director of ABI Research, says that home entertainment has become the largest market for ZigBee, largely for the ZigBee RF4CE spec that defines a remote control network for consumer electronic devices. "Markets that seemed to be sure-fire bets for rapid growth, such as smart meters, have not delivered as expected, while smart home markets continue to flourish."

Research and Markets list ZigBee as a major player in its forecast of emerging wireless sensor network technologies, along with Bluetooth Smart, Z-Wave, Dash7, and Wavenis. Z-Wave, a proprietary wireless standard that connects to home automation devices, announced the latest version of its compliance test tool (Version 2. 4. 7) in early 2014, designed to test all of the new requirements introduced in Z-Wave Plus devices. The Dash7 Alliance, formed in 2009 to promote the use of sub-1 GHz radio technologies, announced a new protocol in September 2013 based on the IEC 18000-7 standard that provides a framework for extensive application development, seamless interoperability, and security for Dash7-enabled apps. Dash7 is also working with the OASIS international open standards consortium to promote interoperability standards in wireless sensor networking. The Wavenis Open Standard Alliance (Wavenis-OSA) came out of technology developed by a company called Coronis for low-power, long distance wireless machine-to-machine (M2M) communications, such as remote monitors. Coronis gave the Wavenis specs to the Wavenis-OSA in June 2008; the alliance manages standardization activities for the royalty-free technology.

11.4　Reading Material

Wind Load Assessment in Marine and Offshore Engineering Standards

International marine and offshore engineering standards are a major tool for engineers designing complex marine and offshore structures. These structures need to comply strictly with standards carefully crafted by groups of leading experts and which are applicable in certain countries and territories. Given that many contemporary offshore engineering structures are of very complex architecture and are huge in size, reaching high into the lower atmosphere, while their structural parts are subjected to sea currents and waves, it is extremely important to precisely determine wind loads acting on these structures, i. e. their portions above sea level. At this point, procedures for assessing wind loads acting on offshore engineering structures as recommended in relevant international marine and offshore engineering standards seem to be inadequate, and substantial improvements may be needed in this regard. This particularly means that the effect of atmospheric turbulence on engineering structures should be taken into account because currently only the mean wind velocity profile (wind shear) is recommended in international marine and offshore engineering standards to be used as input data when calculating wind loads on the portions of offshore engineering structures above sea level. This issue is particularly relevant regarding offshore wind turbines given that this type of structure reaches high into the lower atmosphere where the wind effects on the structures are predominant.

Offshore wind turbine technology has been developing strongly to prevent further global warming and to reduce the depletion of fossil fuel reserves as global awareness rises concerning the relations among humans, society, the economy and nature, particularly regarding the responsible and sustainable exploitation of natural resources, Herbert et al. (2007). Wind energy technology has been receiving more attention as the concepts of sustainable, green, blue, and carbon-free societies have been introduced to the public, Lynn (2012). In addition to harnessing wind energy, carbon-free energy production concepts have also boosted the development of other renewable energy technologies, e. g. solar, geothermal, bioenergy, ocean (current, waves, salinity gradient, thermal) technologies, IPCC (2011). Various aspects of renewable energy technology have been considered, such as resource potential, current technology readiness levels, development prospects, societal and economic issues, project development, design, operation, maintenance, investment costs, Hadˇziˊc et al. (2014a, 2018).

Regarding global wind resource assessment, it was estimated that the maximum global wind energy potential is approximately 6000 EJ/year, while its technical potential ranges from 140 EJ/year to 3000 EJ/year, IPCC (2011). Based on this, it is clear that there is still plenty of space for the further development of wind farms, both onshore and offshore, particularly because the current global electricity consumption is approximately 90 EJ/year, BP (2019). Offshore wind farm developments are particularly motivated by several important factors, i. e. the lack of suitable onshore sites, and the fact that offshore wind farms are less unattractive and cause less noise pollution than those built onshore. In offshore wind farms, it is possible to install larger rotors that yield more energy, while an additional benefit is that there is less turbulence and higher average wind velocity on offshore sites, thus providing higher operating efficiency and lower structural fatigue, Koh and Ng (2016).

There are nevertheless some challenges regarding offshore wind energy harnessing, which are related to increased maintenance, especially at high sea, and the aggressive environment involving intensiffed corrosion processes and complex environmental loading exerted by concurrent wind, wave, and current actions, Hadˇziˊc et al. (2014a). In the case of the typical structural response of an offshore wind turbine, the wave and sea current loads may be assessed using established approaches that may vary depending on the offshore wind-turbine supporting structure and sea depth. However, the aerodynamic load aspect remains complex because of the stochastic nature of the wind, the interaction between the rotating blades and the wind, the aeroelasticity of the blades, the nonlinear loads, and the shadowing effects present in large offshore wind farms, Schafhirt et al. (2016). The complexity of this issue is even more exhibited if other aspects such as network uncertainties, operational costs, and energy management are also taken into account, Motaleb et al. (2016). It is therefore necessary to properly address the modeling procedures of various complex aspects related to offshore wind-turbine design, power output, life-cycle management, and the cost of energy.

The wind load assessment of offshore wind turbines is currently based on the rule-based approach, which assumes the wind is quasi-steady and may be represented by a simple empiric power-law approximation of the mean wind velocity profile without taking into account a myriad of relevant parameters representing atmospheric turbulence as it appears in nature, ABS (2018). Although such an approach is widely accepted and recommended in international marine and offshore engineering standards, it considers wind turbulence only to a limited extent, while neglecting the effect of rotor-induced harmonic loading and irregularities in the power output. Another common approach is the application of actuator disc theory and the blade element momentum theory which addresses the loading conditions of rotor blades, Manwell et al. (2009), Stevens et al. (2018). Unlike the rule-based approach, in the actuator disc and blade element momentum theories it is possible to take into account the harmonic properties of the wind-turbine rotor load. Nevertheless, this approach is highly sensitive to the anticipated wind velocity profile, and thus has the same drawback as the rule-based approach. At the moment, the most advanced approach is Computational Fluid Dynamics (CFD) by using Large Eddy Simulation (LES), the free-vortex method, or aeroelastic fluid-structure interactions, Lee et al. (2018). This methodology is characterized by some important issues, such as the need for high CPU resources and a detailed characterization of local wind flow and turbulence, a drawback present in the main currently used CFD codes and also in the major international marine and offshore engineering standards. This issue is particularly exhibited in the proximity of seaport areas and urban environments, where buildings and port infrastructure may strongly influence wind characteristics usually adopted as a reference for wind loading calculations, Ricci and Blocken (2020).

Several attempts have been made to address aerodynamic loads acting on offshore wind turbines, while most studies rely on the deterministic approach based on the wind energy density to take into account the stochastic nature of the wind. For example, Kim and Hur (2017) proposed a stochastic prediction of the wind by using the probability theory. A similar approach based on the Weibull and Rayleigh distributions was developed in Gyparakis et al. (2014) where the equivalent dynamic load acting on wind turbines is preset. Chen et al. (2020) developed a rotational sampling method that enables an analytic description of the fluctuating wind velocities on rotating blades. Here, the wind field analysis is based on the evolutionary frequency-wavenumber joint spectrum and the stochastic harmonic function representation. Li and Zhang (2020) studied the dependence of six different environmental parameters to enable the long-term formulation of design loads acting on offshore wind turbines at their critical points. The unsteady properties of the wind-turbine load were studied using the two-parameter Weibull distribution as a dominant design load component for the wind-turbine drive train design, Wang et al. (2019), where the wind velocity profile was also considered using the currently proposed (thus inadequate) power-law mean wind velocity profile based on the 1-h mean wind velocity at a 10 m height above the sea surface.

Chapter 12
Business Process Management

12.1 Business Decision

12.1 Professional Terms, Words and Phrases, Sentence Illustration

1. Introduction

Business Process Management (BPM) is the discipline in which people use various methods to discover, model, analyze, measure, improve, optimize, and automate business processes. Any combination of methods used to manage a company's business processes is BPM. Processes can be structured and repeatable or unstructured and variable. Though not required, enabling technologies are often used with BPM.

A business decision, sometimes called an operational decision, is any choice made by a business professional that determines short-term or long-term company activities. Professionals make business decisions in response to a variety of different situations, including determining which job candidate to hire, how to distribute department budgets, when to expand into a new product market, if they should merge branches and other situations that require well-thought out actions.

Successful operational business decisions can be achieved by:

- Managing knowledge and information.
- Getting the corporate culture right.
- Fostering creativity and innovation.
- Focusing on continuous improvement.
- Empowering and mobilising people.
- Fitting operational decisions with the overall strategy.

2. Methods and Tools

Decision-making is an important skill that all employees need. Proper decision-making techniques guarantee that you handle problems in the best manner possible and implement solutions with little risk. Making a decision requires a precise process and there are various possible methods. In this article, we discuss what decision-making is, break down the four primary methods of doing so and list the proper steps on how to find a solution.

When making a decision, it's important to understand how decisions are made and the factors involved in determining the best method. There are four primary methods to choose from: command, consult, vote, and consensus.

（1）Command

The command method involves making decisions without the help or inclusion of others. It's a major component of authoritative leadership as it often provides the fastest solution with little or no input. Emergency situations requiring quick action are where the command method works best. Those who make these decisions are often in managerial or other leadership roles. These decisions come with a high degree of risk compared to other alternatives.

（2）Consult

The consult method involves gaining insight from others but only allowing a single individual to make the final decision. This option often takes more time than the command method because it involves input from others. The consult method is not ideal for emergency situations but provides the opportunity for more people to give their opinions. It also offers solutions that come with little or no risk. Additionally, this method ensures that others feel included and guarantees they're heard within the decision-making process.

（3）Vote

The vote method occurs when all options are openly discussed in a group setting, resulting in the speaker calling for a vote. All those involved either vote for or against the decision in a democratic and fair process. Voting is best in group settings in which all opinions must be heard or when each member represents a larger body of employees. Voting is also a finite solution, creating a quick and effective decision-making process.

（4）Consensus

The consensus method is a group discussion in which all parties present all alternatives and points of view until they reach an agreement. This is a time-consuming method because it requires a large number of people with different ideas and motivations to come to an agreement. It often results in a long period of discussion time spanned across multiple meetings. Additionally, once they reach a decision, the chance of risk is significantly lower than all other methods. Make a sweeping statement that guarantees everyone understands that the decision is final.

The following steps outline the decision-making process:

（1）Identify the Decision

Once you realize a decision must be made, define its nature and conditions. Find any variables that relate to the problem for consideration as well. It's important to understand if a decision is worth making. Not all situations require a difficult decision, especially when other areas have a greater need for similar resources.

（2）Gather Information

Gather all the information you can regarding the situation and the decision. Determine what information is needed and the best sources for it. Additionally, consider seeking out information both internally and externally for every situation. For example, you might gather some information internally through a self-assessment process by simply looking at what's in front of you. Find other information externally online, in books or from other sources.

(3) Identify Potential Alternatives

Throughout your information gathering process, other alternatives may arise. Identify these separate paths and determine if any come with additional benefits. It's also viable to come up with your own alternatives based on the information provided. Collect all potential alternatives within a list for further consideration.

(4) Analyze All Evidence

Using all your information and a combination of both your intuition and reasoning, determine the possible results of each alternative. Look back to the need presented in step one and evaluate which of your chosen alternatives provides the best solution. Narrow down your list and set them in priority order, starting with the most effective and ending with the least effective.

(5) Choose an Option

With all evidence collected and all alternatives measured, choose the best option. Consider that multiple alternatives used in tandem with each other could provide the best solution. Whether you choose a single alternative or a mixture of two or more is dependent upon your unique situation and needs. Identify every possible outcome and the results it poses, positive or negative.

(6) Take Action

With your best course chosen, take the appropriate action. Begin implementing your decision and apply all required resources such as employees, technology or money. Watch how your new solution performs and make adjustments when and where necessary.

3. Model

First, it is essential to identify the decision makers in the organization and understand the process by which they reach their decisions. This is essentially a process of internal marketing and, as with any marketing campaign, you need to understand your customers and their psychology.

This includes looking at the different personality types and decision making processes represented in your organization, although this is not the place for in-depth psychological theory.

The decision-making process within each organization depends on the people involved and the culture of the organization. There may be one sole decision maker to win over or you may have to present your proposal to a group who will take a vote on whether to proceed or not. The process may involve consultation with stakeholders across the organization, or a straightforward pros-and-cons exercise by one individual.

Whatever the situation, you will need to understand this matrix of power. Figure 12−1 shows where these various models lie on the continuum from individual decision at one extreme to group consensus at the other.

Whatever the decision-making model, it will inevitably be affected by the bias of the individual or individuals involved. We cannot help being influenced by our likes, our dislikes, our past experiences and so on. So if at all possible, try to establish whether your decision makers have any previous experiences or influencers that may affect their thinking. You will then be able to make your presentation more relevant and also identify in advance any potential objections, which will help you to overcome them.

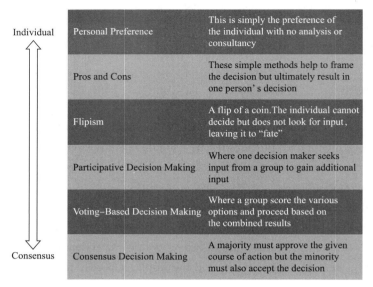

Individual	Personal Preference	This is simply the preference of the individual with no analysis or consultancy
	Pros and Cons	These simple methods help to frame the decision but ultimately result in one person's decision
	Flipism	A flip of a coin. The individual cannot decide but does not look for input, leaving it to "fate"
	Participative Decision Making	Where one decision maker seeks input from a group to gain additional input
	Voting-Based Decision Making	Where a group score the various options and proceed based on the combined results
Consensus	Consensus Decision Making	A majority must approve the given course of action but the minority must also accept the decision

Figure 12-1　Types of decision making

Here are some examples of bias that might impact on the process of decision making, with some ideas on how you can address each-note, however, that this is not an exhaustive list:

● Selective search for evidence: people tend to seek out or pay attention to facts that support the decision they favour.

Address this by: ensuring your proposal is well balanced.

● Peer pressure: some individuals will be influenced by stronger personalities.

Address this by: gathering a strong network of advocates in advance, and making sure that every decision maker has the opportunity to put questions and offer comments.

● Anchoring and adjustment: the information you present first has a tendency to shape how people perceive the rest of the message, and to influence their decisions.

Address this by: paying attention to the way in which your presentation/proposal tells a clear story. We discuss this in more detail below.

● Recency: most people tend to favour recent information over historic data in their decision making.

Address this by: ensuring your proposal is well balanced and that it includes data that covers all the key factors.

● Credibility: if someone has a low opinion of the presenter, or conversely someone they value highly appears not to support the idea, they will be likely to view the proposal negatively.

Address this by: getting support from others in place up front. Make sure the decision maker has a high opinion of you. Find out who it is they respect and get that person on your side, or consider having a credible advocate present on your behalf.

One well-known model that is particularly useful when analysing the psychology of decision making is the Myers-Briggs Type Indicator (MBTI), developed by Katharine Cook Briggs and her daughter Isabel Briggs Myers. This family team developed a set of four cognitive-behavioural dichotomies, which are widely used to assess the personalities and attributes of employees. The four dichotomies or scales are:

- thinking and feeling (T/F).
- extroversion and introversion (E/I).
- sensing and intuition (S/I).
- judgement and perception (J/P).

The theory is that these will dictate whether an individual will make decisions on an analytical or an emotional basis; there is some debate over its predictive accuracy but it remains a useful perspective, and it is worth reading up on the model to help you frame your thinking on the decision making style of your decision maker (s) and therefore the best way in which to present your case.

Another key factor will be the criteria used by boards in their standard decision-making process. These criteria will vary depending on the business but you should aim to cover these five areas in your proposal:

- Logic: how does this proposed investment fit with our agreed strategy?
- Reward: what is the size of the prize, and how quickly can we realize the benefits?
- Risk: if this doesn't work, what is the worst that can happen? Can we recover quickly?
- Execution: do we have the right resources-staff, skills, knowledge, time-to carry out this plan?
- Competition: if we Don't do this, will we fall behind our competitors?

12.2   Process Control

1. Introduction

12.2 Professional Terms, Words and Phrases, Sentence Illustration

The technology of controlling a series of events to transform a material into a desired end product is called process control. For instance, the making of fire could be considered a primitive form of process control. Industrial process control was originally performed manually by operators. Their sensors were their sense of sight, feel, and sound, making the process totally operator-dependent. To maintain a process within broadly set limits, the operator would adjust a simple control device. Instrumentation and control slowly evolved over the years, as industry found a need for better, more accurate, and more consistent measurements for tighter process control. The first real push to develop new instruments and control systems came with the Industrial Revolution, and the First and Second World Wars added further to the impetus of process control. Feedback control first appeared in 1774 with the development of the fly-ball governor for steam engine control, and the concept of proportional, derivative, and integral control during the First World War. The Second World War saw the start of the revolution in the electronics industry, which has just about revolutionized everything else. Industrial process control is now highly refined with computerized controls, automation, and accurate semiconductor sensors.

2. The Form of Process Control

Process control can take two forms: ① sequential control, which is an event-based process in which one event follows another until a process sequence is complete; or ② continuous control, which requires continuous monitoring and adjustment of the process variables. However, continuous process control comes in many forms, such as domestic water heaters and heating, ventilation, and air conditioning (HVAC), where the variable temperature is not required to be measured with great precision, and complex industrial process control applications, such as in the petroleum or chemical industry, where many variables have to be measured simultaneously with great precision. These variables can vary from temperature, flow, level, and pressure, to time and distance, all of which can be interdependent variables in a single process requiring complex microprocessor systems for total control. Due to the rapid advances in technology, instruments in use today may be obsolete tomorrow. New and more efficient measurement techniques are constantly being introduced. These changes are being driven by the need for higher accuracy quality, precision, and performance. Techniques that were thought to be impossible a few years ago have been developed to measure parameters.

(1) Sequential Process Control

Control systems can be sequential in nature, or can use continuous measurement; both systems normally use a form of feedback for control. Sequential control is an event-based process, in which the completion of one event follows the completion of another, until a process is complete, as by the sensing devices.

(2) Continuous Process Control

Continuous process control falls into two categories: ① elementary On/Off action, and ② continuous control action.

On/Off action is used in applications where the system has high inertia, which prevents the system from rapid cycling. This type of control only has only two states, On and Off; hence, its name. This type of control has been in use for many decades, long before the introduction of the computer. HVAC is a prime example of this type of application. Such applications do not require accurate instrumentation. In HVAC, the temperature (measured variable) is continuously monitored, typically using a bimetallic strip in older systems and semiconductor elements in newer systems, as the sensor turns the power (manipulated variable) On and Off at preset temperature levels to the heating/cooling section.

Continuous process action is used to continuously control a physical output parameter of a material. The parameter is measured with the instrumentation or sensor, and compared to a set value. Any deviation between the two causes an error signal to be generated, which is used to adjust an input parameter to the process to correct for the output change.

3. Process Control Methodologies

The principal objective for the process industries represented by the IOF is to develop technology to enable the transition of controls from the environmental level to the in-situ level. Areas where process control technology can be significantly improved include:

- effective use of process measurements.
- robust on-line learning (intelligence applications).
- autonomous control reconfigurations.
- automatic diagnostics and maintenance.
- management of abnormal situations (e. g. , start-up, shutdown, and fault recovery).
- plantwide process optimization.

Control input signals must be accurate and repeatable with few variations; sensor drift, faults, and noise corruption can compromise the data. If multiple sensors are required, there may be high costs for wiring and installation. Even when reliable data are available, information must be rapidly extracted from a mass of data.

Many advanced control algorithms require more accurate process modeling than is available in most industries. Most process models do not adequately address real-world issues of process nonlinearity, instability, inaccuracies in input signals, and the number and complexity of variables. All of these factors have meant that industry now uses complex systems that have long development times and high implementation costs and risks to end users.

The panel suggests the following research areas to address these common needs:

- Intelligent control algorithms would address process nonlinearity, capture heuristic knowledge, and fill voids in first-principles knowledge.

- Neural networks would generate multivariable, nonlinear, reduced-order models from process data. However, ① the current state of knowledge makes it extremely difficult to develop process understanding from "learned" weighting factors; and ② neural networks require large process data sets that accurately represent the entire process space over which the control is to be applied.

- Fuzzy logic strategies can capture heuristic knowledge but require "expert" knowledge that can be translated into rules.

- Chaos theory is already being applied to industrial processes, such as power generation, to extract ordered models of global behavior from apparently random signals.

Recently, advances have been made in several technologies relevant to process controls. Business system models for scheduling production, pull systems, and flow-time minimization are being widely used, as are computer-based systems to monitor maintenance data and schedule preventive maintenance. Reliability techniques are being used to design equipment and analyze data to estimate maintenance schedules from mean time between failures and other statistics.

Improving the state of practice in the IOF industries will require both improving the technologies described above and combining them to cover the large range of issues presented by real processes. Stability criteria must be developed, for example, for the intelligent, nonlinear algorithms to reduce processing risk. Control systems must be able to "learn" on line as processes change and to reconfigure themselves autonomously. This learning must be robust to ensure process reliability. Modeling techniques (first principle, heuristic, neural network, and fuzzy logic) should be integrated into hybrid models in which each technique is applied to the part of the larger process or plant for which it is best suited.

4. Process Modeling

To perform an effective job of controlling a process, we need to know how the control input we are proposing to use will affect the output of the process. If we change the input conditions we shall need to know the following:

- Will the output rise or fall?
- How much response will we get?
- How long will it take for the output to change?
- What will be the response curve or trajectory of the response?

The answers to these questions are best obtained by creating a mathematical model of the relationship between the chosen input and the output of the process in question. Process control designers use a very useful technique of block diagram modeling to assist in the representation of the process and its control system. The principles that we should be able to apply to most practical control loop situations are given below.

The process plant is represented by an input/output block as shown in Figure 12-2.

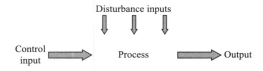

Control inputs are also known as "manipulated variables".
The output is the process varible to be controlled.

Figure 12-2　Basic block diagram for the process being controlled

In Figure 12-2 we see a controller signal that will operate on an input to the process, known as the MV. We try to drive the output of the process to a particular value or SP by changing the input. The output may also be affected by other conditions in the process or by external actions such as changes in supply pressures or in the quality of materials being used in the process. These are all regarded as disturbance inputs and our control action will need to overcome their influences as best as possible.

The challenge for the process control designer is to maintain the controlled process variable at the target value or change it to meet production needs, whilst compensating for the disturbances that may arise from other inputs. So, for example, if you want to keep the level of water in a tank at a constant height whilst others are drawing off from it, you will manipulate the input flow to keep the level steady.

The value of a process model is that it provides a means of showing the way the output will respond to the actions of the input. This is done by having a mathematical model based on the physical and chemical laws affecting the process. For example, in Figure 12-3 an open tank with cross-sectional area A is supplied with an inflow of water Q_1 that can be controlled or manipulated.

The outflow from the tank passes through a valve with a resistance R to the output flow Q_2. The level of water or pressure head in the tank is denoted as H. We know that Q_2 will increase as H increases, and when Q_2 equals Q_1 the level will become steady.

The block diagram version of this process is drawn in Figure 12-4.

Note that the diagram simply shows the flow of variables into function blocks and summing points, so that we can identify the input and output variables of each block.

We want this model to tell us how H will change if we adjust the inflow Q_1 whilst we keep the outflow valve at a constant setting. The model equations can be written as follows:

$$\frac{\mathrm{d}H}{\mathrm{d}t} = \frac{Q_1 - Q_2}{A} \quad \text{and} \quad Q_2 = \frac{H}{R} \tag{12-1}$$

The first equation says the rate of change of level is proportional to the difference between inflow and outflow divided by the cross-sectional area of the tank. The second equation says the outflow will increase in proportion to the pressure head divided by the flow resistance R.

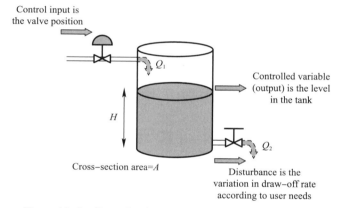

Figure 12-3　Example of a water tank with controlled inflow

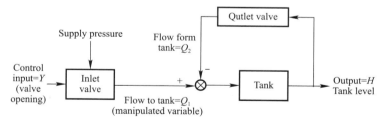

Figure 12-4　Elementary block diagram of tank process

Cautionary note: For turbulent flow conditions in the exit pipe and the valve, the effective resistance to flow R will actually change in proportion to the square root of the pressure drop so we should also note that R = a constant $x \times H$. This creates a non-linear element in the model which makes things more complicated. However, in control modeling it is common practice to simplify the nonlinear elements when we are studying dynamic performance around a limited area of disturbance. So, for a narrow range of level we can treat R as a constant. It is important that this approximation is kept in mind because in many applications it often leads to problems when loop tuning is being set up on the plant at conditions away from the original working point.

The process input/output relationship is therefore defined by substituting for Q_2 in the linear differential equation

$$\frac{\mathrm{d}H}{\mathrm{d}t}=\frac{Q_1}{A}-\frac{H}{RA} \tag{12-2}$$

which is rearranged to a standard form as

$$(RA)\left(\frac{\mathrm{d}H}{\mathrm{d}t}\right)+H=RQ_1 \tag{12-3}$$

When this differential equation is solved for H it gives

$$H=RQ_1(1-e^{\frac{-t}{RA}}) \tag{12-4}$$

Using this equation we can show that if a step change in flow ΔQ_1 is applied to the system, the level will rise by the amount $\Delta Q_1 R$, by following an exponential rise vs time. This is the characteristic of a first order dynamic process and is very commonly seen in many physical processes. These are sometimes called capacitive and resistive processes, and include examples such as charging a capacitor through a resistance circuit (Figure 12-5) and heating of a well-mixed hot water supply tank (Figure 12-6).

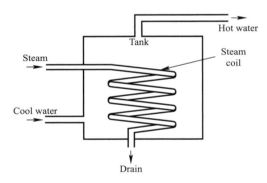

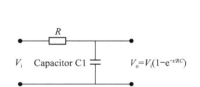

Figure 12-5　Resistance and capacitor circuit with first order response

Figure 12-6　Resistance and capacitance effects in a water heater

12.3　Process Management

1. Definition

Process management refers to a group of interrelated activities implemented by enterprises that transform input into output for the purpose of obtaining stable and maximum "added value".

12.3 Professional Terms, Words and Phrases, Sentence Illustration

Process management is a systematic method centering on the standardized construction of end-to-end excellent business processes and aiming at continuously improving the business performance of an organization. Common business management education such as EMBA and MBA has introduced "process management", which is sometimes called BPM business process management. Process management is the selection of the inputs, operations, work flows, and the methods that transform inputs into outputs.

2. Theory

Process management is the core of the process, the process is the foundation of any business operation, all the business process is needed to drive, just like the body's blood flow to the relevant information data according to certain conditions (department) from one person to the other personnel (department) to get corresponding results later returned to the relevant person (or department). An enterprise from different departments, different customers, different people and different suppliers are on the process to work together, the process in May with the corresponding data transfer process: document/product/financial data/project/task/personnel/customer information such as flow, if poor circulation will lead to the enterprise operation.

Strategy: strategy determines process management, process needs to support the implementation of strategy, strategic initiatives to be implemented in the corresponding process. Not only must the process be identified to implement strategic initiatives, but it must also be organically integrated and managed. Strategic maps, or value chains, must ultimately be aligned with process systems.

Process: Process management itself starts with the top-level process architecture and forms an end-to-end hierarchical process system. Define and design methods and standards for the process management lifecycle, and design end-to-end Process Performance Indicators (PPI). The establishment of central process library is an important feature of process-centered thought.

Personnel: Process management is a very professional work. To realize the organization's process-centered thinking, the first step is to realize the training of process management promoters and the training and development of internal process management personnel. Process learning community construction and process management knowledge exchange mechanism construction are important embodiment. Certification in process management will promote process-centric thinking among leaders, managers, and employees, leading to organizational change.

Tools: The application of IT and non-IT management tools plays an important role in the commonality and implementation of process ideas. Establishing an enterprise-level process management platform, combining the process with the strategic goal of the enterprise, and then associating with IT system effectively, can effectively realize the process thinking of the organization.

Sub-process: According to different industries, the process framework of the enterprise is sorted out based on the value chain, the phased process is defined, and then the hierarchical process is sorted out. Enforce the execution of the process. The superior process cannot be started until the sub-process is completed.

Process nesting: Generally speaking, it is the associated view and preposition relationship between processes. The operation of the process system is based on the construction and implementation of the process system.

3. Methods or Tools

(1) Find a starting point tools: learn pentagram.

It is a best practice process for companies to identify areas for improvement from a variety of sources: customers, suppliers, employees, consultants, and benchmarking.

① Customers are an important source of information that enterprises need to know. The most important customers are often the best place to start in the improvement area, and it is necessary to include very creative customers and world-class operational customers. Sometimes, a particularly critical client's point of view may be the target of a new design approach.

② Suppliers can provide similar assistance to enterprises, and this assistance is not limited to the lower end of the process. A good supplier's interest extends to the entire supply system.

③ The employees of the enterprise have an in-depth understanding of the process, which is also an important source of improving the process ideas.

④ Consultants can provide a useful "outside observer" perspective to drive the BPR project.

⑤ Benchmarking. Companies seek knowledge and inspiration through benchmarking and learning examples.

(2) Process selection tool: 80/20 principle.

Process selection is to determine the objectives of process combing, optimization and reengineering. Process selection follows the "Jewish law" (80/20 principle).

Focus first on the "critical processes", which may account for only 20% of the total number but account for 80% of the organization's performance. Therefore, instead of stopping at every platform on the way of "process management", choose to stop at the place of concern along the way of "process management".

(3) Process selection tool: performance-importance matrix process or the result of the process on the matrix of location on behalf of its importance as well as the organization on the degree of how they run, the degree of importance degree and running performance respectively from low to high, combining with the compare customer feedback data and internal data often get unexpected results. If both aspects are evaluated on a scale of 1 to 5, the project can be divided into four types, of which the areas with high importance and low performance are the areas that need improvement most.

(4) Process selection tool: Process sorting can select the process sorting method to select the key process.

① Evaluate each related process with three indicators: Impact, Scale and Scope; among them, "Impact" refers to the possible contribution to the enterprise's future business goals after the process reengineering, "scale" refers to the amount of enterprise resources consumed during the process reengineering, and "Scope" refers to the cost, personnel and risk affected during the process reengineering.

② "Impact" can be used to evaluate the benefits of ten scales; "Scale" is measured in terms of full-time man-hours (FTE) and estimated costs; "Scope" can be measured in terms of time, cost, risk, and personnel complexity on a scale of three to five.

③ After the 2d table is listed, the reengineering team members discuss and decide the priority of the reengineering process.

④ It is not necessary to use accurate data for cost, risk and time assessment, but only need to reach consensus on the trade-offs of various factors.

（5）Process optimization or reengineering target selection tool: Benchmarking method.

Benchmarking method can be used to set up the goals and prospects of reform, determine the benchmark of process reengineering and so on. There are some successful enterprises in many industries, and the practices of these enterprises can be emulated by other enterprises in the industry. Therefore, some specific indicators of these enterprises can also be used as benchmarks for other enterprises.

（6）The process description tool describes the activities between organizational entities (positions) and the various interactions between the entities. It can be realized with various process description software, such as Aris, Visio, Smartdraw and so on.

（7）Process problem analysis tool: Fishbone diagram analysis with the help of fishbone diagram, from six aspects to find the causes of process problems. This is 5M1E: Management, Man, Method, Material, Machine, Environment.

Finally, identify the primary cause (the process bottleneck) and use it as a feature of the problem. Repeat the steps until the cause is clear and the basis for the solution is formed.

（8）Process problem thinking tool: 5W3H analysis method.

（9）Process optimization tools: ECRS Technique.

ECRS technique refers to the Elimination, Combination, Rearrangement and Simplification techniques and refers to the Elimination and Simplification of existing working methods. Through the "cancel-merge-rearrange-simplify" four technologies to form the existing organization, workflow, operating procedures and working methods of continuous improvement.

① Elimination: Ask the first question of any job: Why do you do it? Can you quit?

a. Cancel all organizations, workflows, operations or actions without added value.

b. Reduce the irregularity in the work, such as determining the fixed location of the workpiece and tools, and forming habitual mechanical actions.

② Combination, if it cannot be cancelled, consider whether it can be combined with other organizations, workflows, operations, actions, implementation tools, use resources, etc.

③ Rearrangement: To scientifically rearrange the order of work as needed.

④ Simplification refers to simplification of organizational structure, working procedures, operations and actions.

4. Models

Individual audits or post project retrospectives can yield valuable lessons and recommendations that team members can apply to future project work. When done on a consistent basis, they can lead to significant improvements in the processes and techniques that organizations use to complete projects. A more encompassing look from an organization wide point of view is to use a project maturity model. The purposes of all maturity models (and there are many available) are to enable organizations to assess their progress in implementing the best practices in their industry and move to improvement. It is important to understand that the model does not ensure success; it only serves as a measuring stick and an indicator of progress.

The term maturity model was coined in the late 1980s from a research study by the United States government and the Software Engineering Institute (SEI) at CarnegieMellon University. The government wanted a tool to predict successful software development by contractors. The outcome of this research was the Capability Maturity Model (CMM). The model focuses on guiding and assessing organizations in implementing concrete best practices of managing software development projects. Since its development, the model is now used across all industries. Currently, over 2400 organizations around the world report their maturity progress to the Software Engineering Institute.

One newer model has received a great deal of publicity. In January 2004, after eight years of development, the Project Management Institute rolled out its second version of the "Organizational Project Maturity Model." The latest version is called OPM3TM. Typically, these models are divided into a continuum of growth levels: Initial, Repeatable, Defined, Managed, and Optimized. Figure 12-7 presents our version, which borrows liberally from other models. What we have tried to do is focus less on a process and more on the state an organization has evolved to in managing projects.

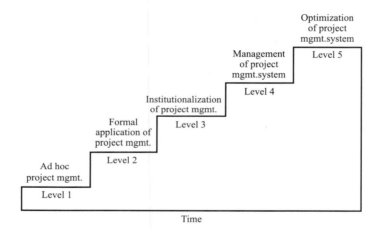

Figure 12-7　Project management maturity model

(1) Level 1: Ad Hoc Project Management

No consistent project management process is in place. How a project is managed depends upon the individuals involved. Characteristics of this level include:

- No formal project selection system exists—projects are done because people decide to do them or because a high-ranking manager orders it done.

- How any one project is managed varies by individual—unpredictability.

- No investment in project management training is made.

- Working on projects is a struggle because it goes against the grain of established.

- Policies and procedures.

(2) Level 2: Formal Application of Project Management

The organization applies established project management procedures and techniques. This level is often marked by tension between project managers and line managers, who need to redefine their roles. Features of this level include:

- Standard approaches to managing projects including scope statements, WBS, activity lists are used.

- Quality emphasis is on the product or outcome of the project and is inspected instead of built in.

- The organization is moving in the direction of stronger matrix with project managers and line managers working out their respective roles.

- Growing recognition of need for cost control, not just scope and time management, exists.

- There is no formal project priority system established.

- Limited training in project management is provided.

(3) Level 3: Institutionalization of Project Management

An organization wide project management system, tailored to specific needs of the organization with the flexibility to adapt the process to unique characteristics of the project, is established. Characteristics of this level include:

- An established process for managing projects is evident by planning templates, status report systems, and checklists for each stage of project life cycle.

- Formal criteria are used to select projects.

- Project management is integrated with quality management and concurrent engineering.

- Project teams try to build in quality not simply inspect it.

- The organization is moving toward a team-based reward system to recognize project execution.

- Risk assessment derived from WBS and technical analyses and customer input is in place.

- The organization offers expanded training in project management.

- Time-phased budgets are used to measure and monitor performance based on earned value analysis.

- A specific change control system for requirements, cost, and schedule is developed for each project, and a work authorization system is in place.

- Project audits tend to be performed only when a project fails.

(4) Level 4: Management of Project Management System

The organization develops a system for managing multiple projects that are aligned with strategic goals of the organization. Characteristics of this level include:

- Portfolio project management is practiced; projects are selected based on resource capacity and contribution to strategic goals.

- A project priority system is established.

- Project work is integrated with ongoing operations.

- Quality improvement initiatives are designed to improve both the quality of the project management process and the quality of specific products and services.

- Bench marking is used to identify opportunities for improvement.

- The organization has established a Project Management Office or Center for Excellence.

- Project audits are performed on all significant projects; lessons learned are recorded and used on subsequent projects.

- An integrative information system is established for tracking resource usage and performance of all significant projects.

（5）Level 5：Optimization of Project Management System

The focus is on continuous improvement through incremental advancements of existing practices and by innovations using new technologies and methods. Features include：

- A project management information system is fine-tuned；specific and aggregate information is provided to different stakeholders.

- An informal culture that values improvement drives the organization，not policies and procedures.

- There is greater flexibility in adapting the project management process to demands of a specific project.

A major theme of this book is that the culture of the organization has a profound impact on how project management methodology operates. Audits and performance evaluation require informed judgment. Good decision making depends not only on the accuracy of the information，but also on the right information. For example，imagine how much different your response might be if you made an honest mistake but did not trust management and felt insecure versus if you had confidence and trust in management. Or think how different the quality of information that would surface from a team would be where trust was divided versus a team that works in a Level 5 environment.

Progress from one level to the next will not occur overnight. The Software Engineering Institute estimates the following median times for movement：

Maturity level 1 to 2 is 22 months.

Maturity level 2 to 3 is 19 months.

Maturity level 3 to 4 is 25 months.

Maturity level 4 to 5 is 13 months.

12. 4　Reading Material

Process management is the management of the review and approval process of financial data. You can use process management to submit budget plans and have them approved efficiently，and to transfer ownership of data. In a centralized environment，you can also use process management to provide review control and to ensure data privacy.

For the purpose of review，data is organized into process units. A process unit is the combination of data for a specific Scenario，Year，Period，Entity，and Value dimension. In the Value dimension，you can select Local，Translated，or Contribution data. For example，a process unit could be a combination of data for Actual，2014，January，WestSales，and USD. During the review cycle，you use process management to submit，promote，approve，reject，and publish process units.

Before you can use Process Management，the administrator must enable process management using the Support Submission Phase attribute for the Scenario dimension in the metadata file. When this attribute is enabled, Process Management is available for the specified scenarios.

When you select a cell, Process Management is available only for the input frequency of the scenario. For example, if the input frequency is months, Process Management is available when you select January, but is not available when you select a quarter, such as Q_1. If you select multiple cells and your selection includes a data cell in which Process Management is not supported, the Process Management option is not available.

If Process Management is enabled for a scenario, the system performs validation checks for each process unit as the data moves from one level to the next. Validation checks are defined by the administrator to ensure that accounts are in balance. See Process Management Validation.

Chapter 13
Innovation and R&D Management

13. 1　New Product Development

13. 1 Professional Terms, Words and Phrases, Sentence Illustration

1. Overview of NPD Theories

The early stages of the new product development process are most usually defined as idea generation, idea screening, concept development and concept testing. They represent the formation and development of an idea prior to its taking any physical form. In most industries, it is from this point onwards that costs will rise significantly. It is clearly far easier to change a concept than a physical product. The subsequent stages involve adding to the concept as those involved with the development (manufacturing engineers, product designers and marketers) begin to make decisions regarding how best to manufacture the product, what materials to use, possible designs and the potential market's evaluations.

The organizational activities undertaken by the company as it embarks on the actual process of new product development have been represented by numerous different models. These have attempted to capture the key activities involved in the process, from idea to commercialization of the product. The representation of these tasks has changed significantly over the past 30 years. For example, the pharmaceutical industry is dominated by scientific and technological developments that lead to new drugs; whereas the food industry is dominated by consumer research that leads to many minor product changes. And, yet, the vast majority of textbooks that tackle this subject present the NPD process as an eight-stage linear model, regardless of these major differences (Figure 13−1 shows how the process is frequently presented). Consequently, this simple linear model is ingrained in the minds of many people. This is largely because new product development is viewed from a financial perspective where cash outflows precede cash inflows. This graph shows the cumulative effect on cash flow through the development phases, from the buildup of stock and work in progress in the early stages of production, when there is no balancing inflow of cash from sales, to the phase of profitable sales that bring the cash inflow.

Figure 13−1　Commonly presented linear NPD model

Virtually all those actually involved with the development of new products dismiss such simple linear models as not being a true representation of reality. More recent research suggests that the process needs to be viewed as a simultaneous and concurrent process with cross-functional interaction.

For the reasons outlined above, the different perspectives on NPD have produced a wealth of literature on the subject. In addition, the subject has attracted the attention of many business schools and business consultants, all interested in uncovering the secrets of successful product development. Numerous research projects have been undertaken, including in-depth case studies across many industries and single companies and broad surveys of industries.

As a result, research on new product development is varied and fragmented, making it extremely difficult toorganize for analysis. Brown and Eisenhardt (1995) produced a highly regarded review of the literature. In their analysis, they identify three main streams of literature, each having its own particular strengths and limitations (Table 13 − 1). These streams have evolved around key research findings and, together, they continue to throw light on many dark areas of new product development. Slateretal (2014) offer a more recent literature review of radical new product development.

The three main streams of research within NPD literature   Table 13−1

Item	Rational planning	Communication web	Disciplined problem solving
Aim/objective/title	Rational planning and management of the development of new products within organisations	The communication web studies the use of information and sources of information by product development teams	Disciplined problem solving focuses on how problems encountered during the NPD process were overcome
Focus of the research	The rational plan research focuses on business performance and financial performance of the product	The communication web looks at the effects of communication on project performance	The third stream tries to examine the process and the wide range of actors and activities involved
Seminal research	The work by Myers and Marquis (1969) and SAPPHO studies (Rothwell et al., 1974) was extremely influential in this field	Thomas Allen's (1969, 1977) research into communication patterns in large industrial laboratories dominates this perspective	The work by the Japanese scholars lmai et al. (1985) lies at the heart of this third stream of literature

Source: Brown S L, Eisenhardt K M. Product development: past research, present findings and future directions [J]. Academy of Management Review, 1995, 20(2): 343-378.

Whilst this is an important development and a useful contribution to our understanding of the subject area, it offers little help for the practising manager on how he or she should organize and manage the new product development process. An analysis of the models that have been developed on the subject of new product development may help to identify some of the activities that need to be managed.

(1) The Fuzzy Front End

Within the new product development literature, the concept of the so-called "fuzzy front end" is the messy getting started period of new product development processes. It is at the beginning of the process, or the front end, where the organization develops a concept of the product to be developed and decides whether or not to invest resources in the further development of an idea. It is the phase between first consideration of an opportunity and when it is judged ready to enter the structured development process. It includes all activities from the search for new opportunities through the formation of a germ of an idea to the development of a precise concept. The fuzzy front end disappears when an organisation approves and begins formal development of the concept.

Although the fuzzy front end may not require expensive capital investment, it can consume 50 percent of development time and it is where major commitments typically are made involving time, money and the product's nature, thus setting the course for the entire project and final end product. Consequently, this phase should be considered as an essential part of development rather than something that happens "before development", and its cycle time should be included in the total new product development cycle time. This is even more critical for discontinuous new products, which are particularly challenging at this early stage in what is, by definition, intrinsically complex and risky, but offering high potential rewards.

There has been much written in NPD literature about the need to involve customers at an early stage in the process and to integrate them into the process in order to fully capture ideas. Despite this, customer involvement in NPD has been limited and largely passive in most industries. There are many reasons for this limited utilisation of consumers in NPD and some we have touched on above, but perhaps the most limiting factor is the disconnection between customers and producers.

Nowadays, technology enables an innovative way of involving and integrating customers to the product development process. In this context, it is here that new technologies, most notably in the form of "toolkits", offer considerable scope for improving connection between consumers and producers. Franke and Piller's (2004) study analysed the value created by so-called "toolkits for user innovation and design". This was a method of integrating customers into new product development and design. The so-called toolkits allow customers to create their own product, which, in turn, is produced by the manufacturer. An example of a toolkit in its simplest form is the development of personalised products through uploading digital family photographs via the internet and having these printed on to products, such as clothing or cups, etc., thereby allowing consumers to create personalised individual products for themselves. User toolkits for innovation are specific to given product or service types and to a specified production system. Within those general constraints, they give users real freedom to innovate, allowing them to develop their custom product via iterative trial and error.

Nambisan (2002) offers a theoretical lens through which to view these "virtual customer environments". He considers the underlying knowledge creation issues and the nature of the customer interactions to identify three roles: customer as resource; customer as co-creator and customer as user. These three distinct but related roles provide a useful classification with which to examine the process of NPD. This classification recognises the considerably different management challenges for the firm if it is to utilise the customer into the NPD process (Table 13-2).

Customer roles in NPD   **Table 13-2**

Customer role	NPD phase	Key issues/managerial challenges
Customer as resource	Ideation	Appropriateness of customer as a source of innovation Selection of customer innovator Need for varied customer incentives Infrastructure for capturing customer knowledge Differentia role of existing (current) and potential (future) customers
Customer as co-creator	Design and development	Involvement in a wide range of design and development tasks Nature of the NPD context: industrial/consumer products Tighter coupling with internal NPD teams Managing the attendant project uncertainty
Customer as user	Product testing	Enhancing customers' product/technology knowledge Time-bound activity Ensuring customer diversity
	Product support	Ongoing activity Infrastructure to support customer-customer interactions

Source: Nambisan S. Designing virtual customer environments for new product development: toward a theory[J]. Academy of Management Review, 2002, 27(3): 395.

(2) Customer Cocreation of New Products

Research by Mahr (2014) sheds light on opportunities and limitations of customer cocreation. They find customer cocreation is most successful for the creation of highly relevant, but moderately novel, knowledge. Cocreation with customers who are closely related to the innovating firm results in more highly relevant knowledge at a low cost. Yet, cocreation with lead users produces novel and relevant knowledge. Recent research by Bogers and Horst (2014) shows how collaborative prototyping across functional, hierarchical and organisational boundaries can improve the overall prototyping process.

(3) Time to Market

Time to Market (TTM) is the length of time it takes from a product being conceived to it reaching the market place. TTM is important in industries where products are outdated quickly. A common assumption is that TTM matters most for innovative products, but, actually, the first mover often has the luxury of time, whilst the clock clearly is running for the followers. TTM can vary widely between industries, say 15 years in aircraft and 6 months in food products. Yet, in many ways, it is a firm's TTM capability relative to its direct competitors that is far more important than the naked figure. Whilst other industries may be much faster, they do not pose a direct threat-although one may be able to learn from them and adapt their techniques.

As usual, there are some other factors that need to be considered when analysing a firm's TTM. For example, rather than reaching the market as soon as possible, delivering on schedule may be more important: to have the new product available for a trade show could be more valuable. Many managers argue that the shorter the project the less it will cost, so they attempt to use TTM as a means of cutting expenses. Unfortunately, a primary means of reducing TTM is to staff the project more heavily, so a faster project may actually be more expensive. Finally, as we have seen throughout this chapter, the need for change often appears midstream in a project. Consequently, the ability to make changes during product development without being too disruptive can be valuable. For example, one's goal could be to satisfy customers, which could be achieved by adjusting product requirements during development in response to customer feedback. Then TTM could be measured from the last change in requirements until the product is delivered. The pursuit of pure speed of TTM may also harm the business.

(4) Agile NPD

Flexible product development is the ability to make changes to the product being developed or in how it is developed, even relatively late in the development process, without being too disruptive. Consequently, the later one can make changes, the more flexible the process is; and the less disruptive the change is, the greater the flexibility. Change can be expected in what the customer wants and how the customer might use the product, in how competitors might respond, and in the new technologies being applied in the product or in its manufacturing process. The more innovative a new product is, the more likely it is that the development team will have to make changes during development. In his book *Flexible Product Development* (2007), Preston Smith uses the software industry to show that having an agile NPD process enables the firm to adapt to changing markets. These days, many industrial New Product Development (NPD) software projects apply agile methodologies, such as Scrum, eXtreme Programming (XP) and Feature-Driven Development (FDD). Petri Kettunen from Siemens studied some of these systems and found that agility in embedded software product development can be enhanced further by following typical NPD principles (Kettunen, 2009).

2. NPD Research Techniques

The following is a brief guide to some of the research techniques used in consumer testing of new products. Some products and services go through all the stages listed, but few do or should go through all these. The techniques would have to be adapted to meet the specific requirements of the product or service under consideration.

(1) Concept Tests

Qualitative techniques, especially group discussions, are used to obtain target customer reactions to a new idea or product. Question areas would cover:

- Understanding and believability in the product.
- Ideas about what it would look like.
- Ideas about how it would be used.
- Ideas about when and by whom it might be used.

This would help to reveal the most promising features of the new product, and groups to whom it might appeal. It might be argued that the assessment of purchase intent is the primary purpose of concept testing, so that products and services with poor potential can be removed. The most common way to assess purchase intention is to provide a description of the product or take the product to respondents and ask whether they:

- definitely would buy.
- probably would buy.
- might or might not buy.
- probably would not buy.
- definitely would not buy.

（2）Test Centres

These are used for product testing when the product is too large, too expensive or too complicated to be taken to consumers for testing. One or more test centres will be set up and a representative sample of consumers brought to the test centre for exposure to the product and questioning about their reaction to it.

（3）Hall Tests/Mobile Shops

These are used commonly for product testing or testing other aspects of the marketing mix, such as advertising, price, packaging, etc. A representative sample of consumers is recruited, usually in a shopping centre, and brought to a conveniently located hall or a mobile caravan, which acts as a shop. Here they are exposed to the test material and asked questions about it.

（4）Product-Use Tests

These are used frequently in business-to-business markets. A small group of potential customers are selected to use the product for a limited period of time. The manufacturer's technical people watch how these customers use the product. From this test, the manufacturer learns about customer training and servicing requirements. Following the test, the customer is asked detailed questions about the product, including intent to purchase.

（5）Trade Shows

Such shows draw large numbers of buyers who view new products in a few days. The manufacturer can see how buyers react to various products on display. This technique is convenient and can deliver in-depth knowledge of the market because the buyers' views may differ considerably from those of the end-user consumers.

（6）Monadic Tests

The respondents are given only one (hence the name) product to try, and are asked their opinion of it. This is the normal situation in real life when a consumer tries a new product and draws on recent experience with the product they usually use, to judge the test product. The method is not very sensitive in comparing the test product with other products because of this.

（7）Paired Comparisons

A respondent is asked to try two or more products in pairs and asked, with each pair, to say which they prefer. This is less "real" in terms of the way consumers normally use products, but does allow products to be deliberately tested against others.

（8）In-Home Placement Tests

These are used when an impression of how the product performs in normal use is required. The products are placed with respondents who are asked to use the product in the normal way and complete a questionnaire about it. Products may be tested comparatively or sequentially.

（9）Test Panels

Representative panels are recruited and used for product testing. Test materials and questionnaires can be sent through the post, which cuts down the cost of conducting in-home placement tests. Business-to-Business firms may also have test panels of customers or intermediaries with whom new product or service ideas or prototypes can be tested.

3. Models of New Product Development

Amongst the burgeoning management literature on the subject, it is possible to classify the numerous models into eight distinct categories:

① Departmental-stage models.

② Activity-stage models and concurrent engineering.

③ Cross-functional models (teams).

④ Decision-stage models.

⑤ Conversion-process models.

⑥ Response models.

⑦ Network models.

⑧ Outsourced.

Within this taxonomy, decision-stage models and activity-stage models are the most commonly discussed and presented in textbooks.

It is worthy of note that there are many companies, especially small specialist manufacturing companies, that continue to operate a craftsman-style approach to product development. This has been the traditional method of product manufacture for the past 500 years. For example, in every part of Europe, there are joinery companies manufacturing products to the specific requirements of the user. Many of these products will be single, one-off products manufactured to dimensions given on a drawing. All the activities, including the creation of drawings, collection of raw materials, manufacture and delivery, may be undertaken by one person. Today, when we are surrounded by technology that is sometimes difficult to use, never mind understand, it is possible to forget that the traditional approach to product development is still prevalent. Many activities, moreover, remain the same as they have always been.

（1）Departmental-Stage Models

Departmental-stage models represent the early form of NPD models. These can be shown to be based around the linear model of innovation, where each department is responsible for certain tasks. Usually, they are represented in the following way. R&D provides the interesting technical ideas; the engineering department will then take the ideas and develop possible prototypes; the manufacturing department will explore possible ways to produce a viable product capable of mass manufacture; then the marketing department will be brought in to plan and conduct the launch. Such models are also referred to as "over-the-wall" models, so called because departments would carry out their tasks before throwing the project over the wall to the next department (Figure 13-2).

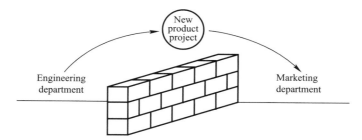

Figure 13-2   Over-the-wall model

It is now widely accepted that this insular departmental view of the process hinders the development of new products. The process usually is characterised by a great deal of reworking and consultation between functions. In addition, market research provides continual inputs to the process. Furthermore, control of the project changes on a departmental basis, depending on which department currently is engaged in it.

(2) Activity-Stage Models and Concurrent Engineering

These are similar to departmental-stage models, but because they emphasise activities conducted, they provide a better representation of reality. They also facilitate iteration of the activities through the use of feedback loops, something that the departmental-stage models do not. Activity-stage models, however, have also received fierce criticism for perpetuating the "over-the-wall" phenomenon. More recent activity-stage models have high-lighted the simultaneous nature of the activities within the NPD process, hence emphasising the need for a cross-functional approach.

In the late 1980s, in an attempt to address some of these problems, many manufacturing companies adopted a concurrent engineering or simultaneous engineering approach. The term was first coined by the Institute for Defense Analyses (IDA) in 1986 to explain the systematic method of concurrently designing both the product and its downstream production and support processes. The idea is to focus attention on the project as a whole, rather than the individual stages, primarily by involving all functions from the outset of the project. This requires a major change in philosophy from functional orientation to project orientation. Furthermore, technology-intensive businesses with very specialist knowledge inputs are more difficult to manage. Such an approach introduces the need for project teams.

(3) Cross-Functional Models (Teams)

Common problems that occur within the product development process revolve around communications between different departments. In addition, projects frequently would be passed back and forth between functions. Moreover, at each interface, the project would undergo increased changes, hence lengthening the product development process. The Cross-Functional Teams (CFT) approach removes many of these limitations by having a dedicated project team representing people from a variety of functions. The use of cross-functional teams requires a fundamental modification to an organisation's structure. In particular, it places emphasis on the use of project management and interdisciplinary teams.

（4）Decision-Stage Models

Decision-stage models represent the new product development process as a series of decisions that need to be taken in order to progress the project. Like the activity-stage models, many of these models also facilitate iteration through the use of feedback loops. However, a criticism of these models is that such feedback is implicit rather than explicit. The importance of the interaction between functions cannot be stressed enough—the use of feedback loops helps to emphasise this.

13. 2　Innovation

1. Definitions of Innovation

13. 2 Professional Terms, Words and Phrases, Sentence Illustration

"Innovation is the successful exploitation of new ideas"—Innovation Unit (2004) UK Department of Trade and Industry.

"Industrial innovation includes the technical, design, manufacturing, management and commercial activities involved in the marketing of a new (or improved) product or the first commercial use of a new (or improved) process or equipment".

"... Innovation does not necessarily imply the commercialization of only a major advance in the technological state of the art (a radical innovation) but it includes also the utilization of even small-scale changes in technological know-how (an improvement or incremental innovation)".

"Innovation is the specific tool of entrepreneurs, the means by which they exploit change as an opportunity for a different business or service. It is capable of being presented as a discipline, capable of being learned, capable of being practised".

"Companies achieve competitive advantage through acts of innovation. They approach innovation in its broadest sense, including both new technologies and new ways of doing things".

"An innovative business is one which lives and breathes ' outside the box'. It is not just good ideas, it is a combination of good ideas, motivated staff and an instinctive understanding of what your customer wants".

Management of technological innovation is a unique field of study that focuses on a technology company's ability to grow through activities relating to advancement of R&D, new product development, new technological knowledge creation, and improvements to existing products and processes. Management of technological innovation (MTI) involves strategic alignment of business goals with opportunities for innovation using tools of forecasting, planning, and market adoption. Although data and analytics play an important role in making decisions, the people aspect must be highly regarded throughout all processes. Impacts on organizational culture, internal capabilities, and external networks must be considered as to not create any additional barriers to the innovation process. "Technological barriers are those instances where the use of the technology is perceived as not being sufficient to perform the tasks or accomplish the objectives for which the technology was initially utilized". Many industry experts agree that real value is created by the people, and technological innovation can ultimately become self-sustaining by maintaining knowledge creation and motivation within a properly selected working group or organization.

2. Innovation Theories

Triple Helix of university-industry-government relationships that drives innovation: University research and research-related activities contribute in many important ways to modern economies: notably through increased productivity of applied R&D in industry due to university-developed new knowledge and technical know-how; provision of highly valued human capital embodied in staff and students; development of equipment and instrumentation used by industry in production and research; and creation of concepts and prototypes for new products and processes, which may have some unexpected and large social and economic impacts. Major discoveries emanating from academic and/or publicly funded research have had enormous global economic and social impacts that are obvious but difficult to predict and quantify (e. g. , Google, the World Wide Web, Nanotechnologies, etc.). Roessner et al. (2013) offers quantitative evidence that the economic impact of university research and technology transfer activities is significant.

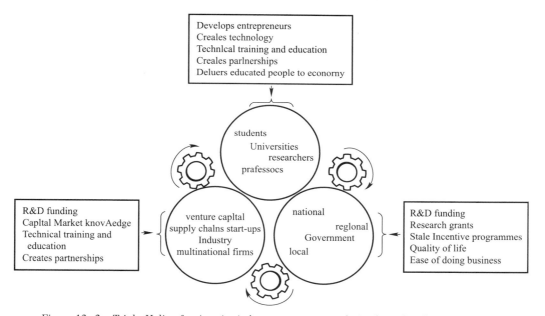

Figure 13-3   Triple Helix of university-industry-government relationships that drives innovation

Lundvall (1988) first introduced the concept of "national systems of innovation" by elaborating on Christopher Freeman's (1987) study entitled Technology, Policy, and Economic Performance: Lessons from Japan. In Freeman's study he argued that Western nations could learn from Japan's experience in the coordination, at the national level, of S&T policies orchestrated by the Japanese Ministry of Trade and Industry (MITI). More recently, the Japanese economy has not been viewed with much admiration. Nonetheless, the Japanese model or system knew what was expected technologically in order to meet (economic) demands and (political) objectives. In this integrative model, university-industry-government relations were synchronised at the national level. Similarly, the Triple Helix of university-industry-government relation-ships initiated in the 1990s by Etzkowitz and Leydesdorff (1995), interprets the shift from a dominating industry-

333

government dyad in the Industrial Society to a growing triadic relationship between university-industry-government in the Knowledge Society. The Triple Helix thesis is that the potential for innovation and economic development in a Knowledge Society lies in a more prominent role for the university. Specifically, regarding the production, transfer and application of knowledge.

Emerging technologies can be expected to be more diversified and their life cycles are likely to become shorter than before. According to Ivanova and Leydesdorff (2014), government policy makers need to take account of a shift from the production of material objects to the production of innovative technologies.

The right business environment is key to innovation. Schumpeter preached technology as the engine of growth but also noted that to invest in technology there had to be spare resources and long time-horizons. So the business environment must give the right signals to the business units for them to invest in such operations. In this regard, not only does macroeconomic stability play a significant role, but also the availability of quick (short-term) returns and opportunistic trends needs to be suppressed so that the money can flow into basic research and R&D. Likewise, the approach of business would differ if it faced strong (external or internal) competition. A protected domestic market more often than not amounts to signalling to business units that they should seek monopolistic or oligopolistic returns by not making enough investment into new product development or even product improvement.

3. Doing, Using and Interacting (DUI) Mode of Innovation

Researchers have recognised for many years that in Low and Medium Technology (LMT) intensive industries the traditional science and technology model of innovation is not applicable and cannot explain continued product and process innovations (see Arrow, 1968; Bush, 1945; Fitjar and Rodriguez-Pose, 2013; Maclaurin, 1953; Pavitt, 2001). Further, in the classic article by Pavitt he spelt out, in his typology of firms, that "LMT industries are characterised by process, organisational and marketing innovations, by weak internal innovation capabilities and by strong dependencies on the external provision of machines, equipment and software". LMT sectors are central to economic growth. Whether measured in terms of output, capital invested or employment, they dominate the economies of highly developed as well as developing nations, providing more than 90 percent of output in the European Union, the USA and Japan. Given this dominant position within modern industrialised economies, attempting to better understand the nature of innovation within this sector is of concern to policymakers and industrialists.

The role of low technology intensive firms and industries in modern economies is complex and frequently misunderstood. This is due partly to Hatzichronoglou's (1997) widely used revision of the OECD classification of sectors and products that refers only to high technology (defined as spending more than 5 percent of revenues on research and development). This has contributed to an unfortunate tendency to understate the importance of technological change outside such R&D-intensive fields. Products and production processes in these industries may be highly complex and capital intensive. Research in the area of low technology intensive industries shows a dominance of incremental, mostly process-driven innovations where disruptive innovation activities are scarce.

The food industry traditionally has experienced very low levels of investment in R&D, yet has delivered both product and process innovation over a sustained period. In such environments, innovation can be explained through learning by doing and the use of networks of interactions and extensive tacit knowledge. Similarly, Jensen et al. (2007) characterised a learning by "Doing, Using and Interacting" (DUI) mode of innovation where extensive on-the-job problem solving occurs and where firms interact and share experiences. More recently, Fitjar and Rodriguez-Pose (2013) developed a classification of DUI firm interactions in a study of firm-level innovation in the food industry in Norway. They found that "firms which engage in collaboration with external agents tend to be more innovative than firms that rely on their own resources for innovation".

(1) Building a Strategic Portfolio

All but the smallest organizations are likely to want to include more than one innovation project in their strategy. While a decision matrix helps you compare projects, you also need diversity in your innovation portfolio. Portfolio management helps you to achieve this.

(2) Balancing Your Portfolio

For a balanced portfolio you need a mix of decision criteria: the risk of failure must be balanced with the rewards of success. This requires analysis of potential obstacles against potential benefits. In general, a safe innovation will be based on what your company does well. More risky innovations are radical in nature. While the risks of such innovations are greater, the potential rewards are also significantly more attractive. You may decide to back a couple of high-risk projects if they are small because they could move you to a new game—and if they fail only a small amount of resources will be wasted—but it would be foolish to base all your hopes of progress on risky ventures that may never work out.

(3) Gaining an Overview

It is useful to develop an overview of your portfolio not just in terms of the risks and rewards, but also in terms of how much you are allocating to each project (Figure 13-4). This can be done by using a bubble chart, which is generated by plotting your projects as circles on a graph against potential risk and potential reward. The more resources a project requires, the larger its corresponding circle on the chart. This chart gives you an instant view of what resources are allocated to what levels of risk and reward. It can show you immediately if you have too many resources tied up in risky projects that are unlikely to succeed in the end. Equally, you can see if you are putting too much investment in a safe bet that is unlikely to generate significant rewards.

(4) Promoting Ideas for Change

Unless you are a top manager in your organization, chances are that you will need to "sell" your ideas for change at some point. Maybe you are an entrepreneur pitching an idea to a potential investor, or you have a great idea about how to make things work more efficiently in your organization. In either case, you will need support if your idea is to become a reality.

(5) Making the Business Case

Whatever the starting point, the destination will be the same: you need to convince someone else that your idea is great and that it will work, and that they will get their investment (of time

MANAGING YOUR PORTFOLIO	
FAST TRACK	**OFF TRACK**
The number of innovation projects in progress at any one time is limited.	There is no limit to the projects you can take on, so you spread your resources too thinly.
Innovation projects have targets and are abandoned if targets are not met.	You are reluctant to kill off projects if they are not working out.
Priority is given to innovations that meet strategic goals.	Unimportant projects succeed at the cost of strategically valuable innovations.
Innovation projects are subject to careful selection.	You do not have a clear criteria for selecting projects.

Figure 13-4　Managing Your Portfolio

and money) back. And they need to believe in you and your capacity to deliver all of this. The problem is that you believing in your idea is unlikely to be enough—you need to put together a compelling business case to convince others that your idea has practical potential.

(6) Gaining Support

Organizations need to innovate, but they cannot do everything. They need to explore options and then make tough decisions about which ideas they will back and why. You can influence these decisions to your advantage—if you know your organization is trying to put together a portfolio of projects that balances risk and reward, you can try and make them include yours in the mix. But you need to present your idea in such a way that its merits are clear. Ask yourself how you can engage them—can you show them a prototype so they can add their comments? Do you have the answers to questions they might ask you? And do you come across as being passionate about the project—will they believe in you?

(7) Covering All the Angles

Making a compelling business case is at the heart of innovation (Figure 13-5). Decisions will not get made on the basis of personality and passion alone—you need to be able to convince decision-makers to spend resources on a project that will work. Is there a market, will the technology work, can you protect the idea, what will it cost, and what are the likely benefits? Showing that you have thought the project through and have answers to any difficult questions they might throw at you will enhance your chances of a successful pitch.

4. Models of Innovation

Traditional arguments about innovation have centred on two schools of thought. On the one hand, the social deterministic school argued that innovations were the result of a combination of external social factors and influences, such as demographic changes, economic influences and cultural changes. The argument was that when the conditions were right, innovations would occur. On the other hand, the individualistic school argued that innovations were the result of unique

BUILDING A GOOD BUSINESS CASE	
FEATURE	WHAT TO INCLUDE
Outline your idea	A short and simple explanation of your idea—how it is new and what it will do. Remember it is not what you think but how "they" see it, so try and present it in terms of what it will do for them. You might try mapping it on a strategic position map.
Market analysis	Who is it targeted at? Who wants it, why do they need it, and why don't they have it yet? How big is this market? Is it growing, declining, or static?
Competitors	Who else is out there, what do they offer, how will this idea get ahead of them, how might they react, and how do you protect yourself from that?
Why it will work	What do you know, and what prior knowledge, skills, experience, and networks can you bring to the table?
Rewards	What will you get if you succeed—money, market share, customer satisfaction—and how long you will have to wait until you get them?
Costs	How much will it cost, and what do you need to make it happen?
Risk factors	What might pose problems and how will you get around them?
Project management	Who will take this forward and how? What reassurances can you offer that you can do it?

Figure 13-5　Building a good business case

individual talents and such innovators are born. Closely linked to the individualistic theory is the important role played by serendipity; more on this later.

Over the past 10 years, the literature on what drives innovation has tended todivide into two schools of thought: the market-based view and the resource-based view. The market-based view argues that market conditions provide the context that facilitates or constrains the extent of firm innovation activity. The key issue here, of course, is the ability of firms to recognise opportunities in the marketplace. Cohen and Levinthal (1990) and Trott (1998) would argue that few firms have the ability to scan and search their environments effectively.

The resource-based view of innovation considers that a market-driven orientation does not provide a secure foundation for formulating innovation strategies for markets that are dynamic and volatile; rather a firm's own resources provide a much more stable context in which to develop its innovation activity and shape its markets in accordance with its own view. The resource-based view of innovation focuses on the firm and its resources, capabilities and skills. It argues that when firms have resources that are valuable, rare and not easily copied they can achieve a sustainable competitive advantage-frequently in the form of innovative new products.

(1) Serendipity

Many studies of historical cases of innovation have highlighted the importance of the unexpected discovery. The role of serendipity or luck is offered as an explanation. As we have seen, this view is also reinforced in the popular media. It is, after all, everyone's dream that they will accidentally uncover a major new invention leading to fame and fortune.

On closer inspection of these historical cases, serendipity is rare indeed. After all, in order to recognise the significance of an advance, one would need to have some prior knowledge in that area. Most discoveries are the result of people who have had a fascination with a particular area of science or technology and it is following extended efforts on their part that advances are made. Discoveries may not be expected, but in the words of Louis Pasteur, 'chance favours the prepared mind'.

(2) Linear Models

It was US economists after the Second World War who championed the linear model of science and innovation. Since then, largely because of its simplicity, this model has taken a firm grip on people's views on how innovation occurs. Indeed, it dominated science and industrial policy for 40 years. It was only in the 1980s that management schools around the world began seriously to challenge the sequential linear process. The recognition that innovation occurs through the interaction of the science base (dominated by universities and industry), technological development (dominated by industry) and the needs of the market was a significant step forward (Figure 13-6). The explanation of the interaction of these activities forms the basis of models of innovation today. Students may also wish to note that there is even a British Standard (BS7000), which sets out a design-centred model of the process (BSI, 2008).

Figure 13-6　Conceptual framework of innovation

There is, of course, a great deal of debate and disagreement about precisely what activities influence innovation and, more importantly, the internal processes that affect a company's ability to innovate. Nonetheless, there is broad agreement that it is the linkages between these key components that will produce successful innovation. Importantly, the devil is in the detail. From a European perspective, an area that requires particular attention is the linkage between the science base and technological development. The European Union (EU) believes that European universities have not established effective links with industry, whereas in the United States universities have been working closely with industry for many years.

As explained above, the innovation process has traditionally been viewed as a sequence of separable stages or activities. There are two basic variations of this model for product innovation. First, and most crudely, there is the technology-driven model (often referred to as technology push) where it is assumed that scientists make unexpected discoveries, technologists apply them to develop product ideas and engineers and designers turn them into prototypes for testing. It is left to manufacturing to devise ways of producing the products efficiently. Finally, marketing and sales will promote the product to the potential consumer. In this model, the marketplace was a passive recipient for the fruits of R&D. This technology-push model dominated industrial policy after the Second World War (Figure 13-7). Whilst this model of innovation can be applied to a few cases, most notably the pharmaceutical industry, it is not applicable in many other instances; in particular where the innovation process follows a different route.

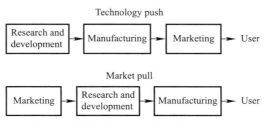

Figure 13-7　Linear models of innovation

It's only by understanding what the customer wants that we can identify the innovative opportunities. Then we see if there's technology that we can bring to bear on the opportunities that exist. Being innovative is relatively easy-the hard part is ensuring your ideas become commercially viable.

(*Murray*, 2003)

13.3　Technological Innovation

13.3 Professional Terms, Words and Phrases, Sentence Illustration

1. Definitions of Technology and Innovation

Technology is a replicable artefact with practical application, and the knowledge that enables it to be developed and used. Technology is manifested in new products, processes, and systems, including the knowledge and capabilities needed to deliver functionality that is reproducible.

Innovation is much more than invention—the creation of a new idea and its reduction to practice—and it includes all the activities required in the commercialization of new technologies. Essentially, innovation is the successful commercial exploitation of new ideas. It includes the scientific, technological, organizational, financial, and business activities leading to the commercial introduction of a new (or improved) product or service.

2. Types and Extent of Technological Innovation

The type and extent of technological innovation varies, with consequences for its management. Researchers have analysed extent and type of innovation according to whether it is:

● Radical or incremental—that is, the extent to which a technology has changed, or the degree of novelty of an innovation. Radical innovations include breakthroughs that change the nature of products and services, such as synthetic materials, and may contribute to the "technological revolutions". Incremental innovations include the "million little things" that involve minor changes to existing products, which cumulatively improve the performance of products and services. Radical innovation usually requires greater investment in basic research than incremental changes, and more links with research institutes, and may follow different diffusion patterns.

Continuous or discontinuous—that is, whether it affects existing ways of doing things, or whether it is sustaining or disruptive. Firms commonly find it very difficult to break away from previous technologies and ways of innovating, and managers may need to explore new ways of doing things that are destructive of existing successes.

Change over life cycles—that is, how it relates to early emergence of an innovation, a period of ferment and uncertainty, progress to a takeoff period of growth, and maturity in a satiated market.

- Modular—that is, occurs in components and subsystems without addressing the system of which it is a part; or architectural—that is, attempts systemic improvements without great attention to its component parts. The management of Systems Integration (SI) poses very different MTI challenges to innovation in modules or components.

- Results in the emergence of a dominant design. MTI changes once a dominant design—the winning product class in the market, the one competitors and innovators must adhere to—is established.

- Occurs within open or closed innovation strategies. The innovation involves different strategies for buying, selling, and collaborating.

3. Choosing the Right Tools

Innovation strategy formulation involves making choices about which tools to use and when to use them. This box provides some broad guidance on making sensible choices about gathering and analysing evidence and monitoring activities to inform MTI decision-making. As we have seen, however, innovation can be inherently uncertain and reliable evidence is often difficult to obtain and decisions usually involve judgement based on experience.

A plethora of tools and techniques is available to support decision-making, including techniques for performance measurement and evaluation of cost benefit. Many are adapted from general strategy and project management. Choosing the right technique, using it at the right time, and understanding the benefits and limitations of qualitative and quantitive data present major challenges in MTI. It must be remembered that the reliability of results from data-gathering and analytical exercises is likely to diminish in more radical innovation environments where novelty and uncertainty are higher. In contrast, the use of tools to set targets, measure and monitor performance in incremental innovation, and continuous improvement environments is commonplace. A distinction needs to be made between tools and techniques that assist decision-makers on what to do, as inputs into strategy, and those that assist with how to do it, which are more tactical and operational. A key requirement is for managers to have a well-grounded perspective on the level of risk and uncertainty in possible future courses of action. Failure to do so can lead to major mistakes in choice of tools and techniques.

Figure 13-8 provides some examples of tools and techniques used to assist innovation strategy. They are not exclusive; many different methods exist. The particular tools depicted in the figure are in the "what to do" categories, and those in the larger box are in the "how to do it" categories. Some tools are used in several phases of the innovation process.

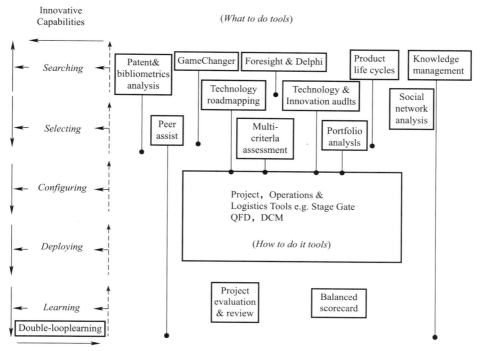

Figure 13-8　Some examples of tools and techniques supporting innovative capabilities

There are no hard and fast rules about which to use and when to use them, but some tools are more helpful than others at particular stages of innovation strategy development. Reliance on particular techniques and their results can focus managers' attention narrowly on detailed issues that do not allow decisions to be made in a way that connects with the wider business context. In general, it is better to keep data gathering, measurement, and analysis as simple as possible and to see the results of tools as an input to decision-making rather than letting them drive the direction of future events. Overly elaborate instruments can use up scarce resources and may not provide results that are any better than simple approaches. In either case, firms need the capacity to absorb and make use of results in a systematic fashion. The choice of a particular tool therefore has to fit within a wider framework of decision-making and capability in the firm. Some tools will need to be used repeatedly in particular innovation processes; others evolve as the process develops.

In general, tools and techniques that support strategic thinking are useful if they provide a means for managers to reflect upon issues and decisions in what Schön (1991) describes as reflective development, using a common language across disciplines and functions involved in innovation processes. For this reason, the double-loop learning processes are particularly useful in helping firms develop capabilities and avoid investigating unproductive ideas again and again.

4. Models

Social sciences emerged under the shadow of the physical sciences and to some extent the methods, epistemologies and strategies they employed mirrored those of the established physical sciences. Indeed, the Enlightenment in Europe heralded a new scientific revolution, which has influenced all the different types of knowledge-development in the modern era. We also suggested that knowledge-development in the social sciences took a number of different forms, resulting in phenomenological, critical and post-modernist epistemic revolutions. One of these new epistemic forms was an intensely practical one, that of knowledge-development through the Research and Development (R&D) sector. Research and Development activities range from very practical and quick problem solving to basic research, essentially driven by curiosity and with less concern as to its immediate application.

In 1963, the Organization for Economic Cooperation and Development (OECD) in Frascati, Italy, published a manual for policy-makers describing and proposing a standard practice for surveys of research and development. In the Frascati Manual, R&D is described as having three elements: (1) basic research in experimental or theoretical work undertaken primarily to acquire new knowledge of the underlying foundation of phenomena and observable facts, without any particular application or use in mind; (2) applied research is also considered to be original investigation undertaken in order to acquire new knowledge (however, it is directed primarily towards a specific practical aim or objective); and (3) experimental development is systematic work, drawing on existing data gathered from research and/or practical experience, where the aim is to produce new processes, systems, and services, or to improve substantially those already produced or installed.

Basic and applied forms of research are points on a continuum, with many interconnections. A generalized linear model was produced in the twentieth century, which suggested that innovation starts with basic research. It then becomes applied research, is developed as a product, and finally, is used by people in society. The last two steps are more associated with innovation. What we can observe today is that innovation is no longer a distant consequence of basic research. Innovation becomes in many instances the origin of the research programme and, as a consequence, moderates and stimulates the science itself. At the same time, the traditional assumption that innovation results from meeting demand is replaced by the idea that sometimes innovation also generates demand which previously had never been imagined. This suggests a simplified knowledge management scheme (Figure 13-9).

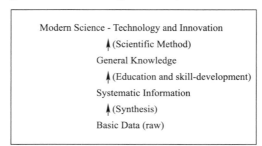

Figure 13-9　Knowledge-development management scheme

Starting from basic data, through its synthesis and organization, systematic information is generated. This in part promotes education and skills development, allowing for general knowledge to be transferred from generation to generation. The specific fraction of general knowledge, which is based on the scientific method, is recognized as modern science, which is closely associated with technology and innovation.

With regards to science, traditionally, the model in Figure 13-10 was considered to be the norm. However, a new model (Figure 13-11) now has more credence.

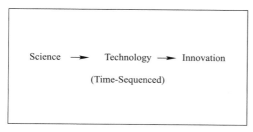

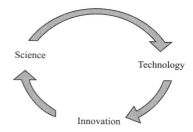

Figure 13-10   Science-Technology-Innovation
time-sequence traditional model

Figure 13-11   Science-Technology-Innovation
model, time-sequenced in accordance
with a contemporary circular relationship

Innovation is becoming more central in the knowledge-development process, broader in scope and it is both an end-product and a stimulant for knowledge in its own right.

Suh (2010) argues that there are three necessary conditions for the occurrence of innovatory practices. The first of these is that all steps or elements of an innovation continuum are present. The second is that an innovation hub can be nucleated if the initial size of the nucleate is larger than a critical size and if the activation energy barrier for nucleation can be overcome. Finally, the last requires that the nucleation rate must be faster than the rate at which innovative talents and ideas can diffuse away from the region. In this new scenario, educational institutions have increasingly played a central role in science, technology and innovation-based economic development, and the role of universities and research centres has evolved from performing conventional research and educational functions to serving as innovation promoting knowledge hubs.

The traditional university, in general, looks backwards and understands itself as a storehouse or accumulator of old knowledge. On the other hand, the modern university sees itself as a generator of technological innovation and economic development in its region. Where innovation is the central issue, universities are simultaneously central generators, essentially motivated by external demands, and repositories of knowledge. The way that knowledge is developed, disseminated and applied affects not only the cultural richness of the society, but also its global competitiveness. To meet the challenges of competitiveness, appropriate policies are necessary to encourage and facilitate closer understanding and joint work between universities and the productive sector.

13. 4 Professional
Terms, Words and
Phrases, Sentence
Illustration

13.4   Engineering Innovation

1. Definitions of Engineering Innovation

Let's start by looking at the terms "engineering" and "innovation". An engineer is someone who approaches situations and problems in a methodical and systematic way. Due to this style of problem solving, engineers are often considered rigid and inflexible.

On the other hand, "innovation" brings to mind words such as creativity, brilliance, novelty, and inspiration. "Innovation" is a vague term that refers to anything that has not been done before. By way of example, "innovation" could mean developing a software program that merges information from multiple sensors in a new way, developing a platform service that revolutionizes the way people perform daily tasks, or developing a noninvasive technique to deliver gene therapy to specific cells in the body. But innovation does not need to be as complicated or technical as these examples. Innovation could simply be developing a cell phone case that also holds credit cards or a no-drip, homemade popsicle stick.

An innovation does not have to be one significant or disruptive technological development that will make billions of dollars. Rather, innovations can be small or incremental, but more importantly, innovations change how the process was done before. Innovation is often a response to the grueling redundancy of performing the same duties day in and day out in the workplace. As discussed in this book, innovation can also be formulated to increase the likelihood of commercial success.

Engineering Innovation outlines what it takes to transition a creative and inspiring new concept into a successful product/process/service using a methodical, structured plan, and approach.

2. Business Development & Product or Technology Development

Taking an innovation from ideation to market success involves two separate processes that must occur simultaneously: building a business around the innovation (i.e., Business Development) and evolving the innovation from an idea to a viable product or service from a technical standpoint (i.e., engineering the innovation through Product or Technology Development). Both the Business Development Process and the Product/Technology Development Process run in parallel and generally correspond to the life cycle stages of the company, which also coincidentally correspond to stages of funding that companies often encounter as they grow from a startup to an established business.

Figure 13 – 12 shows the relationship between the Business Development Process and the Product/Technology Development Process. Figure 13 – 12 also shows the corresponding business life cycle stages of a company and the typical corresponding funding stages. Color has been used to indicate the life cycle stage of the company: the due diligence stage is represented by orange, the startup stage is represented by yellow, the growth stage is represented by green, and the expansion stage is represented by blue. The graphics within Figure 13 – 12 will be referred to frequently throughout the text of this book to orient readers as to how the various processes of building a business and bringing a product to market interplay. Engineering Innovation consists of two parts: Part A: The Business Side of Innovation; Part B: Engineering the Innovation.

3. Method

Concept Generation Process:

Once the team chooses an unmet need (and alternative unmet needs are identified, in case continued In-Depth Validation uncovers disqualifying information), then it is time for Concept Generation. Concept Generation is a system designed to exhaustively and categorically identify solutions for each stage of a process, then assess and aggregate the independent ideas into a single cohesive solution (i. e. , concept). The process of Concept Generation is a technique used to ideate solutions, rank the solutions using a decision-making process, and deliver a thoroughly researched and ranked final concept that has been analyzed from component to full concept. The structure of the analysis translates the individual ideas and full concepts into IP that can be captured in a provisional patent application (Figure 13-13).

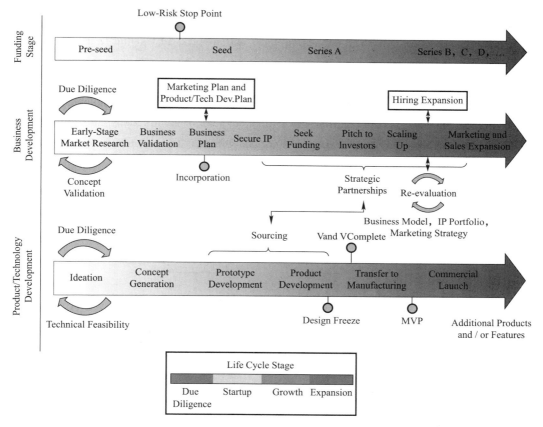

Figure 13-12　Graphic representation of the various processes involved in simultaneously developing a business and bringing a product/technology to market

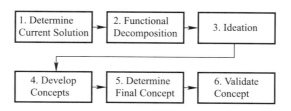

Figure 13-13　Concept Generation pathway

（1）Determine Current Solution

Even if there are not any products on the market that directly solve your unmet need, there is still at least one process or solution that exists to circumvent the unmet need. If there is a process or "gold standard", then it, and alternative processes, should be identified.

（2）Functional Decomposition

Functional Decomposition is the process of analyzing a product, device, system, or procedure to break it down into its smaller, simpler parts or functions. Within a Functional Decomposition, a function is the simplified task or procedure, whereas the decomposition is the process of breaking down the overarching product, device, system, or procedure into functions and/or subfunctions. A Functional Decomposition begins by creating a functional decomposition diagram (i. e. , a picture to help understand how all of the general tasks and subtasks fit together). The development of the diagram begins by taking the identified process (i. e. , process pathways) of the current solution and breaking it down to its essential, simplified components (Figure 13-14). Since every product, device, system, and process is unique, there are varying levels of complexity. A general function is a function that is dependent on other functions and/or subfunctions. A subfunction is a function that has to work in order for a more general function to take place. Finally, a basic function is a function that has no remaining subfunctions.

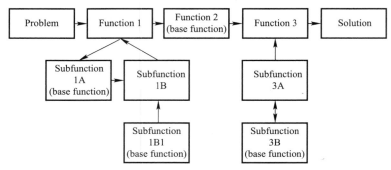

Figure 13-14　Basic example of functions, subfunctions, and base functions
within a Functional Decomposition diagram

Work as a team to determine the multiple known process pathways currently addressing the unmet need. There are usually several different process paths toward a single existing solution. Undoubtedly, there can be multiple functional decomposition diagrams for a single problem or solution.

（3）Ideation

Ideation is the creative process used to exhaustively and categorically develop solutions to address a function or subfunction from the Functional Decomposition. Ideation begins by outlining a list of approaches. For example, when developing a physical manufacturing process or medical device, the use of the MECE principle is helpful for ideation, so that all different types of ideas are represented. Different industries will use different terminology to group ideas. For example, terminology that is used in computer science may include computational techniques, computer languages, database structures, and so on.

The MECE list of approaches should be extensive and encompassing. The process for making diesel fuel is a good example. You may not have thought of including the Biological approach when assessing oil refining processes, though biodiesel is a viable internal combustion engine fuel type. The next innovative separation technique used during making fuel could be acoustic-based or magnetic-based. Thinking about "outside-the-box" solutions offers a key to finding something truly innovative. Sometimes the simplest solution is the most innovative.

To maximize effectiveness of the Ideation exercise, attempt to first ideate individually, then collectively as a team. During independent ideation, each team member can retreat to a comfortable place to conduct ideation. Use a blank piece of paper or a template to record the:

- Team Member's Name.
- Function Identification.
- Approach (e. g. , Thermal).
- Concept Description.
- Drawing (if possible).

Each team member should come up with as many concepts as possible per approach. It does not matter how far-fetched or outlandish an idea is, as long as it provides a solution to perform the function (or task). Each concept should be documented on its own record and include diagrams, if possible.

Once the individual team members return from their Ideation exercises, each person should have a collection of completed templates with concepts for all of the approaches. Each concept should be logged in a central spreadsheet or database with the appropriate identifiers. The concepts should be organized by function and approach. Often during the organization process, the team will brainstorm additional ideas and idea hybrids can be added to the central concept database. Scan all of the drawings and link them to their descriptions within the database.

A team brainstorming session to establish the selection criteria and ranking system will provide insightful discussion about the different ideas that have been developed. The ranking (or scoring) of the ideas will filter out the ideas that do not seem like a good fit.

(4) Developing Concepts

It is recommended to leave a couple of days in between the Ideation and Concept Generation activities because ① decision-making processes can be labor intensive and time consuming, and ② the extra time will allow each team member to reflect on the independent ideas and formulate them into unrefined concepts. When beginning the generation of full concepts, the team will take the ideas that scored well during Ideation and organize them together under the functions and subfunctions that were listed in the Functional Decomposition.

The established selection criteria (e. g. , quality, estimated costs, feasibility, and team interest) will identify low-ranking concepts that can be set aside. Decisionmaking tools can be used to correlate ideas with functions and subfunctions (as illustrated in Figure 13-15) within the functional decomposition diagram. Repeat the decision-making model (as many times as needed) with the highest scored collection of ideas to arrive at a complete concept.

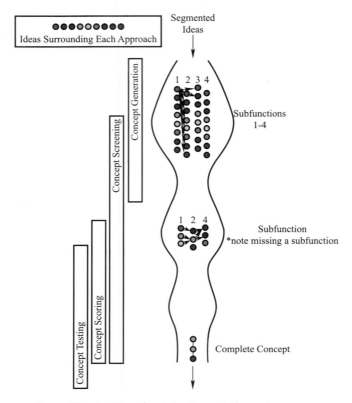

Figure 13-15　Example of the Concept Generation process

Innovation often occurs when a function or subfunction can be removed from a process to improve efficiency, improve profitability, reduce waste, and so on. Note that some concepts (and sometimes whole processes) are not technically possible, not cost effective, not optimal for the environment it is performed in, or may take too many resources to develop.

Turning to IP for a moment; even though the team has selected a "most viable" concept and identified a couple alternatives, an invention disclosure encompassing all concepts should be developed in accordance with the instructions provided by your patent attorney. Your team's organized spreadsheet with linked diagrams will then be translated from the invention disclosure into a provisional patent application by your patent attorney. This approach provides comprehensive protection for the company's IP assets, while the team is developing prototypes and testing and validating the concept. Additionally, while conducting extensive due diligence, if you find that your concept infringes on another's patent rights or you cannot get a freedom to operate legal opinion, then the alternative concepts included in the provisional patent application afford some "wiggle room" for shifting the development of the final concept within the first year after filing.

(5) Determine Final Concept

Using decision-making tools, establish selection criteria and ranking scales to objectively rank the possible concepts that were previously generated. The ranking process will also establish alternative concepts or variations of a concept, in case the chosen concept encounters problems during concept validation.

(6) Validate Concept

As discussed earlier, once the final concept is selected by the team, then the Concept Validation process should continue. When conducting Concept Validation, stakeholders will be able to help determine usability and assess human factors of the final concept. If validation of the concept uncovers a disqualifying feature, then referring back to the Concept Generation ranking can offer alternative solutions.

4. Model

SWOT Analysis:

An exercise worth completing during business validation is a Strengths, Weaknesses, Opportunities, Threats (SWOT) evaluation of your business model (refer to Figure 13 – 16). SWOT analysis is typically conducted as a team brainstorming session. In a SWOT analysis, strengths and weaknesses are typically categorized as internal to a business (such as customer loyalty to a brand, a product's share of the market) and opportunities and threats are typically categorized as external to a business (for instance, substitute products are decreasing customer demand, buyers of your product are trying to reduce prices, and supplier diversification). The goal of the SWOT analysis is to match a business's internal strengths with external market opportunities. For example, by utilizing your business's current market share, you can increase the technology/product portfolio (for instance, via internal or outsourced innovation projects) to take advantage of additional potential revenue streams.

Through market research, business model validation and SWOT analysis utilize the knowledge learned to define an innovation and technology development strategy for the company that will generate the optimal portfolio of products and solutions for realizing the highest profits. This strategy should take advantage of market opportunities and should match those

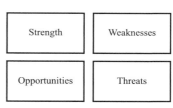

Figure 13–16   SWOT model

opportunities to a company's strengths in design, development, engineering, testing, project management, supply chain management and marketing, and so on. The data gathered during business model validation informs the decision-making process and should be in alignment with the company's mission, vision, and business goals.

13.5   R&D Management

1. Definitions of R&D Management

The National Science Foundation (NSF) classifies and defines research as follows:

(1) Basic Research. Basic research has as its objective "a more complete knowledge or understanding of the subject under study, without specific applications in mind." To take into account industrial goals, NSF modifies this definition for the

13.5 Professional Terms, Words and Phrases, Sentence Illustration

industry sector to indicate that basic research advances scientific knowledge "but does not have specific immediate commercial objectives, although it may be in fields of present or potential commercial interest."

(2) Applied Research. Applied research is directed toward gaining "knowledge or understanding to determine the means by which a specific, recognized need may be met." In industry, applied research includes investigations directed "to discovering new scientific knowledge that has specific commercial objectives with respect to products, processes, or services."

(3) Development. Development is the "systematic use of the knowledge or understanding gained from research, directed toward the production of useful materials, devices, systems or methods, including design and development of prototypes and processes."

In its publication The Measurement of Scientific and Technical Activities (1993), the Organization for Economic Co-operation and Development (OECD) defines some research activities as follows:

Basic research is experimental or theoretical work undertaken primarily to acquire new knowledge of the underlying foundations of phenomena and observable facts, without any particular application or use in view. Basic research analyzes properties, structures, and relationships with a view to formulating and testing hypotheses, theories or laws. The results of basic research are not generally sold but are usually published in scientific journals or circulated to interested colleagues. Pure basic research is carried out for the advancement of knowledge, without working for long-term economic or social benefits and with no positive efforts being made to apply the results to practical problems or to transfer the results to sectors responsible for its applications. Oriented basic research is carried out with the expectation that it will produce a broad base of knowledge likely to form the background to the solution of recognized or expected current or future problems or possibilities. Applied research is also original investigation undertaken in order to acquire new knowledge. It is, however, directed primarily towards a specific practical aim or objective. Applied research develops ideas into operational form. Experimental development is systematic work, drawing on existing knowledge gained from research and practical experience that is directed to producing new materials, products and devices; to installing new processes, systems and services; or to improving substantially those already produced or installed.

Research and development covers many of these activities. The OECD defines R&D as "creative work undertaken on a systematic basis in order to increase the stock of knowledge of man, culture and society, and the use of this stock of knowledge to devise new applications."

In order to provide functional and understandable definitions for various research activities, Science Indicators categorizes R&D activities as efforts in science and engineering as follows:

● Producing significant advances across the broad front of understanding of natural and social phenomena—basic research.

● Fostering inventive activity to produce technological advances—applied research and development.

● Combining understanding and invention in the form of socially useful and affordable products and processes—innovation.

Many United States governmental agencies have categorized research and development activities to provide a better focus on these activities and, ostensibly, to facilitate technology transfer. Since DOD accounts for approximately 60 percent of the federal government's R&D expenditures, some understanding of its research program categorization would be helpful to those seeking research support from the DOD.

2. R&D Project Management

In applying project management to R&D, it is necessary to

- minimize the dividing line and strict categorization for what constitutes a project.
- constrain the typical R&D activities into a time frame.
- identify the basic outcomes that are desired, either from a tactical or strategic perspective.
- define success differently than within a standard project.
- R&D success is in the decisions that move the experiments along and prove or disprove the theory or hypothesis within some set of constraints.

In traditional project management methodology, only defined subsets of activities meet the definition of a project and, therefore, are the best candidates for the application of the methodology. However, in applying project management to R&D, it becomes necessary to minimize the dividing line and strict categorization for what constitutes a project. It is possible to categorize any activity as a project and gain the benefits of applying the right level of managemen. All activities can be artificially bounded during a defined period, such as one year, allowing a baseline against which statuses can be obtained.

The ranges of activities that make up R&D do not easily lend themselves to rigid structures of management over long time periods. That is because of the nature of this highly creative activity. However, that does not mean that project management cannot be applied to R&D, which is a common misperception. Generally, R&D is used to learn and apply learning in an area that is undefined, conceptual, complex, and ambiguous. The research often has no defined outcome, or has an outcome identified; however, the means to reach the outcome may be unknown. That being said, it is still possible to choose a time frame during which the R&D project will occur, and to identify the known tasks that will be completed during that time frame. By constraining the typical R&D activities to this time frame and identifying the basic outcomes (including anticipated experiments or completion of research, the submission of scientific or technical papers, the completion of a prototype, or other activities), one can treat R&D as a project.

One of the most significant challenges of implementing project management on R&D projects can be in dealing with individuals or established cultures that have not applied a disciplined approach to creative activities. It is sometimes the case that individuals in these environments will often insist that they are not following any type of a process and may even rebel against the application of structure and methods. They are generally concerned that doing so will impede their ability to implement change and, thereby, impact their creativity. It turns out that, although they may not be able to articulate their methods, if one was to follow the steps that they take within the implementation of his or her work, it would become apparent that they are indeed following a process, albeit one of their own development, often at the expense of valuable time and energy.

In most cases, processes built this way are not built on any true discipline. Therefore, not only are these creative individuals spending time reinventing the wheel, but also they are doing so without the benefit of the discipline, knowledge, and experience that went into an established and standard process. Implementing processes outside of a discipline increases the probability that key critical steps will be left out, and, thus, impact the project downstream.

R&D projects do benefit from the application of project management discipline if applied correctly. R&D does not require a thorough definition of a project scope. However, it does require a careful description of the hypothesis to be tested and of the experiments to be attempted. The explanation of the anticipated outcomes and trajectory, or the direction they are headed, is essential. Decision points become more important because, as the experiments and testing are carried out, results should lead to decisions on how to proceed. Success is defined differently than within a standard project, although it is still imperative that the project is completed within a specific budget (unless money is no object), schedule (even if multiple years in length), and in the progress it makes in evolving a product, service, technique, or other area of focus. R&D success is in the decisions that move the experiments along and prove or disprove the theory or hypothesis within some set of constraints.

3. Models

(1) Simultaneous Coupling Model

Whether innovations are stimulated by technology, customer need, manufacturing or a host of other factors, including competition, misses the point. The models above concentrate on what is driving the downstream efforts rather than on how innovations occur. The linear model is able to offer only an explanation of where the initial stimulus for innovation was born, that is, where the trigger for the idea or need was initiated. The simultaneous coupling model shown in Figure13−17 suggests that it is the result of the simultaneous coupling of the knowledge within all three functions that will foster innovation. Furthermore, the point of commencement for innovation is not known in advance.

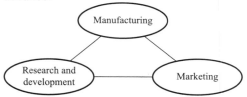

Figure 13−17 The simultaneous coupling model

(2) Economic Index Model

Under this model, research needs are defined as those needs designed to improve the operation or manufacturing efficiency of the organization or the enterprise. The emphasis is on building a "better mousetrap" to reduce the cost of doing things. Inputs for such needs come from the users, operation units, and scientists, as well as from looking at competitive products and operations.

(3) Portfolio Model

Under this model, normative, comparative, and forecasted research needs are considered. Normative needs are those of the user (a user being the primary or follow-on beneficiary of the research product). Comparative needs relate to research needs derived from reviewing comparable organizations, competitive product lines, and related enterprises. Forecasted research needs focus on trend analysis in terms of consumer or organization needs derived from new requirements, changed consumer behavior, new technological developments, new regulations (e. g. , environmental, health, and safety regulations), and new operational requirements. Often the effectiveness of a commercial enterprise or of a national defense effort depends not only on how well the organization itself does but also on how well the organization does in comparison with its competitor or adversary. Consequently, it is necessary to have effective intelligence concerning the portfolio of a competitor in order to focus properly on comparative and forecasted research needs.

After defining research needs using these two models, some research projects would be essentially modifying, adapting, or adopting existing scientific knowledge and would correspond to applied research and development; other research projects would fill technology gaps and would correspond to basic or fundamental research.

Inevitably, there are more projects to be researched than there are funds available. This is a normal and a healthy situation. A model derived from the work of Keeney and Raiffa (1993), which takes into account multiple objectives, preferences, and value tradeoffs, is suggested for deciding which projects to select among competing requirements. The main problem in using such an approach is the tendency on the part of many technical users to quantify items that do not lend themselves to quantification.

In developing a policy (at higher levels) or in making specific project choices among competing demands (at lower levels), the decision-maker can assign utility values to consequences associated with each path instead of using explicit quantification. The payoffs are captured conceptually by associating to each path of the tree a consequence that completely describes the implications of the path. It must be emphasized that not all payoffs are in common units and many are incommensurate. This can be mathematically described as follows:

$$a' \text{is preferred to } a'' \Leftrightarrow \sum_{i=1} P_i' U_j' > \sum_{j=1} P_j'' U_j'' \qquad (13-1)$$

Where a' and a'' represent choices, P represents probabilities, and U represents utilities; the symbol⇔reads "such that".

Utility numbers are assigned to consequences, even though some aspects of a choice are not in common units or are subjective in nature. This, then, becomes a multiattribute value problem. This can be done informally or explicitly by mathematically formalizing the preference structure. This can be stated mathematically as:

$$v \ (x_1, \ x_2, \dots, \ x_n) \geqslant v \ (x_1', \ x_2', \dots, \ x_n')$$
$$\Leftrightarrow (x_1, \ x_2, \dots, \ x_n) \gtrsim (x_1', \ x_2', \dots, \ x_n') \qquad (13-2)$$

Where v is the value function that may be the objective of the decision-maker, x_i is a point in the consequence space, and the symbol $\gtrsim$ reads "preferred to" or "indifferent to".

After the decision-maker structures the problem and assigns probabilities and utilities, an optimal strategy that maximizes expected utility can be determined. When a comparison involves unquantifiable elements, or elements in different units, a value tradeoff approach can be used either informally, that is, based on the decision-maker's judgment, or explicitly, using mathematical formulation.

After the decision-maker has completed the individual analysis and has ranked various policy alternatives or projects, then a group analysis can further prioritize the policy alternatives or specific projects. A modified Delphi technique (Jain et al., 1980) is suggested as an approach for accomplishing this.

After research project selection and prioritization, an overall analysis of the research portfolio should be made. The research project portfolio should contain both basic and applied research. The mix would depend on the following:

- Technology of the organization.
- Size of the organization.
- Research staff capabilities.
- Research facilities.
- Access to different funding sources.

It should be noted that the distinction between basic and applied research can become rather blurred. What is basic research to one organization can be applied to another and what is basic one year can be applied the next. Also, given the same general research project title, different emphases during project execution can affect the nature of research. As will be discussed below, to maximize R&D organizational effectiveness, scientists and work groups should be involved in a mix of basic and applied research.

13.6   Reading Material

Reading Material 2: Managing the New Innovation Process

The innovation process will become ever more complex, involving larger numbers of actors and displaying more emergent and unpredictable properties. This complexity will occur for a number of reasons and will manifest itself in a number of forms. First, the business, technological, and regulatory contexts in which firms operate will become increasingly intricate. Change is rapid and unpredictable and, as the chapters in this volume show, often requires networking and collaboration within communities, and engagement with governments to gain some control over the pace and direction of technological change (essentially sharing control in order to retain it). The scale and scope of scientific advice will multiply, increasing the challenges for firms to be appropriately receptive. Second, the internal organizational structures and ways of engaging with external parties will become more multifaceted. The need to ensure effective communications and engagement between a broader range of technical and other specialists will require continuous network, project, and team configuration and reconfiguration, and constant experimentation with new organizational forms. This is especially the case where innovations have social or environmental implications and a wide range of interested bodies demand involvement. Third, complexity will manifest itself in the configuration of "products", involving ever-closer integration of recent basic research, and combined and merged service features, and may take the form of "integrated solutions".

One way of dealing with an increasingly complex and unpredictable innovation process is by encouraging the use of play. The innovation process will become a much more "playful" series of activities. Michael Schrage's (2000) excellent book *Serious Play* analyzes how "the world's best companies" simulate, and in particular use prototyping, to innovate. In fact, play has always been central to creativity, knowledge, and development. Plato said that life must be lived as play, and Charles Dickens said: "There can be no effective and satisfactory work without play... there can be no sound and wholesome thought without play".

So play is a serious business and it needs to be incorporated centrally into the innovation process. It needs to be combined with the creative thinking and formalized research that occur inside and outside of companies and the operations and process capabilities that firms need to deliver value. *Homo cogito*—man the thinker—and *homo faber*—man the maker—need to be complemented by *homo ludens*—man the player.

Technologies, especially simulation and prototyping, will play an important role in encouraging play and its integration with thinking and doing in the management of the new innovation process. These innovation technologies, which we call IvT—e-science, simulation and modelling, artificial intelligence, and rapid and virtual reality prototyping—will increasingly become essential tools of the innovation process. Companies will utilize computer-integrated operations systems linking all elements of the design and delivery of new products and services. Firms will have real time access to information in those systems to help control the entire value chain. Local area networks will integrate activities within operations; electronic data interchange will link the activities of those sites with suppliers and customers; the Internet will assist the iterative and playful processes of information exchange between firms and across all the activities within a firm. In its most advanced form, the capacity to simulate and model innovations prior to their production (to see if anyone will buy them) will be extended to the simulation and modelling of the operations used to deliver them (to see if they can be made), and the simulation and modelling of the business models used to maximize returns from them (to see which will be most profitable).

ICT and IvT may on the one hand assist in dealing with complexity through facilitating the exchange and integration of information, but on the other hand will add to the complexity by multiplying its potential sources (and placing greater technical demands on the security of commercially sensitive information), and raising new challenges around the skills and organization required to co-produce and co-utilize knowledge.

The use of ICT and IvT in the innovation process raises questions about whether knowledge that previously was tacit can be codified. If it can, there are implications for appropriability and the use of collaborations (codified knowledge is more easily protected, and can be transferred via markets or hierarchies rather than alliances). Whereas the new electronic tools can store, transfer, and process information, their ability to do this with knowledge is more limited. Firms will increasingly experiment with new organizational forms using technologies, including virtual worlds and new forms of visualization and representation, that improve understanding between diverse groups and engage multiple parties in the design of new products, services, and processes. Diverse groups playing collaboratively around common technology platforms will become a key feature of the future innovation process. Firms will face the challenge of providing people with sufficient time away from everyday demands to play, and create physical working environments conducive to experimentation and learning.

Technology is only a tool. It has no value until it is used productively by people. Tacit knowledge will remain a major differentiating factor for a firm's competitiveness, with the implication that rewards derive from investments in people. Particularly important will be investments in staff, whose ability to generate and assimilate new knowledge—that is, to learn, as a result of investments in R&D and technology, will improve. As Chapter 8 showed, there are many examples of technology initially being used to deskill and limit the discretion of those using it. Creating the managerial strategies, organizational structures, skills, and incentives to encourage the innovative use of technology presents a continuing challenge for managers. There will be particular demands for skilled people able to use the new technologies to work across organizational, professional, and disciplinary boundaries. There will be pressure on education institutions to produce graduates with more broadly based skills to operate effectively with new innovation processes. Creative staff will need to be skilled at co-simulating and developing their ideas (playing with others); systems thinkers will need to be skilled at integrating complex systems involving many different parties. Every employee in the innovation space—which increasingly will include everyone in the organization—will need to be skilled at teamwork and communicating across boundaries.

Reading Material 2

1. Introduction

The current transportation and transit systems in the USA are reaching a critical focal point in its major urban areas. Carbon emissions, congestion, traffic mortality, and aging infrastructure are just a few of the problems that need to be urgently addressed by creating a sustainable system that integrates all transport modes to meet the economic and environmental mobility needs of today and tomorrow.

It has been 100 years since the last disruptive change in the transportation industry happened. According to Inrix statistics research, we are having a major problem with traffic congestion, the number of cars on the streets keeps increasing and the chaos on the roads is getting worse every year. This Inrix research, published by Forbes Statista, shows how only in one year, 2017, people in Los Angeles spent 102 h stuck in traffic, almost 4 days and a half just waiting in the car. A critical problem that does not seem to have a clear solution.

The inability for people to use a transportation method that allows them to reach long distances faster is one of the weaknesses of our current transportation modes. Germany, France, and Japan are trying to find ways to make their trains travel faster. However, they have been fighting the problem of friction for decades. Rolling and air resistance are the two major components they have not been able to fix.

Safety is another component we need to mention. We often see cars, trains, trucks, ships, and planes' accidents. According to the National Transportation Safety Board, 39 339 people died in 2016 in a transportation accident (CO_2 and other greenhouse gas emissions n. d.). The question here is: Could a new transportation mode help to decrease this number?

The last two components to mention are the increasing amount ofcarbon footprint emissions and the lack of transportation modes using sustainable energy sources. The emissions of CO_2 have never stopped increasing, there are some countries that contribute more than others, as well as other industries. This is a major global problem that now is taking the attention of the majority of people, most of them with intentions to help to solve this issue by proposing disruptive solutions. One of them, the Hyperloop model. In this paper, we are analyzing the implementation of the Hyperloop system which is the fifth mode of transportation after air, rail, road, and water. As a brief description, the Hyperloop is a steel construction medium vacuum pressure tube that accelerates capsules through the tube at up to 760 mph on proposed air bearings. It is meant to be propelled by solar power in a low-pressure environment.

2. Current Hyperloop Industry

The Hyperloop industry is a burgeoning one with whole new possibilities when it comes to the development, implementation, and technology of the system. The complexity of the technology and implementation requires close coordination between the different parties at work. In the end, the purpose is to develop an entire ecosystem that provides an alternate transport option to the passenger or end customer. The first Hyperloop system is scheduled to be deployed in 2022. In the first year of deployment, it is expected to generate a revenue of US $ 1. 35 billion. This is expected to grow at a Compounded Annual Growth Rate (CAGR) of 47. 2% for the next 4 years and reach US $ 6. 34 billion. by 2026.

3. Conclusions

The milestone of conducting a full flight test of the Hyperloop in Q4 2017 has been missed by Hyperloop One. Just by December 15th (Q4 2017) they finished the third phase of testing of the Hyperloop, that means the first full flight test to be conducted still has a long way to go as the regulations of a new classification system for freight pricing still needs to be established, the milestone of cargo trips to begin from LA to San Francisco in 2020 could be still under speculation. As these two important milestones are not achieved by Hyperloop One due to political and regulatory factors, the milestones discussed in the literature might still be pushed further in the timeline. Therefore, it is expected that to become a reality and transportation of the future, Hyperloop might still be a few years away.

Hyperloop One has to put efforts in the political and legal fronts to develop Hyperloop in the planned routes. It would be easier for the company to rather build public-private partnerships, instead of waiting for the government through a 15-to 20-year process to reach a consensus. Also, the company should actively pursue projects in countries with friendly regulatory environments and economically viable routes instead of contending with overbearing regulators.

The hype around Hyperloop technology and its benefits may have gotten the prospective customers excited to use it. But, to establish it as a preferred mode of transport, the companies should focus on meeting the safety requirements, and provide a top-notch overall user experience.

The technological advancements taking place are huge that make a great difference and will continue the same in the upcoming years. But there is still, lot to work on and to achieve further advancements in the innovation. The phase testing process has achieved good results, setting new records with every phase. These new achievements can set the road map on the right path and can turn this mode of transportation into reality.

Once the system is finished, Hyperloop has the potential to become the best environmentally friendly transportation mode. However, it is also important to keep in mind the amount of pollution and contamination that this project will generate during the construction and testing phases. These are factors that will need to be included in the environment impact report to leverage the importance and benefits of having a fifth transportation mode versus the damage this project could cause to the environment.

Finally, the project's costs have been underestimated since operational and maintenance expenses have not been considered thoroughly. Therefore, a fare ticket of 20 USD for a one-trip may not be accurately estimated making it necessary to seek agreements with the US government for subsides.

Chapter 14
Investment Decision and Economic Evaluation

14.1　Economic Evaluation

1. Introduction

The financial evaluation of a project involves studying its performance and return (profitability) from the points of view of the industry (the utility and the firm), the owner and the investor (IPP). Economic evaluation, on the other hand, involves studying project benefits and returns from the national well-being point of view and assessing the effect the project will have on the overall economy and society of the country. While small projects have limited, if any, impact on the national economy, large projects have social and environmental effects, which cannot be ignored (referred to earlier as externalities). The electrical power industry is highly capital intensive and is also a major emitter. A modern power station normally costs hundreds of millions of pounds, and so do some network projects. In high-capital projects of this nature it is necessary to find the least-cost solution not only from the point of view of the industry but from that of the national economy as well. The project evaluation should not be restricted to its profitability and should also evaluate its national economic and environmental impacts (social impacts) and compare them with those of other competing projects in the resource-limited national economy to ensure economic efficiency.

Economic analysis of major projects involves, therefore, evaluating two things:

(1) the priority of the project in the national plans of the country.

(2) its effect on the overall economy of the country, and its environmental (social) impacts.

The ultimate purpose of the analysis would be to provide a measure of the impact of the project on the national welfare as exemplified by the increased consumption of goods and services (including electrical energy) that serve as a proxy to increased welfare.

2. Method

In economic evaluations, static and dynamic methods are distinguished, although static methods are seldom applied nowadays. On an international level, economic assessment of deposits is done through dynamic methods which take the time factor for investments and returns, i. e. the time value of money, into account and are based on compound interest formulae. The following notations and abbreviations will be applied:

Everybody knows intuitively what the time value of money is. If I invest US $1000 today and after a year get US $1200 in return, I consider this a good bargain. If I get the money after only 20 years, I would not invest the US $1000, i. e. a profit of US $200 within a year has a

14.1 Professional Terms, Words and Phrases, Sentence Illustration

considerably higher value than a profit of US $200 after 20 years.

The time value is calculated by means of the compound interest formula. If an investment of $I = $ US $1000 is made today at an interest rate of 10%, the value is

- after 1 year: $I \times (1+i) = 1000 \times (1+0.1) = $ US $1100
- after 2 years: $I \times (1+i) \times (1+i) = 1000 \times (1+0.1)^2 = $ US $1210
- after 10 years: $I \times (1+i)^{10} = 1000 \times (1+0.1)^{10} = 1000 \times 2.594 = $ US $2594
- generally after n years: $I \times (1+i)^n$

This procedure can also be reversed. At an interest rate of 10%, US $1000 will be worth US $2594 in 10 years. If $R = $ US $2594 is the target value my investment is to reach in 10 years time, I will have to invest

$$I = \frac{R}{(1+i)^{10}} = \frac{2594}{(1+0.1)^{10}} = \frac{2594}{2.594} = \text{US} \ \$ 1000 \tag{14-1}$$

In other words: If I get US $2594 in 10 years, the present value at an interest rate of 10% is US $1000. Thus US $1000 is the present value of US $2594 at an interest rate of 10% over 10 years.

This, for example, is the principle of special government bonds in Canada, the called stripped bonds. They are stripped of their annual interest coupon. These interests are accumulated and paid out at the payback date of the bond. To take the example of above, if the interest rate would be 10% and the lifetime of the bond 10 years, one would pay CA $1000 and get back CA $2594 after 10 years.

To find out how much today's investment will be worth in n years, we have to compound by $(1+i)n$. The factors $(1+i)n$ are therefore called compounding factors. If, however, we want to project the value R into the future and want to know how much R is worth today, we have to discount R by

$$\frac{1}{(1+i)^n} \tag{14-2}$$

$$\frac{1}{(1+i)^n} \quad \text{or} \quad (1+i)^{-n} \tag{14-3}$$

The factor therefore is called the discounting factor $q - n$. As will be shown below, the discounting factor is the most important entity for our calculations.

Two dynamic methods, also called DCF (Discounted Cash Flow) techniques, will be dealt with

- the calculation of the Net Present Value (NPV).
- the calculation of the Internal Rate of Return (IRR or IROR); it is also called the DCF rate or the earning power of a project.

The cash flow calculation is the summary of a feasibility or prefeasibility study. During the feasibility stage a team of geologists, mining engineers, metallurgists, economists etc. work together. The cash flow calculation, which can be very time-consuming, is usually prepared by economists.

This study will only deal with simple cash flow calculations a geologist or mining engineer will have to make at the prefeasibility stage of a project in order to establish whether an exploration project is worth pursuing. Once the principles are understood the actual calculation can be carried out using spread-sheet computer programmes.

14. 2   Engineering Cost

1. Introduction

During the construction stage, the focus of QS (Quantity Surveying) shifts from cost estimation to cost control. Cost control is the process of "monitoring the status of the project to update the project costs and managing changes to the cost baseline". According to PMI (2013), the main benefit of cost control is to help

keep the final construction cost within the client's approved budget by determining the cost variations, evaluating possible alternatives, and taking appropriate actions. In order to maintain effective cost control, the key point is to manage the approved cost baseline and the changes to that base line. An illustration of the baseline is presented in Figure 14-1. One can easily see from the Figure that the actual accumulative cost is above the baseline, indicating that the project is performing over budget, and discretionary interventions should be taken immediately if aiming to complete the project within the approved budget.

Cost control becomes rather important due to increasingly complex construction projects, inadequate planning and preparation at the preliminary stages, and incessant fluctuation in construction costs. To effectively control expenditure, QS regularly scrutinise their construction project's progress by comparing the actual expenditures with the baseline cost plan and preparing monthly valuations and cost reports for further control actions. Specifically, cost control methods include:

● Preparing an overall cost control plan, which warns of undesirable trends, deviations, slippages, and other project problems.

● Reviewing and approving the work breakdown structure.

● Making and monitoring the cash flow.

● Monitoring and reporting cost during the construction stage.

● Initiating and approving financial reports to the owner and contractor management.

QS normally call themselves consultants, as the chief architect or engineer would. They are

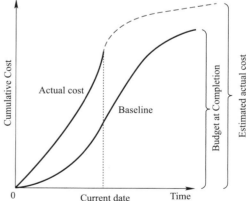

Figure 14-1   Illustration of the baseline and actual cost

also key coordinators between the client and the client's principal consultant, the lead contractor, or independent project manager, to settle interim payments. The principal consultant will rely on the valuations provided by QS to issue the certificate confirming work completed by the contractor. Only by presenting this certificate to the client can the contractor receive payment for work completed. QS will also manage the evaluation of variations when changes occur unavoidably against the contract documents, as well as to provide advice on contractual claims.

2. Theories

Establishing Baselines for Control:

The primary mission, or goal, of a project is the completion of a set of objectives that, when achieved, represents completion of the project. All contracting parties, whether the owner, the architect, the engineers, or the contractors, are interested in knowing how the project is coming along. To satisfy such an interest, a standard or baseline must be developed, against which progress may be measured. Identification of objectives is important, and should be done in the early stages of a project. Therefore, before data is collected or progress measured, a budget baseline is established to use as a yardstick to measure progress. Budget baselines are generated through the estimating process. If the project scope is not fully defined, this estimate will be approximate and may vary. As the scope becomes more defined, the budget estimates are updated (Figure 14-2).

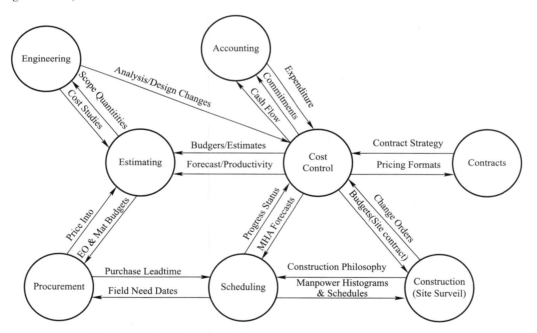

Figure 14-2 Information flow between cost control and other disciplines

(From K. Eckhoff and K. E. Harto. *Ninth International Cost Engineering Congress*, *Congress Papers*. Norwegian Association of Cost and Planning Engineering, International Cost Engineering Council, and Norwegian Petroleum Society, 1986, Oslo, N3. 3, p. 2.)

3. Methodology

The Three-Quarters Rule:

The three-quarters rule provides a simple method of developing the estimate for the total cost of a proposed project by comparing the capacity of the existing and proposed deliverable. The capacity index can be the size, speed, complexity, or accuracy of the deliverable in question. The decision of which one of these indices to use for the rough estimate depends on the objectives of the project, on whatever information is available when the estimate is made, and finally, on the experience of the project manager. Given that the relationship between any two facets of the project and the total cost may not follow the same pattern, two different size/capacity indices might produce different estimates for the new project. Therefore, for best results, as many indices as possible should be used in determining the estimate. Then, by simple averaging, or by weighted averaging, of these individual estimates, a more tempered project estimate will be obtained.

This estimating rule is a slightly more sophisticated version of the ratio estimating technique, where there is an assumed equality between the ratios and the exponents of equipment sizes and overall project costs. The three quarters rule, aptly named, is based on the following formula:

Analogous Estimating Rules of Thumb:

- Three-Quarters Rule

$$C_p = C_e (S_p / S_e)^{0.75} \qquad\qquad (14-4)$$

- Square Root Rule

$$T_p = T_e (C_p / C_e)^{0.5} \qquad\qquad (14-5)$$

- Two-Thirds Rule

$$T_p = T_e (N_p / N_e)^{0.66} \qquad\qquad (14-6)$$

The premise of this rule is that if the ratio of the capacities, or sizes, of the proposed and current projects is raised to the power of ¾, it will provide an indicator of the ratio of the cost of the two projects. This technique can be used to make extrapolations or interpolations either graphically or computationally and both can be performed with the use of spreadsheet software. The following display shows the computational application of this rule to predict the cost of houses with two, five, or six bedrooms, where the project manager has only the cost for a three-bedroom house.

The Three-Quarters Ruie:

Estimate Cost of a House Based on the Number of Bedrooms:

Current House: 3 Bedrooms, $37,500

Proposed House: 5 Bedrooms

(Cost of New Facility)/(37,500) = ((5)/(3)) ** (3/4)

Cost of a Five Bedroom House = $55,007

Cost of a Six Bedroom House = $63,067

Cost of a Two Bedroom House = $27,667

Figure 14-3 shows a graphic application of the same example. If one uses a log-log scale when using the graphic application of this method, the model data will be displayed in a straight line, making visual interpolation very easy. Figure 14-4 shows the application of this technique to the cost of apartment complexes based on the number of units in each complex.

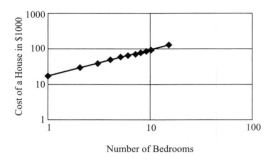

Figure 14-3　Estimate cost of a house based
on the number of bedrooms

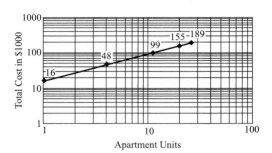

Figure 14-4　Estimate cost of a complex based
on the number of apartment Units

If enough industry-specific or organization-specific data are available, this technique can be refined to reflect the specifics of that industry in conjunction with that particular capacity index used for extrapolation. Then, for future estimates, a customized variation of this technique will be used to arrive at more accurate conceptual estimates. This modification is referred to as the modified Three-Quarters Rule. Thus, using the existing data, an exponent other than % will be suggested for this particular project environment. Again, it is important to note that the cost exponent will be different for different capacity indices and, therefore, a different exponent needs to be developed for each capacity index. Then the results can be combined to formulate a more refined estimate.

The following modified Three-Quarters Rule shows how an exponent of 0.96 was obtained for a particular class of construction projects. It is an important point that computation and recording of the value of the exponents is necessary only in the computational method. If the graphic method is used, it is not necessary to be aware of the value of the exponent; using a straight-line extrapolation or interpolation, the cost of the proposed project can be determined.

The Modified Three-Quarters Rule:

Estimate Cost of a House Based on the Number of Bedrooms.

Current Facility: 3 Bedroom House, $70,000

Current Facility: 4 Bedroom House, $90,000

Proposed House: 6 Bedroom House?

$(90/70) = ((4/3)^{**} ?)$　　　$? = 0.96$

$(\text{Cost of New Facility})/(70,000) = ((6)/(3))^{**}(0.96)$

Cost of New Facility = $128,000

Figure 14-5 shows a graphic application of this technique without any specific reference to the value of the exponent. Using any two data points, the straight line defining the model can be defined, based on which future estimates can be made very quickly. Figure 14-6 shows the application of this model to develop a model to estimate the cost of airport expansions. This model used the cost of completed airports, such as Newark, JFK, and Hartsfield, to develop a conceptual estimate for the total cost of the Denver Airport. The index that was used for comparison was the terminal's size in square feet.

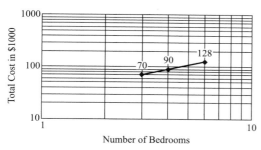

Figure 14-5　Estimate cost of a house based
on the number of bedrooms

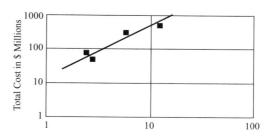

Figure 14-6　Estimate cost from
capacity or size

4. Modeling

Earned value management shows the relationship among all three of the primary project success criteria: cost, schedule, and performance. The Fgures below illustrate the superiority of EVM in comparison with the other project-tracking mechanisms, such as Gantt charts and S-curves. Essentially, S-curves establish a linkage directly and solely between cost and schedule (Figure 14 – 7). Tracking mechanisms, such as tracking Gantt charts, employ links between schedule and project (or activity) performance (Figure 14 – 8). It is only through earned value that the full nature of the association between the three success metrics of schedule, cost,

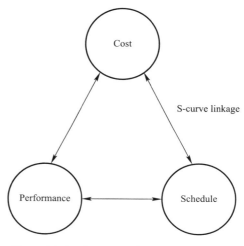

Figure 14-7　Project performance dimensions
linkage in S-curve analysis

and performance can be understood in relation to each other (Figure 14-9).

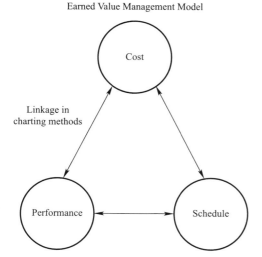

Figure 14-8　Project performance dimensions
linkage in charting methods

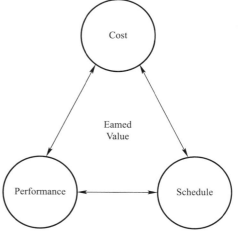

Figure 14-9　Project performance
dimensions linkage in EVA

365

14.3 Investment Feasibility

14.3 Professional Terms, Words and Phrases, Sentence Illustration

1. Introduction

(1) Definition of Project Feasibility Study

A project feasibility report is a comprehensive study which examines in detail the five frames of analysis of a given project in consideration of the four Ps, its risks, POVs, and its constraints (calendar, costs, and norms of quality) in order to determine whether it should go ahead, be redesigned, or else totally abandoned. This is illustrated in Figure 14-10.

In the Québec Multifunctional Amphitheatre (QMA) case, a color coding system was chosen to express changes to the project chart in the *Programme fonctionnel et technologique* (PFT) as follows:

- Green: Proposed changes are accepted conditional to changes.
- Yellow: Proposed changes must be further specified/explained and then validated by the City of Québec.
- Red: Proposed changes refused by the City of Québec.

Figure 14-10 Feasibility choices

(2) Definition of Vulnerability

Vulnerability: condition experienced by any of the four Ps (Plan, Processes, People, Power) of a project that make it susceptible to failure.

(3) Definition of Points of Vulnerability

Points of Vulnerability (POVs): temporal and physical points along the various stages of a project that impede on the calendar, costs, and/or quality of the project as it faces adverse conditions (negative forces), whether these conditions are under human control or not.

(4) Six Laws of a Project Feasibility Assessment

The first law of project feasibility (the law of positive and negative forces) states that a project is not feasible if the positive forces (which play in favor of the project, i.e., which maintain a functional g-spread) are smaller than the negative forces (which play against the project, such as risks). The second law of project feasibility on dependencies notes that the higher the dependencies between the project's tasks, the more vulnerable the project is. High task interdependence engenders high potential vulnerability. The third law of project feasibility (the law of points of vulnerability) stipulates that the higher the total vulnerability is (the sum of all g-spreads along each of the transformation stages) and the weaker the remedial actions are, the less the project is feasible. The fourth law of project feasibility (the law on the Forces of Production) posits that the more FPnc>FPc, the more the probability of collapse augments. Notably, I referred to a deadly interplay between FPnc and poor planning. The fifth law of project feasibility (law on conflicts) states that the more the wrangling among stakeholders is intense, frequent, and covers critical issues, the less likely the feasibility of the project. The sixth and final law of project feasibility (law of complexity) assumes that the more complex a project is, the riskier it is and the more POVs it contains, and the more probabilities of failure exist.

2. Methodology

The term "vulnerability" has been given different meanings by a slew of authors, ranging from adaptability, capacity, exposure, potentiality, resilience, robustness, sensitivity, or even wound. Some scholars propose a methodology to deal with vulnerabilities as follows: There should be a management group assigned to identify vulnerabilities; once POVs are identified, they should be analyzed. Then, a response plan must be prepared (the model excludes the fact that it must be implemented). Finally, monitoring and control must take place with a provision for lessons learned.

The present book proposes a more thorough methodology (the six Ps of strategic management thinking—PRO, the four Ps, POW, POV, POE, and PWP), but at least we are comforted by the fact that attempts have been made to establish a procedure to address vulnerabilities, something that escapes the various versions of PMBOK. In the same vein, some authors envision to measure risks and vulnerabilities along a supply chain. I provide some samples of measurements that could potentially be utilized to gauge the presence of POVs in Table 14-1.

Examples of measurements of potential POVs			Table 14-1
For outputs items	For time	For costs	For norms of quality
Forms processed	Cycle time	Budget variances	Complaints
Items assembled	Equipment downtime	Contingency costs	Defects
Productivity	Late reporting	Cost by account	Error rates
Sales (e.g., ticket sales)	Overtime	Delay costs	Number of accidents
Units produced	Response time to complaints	Overhead costs	Rejects
Work backlog	Repair time	Penalties/fines	Rework
—	Work stoppage	Unit costs	Scrap
—	—	Variable costs	Waste

This is not to say that these items should be actual measurements of POVs, but simply that feasibility analysts and project managers are not short of potential metrics—these are incremental when having to meet norms of quality. In other words, there are no managerial reasons to dodge the reality of POVs.

3. Models

Four Ps:

Since the 1960s, marketing theory has adopted the four Ps system, which stands for "product, price, promotion, and place (distribution)". In project feasibility, four Ps are also used: Plans, Processes, People, and Power.

I suppose that the four Ps normally form positive forces driving the project (I know that there are also negative forces). They are most active during the transformation process, at which point I classify them as Plans', Processes', People', and Power'.

I thus complement the input-transformation-output model by specifying what "inputs" mean, as shown in Figure 14-11.

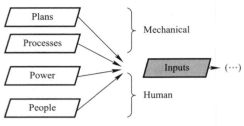

Figure 14-11　The fours Ps

In my basic model, inputs are actually composed of four key elements: "Plans" and "Processes" deal with the internal mechanics of projects; "People" and "Power" represent its human aspect (the psychodynamics or an organization's internal cultural forces). The Plans and Processes, People, and Power, form the four Ps of project management, and are sine qua non elements that the analyst must dutifully take into account when doing a feasibility study. In the Mervel Farm project, roughly speaking, the Plan is the vision of a tourist venue for an old farmhouse; Processes are, for example, the means used to direct the traffic of cars and visitors; People are the tourists, the staff, and the army of volunteers; and Power is the site manager and the promoters.

The sine qua non condition is partly set forth by posing the question: "Can there be a project without a plan?" The answer is "No."; therefore, the plan is likely a sine qua non condition. In the present model, I assume there is no colinearity between the four Ps so that they don't interact with each other before the project actually enters into the transformation phase. The absence of colinearity is proved by the question posed at the input stage, prior to the phase of transformation: "Can the plan be established without team members actually transforming inputs into outputs?" The answer is "Yes." "Can the plan be established without all transformation processes being carved in stone?" "Yes." "Can the plan be set out without having found the right project managers to take on the challenge?" "Yes." Then, the same types of questions are posed for the other variables. For example, "Can the processes take place in the planning stage without committing specific people?" and so forth. Therefore, a sine qua non condition is set when (1) the variable must be present to define the project's inputs and (2) each variable is independent. Of course, as the project moves from being an idea to being a concrete endeavor, colinearity builds up because people will handle certain processes, will need some lines of authority (Power), and will produce deliverables according to plan.

The four Ps will work together during the transformation stage, but for now, the plan is decided by the promoters (Power) independently of the staff (People) that will be hired later on, and the processes are being set but not put in motion just yet. Ultimately, a project is composed of inputs, a transformation process, and outputs, given a calendar of tasks and activities (time).

Time is entered as a constraint because time is what links inputs to transformation and ultimately to outputs. For the four Ps set as inputs, prior to being brought together through the process of transformation, we have

$$\text{Inputs} = \text{Plans} + \text{Process} + \text{People} + \text{Power} \qquad (14-7)$$

Assume that each P has its one beta (B) expressing the contribution of the respective P to the inputs; we then have

$$\text{Inputs} = \beta_1 \text{ Plans} + \beta_2 \text{ Processes} + \beta_3 \text{ People} + \beta_4 \text{ Power} \qquad (14-8)$$

However, during the transformation stage, the four Ps are brought together and interact intensely with one another. In other words, the characteristics of each P affect the other Ps: as an example, what People do has an influence on the line of authority (Power), which could potentially trigger a change in the project plan or on some of its processes. Indeed, changes compared with the initial plan are one of the major complaints that project staff use when trying to explain their shortcomings.

In the case of the QMA for example, about 2 months prior to its completion, there had been no less than 1100 DDM (requests for changes or "demandes de modifications"), for a total value of approximately 17 million dollars, with each and every one having to be reviewed and approved or else dismissed by the chief project manager. On a 400 million dollar project, this represents a change request of roughly 4% (17/400); it turns out that 4% is also a usual measure for waste in a production line. For example, on a printing press, it is generally estimated that 4% of ink and paper loss is due to the warming up of the machines. When I look at the cost of changes related to construction and to equipment, I find that it is an average of 6% (for a budget of 30 million dollars involving 46 requests for change /DDM/). From this perspective and if I expand my thinking a bit (setting each change as a POV), I can estimate that there are a minimum of 4% ~ 7% of POVs in projects in general. On a chessboard, even before starting the game, one POV exists among the 16 pieces of the same color (6%): the pawn on the F2 square is technically less protected compared with any of the other pieces on the board. This measure is by no means scientific, but serves to highlight the fact that there is a real possibility of POVs existing within any project and that, if they do, they are not insignificant. If 100% of projects have POVs and knowing that POVs account for 4% of their content, it seems fair to say that the POVs must be dealt with.

Simply identifying the four Ps in the preliminary analysis of the project is useful (indeed, this is already a more complete view of the project compared with what is done customarily), but it is far from reflecting the manifold aspects of their interactions once the project gets into its transformation stage. In other words, there is plenty of room for points of vulnerability to be avowed after the project has been given the go-ahead; that is, once the project enters into the transformation stage. The project manager may be caught off guard because, on paper, everything seems to be in marching order. The more we can do to understand the four Ps that are tied to a particular project ahead of time, the more equipped we are to avoid unpleasant surprises. To account for this possibility, I add an error term (ε) to my project definition formula, but instead of having a positive sign in front of the error term, I use a negative sign. The reason is that in theory, the sum of the four Ps should deliver a perfect project, but points of vulnerability will come and reduce the potential for perfection. We all know that humans make errors (except for our wives!) and that processes don't always go according to plan, that the plans themselves can be faulty, and that power struggles can spoil a work atmosphere. We thus express the sum of all points of vulnerabilities as they materialize with their devastating effects by ε, which is a measure of chaos (and more particularly, of deviance to norms of quality). We have

$$\text{Inputs} = \beta_1 \text{ Plans} + \beta_2 \text{ Processes} + \beta_3 \text{ People} + \beta_4 \text{ Power} - \varepsilon \qquad (14-9)$$

In terms of a "Plan" for the Mervel Farm project case, one must assume that the weather will be favorable, but nothing is less certain. What if it is a wet summer? Will tourists venture in an outdoor open field to buy regional products they can probably find one way or the other in a close, tidy, and warm environment such as a local specialty store? That is, for sure, a POV (no proper shelter) versus a given risk (that of bad weather).

In terms of Processes, the Mervel Farm concept relies heavily on the willingness of local craftspeople and farmers to adhere to its cooperative: an obligatory step in order to participate in the project. What if these people do not think the setup is worth their time and money? This is a risk.

In this same project, "People" refer to all stakeholders, including clients, fund providers, managers, staff, the media, and so forth. PMBOK would have it that the following groups would be present: initiators (Plans), clients (People), start-up group (Process), process group (Process), execution group (Process), surveillance group (Power), and control group (Power). The start-up group includes the three entrepreneurs that came up with the idea as well as the City of Pierreville and the National Capital Commission. To the process group, I add the project manager, the agronomist that will necessarily have to be hired, as well as disparate sources of financing such as banks, and a head coordinator of the crew of volunteers (as the project relies heavily on the participation of local volunteers). For all intents and purposes, I characterize these "People" as inputs that participate in the chain of transformation, which then produce outputs that will be delivered to the end customers.

The execution group includes people specifically hired to do the work on the site. The surveillance group is simply the project manager and some of his key staff. The same applies to the control group, except that the National Capital Commission and the City of Pierreville will be sending their own inspectors to ascertain compliance with the farm's and city's strict rules of operation.

A typical POV when it comes to People, whom I refer to as Forces of Production (FP) when dealing with a transformation process, is the existence of so-called uncontrolled Forces of Production (FPnc, or the "Unfits"), who are people acting in a detrimental fashion during the transformation stage.

Forces of Production (who are People acting favorably during the transformation phase) are assumed to be under control (FPc): a project manager directs them, evaluates them, and pays them. He thus has control over them. Technically, if one such Force of Production (team member) falls below a preset performance requirement, an action can be taken to rectify the situation, by way of docking bonuses, training, reprimand, or layoff. However, there are Forces of Production that remain amply uncontrolled or uncontrollable (FCnc): these individuals or groups of individuals have their own agendas. An excellent example is the strike by the construction/trade individuals that plagued the construction of the Olympic Stadium in Montréal in 1976 a few months prior to its grand opening. Management had been "painted in a corner" so to speak: over a billion dollars had been invested to show the entire world what Montréal was made of. Evidently, there was a risk and a point of vulnerability (not having an internal specialized trade force) because a large workforce (apart from trade people) was uncontrolled. In the case of the Mervel Farm, there is also a certain number of possible Unfits (FPnc)—the army of volunteers whom the project promoters assume will rush to adhere to the ideology of the project ("a more natural way of life within a city"). However, what if this army of teenagers decides to not show up on the next workday for whatever reason (the teenagers went to bed too late, the nice weather commanded a picnic at the beach with their boy/girlfriends, etc.)? This is an ominous point of vulnerability (taking for granted that there are employees of this sort—albeit unpaid—available to the promoters).

A project is a cluster of people that is bound by a calendar of tasks and activities, costs, and norms of quality; that has specific objectives to meet; and that deals with problems and challenges. For example, a construction project such as the QMA includes agents such as architects, builders, experts responsible for establishing work schedules, subcontractors, and tradespeople (carpenters, electricians, etc.).

There are two broad categories of people: external (e.g., banks), to whom risks can be attributed; and internal (often busy performing daily operations), to whom vulnerabilities can be attributed. In the case of the QMA, external people are trade people hired by the construction manager, Pomerleau. Internal people are the crew headed by Mr. Jean Rochette, from the City of Québec. We can also divide People according to whether they are producers, consumers (such as the Olympic athletes and visitors to the Montréal Games), regulators (such as government or private professional associations), or so-called bad apples (who consist of unethical pressure groups, illegal workers, etc. —they act outside of the social norms and cause collateral damage).

Unfits (uncontrolled Forces of Production) are one category of people acting up. All external uncontrolled people represent a risk, and may negatively affect projects by empowering points of vulnerability; all internal uncontrolled people represent a POV. We can represent People, before they become Forces of Production by way of the transformation process, as shown in Figure 14-12.

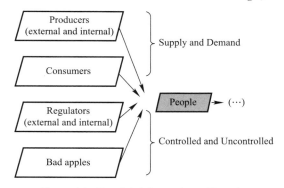

Figure 14-12   A brief overview of People

Some authors have separated people depending on whether they are customers (consumers), the parent organizations (producers), project teams (producers), or the public (consumers). Neither they nor PMBOK mention bad apples, but any experienced project manager will recognize their presence and devastating role without difficulty. By definition, internal bad apples are a POV. External bad apples were especially active in the construction industry in Québec—the 1974—1975 Cliche Commission exposed the fact that the mafia integrated many layers of construction projects with rippling effects in terms of costs and delays.

Power is the line of authority (both formal and informal) that sees that the project comes to a successful end. It includes the project managers and the various jurisdictional authorities who make sure codes and rules are respected.

An example of Power is found in the QMA. Any change to the content of the project had to be formally authorized by the project director and scrupulously entered into a register.

As previously put forth, POVs may exist within each one of the four Ps. With respect to Power, there is a POV readily identifiable in the Mervel Farm project: the fact that the City of Pierreville (of provincial jurisdiction), which is an integral part of the project, must cooperate with the National Capital Commission (of federal jurisdiction). Often such political setups lead to bureaucratic or political upheaval.

Project promoters (acting as producers) design projects and find ways to fund them. Project leaders are more into day-to-day operations: they plan project activities, establish costs and schedules, lead and motivate teams, and implement a certain project culture. They measure risks, plan for the long term, and share their vision. Project managers, on the other hand, execute— they manage activities, costs, resources (including human resources), and schedules. They are task-oriented, they conform and administer and tend to avoid risk. They understand the importance of people in the organization, of competencies, culture, leadership, and performance. Their approach to risk is what differentiates promoters from leaders from managers. Project leaders should be able to foresee POVs and project managers should be able to implement solutions that minimize them in earnest.

Judging from the Mervel Farm project, one can see that on paper all seems quite promising: the Plan is set and approved by expert committees, People who will work at the farm are assumed to be hardcore believers in the value of such an undertaking, Processes have been well laid out, and the promoters are enthusiastic and competent (Power). However, once all four elements (the four Ps) are put together, the scenario may not be as rosy. A group of volunteers (People) may not be willing to abide by the processes set in place. Intentions and reality differ. A project is by definition just that: intentions (hence the term "project").

So far, I have demonstrated that a project is a transformation process that receives inputs and that generates outputs, such as deliverables, thereafter. These inputs consist of the four Ps (Plans, Processes, People and Power) which interact during the transformation stage (Plans', Processes', People', and Power'). All four Ps are susceptible to POVs for whatever type of project, be it a construction endeavor or a touristy park of sorts.

14.4 Reading Material

1. Risk Management

"Risk" and "Management" are over-used words. These days everything has to be risk managed.

There is undoubtedly a need to formalise an approach to identifying and limiting the numerous risks which affect all businesses today. Managers or business owners cannot be expected to comprehend all the risks which might affect their businesses. Spreadsheet analysis of investment opportunities prior to commitment is an obvious way to identify and eliminate risk. The strictest interpretation could be that if the proposed investment is not risk free then do not invest.

The real use of a sensitivity analysis is to identify which parameters are sensitive and thus limit risk. Where a parameter is identified as being sensitive, in that a small change in it will materially adversely affect the project outcome, then the risk should be eliminated or at least "tied down". If it cannot be satisfactorily dealt with then the project should be abandoned.

2. Can There be Too Much Analysis?

Analysing the sensitivity of a spreadsheet model is well established and many quite detailed analyses are carried out. The aim being to identify how much decreases in inflows or increases in outflows can be tolerated or more likely what cannot be tolerated. There is no end to the number of "what if?" situations which may be tested. It is obviously very sensible to carry out extensive and detailed sensitivity analyses. However there is a danger that either too much analysis is done or too pessimistic a view is taken-is it really likely that all parameters go wrong at the same time? Another potential problem with sensitivity analyses is that they may be comprehensible to the preparer of the model but may not really make clear the risks to others involved in the investment and sanctioning process.

3. Need for a Defined Model

Thus a clear base "most likely case" model should be devised and the sensitivities of the parameters demonstrated in as clear and simple a manner as possible. The emphasis of the sensitivity analysis should be to identify sensitive parameters, quantify just how sensitive they are and then identify how the risk of the parameter "going wrong" can be averted. Sensitivity analysis should lead to real risk management.

As described in chapter 5, the process of project appraisal includes more than analysis of spreadsheets for sensitivity. The risks, commercial and otherwise, inherent in any project should be identified by structured thoughtful review of the project. The technical, commercial and ultimately cash flow risks should also be identified. The use of review checklists outlined at the end of chapter 5 may assist. Having made this very important point the use of structured sensitivity analyses of projects is of the greatest support in identifying and thus being in a position to overcome risk.

4. Sensitivity Analysis

The fact that appraisals can be so easily carried out on spreadsheets or by other computer models means that it is possible to look at outcomes based on endless arrangements of input parameter settings. This is fine, but can lead to the overabundance of output information causing the truly sensitive parameters to be missed. Although simple in concept and with the limitation that only one parameter is changed at a time, the "one at a time" sensitivity analysis does reveal both the sensitive parameters and indicates the materiality of changes in input parameters.

The growing tendency to rely on spreadsheet and like calculations may mean that obvious business risks and sensitive parameters are overlooked. Basic arithmetical truths such as the fact that the largest figures will be most sensitive should not be forgotten. As indicated in chapter 5 on the appraisal process, it is important not to rely solely on an arithmetical analysis to identify sensitive and thus potentially risky parameters. Sensitivity analysis should really only be seen as a back up to an individual's understanding of the risks inherent in the business proposition.

5. The Need for the Most Likely Case

By definition, since sensitivity to change in inputs is being reviewed, then there must be a base position. For the analysis to reveal and quantify realistic sensitivities, there should be a "most likely case"—neither optimistic nor pessimistic—base model of the project. The simple but effective approach of carrying out a "one at a time" sensitivity analysis may then be adopted.

As the aim of the sensitivity analysis is to identify and thus quantify the parameters which are most sensitive to change (in an adverse direction), there is no point in carrying out the analysis on figures which are either pessimistic or optimistic. It is the most likely situation which is required. This demand for the most likely situation may also help in focusing on the amount of effort which goes into estimating.

6. No Need for Provisions or Contingencies

A follow-on point is that figures in an appraisal should in no way be loaded by the existence of provisions or contingencies. In fact, the inclusion of a provision or contingency is quite fatuous. No moneys have been committed—this is just the appraisal stage. It is the most likely outcome which should be appraised for sensitivity. It is also arguable that there is no need for provisions on sanctioned projects—if they exist, they will only be used!

However, when carrying out the sensitivity analysis, risks may become evident. The need for an amount of provisions, should the project be sanctioned, may well be capable of quantification. A business may then set up specific provisions for specific projects or may wish to hold central provisions as part of its risk management process or simply for political reasons. It should be noted that with the issue of Financial Reporting Standard (FRS)-12 Provisions, Contingent Liabilities and Contingent Assets, the common practice of carrying provisions against future costs has been very much curtailed.

Words and Expressions:

The students should write down unfamiliar words and expressions which may disorder their reading.

Questions:

How could the simple but effective approach of carrying out a "one at a time" sensitivity analysis be adopted?

Chapter 15
Management of Public Utilities and Government Departments

15.1 Project Decisions for Public Utilities and Government Departments

1. Introduction

The so-called engineering decision-making refers to the trade-off and design of the engineering tasks to be completed and the engineering problems to be solved by the engineering decision-making party or decision-making subject, as well as the choices and decisions made on the direction, procedures, approaches, measures, etc. of future engineering activities. Engineering decision-making is the most important and complex link in the process of engineering activities. The correctness of decision-making directly affects the success or failure of the whole engineering activities and their results.

15.1 Professional Terms, Words and Phrases, Sentence Illustration

In people's production and life, from daily life to national development, we often face various problems. Decision making issues. Decision making generally refers to the collection and processing of various relevant information in order to achieve a certain goal, and the adoption of decisions. The decision-maker's analysis and judgment make a choice for the action plan. Decision making is the premise and guide of action.

Engineering decision-making refers to the behavior that the engineering decision-maker (government, enterprise or individual) establishes the overall deployment for the proposed engineering project, compares, analyzes and judges different engineering construction schemes, and makes a choice for the implementation scheme. Decision making is the main line running through the whole planning stage. It can be considered that the whole project planning stage is a decision-making process and an activity process before the implementation of the project. Engineering decision-making generally includes two levels: one is the overall strategic deployment of engineering construction, and the other is the selection of specific implementation schemes.

Characteristics of engineering decision-making: from the process of engineering decision-making and the factors involved, engineering decision-making has the following characteristics:

(1) The essence of engineering decision-making is a design and decision of future engineering activities on the basis of cognition. Engineering decision-making points to the future, which points to the new engineering existence that has not been completed. It focuses on mining and realizing the possible goals and values in the future by transforming theoretical knowledge into practical knowledge and shaping the practical concept model. Engineering decision-making should

not only face the future, but also be related to the current reality. On the one hand, it must be connected with the current reality. Starting from the inherent provisions of the object and the determined value relationship that people grasp in their ideas, we can realize the search for the future. On the other hand, engineering decision-making is to realize the purpose of transforming reality and promoting development through the planning of people's future goals and activities.

(2) Engineering decision-making is a non-logical integration between technical factors, social factors and environment involved in engineering activities. Decision making must be logical, but the logic of decision-making in the social field is not strict or absolute. In the context of social system, engineering decision-making is a decision-making mode dominated by engineering thinking. It is different from the scientific thinking that pursues logical rigor. Engineering decision-making as a whole shows not strict logic, but often a kind of non-logical integration or super logical coordination between decision-making elements.

(3) Engineering decision-making is a nonlinear social system decision-making. Any engineering project and engineering construction activities should be carried out in the social system. The social system is the basis and environment for engineering activities, and all aspects of engineering activities are affected and restricted by the social system. Social system is also the most complex nonlinear open system in the real world, which has unique attributes and evolution mechanism. The nonlinear characteristics of social system determine the coexistence of randomness and certainty, order and disorder, gradual change and mutation, etc. in the evolution of social system, which requires multi-dimensional understanding and description.

2. Methods and Tools

(1) Improve the laws and regulations on government investment management.

First, improve laws and regulations. Clean up and abolish the laws and regulations that are inconsistent with the central government. Accelerate the legislation of "agent construction system" and comprehensively implement the "agent construction system" for non-profit projects invested by the government. Secondly, government investment should be included in the supervision scope of the whole audit process. Promote the establishment of audit supervision system to be more scientific and better managed, and give play to the function of audit immune system. Thirdly, strengthen supervision regulations. Give full play to the power of professional and comprehensive supervision, prevent fraud, corruption and bribery, and severely punish violations of laws and disciplines.

(2) Establish a scientific management system.

First, strengthen owner management. All projects belonging to fiscal investment projects, organizations of administrative institutions, state-owned companies and state-owned holding companies shall be included in the scope of government investment. Secondly, establish a scientific and democratic government investment management system and decision-making system, strictly implement the basic construction procedures and implement the project management system of "three separation" of investment, construction and operation management in accordance with the principles of "three public and four systems" (i. e. openness, fairness, impartiality and owner responsibility system, bidding comparison and selection system, supervision system and project acceptance system).

(3) Improve the internal control system.

First, strengthen the scientific rationality of decision-making. Carry out the scientific demonstration and process of "expert evaluation, staff evaluation and social evaluation" to avoid losses, waste, low efficiency and blind decision-making. Secondly, implement the system of government investment project bank, enhance the transparency and democratization of government investment project decision-making, and promote the standardization of investment decision-making procedures.

(4) Promote the construction of "agent construction system" for government investment projects.

First, accelerate the reform of the management system of government investment projects. Establish a scientific and standardized project management system and operation mechanism with clear rights and responsibilities, effective constraints. Secondly, establish an effective supervision mechanism for the separation of "investment, construction, management and use", comprehensively implement the "agent construction system", and realize professional and market-oriented management. Thirdly, realize the separation of government and enterprises. The government is no longer directly involved in the micro management of project construction. Ensure that all parties involved in the construction (owners, contractors, supervisors) form an effective check and balance mechanism to ensure the efficiency of government investment in project construction.

(5) Standardize scientific management.

First, strictly implement the bidding. From the aspects of design, construction, equipment, supply, supervision, etc., we should carry out all-round and whole process bidding, select the best, and put an end to unfair competition in the process of project bidding. Secondly, strictly control the legitimacy and rationality of bidding procedures. Adhere to the principle of "openness, fairness and justice" and implement the "sunshine project". Secondly, strengthen the supervision and inspection of bidding work, and strictly deal with and punish violations. Thirdly, check the contract. The bidding and tendering shall be consistent with the contract, and the numbers and words shall be accurate, so as to reduce ambiguity and reduce changes and claims in the process of project implementation. Fourth, ensure quality and safety. Strengthen the monitoring of the construction process and eliminate any form of quality and safety hazards. Fifth, we should ensure good project management. Establish and improve the internal control system, timely complete the visa, and confirm the rationality of the price. Sixth, introduce the supervision mechanism. Standardize project supervision and ensure project quality.

(6) Improve the supervision system.

First, strengthen prevention and integrate supervision. Strengthen the authority supervision of the people's Congress, pay attention to the supervision of the public, form a joint force of discipline inspection, supervision, audit, finance, planning, construction, etc., establish and implement the corresponding project evaluation system, performance audit system, project quality system, project clean government construction system, responsibility accountability system, promote the "action under the sun" of government investment projects, and curb "project corruption". Secondly, strengthen internal supervision. Improve the supervision mechanism and management system of management units. Give play to the operational efficiency of thetrinity of decision-making, implementation and supervision, and ensure that government investment projects become "popular projects", "reassuring projects" and "sunshine projects".

(7) Strengthen financial supervision.

First, improve the financial management system. Strictly examine, approve, implement and supervise funds to prevent the absence of financial supervision. Secondly, establish a centralized financial payment mechanism. Adopt the method of centralized payment by the financial department to improve the efficiency of capital turnover. Thirdly, financial management and accounting should be carried out in accordance with the law, and financial supervision should be strengthened.

(8) Do a good job in performance audit.

First, do a good job in the performance audit of government investment projects. Combine investment audit with performance audit, and focus on investment decision-making, investment management, fund use, and investment effect audit. Secondly, give play to the constructive role of audit. Scientifically evaluate the whole process of the use of funds and the economic and social benefits generated by the project, conduct in-depth analysis and research on the uncontrolled investment, loss and waste, and put forward constructive audit suggestions.

(9) Innovative audit methods.

First of all, we should strengthen the management mode of "must review system" and "bidding pricing, auditing and fixing money" for government investment projects. Secondly, innovate the audit concept. For major investment projects, the whole process follow-up audit shall be carried out, and the supervision gate shall be moved forward. Do a good job in pre, in and post audit, and give play to the function of audit immune system. Thirdly, we should innovate audit methods and use computers to carry out auxiliary audit to improve work efficiency and audit quality. Fourth, establish a stable investment audit team. Cultivate "usable and retained" engineering audit talents to meet the needs of the development of government investment audit.

3. Models

Decision model—this model serves as a basis for the analysis and synthesis of information and is the mechanism used to compare competing alternatives. To be effective, a decision model must be based on a systematic and logical framework for guiding project decisions. A decision model can be a verbal, graphical, or mathematical representation of the ideas in the decision-making process. A project decision model should encompass:

- A simplified representation of the actual situation.
- An explanation and prediction of the actual situation.
- Validity and appropriateness.

- Applicability to similar problems.

The formulation of a decision model involves three essential components:

- Abstraction: Determining relevant factors
- Construction: Combining the factors into a logical model
- Validation: Assuring that the model adequately represents the problem

The five basic types of decision models for project management are described next.

Descriptive models are directed at describing a decision scenario and identifying the associated problem. For example, a project analyst may use a Critical Path Method (CPM) network model to identify bottleneck tasks in a project.

Prescriptive models furnish procedural guidelines for implementing actions. The triple C approach (Badiru 2008) prescribes the procedures for achieving communication, cooperation, and coordination in a project environment.

Predictive models are used to predict future events in a problem environment. They are typically based on historical data. For example, a regression model based on past data may be used to predict future productivity gains associated with expected levels of resource allocation. Simulation models can be used when uncertainties exist in the task durations or resource requirements.

"Satisficing" models provide trade-off strategies for achieving a satisfactory solution to a problem within certain given constraints. Satisficing, a concatenation of the words satisfy and suffice, is a decision-making strategy that attempts to meet criteria for adequacy rather than identify an optimal solution. It is used where achieving an optimum is not practicable. Goal programming and other multi-criteria techniques provide good satisficing solutions. These models are helpful where time limitations, resource shortages, and performance requirements constrain project implementation.

Optimization models are designed to find the best available solution to a problem subject to certain constraints. For example, a linear programming model can be used to determine the optimal product mix in a production environment.

In many situations, two or more of the models may be involved in the solution of a problem. For example, a descriptive model might provide insights into the nature of the problem; an optimization model might provide the optimal set of actions to take in solving the problem; asatisficing model might temper the optimal solution with reality; a prescriptive model might suggest the procedures for implementing the selected solution; and a predictive model may foresee an outcome.

15. 2　Project Management in Public Utilities and Government Departments

1. Introduction

Characteristics of project management:

(1) The management is very strict.

The next step of construction can only be carried out with the approval of the

15. 2 Professional Terms, Words and Phrases, Sentence Illustration

relevant documents of the national, provincial and municipal governments, and the construction can only be carried out under the premise of relevant regulations. We must strictly implement the national procedures and norms, and carefully implement the construction standards and relevant management systems. When such projects are under construction, there are more government supervision and management departments than ordinary projects, and there are also many matters that need to be submitted for approval.

(2) Will be concerned by all sectors of society.

Because most of the projects funded by the government can involve the projects of social and public cultural development or projects that have a close relationship with the lives of the masses, they will certainly receive the attention of all sectors of society, which can also play a good supervisory role.

(3) The workload of project organization and coordination is relatively large.

Because there are many governmental group projects and their distribution area is very wide, the workload of organizing and coordinating them is correspondingly large. It is very cumbersome to coordinate with the management department. For example, the relevant project initiation plan and adjustment work coordinated by the Planning Commission, and the related matters of financial allocation need to be discussed. In addition, it needs to communicate with the Planning Bureau. In addition, it also needs to coordinate and arrange the specific work.

(4) The amount of funds invested is very large, and most of them are public welfare.

Qualitative project. If the project can be completed satisfactorily as planned, it will greatly improve the living conditions of the public and bring benefits to the people. However, if there are problems in the construction, or the construction is not ideal, on the one hand, it will waste a lot of money and cause economic losses, on the other hand, it will affect the image of the government, because the government project itself has been concerned, so once there are problems, it will arouse the dissatisfaction of many people and affect the image of the government.

2. Methods and Tools

(1) Gradually establish and improve the construction management system.

The operation process of construction enterprises has the characteristics of seasonality, liquidity, periodicity, and uneven production capacity load. The project management mode must conform to the characteristics of construction products. The construction of engineering project management in China must start from the situation of Chinese construction enterprises, and gradually establish a scientific and reasonable management mode. This mode is first of all a scientific and reasonable organization system with the characteristics of close to the market, rigid industrial structure and flexible productivity. We should also ensure that this mode can separate the functions of construction operation and construction management. In addition, scientific and practical means of project planning and effective means of project control should be established.

(2) Continuously improve the safety production system.

The first is to strengthen the awareness of construction safety management. Construction enterprises must attach great importance to the safety management of construction, adhere to the principle of people-oriented and safety first, and realize "zero accident". Engineering construction management should pay attention to details and do a good job in related work of construction safety. Secondly, the safety production system should be constantly improved to provide the basis for the safety management of construction and effectively ensure that potential safety hazards are nipped in the cradle. Therefore, for safe construction, it is necessary to set up a special safety team to control these factors within a certain range and take preventive measures.

(3) Strengthen quality management in construction.

Good quality control is an important means to strengthen project quality management in construction. The realization of project quality control is mainly through the construction technology activities, so that the quality of the construction project can meet the requirements of the design and related technical standards, and then the various methods and measures adopted. The quality management of the construction stage is mainly to transform the construction design drawings into the entity of the project. Therefore, the management and control of the project quality should comply with the laws and regulations issued by the state and its relevant departments and the provisions of relevant project contract documents. Strengthening the inspection of the construction site is a powerful means to strengthen the quality management in the construction stage. In addition, effective tests can also be carried out on various construction raw materials and semi-finished products entering the construction site by means of tests, and then the quality of materials can be strictly analyzed and evaluated. Only when the quality of materials meets the standards of relevant specifications can they be put into use.

(4) Strengthening the management of building materials.

The management and control of building materials determine the quality and service life of construction projects to a certain extent. Material management and control include the control of raw materials, finished products, semi-finished products and construction components and accessories. At the same time, we should also realize the importance of the quality of building materials, which is the basis of project construction management and control. The quality of building materials seriously affects the quality of the project. Therefore, strengthening the control and management of building materials is an important means to ensure the quality of the project.

(5) Improve the safety awareness of construction personnel.

In order to reduce the occurrence of safety accidents, construction enterprises need to improve the safety awareness of construction personnel and install some corresponding safety facilities. To improve the safety awareness of construction personnel and ensure the safety of construction personnel, we should pay attention to the following two points: first, we must make construction personnel aware of the importance of safety ideologically, so that they can establish their safety awareness. In the construction of construction projects, construction workers must operate according to the construction requirements, so as to ensure their own safety. If the construction workers are ideologically aware of the consequences of violating the operation, they will improve their prevention ability, so as to avoid unnecessary casualties. Secondly, some necessary safety facilities should be installed at the construction site to ensure the safety of construction workers.

The construction unit should not only improve the safety awareness of construction workers, but also continuously reduce the risk factors existing at the construction site, so as to effectively reduce the occurrence of safety accidents. For example, the dormitory of construction workers should be far away from the construction area, and safety passages should be set up in the areas where construction workers often pass by, as well as safety slogans and warning signs. In addition, when construction workers carry out safety work, they must bring relevant protective equipment. Construction management workers must improve the safety system and carefully manage the construction site, so as to effectively ensure the life safety of construction personnel.

3. Models

（1）Infrastructure division mode.

This mode has the advantages of rapidity and flexibility, and is easy to be approved faster, which is conducive to being put into engineering construction as soon as possible. However, this model also has shortcomings, that is, the power concentration is too strong. In order to obtain more utilization, the demand units will blindly expand the construction scale, resulting in a waste of funds. This is a model that is dying out at present.

（2）Project legal person system.

This system is widely used in current water conservancy, transportation and railway government projects. Its main advantage is that it can effectively specify property rights and distribute interests. The deficiency of this management mode is that a project needs a legal person, resulting in a huge management team. This project legal person management mode is not suitable for small and medium-sized projects and a single investor. But it is more suitable for large-scale projects and government projects with multi-level investment subjects.

（3）Centralized government procurement.

The advantage of this management mode is that it is convenient to effectively regulate and control the regional economy, and can accumulate more accumulation, thereby reducing the cost of management funds. However, there is a relatively significant disadvantage is the concentration of power. Once the supervision is absent, it is easy to produce corruption. Therefore, the adoption of this model must be truly open and transparent. Therefore, the application of public bidding also needs to improve the supervision mechanism. Because the government procurement management mode has these advantages, it will be more applied in the future development.

（4）Agent system.

This is a new management mode, which is mainly for professional management companies to manage government projects under the commission of the government. This model can give full play to the advantages of professional units, effectively decentralize rights, avoid or reduce corruption, and help maintain the market order of fair competition. Especially after the State Council issued relevant regulations, this model has been widely promoted. However, the agent construction system also faces many problems: the lack of detailed and feasible laws and regulations, and the management subject has not been clearly positioned. This mode will be the main mode of management reform of public welfare government engineering projects in the future.

However, judging from the time of its reform and development, it still needs to go through a quite long process.

For quite some time in the future, many new management models will be launched one after another with the help of their unique advantages, thus forming a new situation in which diversified and multi type management models coexist. The models of each group will also develop in the direction suitable for their own development: first, the government centralized procurement management model. It can be reasonably applied in small and medium-sized public welfare projects and simple public welfare projects. The second is the agent construction system. With the development, this mode will be the main mode of public welfare projects in the future. It has strong adaptability and can be applied to large-scale projects, medium-sized projects and small-scale projects. However, the development of this mode starts from small and medium-sized projects, and starts from government engineering projects with low technical difficulty requirements and relatively simple interest relations. It continues to accumulate experience, mature and perfect in practice. Third, the system of project legal person and the mode of institutional legal person. It is mainly applicable to large-scale public welfare government engineering projects with complex relationships. After the agent construction system is popularized in large-scale enclosure, this model will still have stronger adaptability in large-scale projects. Fourth, the government concentrated investment. This mode is mainly applicable to simple and quasi-public welfare government projects, and small projects are also suitable. Fifth, the project legal person system. When faced with complex, large-scale and diversified investment subjects of quasi-public welfare government engineering projects, this management mode will be mainly used in the future. Sixth, the separation mode of public welfare and quasi-public welfare. Theoretically, it has strong rationality, but it is easily limited by many factors in practice, so it needs to be verified and improved in the continuous practical exploration. Seventh, the market operation mode. With the deepening of the transformation and reform of the market economic system, this model will have a broader world. It will be the mainstream model of future development and can be gradually improved in the continuous development in the future.

15. 3 Risk Management in Public Utilities and Government Departments

1. Introduction

Municipal engineering projects are carried out in a complex natural and social environment. Their construction face is long, the construction period is tight, the investment is many, the technical requirements are high, and there are many cross operations with other pipeline units. In the project implementation engineering, there are a large number of uncertain factors, which are constantly changing, and the risks arising from this often affect the smooth implementation of engineering

15. 3 Professional Terms, Words and Phrases, Sentence Illustration

projects. The risk management of municipal engineering project is to evaluate the risk of construction project on the basis of analyzing the risk factors, obtain the possibility and harm degree of each risk of construction project, and use scientific management technology and means to prevent and deal with the possible risks of engineering project, which plays a key role in the success of engineering project.

Risk management runs through the whole process of the project, and is also reflected in all aspects of the main body in the process of project implementation, namely, the owner, the contractor, the consulting agency and the supervising engineer. The owner and the contractor sign the project contract, and both parties share the corresponding project risks. However, due to the fierce competition in the project contracting industry and the restriction of the "buyer's market" rules, the degree of risk borne by the owner and the contractor is not equal, and the main risks often fall to the contractor. According to the situation of project management and the practice of Yuanbai highway reconstruction project in Anqing City, project risk management can be divided into six stages: risk planning, risk identification, risk analysis, risk evaluation, risk response and risk monitoring.

Project risk management refers to the management work of recognizing the risks of the project through risk identification, risk analysis and risk evaluation, and on this basis, reasonably using various risk response measures, management methods, technologies and means to effectively control the risks of the project, properly handling the adverse consequences caused by risk events, and ensuring the realization of the overall objectives of the project at the least cost.

Risk factor refers to the inducement of risk. The risk of municipal engineering project is caused by many uncertain factors. If risk factors are not considered in the process of project implementation, the actual cost will be increased, resulting in lower profits or even losses. Therefore, in order to obtain the target expected profit, we must accurately analyze the risk factors of the engineering project. The risk factors in municipal engineering projects mainly include the following aspects:

Investment risk is the primary risk in the implementation of the project, covering the risks that run through the overall risk factors of the project. Due to the large investment and tight construction period, the physical and economic characteristics of the municipal engineering project itself make the municipal engineering investment also show the inherent characteristics different from other investments. It has the characteristics of long investment return period, large investment amount, many factors affecting the investment effect, poor investment transfer and substitution, complex and difficult investment decision-making. In this process, there are a large number of uncertain factors, random factors and fuzzy factors, and constantly changing, the resulting risks directly threaten the smooth implementation and success of municipal engineering project investment.

In municipal engineering projects, due to people's limited cognitive ability, the project cycle is tight. Objective conditions during the project, such as technology, construction, geology, materials, etc., may interfere with the implementation of the project agreement, and this objective uncertainty in the performance of the contract will bring risks to the contract. The main manifestations are: misunderstanding caused by incomplete and imprecise contract provisions, unilateral binding of the contract, imbalance of responsibilities, rights and interests, risks caused by exculpatory clauses proposed by the employer, risks caused by the owner's breach of contract, overdue payment of engineering mania, substantial rise in materials, changes in the process of performance, visa risks, etc.

Construction period risk refers to the comprehensive influence of various factors in the construction process of municipal engineering projects, which eventually leads to the delay of project construction and the failure to complete the project in time according to the construction period. This is mainly because: on the one hand, the government engineering demolition is not in place and the selection of design and construction teams, and the decision-making is biased, which leads to the poor professional quality of the design and construction personnel, making the designed architectural drawings fail to meet the construction requirements, which will ultimately affect the progress of the project. On the other hand, municipal engineering construction is a complex dynamic process, facing a variety of internal and external environments that are more complex. Any adverse effect or unexpected load will have an adverse impact on the municipal engineering and bring varying degrees of damage, which will lead to the problem of project rework and affect the progress and quality of the project.

Economic risk refers to all kinds of risks that lead to bad luck in the operation of enterprises in the economic field. That is, the potential uncertainties in economic strength, economic situation and the ability to solve economic problems constitute the possible consequences of operation. Such as economic crisis and financial crisis, inflation or deflation, exchange rate fluctuations, etc. There are also economic risks associated with project contracting activities, which only affect specific construction enterprises, such as the owner's ability to perform the contract.

2. Methods and Tools

The goal of risk countermeasures is to minimize the threat brought by risks with the lowest cost disposal steps, so as to obtain the maximum benefits. We can divide the risk treatment methods into risk control type and financial accommodation type according to different risk properties.

The risk control type focuses on reducing or controlling the frequency andamplitude of losses to achieve the purpose of reducing or avoiding losses. Its treatment methods are: risk avoidance, risk prevention, risk transfer, risk separation, and risk dispersion. on reducing or controlling the frequency and amplitude of losses to achieve the purpose of reducing. Its treatment method is divided into financial accommodation type: the risk already exists, and the loss is still difficult to avoid, so it depends on financial accommodation in advance to minimize the financial impact and inconvenience of the loss. Treatment methods usually include loss retention and insurance transfer.

On the basis of the evaluation and analysis of project risks, the probability of project risks, the severity of losses and other factors can be comprehensively considered, and the possibility and harm degree of various risks of the project can be obtained, and then compared with the recognized safety indicators, so as to determine what measures should be taken and to what extent control measures should be taken. For the specific process of construction project implementation, in order to minimize the risk, the following risk prevention countermeasures can be adopted:

（1）Grasp investment decisions and strengthen investment risk management.

The avoidance of investment risks in municipal engineering projects should grasp the following two points: ① grasp investment decisions and prevent investment risks. In the investment decision-making stage, investors in municipal engineering projects should do the following tasks to prevent risks: first, establish a high-level, multidisciplinary investment management team. Second, establish risk awareness. The investment management team, especially the main decision-makers, should establish a correct risk attitude. Third, improve the risk early warning system. The key to prevent risks is to take action in advance, that is, to actively control. The longer the project enters the implementation stage, the higher the cost of risk control. Fourth, implement the risk management responsibility system. Investors should establish a risk management responsibility system and formulate scientific assessment standards and reward and punishment measures. ② Grasp the analysis of investment risk factors and control investment risks. Because there are many risk factors that affect the investment of engineering projects, and various risks often overlap and cross each other, it requires investors to predict, evaluate and control project risks by studying the variability, diversity and hierarchy of project risks. The analytic hierarchy process (AHP) model can decompose the control objectives into different sub objectives according to the nature and requirements of the control objectives, and gather and combine the objectives according to different levels according to the mutual correlation, influence and subordinate relationship between the objectives, so as to form a multi-level structural model and comprehensively obtain the required control results. In the investment risk control of municipal engineering projects, the investable control objectives are divided into three levels: total project, single project and unit project. According to the investment statistical data of national construction projects, the different control ranges of different levels of investment control objectives on the degree of deviation can be represented graphically.

（2）Clarify contract details and strengthen contract risk management.

Municipal engineering contract is not only the legal document of project management, but also the main basis of comprehensive risk management of municipal engineering projects. Project managers must have a strong sense of risk, learn to study every clause of the contract from the perspective of risk analysis and risk management, have a comprehensive and profound understanding of the risk factors that the project may encounter, and reasonably control the occurrence of contract risks. First, specify the contract terms for the project content. At the signing stage, the project manager shall set up a special negotiation team for the project, which must be clear, elaborate and avoid ambiguity on the contract object, project contracting method, project price, project technical requirements, process selection, project quantity, project quality, change terms, settlement method, payment method, liability for breach of contract terms, dispute resolution and other contents. Second, according to the characteristics and reality of the project, the pricing contract form should be appropriately selected to transfer the risk to other people or organizations in the form of contract. Third, strengthen the contract management awareness of project managers in combination with the market situation. In practical work, with the standardized operation of the market and the development and changes of the market situation, contract management will continue to produce new problems and put forward new requirements. This requires project managers to strengthen management awareness and constantly improve the contract management system.

(3) Turn the risk of engineering change into profit through engineering claims.

In view of the factors that cause the construction period or quality risk of the municipal project, such as the change of quantities, the error of design, the acceleration of construction, the change of construction drawings, the change of construction conditions caused by adverse natural conditions or non-Party B's reasons, and the delay of construction period, the project risk shall be converted into profit through engineering claims. Project claim is a kind of claim, which is the redefinition of project risk by the contract subject, and it should run through the whole process of project implementation. The main ways to make engineering claims during the implementation of municipal engineering projects are as follows: ① claim for delay in construction period. It refers to that when the construction unit is responsible for the construction period delay, the construction unit will make a claim against the construction unit, that is, the construction unit will pay liquidated damages for delayed completion. When determining the rate of liquidated damages, the construction unit should generally consider the following factors: the profit loss of the construction unit; the loan interest increases due to the extension of the construction period; additional supervision fees caused by project delay; rental fees for renting other buildings due to project delay. ② Claim for construction defects. If the construction quality of the construction unit does not meet the requirements of the construction technical regulations, or the equipment and materials used do not meet the provisions of the contract, or the project that should be repaired is not completed before the warranty period expires, the construction unit has the right to investigate the responsibility of the construction unit.

(4) Change project objectives and avoid project risks.

Risk avoidance strategy refers to a strategy to actively abandon the project or change the project objectives and action plans to avoid risks when the potential threat of project risks is too likely, the adverse consequences are too serious, and no other strategies are available. For example, the enterprise is currently facing an investment project with immature technology. If it is found through risk assessment that the implementation of the project will face a huge threat, and the project management organization has no other available measures to control the risk, then it should consider giving up the implementation of the project to avoid huge risk accidents and property losses.

3. Models

Process management can be said to be one of the branches of modern management, and its management method is also one of the main management methods. Because the risk factors have the characteristics of concealment and are widely distributed, the management of each process is a dynamic process management. For those risk events caused by the impact of environmental factors, they must be found and analyzed in time, so as to formulate corresponding management countermeasures. The whole process risk management mode of the project is to manage the risk from the perspective of the whole process management, so as to ensure the realization of the objectives of project quality, progress and benefits. The risk management must be based on the overall management, and the project risks must be identified, evaluated and controlled in stages. The overall management mode includes the following parts.

(1) Formulation of risk management plan.

Everything is done in advance, and project risk management is no exception. As a guiding document for project risk management, the management plan mainly covers how to arrange and implement the whole process management of the project. The details include methodology, that is, the methods and tools used in the management process; roles and responsibilities are the roles and responsibilities in each stage of the management process; cost budget, obviously, refers to the cost required in the process of management; at the same time, there are some risk classification and risk assessment reports. Generally, the Risk Management Committee formulates the management plan, and it is worth noting: the risk attitude of the project personnel, the risk tolerance and the specific matters of the project.

(2) Institutional setup.

Any management work requires a special organization; whose main purpose is to exist as a risk management subject. This will help to clarify the position of risk management in the whole project management, improve the risk awareness of employees, and make staff recognize their responsibilities and obligations in management. In addition, this special management organization can ensure the smooth implementation of the management plan and ensure the effect of risk management when conducting risk management. The basic requirements for this institution are independence, authority, experience, skills and comprehensive knowledge.

(3) Risk management in planning and design.

Generally, risk management teams will be established in the management plan, and these teams will identify the risks of the project design in terms of quality, progress, rationality, etc. after these are completed, the identified risks will be analyzed and evaluated in detail, so as to form a risk list, and the management plan will be implemented with this list. At the same time, the risk identification and control of contract signing, planning and other aspects cannot be ignored.

(4) Risk management in implementation and control stage.

The main body of risk management in this link is the construction unit. Under the guidance of the risk management plan, the construction unit should also set up a management team to identify and evaluate the risks of the project in terms of technology, environment, personnel and facilities. This link is the one that invests the most resources, so once there is a problem, it will cause huge losses in human, financial, material and other aspects.

(5) Risk management in the completion stage.

At this stage, the entity of the project has been completed, and its main work is the collation and acceptance of documents and materials. At this stage, the risk management team should judge and identify risks from the aspects of whether documents and materials are complete and whether the acceptance work is reliable, and on this basis, formulate a risk management plan before implementation.

15. 4   Solution Implementation

15. 4 Professional Terms, Words and Phrases, Sentence Illustration

1. Introduction

Government organizations are among the most complex-because they are driven by very specific yet often open-ended missions... where success may not be easily measured, where efficiency is a secondary objective, and where matrix organizations result in lines of authority and accountability that may not be so clear and consistent. Responsible spending of funds in such an environment—to accomplish strategic objectives-can be extremely difficult and challenging. This article explores strategy implementation in government-the challenges and pitfalls, and some of the key drivers to think about that might help improve effectiveness.

Projects necessarily implement strategy, even if only at the most tactical level. Thus, it is important that the PM have an understanding of strategy in general-and of the organization's strategy in particular, especially the aspects that are driving the project. Understanding the strategic drivers of the project shapes the timing, quality standards, and cost variables for the project. It also determines the key metrics for measuring progress toward the strategic objectives of the project. This article looks at the extended challenges and responsibilities of the project manager performing strategy implementation on projects-beyond just meeting cost, schedule, and quality metrics.

2. Methods and Tools

Understand the Strategy-In the past, it may have seemed acceptable for the PM to manage the project as prescribed-and pay little or no attention to the strategic drivers that were the basis for the project. That is no longer acceptable, as evidenced by the emphasis over the past few years by the Project Management Institute (PMI) on requiring of certified Project Management Professionals (PMP) continuing education in the subject of strategy.

Define Strategy-Driven Metrics-The PM asks, "How will we know we are progressing toward the end goal of the project?" While there are the typical cost, schedule, and quality parameters, there also need to be metrics derived from the strategic objectives of the project that need to be monitored for progress throughout the life cycle.

Strategy and Timing-As there often is a temporal nature to strategic objectives, the PM and team need to be keenly aware of the need to get certain things in place within a specified time frame-and raise the flag and re-evaluate if there is trouble meeting the deadline.

Cross-Project Communication-Projects within a program or even across the organization are related in some ways. There could be commonalities related to timelines, dependencies, overlapping objectives. ... Successful strategy implementation within the organization requires a healthy degree of association among PMs across projects to socialize problems, approaches, best practices... and strategic alignment.

Identify Strategy-Related Risks-PMs need to ensure that risks related to veering "off strategy"-or strategy changing or becoming no longer valid-are identified as part of the risk management process.

Stakeholder Involvement-It is the right thing always to have direct involvement of stakeholders... but it is also important to involve key members from within the organizational hierarchy to ensure continued strategic relevance.

Here are just a few of the key areas requiring attention to more effectively implement strategies in government environments:

Manage the Matrix-On of the reasons government organizations are so complex is matrix organization. In other words, there are multiple lines of authority, where in essence any individual has multiple bosses. Much or most of this cannot be changed... but projects and programs within the matrix can be isolated and defined as much as possible "below the radar" where, while they are subject to the authorities inherent in the matrix, they also provide some room to get something done more freely.

Subject Matter Expert (SME) and Authoritative Support-Often projects and programs in government are limited in capability to get things done within the organization. While technical SMEs are helpful on the team, sponsorship or some degree of connectedness to individuals with authority is indispensable to having the ability to get things done-like removing obstacles-in a crunch.

Contract Flexibility-There are a variety of contract vehicles available, and it's good to have a "portfolio" of them in place to bring some flexibility when situations demand it. There will be needs for more-or fewer-resources. There are times to define statements of work in detail-and others more broadly. Keeping the implementation of the strategy in mind, you need to maintain a certain degree of flexibility to have enough control.

Stability of Leadership-Like any organization, there is a certain amount of movement around-and things change when someone new in authority comes in. This is especially true in military organizations, where changes occur every one to three years. To keep things moving toward strategic goals that are independent of the personnel in place, you need to identify the risks to the project or program and a way to minimize.

Timing of Funding-You need to line up funding with the milestones associated with strategic implementation-or run the risk of not having the resources in place when you most need them. This may lead to "over resourcing"-but whatever it takes, you need the resources in place to meet the timelines.

3. Models

The management mode of government investment projects includes macro and micro levels. From a macro point of view, the government investment project management mode refers to a set of processes that a country needs to go through from decision-making to implementation and the setting arrangement of a series of management systems to implement government investment projects in accordance with its own laws and regulations.

From a micro perspective, according to the sequence of project development, the concept of government investment project management mode can be extended to three levels: project financing mode, project management organization mode and project construction implementation mode. The primary problem of project construction is to raise construction funds and choose the appropriate project financing mode; How to select the owner and make him manage and be responsible for the project involves the selection of project management organization mode; After the confirmation of the owner, how to carry out the project contracting and select contractors to complete the construction and implementation of specific projects involves the selection of project construction and implementation mode.

(1) Project Financing Mode

With the development of social economy, the investment scale of engineering projects is becoming larger and larger, and a single way of financing and financing channels cannot meet the needs of engineering construction. Therefore, modern engineering construction often needs to comprehensively use a variety of financing methods to raise the required construction funds from different channels. Project financing mode refers to the combination of different financing methods adopted by project sponsors or investors to meet the needs of project construction funds, as well as the economic and legal relations of financing parties involved.

① Corporate Financing

The main advantages of the corporate financing model include: the financing structure is simple and easy to operate; The project company has the full right to use the funds; In the process of project implementation, it is less supervised and controlled by banks and financial institutions.

② BOT Mode

The main advantages of BOT mode include: reducing the impact of the project on the government budget; It can overcome the disadvantages of government investment, such as over construction period, over cost and poor operation service; The cash flow of public infrastructure projects is stable, and the investment risk is relatively small, which can bring stable and long-term investment income to investors; As the concession agreement of the project is signed between investors and the government, the legal binding force is strong, and investors can obtain effective legal protection.

③ TOT Mode

The main advantages of TOT mode include: Based on the existing infrastructure projects put into operation, it reduces the risks of private enterprises during the construction period and reduces the barriers for private enterprises to enter the infrastructure industry; In the process of transfer, the state-owned and private mode of infrastructure industry is formed through the transfer of management rights. Make the operating benefits of infrastructure industry directly linked to the interests of managers, so as to effectively stimulate enterprise managers and employees, and also increase fiscal revenue for local, regional and central governments.

（2）Project Management Organization Mode

With the transformation of China's economy from planned economy to socialist market economy, affected by the reform of macro politics and economic system, the organization mode of government investment project management in China has also experienced a historical development process from planning to marketization.

① Self-Support Mode of the Construction Unit

From 1949 to 1957, China was faced with the task of restoring and developing the national economy, which required a large amount of capital construction investment. However, at that time, the design and construction forces were very weak and scattered. The state could only integrate the production units and the construction units and organize the project construction in the self-supporting way of the construction units.

② Engineering Headquarters

After 1958, the management system in the form of Engineering Headquarters appeared in China. Many large and medium-sized projects are constructed in the form of Engineering Headquarters, led by the competent government departments, to organize the construction units, design units, and construction units to set up headquarters, preparation offices, offices, etc. for specific projects, separating the functions of managing construction projects from those of managing production projects. The Engineering Headquarters is responsible for the design, procurement, and construction management during the construction period. After the completion of the project, it will be handed over to the production management organization for operation, and the project headquarters will complete its mission.

③ Infrastructure Department Type

This model came into being in the 1950s and is still a relatively common model. Its main feature is self-construction and self-use. Various administrative departments (such as education, culture, health, sports) and some units with more engineering projects have infrastructure offices, which are responsible for the implementation of specific projects, while the administrative departments mainly carry out routine administrative management.

（3）Project Construction Implementation Mode

The implementation mode of project construction refers to the trading activities between different subjects in the construction market and the economic and legal relations they form. After long-term development, the project construction implementation mode and the corresponding contract form have been constantly innovated and improved, forming a variety of widely recognized forms.

Traditional Mode：

The traditional mode is the most common project management mode at present, which is also called design bid build method or sequential construction approach. This mode is adopted in the world bank, Asian Development Bank loan projects and projects using the civil engineering contract conditions of the International Federation of Consulting Engineers（FIDIC）.

In this mode, the project owner should first entrust architects or consulting engineers to carry out the preliminary work of the project, such as project approval analysis, feasibility study, etc., and then carry out project evaluation and project design. In the design stage, the construction bidding documents are prepared, followed by the project construction bidding. The owner and the contractor sign the project construction contract, which can be in the form of parallel contracting or general construction contracting. The subcontracting of the project, the supply of materials and equipment shall be directly contracted and implemented by the contractor with subcontractors and suppliers. Some suppliers can also be designated by the owner, but they must sign a contract with the contractor. During the implementation of the project, the owner will contact the consultant and the contractor through its representatives to be responsible for project management, or authorize architects, consulting engineers and supervising engineers to carry out project management.

(4) Project Management Mode

Project management refers to the management and service of the whole process or several stages of the organization and implementation of the project on behalf of the owner entrusted by the enterprise engaged in project management according to the contract. Its main forms are as follows:

① PMC Mode

PMC mode (Project Management Contractor) refers to the mode of project management contracting, which means that the project owner hires a company (generally an engineering company or consulting company with considerable strength) to provide project consulting services for the owner or manage the whole process of the project on behalf of the owner. PMC, as the owner's representative or the extension of the owner, helps the owner effectively control the project quality, progress and cost in the whole implementation process of project preliminary planning, feasibility study, project definition, plan, project budget, financing scheme, subcontracting scheme, design, procurement, construction, commissioning, etc., so as to ensure the successful implementation of the project and achieve the optimization of technical and economic indicators in the whole life cycle of the project.

② PM Mode

PM mode (Project Management) refers to the project management service mode. According to the contract, the owner entrusts a professional organization to manage the whole process on behalf of the owner. The project management services provided by PM mode usually include consulting in the early stage of the project and management services during the implementation period. Although it is similar to the Project Management Contracting mode (PMC), the project management company and the contractor do not enter into a contract, and the two are just management and coordination relations.

③ CM Mode

CM mode (construction management approach) is also known as phased construction method or fast track method. It is a joint group formed by the owner and the CM manager entrusted by the owner and the architect, which is jointly responsible for organizing and managing the project planning, project design and project construction.

15.5　Reading Material

Why Environment?

Perhaps as a legacy from Marxism, some professionals still believe that economics is the main factor in explaining events. However, it may appear that as the time goes by, in the confrontation between economics and ecology, it is the ecology that will have the upper hand. It seems that we are now living in a paradigm shift era where in fact just the reverse has happened as documented in Figure 15−1.

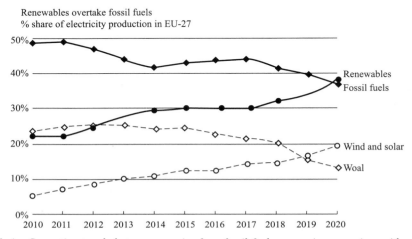

Figure 15−1　Competing trends between energies from fossil fuel sources in comparison with renewables

Figure 15−1 clearly shows since almost a decade ago that the trend for renewables has started to show gradual improvement over conventional, fossil energies. It is important to bear in mind that one of the most serious critics against renewables has always been that in comparison with fossil fuels, the former has not been economically a good choice. Environmental considerations and field data, though, show just the opposite.

Indirect costs related to corrosion can be listed verbatim as below:

(1) Loss of a product from a container that has corroded.

(2) Damage caused by leakage of a material such as oil or water from a corroded vessel.

(3) Contamination of a product; for example traces of metal may alter the color of dyes, or food may be spoiled in corroded metal containers.

(4) Loss of production because of a corrosion failure or loss of efficiency, for example, due to corrosion product reducing heat transfer. Replacement of a corroded tube in a plant may cost only a few hundred dollars, but shutdown while repairs are underway may mean a cost of many thousands of dollars in lost production.

(5) Effect on safety; for example, failure may cause fire, explosion, or release of a dangerous product.

(6) Appearance; a corroded material is unpleasant to the eye, so commercial establishments may use expensive trim for the sake of appearances.

Of the six items above, items 2 and 5 can be related directly to what we mean as corrosion impact in the context of this chapter. The other four items can be referred to as proprietary damages where the product itself or the factory in which production takes place are affected.

In other words, the items 2 and 5 signify the areas in which the impacts of corrosion go far from locality of a given production plant; these two items of indirect corrosion costs can affect one or all environmental components, and due to this very nature of them, their careful studies need to be prioritized in relation to the other four items listed.

It may seem more logical, then, to categorize costs of corrosion into direct and indirect, and classify them as "proprietary" and "universal" depending on the damage range they create. By this approach, the damage impact created by the corrosion impacts on universal costs, one of which being the environment will make sense.

For a balance between economy-based and ecology-based proprietary costs, our personal/ professional choice is to concentrate on the ecology-based proprietary costs. Our reason is simple; you can always make money and recover from financial loss, but you can never remake the environment again and recover it.

Appendix
Research Methodology

1. Research Criteria

An authentic paper is generally composed of the following criteria:

(1) Necessity of research. If your answer to one of the following questions is YES, your published paper is required:

- Should the area be addressed because it has been neglected?
- Would the area fill a gap in current scientific knowledge?

(2) Significance of research. If your answer to one of the following questions is YES, your published paper is important:

- Does your paper advance understanding?
- Does your paper make a useful contribution?
- Can you show a specific instance of the possible useful contribution?
- Are your findings original?

(3) Relevance of research. If your answer to one of the following questions is YES, this is an appropriate place for your possible publication:

- Is your research of interest to the journal audience?
- Is this topic relevant to the publication?

(4) Clarity of research. If your answer to one of the following questions is YES, your paper is easily acceptable:

- Is your topic clearly mentioned?
- Does your paper follow through by addressing this topic consistently and cogently?

(5) Relation to literature. If your answer to one of the following questions is YES, your paper is reliable:

- Does your paper show an adequate understanding of the current literature in the field?
- Does your paper connect with the literature in a way which might be useful to the development of our understanding in the area it addresses?

(6) Reference of research. If your answer to one of the following questions is YES, your findings from other research are very useful:

- Does your paper use theory in a meaningful way?
- Does your paper develop or employ theoretical concepts in such a way as to make plausible generalizations?
- Does your paper develop new theory?
- Does your paper apply theory to practice?

(7) Methodology of research. If your answer to one of the following questions is YES, your

research design and data collection methods are suitable:

- Has the research, or equivalent intellectual work upon which the paper is based, been well designed?
- Does the paper show adequate use of evidence, informational input, or other intellectual raw materials in support of its case?

(8) Data analysis. If your answer to one of the following questions is YES, you can use data correctly:

- Can you correctly use data analysis techniques?
- Can you make right interpretations from the data collected?
- Have the data been used effectively to advance the themes that the paper sets out to address?

(9) Critical qualities. If your answer to one of the following questions is YES, your paper has good quality:

- Does your paper demonstrate a critical self-awareness of the author's own perspectives and interests?
- Does your paper show awareness of the possibility of alternative or competing perspectives, such as other theoretical or intellectual perspectives?
- Does your paper show an awareness of the practical implications of the ideas it is advancing?

(10) Clarity of conclusions. If your answer to one of the following questions is YES, your paper is cohesive:

- Are the conclusions of the paper clearly stated?
- Do the conclusions adequately tie together the other elements of the paper (such as theory, data, and critical perspectives)?

(11) Quality of communication. If your answer to one of the following questions is YES, your paper is well written:

- Does your paper clearly express its case, measured against the technical language of the field and the reading capacities of an academic, tertiary student, and professional readership?
- What is the standard of writing, including spelling and grammar?

If you say YES for almost every criteria, this means that your authentic paper possibly makes it clear how the findings advance understanding of the issue under study. In addition, your paper provides an important critical and/or analytical insight that contributes something new to the field of higher education. Moreover, your issue/problem is well situated in appropriate literature. Furthermore, your paper demonstrates methodological soundness. Last, your conclusion is well supported and persuasively argued. Your paper is also succinct and coherent.

2. Format of Paper

Generally, there are many types of the authentic papers. Herein we focus on research paper and review paper, which many researchers usually publish for their experimental and/or theoretical works.

（1）Research paper. A research paper can be quantitative, qualitative, or mixed methods. This paper shows important and original findings.

（2）Review paper. A review paper is usually commissioned by editors. This paper raises technical or scientific questions about the published work.

A general set of sequential components of the research and review papers should have the following details:

- Title. The title length is usually around 5~20 words. Context must be short and specific.
- Abstract. Abstract is a brief summary of about 75~300 words. You can use the suitable tense in the sentence.

You should avoid citations, tables, equations, figures, and references.

- Keywords or PACS numbers. You must provide at least five keywords or the Physics and Astronomy Classification Scheme (PACS) numbers so that these are useful to select reviewers who are familiar with your papers. PACS was developed by the American Institute of Physics. It is used to identify the fields in physics, astronomy, and related sciences.
- Introduction. The introduction must show a statement of the problem, significance of the study, and objective.
- Methodology. The methodology identifies the type of experimental study and general design and construction. We normally use the past tense but the active voice in this section.
- Results and discussion. Data analysis must be accurate. This must be based on the research questions you have formulated. Results and discussions can be either in the same section or in separate sections. You should show and compare your findings with other studies. In addition, you should purpose your own suggestions.
- Conclusion. The content can be similar to the introduction plus abstract sections, but you can just restate it.
- Acknowledgment (if any). You mention the financial support and thank your college at this section.
- References. You must show the references cited in the paper using the reference format according to the publisher's format (Table 1).

	Sequential components of the paper	**Table 1**
1	Title *You write a few tentative titles and select the best one later.*	
2	Abstract *You write an abstract when the whole content of the document is completed.*	
3	Keywords and/or PACS numbers	
4. 1	State a conceptual framework *You show a block diagram and connect your variables to the theories*	

continued

4. 2	Literature review based on the research problem to solve/explain/test and develop. You provide the evidence of the existence of the problem. *You cite the previous studies that are inconclusive or contradictory.* *You prove that there is lack of studies in this area and it is important to fill this gap.*
4. 3	Objective *Based on the research problem, state what your study intends to do and what the significance of this study is.*
5	Methodology *What the sample would comprise, how sampling would be done, and what instruments would be used for sampling?*
6. 1	Results *You state the results based on each research problem.*
6. 2	Discussion *You compare findings with the findings from previous studies reviewed in the literature review You give reasons why your findings support/do not support the previous findings.*
7	Conclusion
8	References

3. Clarity of Abstract and Conclusion

In this chapter, I will explain how to write abstracts and conclusions. An abstract is a description of the entire document and is the first paragraph of a paper. Conclusion is the last paragraph of the paper. It is like the final chord in the song. It makes the listeners/readers understand that the piece is completed.

(1) Abstract

You can write an abstract only when the whole document is complete. When you write an abstract, you should keep in mind two purposes: giving readers useful information included in the document and helping them to get basic information about the document.

Some general guidelines for writing an abstract are as follows:

① An abstract is a brief summary of about 75 ~ 300 words. It should be short and should contain concise sentences in one paragraph.

② An informative abstract should have the following order:

- You make a statement of purpose indicating the situation, problem, or issue that will be studied and why the research should be undertaken (i. e. , objective or hypothesis).

- You indicate the variables involved and how these will be measured (i. e. , technique or method).

- You indicate what data analyses will be undertaken and show the results that will explain or solve the issue. (i. e. , observation or evaluation).

- You make a conclusion and provide recommendation for further research.

③ While writing an abstract, you should avoid some tactics. You should not mention the names of authors. You should avoid tables, equations, graphs, references, or other citations.

(2) Conclusion

Conclusion is the last paragraph in a paper. The conclusion is like the final chord in a song. It makes the listener realize that the piece is completed. You want them to understand the issues you have raised in your paper, synthesize your thoughts, and show the importance of your ideas (your findings). You then become a reliable author and create a lasting impression for them. They are more likely to read your paper in the future. They may also have learned something, and what you have reported might have changed their opinion. The conclusion is, in some ways, like the introduction section plus the abstract section. You can restate the main points of evidence in these sections for the readers. Finally, you can report conflict of interests (financial, personal assistance) in the acknowledgment section after the conclusion section.

When you write the conclusion, you should avoid some tactics:

① You should not make sentimental, emotional appeals that are out of character with the rest of the analytical paper.

② You should exclude the evidence (i. e. , quotations, statistics, etc.) that should be in the body of the paper.

4. Introduction to Report

After you select the topic of your research from the defined problem (basic and/or applied research), you have to search for all relevant literature related to your topic. This will get the reader's attention and interest. This chapter will show how to carry out literature survey.

(1) Literature Survey and Developing a Conceptual Framework

You first build your research framework of relevant and current studies (summary of previous research) that you may get from journals, textbooks, and the Internet. Then you use the framework to write your literature review cogently, which will lead your argument to research objectives, research questions, or hypothesis. The framework can be conceptual. You must draw a simple diagram showing how the variables in your study are related to the theories (Figure 1).

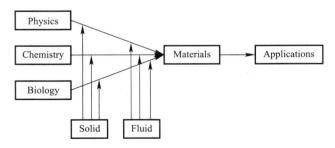

Figure 1　Research framework

(2) Examples of Conceptual Frameworks

Conceptual Framework: Example 1

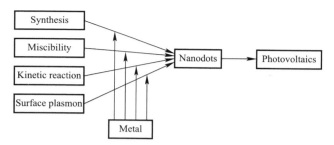

Figure 2   Conceptual framework 1

Conceptual Framework: Example 2

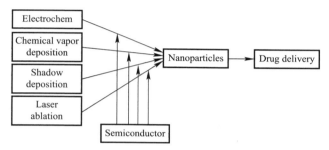

Figure 3   Conceptual framework 2

Conceptual Framework: Example 3

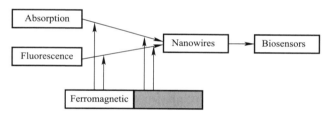

Figure 4   Conceptual framework 3

5. Data Collection Methods

Data collection method is the second major part of a paper. In this chapter, you will see how to present a detailed methodology, which readers can replicate to check your study. The methodology can be presented in terms of experiment or design and construction or even both.

(1) Experiment Method

The methodology identifies the type of experimental study. You should normally use past tense and active voice in this section. First, you show what the sample is, how to ensure ethics in research with animal or human subjects (e. g. , permission, etc.), and what instruments to be used. You should state the name of the instruments, validity, and reliability. Then you show the data collection procedure for the study. Finally, you propose analysis of data based on your research questions or hypothesis.

(2) Design and Construction

In addition to experiment method, the methodology can be of the type of general design and/

or construction. First you show what the specimens are and what materials will be designed and constructed. Then you show the data collection procedures for the study.

(3) Quantitative and Qualitative Methods

Basic and applied researches can be quantitative or qualitative or even both.

① Quantitative data are based on the measurement of quantity. A process is described in terms of one or more quantities. The data of this research are a set of numbers by using statistical or mathematical analysis. The results are often presented in tables and graphs.

② Qualitative data are concerned with quality. Qualitative methods can be used to understand the meaning of the numbers that we obtain from quantitative research. The data of this research cannot be graphed. Experimental and simulation studies are quantitative research.

(4) Problems

Pb. 1. Discuss the difference between experiment method and design and construction method.

Pb. 2. Indicate the details needed for experiment method.

Pb. 3. Indicate the details needed for design and construction.

Pb. 4. If you are dealing with theoretical simulation, write how the experiment looks like.

Pb. 5. Comment on the following experiment methods.

6. Data Analysis of Report

In this chapter, I will show how to perform data analysis to obtain accurate results so that readers can replicate them. The third major section of a research paper includes results and discussion. The results section contains facts related to your experiment. You should use figures, tables, and equations so that understanding your data becomes easier. The results are interpreted in the discussion section.

(1) Results and Discussion

After performing the experiment on your chosen problem, you should prepare the section on results and discussion. In this section, you should give all evidence relevant to the research problem and its solution. A bare statement of the findings is not enough; the implications need to be informed. Data analysis and the report must be accurate. These must be based on the research questions you have formulated. This section must include statistical operations. You compare your findings to see whether they agree with previous research. You inform the strengths and weaknesses of your work and your suggestions for the study. Also you can show the direction of your future research.

The organization of the results section should be as follows:

① You start with a paragraph, not tables or figures.

② You produce Tables and Figures after mentioning them in the text.

③ You can explain if any data are missing or problems exist.

④ You explain the main results and compare your expectation (hypothesis) with that of other researchers.

⑤ You explain all other interesting trends in your data.

The results and discussion section can be revised anytime based on the following:

① Quantitative and qualitative analyses are adequately performed to draw the conclusion.

② The results and discussion are general.

③ The results and discussion are valid for the situation considered in the present work.

④ The discussion is not too broad considering the analysis performed.

⑤ The evidence is not too weak for the discussion.

(2) Table Format

Tables are good for showing exact values or a lot of different information. Tables (refer them with Table 1, Table 2,...) should be presented as part of the text, but avoiding confusion with the text. A descriptive title should be placed above each Table. Units in Tables should be given in square brackets /meV/. If square brackets are not available, use curly {meV} or standard brackets (meV). Special signs are always written in the fonts Times New Roman or Arial. Here is an example of the Table format (Table 2).

Geometrical and deposition parameters of the fabricated samples   **Table 2**

Sample	Wire width (nm)	Nominal thickness (nm)	Peiodicity (nm)	Homoepitaxial growth temperature (℃)
C7	17	20	27	200
C8	14	10	27	200
C9	19	20	40	400
C10	15	10	40	400
C12	$r^* = 5$	5	22	200

r^* is the radius of nanodots.

(3) Figure Format

Graphs are good for showing the overall trends and are much easier to understand. Graphs and Tables should not depict the same data. Figures should be presented as part of the text, leaving enough space so that the caption is not confused with the text. The caption should be self-contained and placed below or beside the figure. Generally, only original drawings or photographic reproductions are acceptable. Utmost care must be taken to correctly align the Figures with the text. If possible, you should include your Figures as images in the electronic version.

For the best image quality, the pictures should have a resolution of 300 dpi (dots per inch). Color Figures are good for the online version of the journal. Generally, these Figures will be produced in black and white in the print version, partly for reducing the cost of publication. You should indicate on the checklist of the publication if you wish to have the Figures printed in full color and make the necessary payments in advance. You can use many different types of graphs to show your results (Figure 5~ Figure 7): line graph, scatter plot, bar graph, histogram, etc.

(4) Equation Format

Equations should be indented 5mm (0. 2″). There should be one line of space above and below the equations. They should be numbered sequentially, and the number should be put in parentheses at the right-hand margin. Equations should be punctuated as if they were part of the text. Punctuation appears after the equation but before the equation number, such as

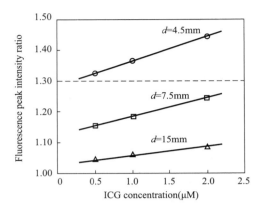

Figure 5　Indocyanine Green（ICG）concentration as a function of fluorescence peak

intensity ratio at a detection point of $30°/-30°$

（The target was 6 mm in diameter and was located at $d=4.5$mm, 7.5mm, or 15mm,

measured from the phantom surface to the target center）

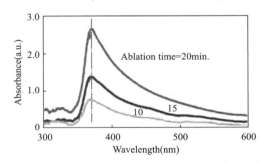

Figure 6　Measured absorption spectra of the zine oxide nanoparticles with various ablation times

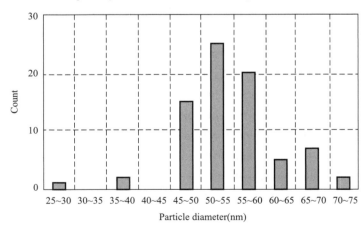

Figure 7　Distribution diagram of the zine oxide nanoparticles

$$C^2 = a^2 + b^2 \qquad (1)$$

7. Presentation Format

After your paper is accepted, the presentation of your work（although optional）can help you
share the idea and/or get financial support from audiences/readers. In a conference, seminar, or

workshop, you can select your preferred presentation format during the online abstract submission process: oral or poster presentation. On the other hand, you can present your research proposal for receiving financial support when you would like to carry out further studies in the future.

(1) Oral Presentation

For oral presentation, the time generally allocated for a plenary speaker is 45 min, for a keynote speaker is 25min, and for a contributory speaker is 15min, which accommodates the presentation followed by a short discussion. You should prepare your presentation with 1~2 slides/min. The content of the presentation is similar to manuscript submission: Introduction, Experiment, Results and Discussion, and Conclusion.

The following guidelines are very useful for oral presentation when you present your work in a conference, seminar, or workshop:

① Introduce yourself, your advisor, and committee members.

② Give an introduction and background information on your topic. What relevant research has been performed previously?

③ State the problems that remain unanswered.

④ State your objectives clearly and give the specific hypotheses you wish to show.

⑤ Describe the methodology. Be sure you fully understand your chosen methods. Give reasons why you chose these methods over other approaches.

⑥ Present any data you have collected.

⑦ Explain the significance of your findings or potential future findings.

(2) Poster Presentation

Poster presentation is a casual demonstration of a novel and applicable idea in a simple and concise manner. It is an effective mode for discussion and for receiving responses, which can help you to refine your research and develop new ideas for future studies. A poster is generally displayed during a conference. It should fit within the offered area. Each poster is normally allocated a board of width 841mm and height 1189mm. The presenter should stand beside the poster for about 1~2h during the display period.

(3) Research Proposal

A research proposal is a request for supporting the sponsored research, instruction, or extension projects. The proposal for sponsored activities generally follows a format similar to that of the manuscript, although there are variations depending on whether the proposer is seeking support for a research grant, a conference, or curriculum development project. The following outline covers the primary components of a research proposal: Title, Aim, Background and Outline, Method, Schedule, and References. Your proposal will be a variation on this basic outline.

(4) Problems

Pb. 1. Show the difference between oral and poster presentations.

Pb. 2. Select one paper of your interest and present it in terms of oral or poster format.

Pb. 3. Write a new research proposal when you need to get the financial support from your affiliation.

References

［1］ Urs B Meyer. Process Oriented Analysis Design and Optimization of Industrial Production Systems ［M］. Boca Raton: CRC Press, 2007.

［2］ Dan Olsen. The Lean Product Playbook ［M］. Hoboken: John Wiley & Sons, Inc. , 2015.

［3］ John Stewart. A Practical Guide to Implementing Lean ［M］. Boca Raton: CRC Press, 2011.

［4］ Masoud Soroush. Smart Manufacturing ［M］. Netherlands: Elsevier Inc, 2020.

［5］ Joseph Eli Kasser. Systems Engineering A Systemic and Systematic Methodology for Solving Complex Problems ［M］. Boca Raton: Taylor & Francis Group, LLC, 2020.

［6］ Thomas, Willis H. The Basics of Project Evaluation and Lessons Learned ［M］. Boca Raton: CRC Press, 2015.

［7］ Michael W Carter, Camille C Price etc. Operations Research A Practical Approach ［M］. Boca Raton: Taylor & Francis Group, LLC, 2019.

［8］ Hamdy A Taha. Operations Research: An Introduction ［M］. London: Pearson Education Limited, 2017.

［9］ Mohammad S. Obaidat. Applied System Simulation: Methodologies and Applications ［M］. New York: K1uwer Academic Publishers, 2003.

［10］ Radu-Emil Precup, Tariq Kamal, Syed Zulqadar Hassan. Solar Photovoltaic Power Plants: Advanced Control and Optimization Techniques ［M］. Singapore: Springer Nature Singapore Pte Ltd. 2019.

［11］ Evelyn C Fink. Game Theory Topics ［M］. Thousand Oaks: Sage Publications, Inc. , 1998.

［12］ Andrew M Colman. Game Theory and Experimental Games ［M］. Oxford: Pergamon Press, 1982.

［13］ Ya. Ravi Ravindran. Operations Research Applications ［M］. Boca Raton: CRC Press, 2009.

［14］ Babak Jafarizadeh. Economic Decision Analysis For Project Feasibility Studies ［M］. Cham: Springer Briefs in Petroleum Geoscience & Engineering.

［15］ Granino A Korn. Advanced Dynamic-system Simulation: Model-replication Techniques and Monte Carlo Simulation ［M］. Hoboken: John Wiley & Sons, Inc.

［16］ J Murray-Smith. Continuous System Simulation ［M］. London: Chapman & Hall, 1995.

［17］ Richard H Clough, Glenn A Sears, S Keoki Sears, Robert O Segner, Jerald L Rounds. Construction contracting: a practical guide to company management ［M］. Hoboken: John Wiley & Sons, Inc. 2015.

［18］ Shoshanah Cohen, Joseph Roussel. Strategic Supply Chain Management ［M］. New York: The McGraw-Hill Companies, Inc. 2005.

［19］ Eugenio Pellicer, Víctor Yepes, José C. Teixeira, Helder P. Moura, Joaquín Catalá. Construction Management ［M］. Chichester: John Wiley & Sons, Ltd. 2014.

［20］ Alan Moylan. Understanding Computer Aided Design (CAD) and Building Information Modelling (BIM) ［M］. America: Alan Moylan. 2016.

［21］ Joseph Y-T. Leung. Handbook of Scheduling: Algorithms, Models, and Performance Analysis ［M］. Boca Raton: CRC Press LLC, 2000.

［22］ Harold Kerzner. Project Management: A Systems Approach to Planning, Scheduling, and Controlling ［M］. Hoboken: John Wiley & Sons, Inc. 2017.

［23］ Richard S Sutton, Andrew G Barto. Reinforcement Learning: An Introduction ［M］. Cambridge, MA: The MIT Press. 2018.

[24] National Academy of Sciences. Advanced Engineer Environments: Achieving the Vision [M]. Washington, D. C.: National Academy Press. 2003.

[25] James A Brickley, Clifford W Smith, Jerold L Zimmerman. Managerial Economics and Organizational Architecture [M]. New York: McGraw-Hill Education. 2016.

[26] Joseph Phillips. PMP Project Management Professional All-in-One Exam Guide [M]. New York: McGraw Hill. 2022.

[27] Christian Artigues, Sophie Demassey, Emmanuel Néron. Resource-constrained project scheduling: models, algorithms, extensions and applications [M]. Hoboken: John Wiley & Sons, Inc. 2008.

[28] PMBOK Guide. A Guide to the Project Management Body of Knowledge [M]. U. S.: Project Management Institute. 2017.

[29] José Ramón San Cristóbal Mateo. Management Science, Operations Research and Project Management [M]. Farnham: Gower Publishing Limited, 2015.

[30] Martin E Liggins, James, Ph. D. Llinas etc. Handbook of Multisensor Data Fusion Theory and Practice [M]. Boca Raton: Taylor & Francis Group, LLC. 2009.

[31] Charles Yoe. Principles of Risk Analysis Decision Making Under Uncertainty [M]. Boca Raton: Taylor & Francis Group, LLC. 2019.

[32] Thomas McCarty, Lorraine Daniels etc. The Six Sigma Black Belt Handbook [M]. New York: The McGraw-Hill Companies. 2004.

[33] Guido Grüne · Stephanie Lockemann, Volker Kluy · Stefan Meinhardt. Business Process Management within Chemical and Pharmaceutical Industries Markets, BPM [M]. Berlin: Springer-Verlag Berlin Heidelberg. 2014.

[34] Stephen E Hargitay, Shi-Ming Yu. Property Investment Decisions A quantitative approach [M]. London: E & FN Spon. 2005.

[35] Winston Ma, Xiaodong Lee, Dominic Barton. China's mobile economy opportunities in the largest and fastest information consumption boom [M]. Hoboken: John Wiley & Sons. 2017.

[36] Albert lester. Project Management, Planning and controlling [M]. Oxford: Butterworth-heinemann ltd. 2017.

[37] George J Ritz. Total Construction Project Management [M]. New York: McGraw-Hill, Inc. 1996.

[38] Len Holm. Cost Accounting and Financial Management for Construction Project Managers [M]. London: Routledge. 2018.

[39] James P Lewis. Project planning, Scheduling and Controlling [M]. New York: McGraw-Hill, Inc. 2011.

[40] James OBrien, George Marakas. Management Information Systems, 10th Edition [M]. New York: McGraw-Hill/Irwin. 2011.

[41] Hector Garcia-Molina, Jeffrey D. Ullman etc. Database Systems The Complete Book [M]. America: Pearson Education Inc. 2009.

[42] Turner, Keith A. Three-Dimensional Modeling with Geoscientific Information Systems [M]. Dordrecht: Kluwer Academic Publishers, 1992.

[43] Marianne Bradford. Modern ERP Select, Implement, and Use Today's Advanced Business Systems [M]. America: SAS Institute Inc. 2014.

[44] M Ralph. Principles of information systems: a managerial approach [M]. Boston: Boyd & Fraser Pub. Co, 1995.

[45] Liu K. Semiotics in information systems engineering [M]. Beijing: Tsinghua University Press, 2005.

[46] Delone W H, Mclean E R. Information Systems Success: The Quest for the Dependent Variable [J].

Information Systems Research, 1992, 3(1):60-95.

[47] Seddon P B, Staples S, Patnayakuni R G R, et al. Dimensions of information systems success [J]. Communications of the Ais, 1999.

[48] Ramakrishnan R. Database Management Systems [M]. Beijing: Tsinghua University Press, 2000.

[49] Ghafoor A. Multimedia database management systems [M]. Boston: Artech House, 1997.

[50] Vossen G. Data models, database languages and database management systems [M]. Boston: Addison-Wesley Longman Publishing Co. Inc. 1991.

[51] Mccarthy D R. The Architecture of An Active Database Management Systems [J]. Proc of Acm Sigmod, 1989.

[52] Dayal U. Active Database Management Systems [J]. Proceedings of the Third International Conference on Data and Knowledge Bases, 1988:150-169.

[53] Stephen Haag, Maeve Cummings. Management Information Systems for the Information Age [M]. New York: McGraw-Hill Education. 2009.

[54] Kenneth C. Laudon, Jane P. Laudon. Management Information Systems: Managing the Digital Firm [M]. Upper Saddle River: Prentice Hall PTR. 2011.

[55] Jiawei Han, Micheline Kamber. Data Mining Concepts and Techniques Third Edition. [M]. Waltham: ElSevier. 2012.

[56] Raghu Ramakrishnan, Johannes Gehrke. Database Management Systems [M]. New York: McGraw-Hili. 2003.

[57] Bhaskar Mondal. Artificial Intelligence: State of the Art. Recent Trends and Advances in Artificial Intelligence and Internet of Things Valentina E. Balas, Raghvendra Kumar, Rajshree Srivastava [EB/OL]. 390-391.

[58] Tijn van der Zant, Matthijs Kouw, and Lambert Schomaker. Generative Artificial Intelligence. Philosophy and Theory of Artificial Intelligence (Vincent Müller) [EB/OL]. 107-108.

[59] Mohsen Hesami & Andrew Maxwell Phineas Jones. Application of artificial intelligence models and optimization algorithms in plant cell and tissue culture. [EB/OL]. https://link. springer. com/article/10. 1007/s00253-020-10888-2.

[60] Vivek Kothari&Edgar Liberis&Nicholas D. Lane Authors Info & Claims. The Final Frontier: Deep Learning in Space [EB/OL]. https://dl. acm. org/doi/abs/10. 1145/3376897. 3377864.

[61] Ying Feng & Xiaojing Lv(U). Frontier Application and Development Trend of Artificial Intelligence in New Media in the AI Era [EB/OL]. https://link. springer. com/chapter/10. 1007/978-3-030-89508-2_8.

[62] Itamar Arel, Derek C. Rose, Thomas P. Karnowski. Deep Machine Learning - A New Frontier in Artificial Intelligence Research [Research Frontier] [EB/OL]. https://ieeexplore. ieee. org/document/5605630.

[63] Jason Underwood, Umit Isikdag. Handbook of Research on Building Information Modeling and Construction Informatics: Concepts and Technologies [EB/OL]. https://p303. zlibcdn. com/dtoken/f5c2b51d4277dff0aae4602763fc386c.

[64] Jason Underwood, Umit Isikdag. Handbook of Research on Building Information Modeling and Construction Informatics: Concepts and Technologies [EB/OL]. https://p303. zlibcdn. com/dtoken/f5c2b51d4277dff0aae4602763fc386c.

[65] Jason Underwood, Umit Isikdag. Handbook of Research on Building Information Modeling and Construction Informatics: Concepts and Technologies [EB/OL]. https://p303. zlibcdn. com/dtoken/f5c2b51d4277dff0aae4602763fc386c.

[66] Geoff Zeiss. Building information modeling [EB/OL]. https://dl. acm. org/doi/10. 1145/1999320.

1999394.

［67］ Xiaofang Xue, Guocheng Qin, Yin Zhou, Chunli Ying, Yupeng Yang, Qian Meng, Yanhui Liu, Tong Guo, Daguang Han. Modeling Method and Application of BIM in Design Stage of Long-span Suspension Bridge ［EB/OL］. https://dl. acm. org/doi/abs/10. 1145/3518781. 3519225.

［68］ Stephen Mulva. Building Information Modeling: A New Frontier For Construction Engineering Education ［EB/OL］. https://peer. asee. org/building-information-modeling-a-new-frontier-for-construction-engineering-education. pdf.

［69］ L Tabb, C Herrmann. Methods for hypertext reporting in a relational database management system ［EB/OL］. https://xueshu. baidu. com/usercenter/paper/show? paperid = 431329d00b02c3eb5d0aa739f4f5e3e8& site = xueshu_se.

［70］ F Elias. Systems and methods for managing data in relational database management system ［EB/OL］. https://xueshu. baidu. com/usercenter/paper/show? paperid = 86e4e643f9c8aa1670b55fffdd63f307&site = xueshu_se.

［71］ J G Wright, C L Bieniewski, R Pifarre, R M Gunnar, P J Scanlon. A database management system for cardiovascular disease ［EB/OL］. https://xueshu. baidu. com/usercenter/paper/show? paperid = 806561ad7429504f9f3947e50ce555f9&site = xueshu_se.

［72］ Marcus Paradies, Wolfgang Lehner & Christof Bornhövd. GRAPHITE: an extensible graph traversal framework for relational database management systems ［EB/OL］. https://dl. acm. org/doi/abs/10. 1145/2791347. 2791383.

［73］ Bin Cui, Hong Mei, Beng Chin Ooi. Big data: the driver for innovation in databases［EB/OL］. https://doi. org/10. 1093/nsr/nwt020.

［74］ Young B. Moon. Enterprise Resource Planning (ERP): a review of the literature ［EB/OL］. https://surface. syr. edu/cgi/viewcontent. cgi? article = 1007&context = mae.

［75］ Shobhit Seth. Top Tools for ERP Enterprise Resource Planning ［EB/OL］. https://www. investopedia. com/articles/investing/110614/top-tools-erp-enterprise-resource-planning. asp.

［76］ Julie Young. Case Studies of Successful Enterprise Resource Planning ［EB/OL］. https://www. investopedia. com/articles/investing/111214/lg-case-study-successful-enterprise-resource-planning-system. asp.

［77］ Peter Gomber, Robert J. Kauffman, Chris Parker & Bruce W. Weber. On the Fintech Revolution: Interpreting the Forces of Innovation, Disruption, and Transformation in Financial Services ［J］. Journal of Management Information Systems. 2018.

［78］ Sherif Barrad, Raul Valverde. The Impact of e-Supply Chain Management Systems on Procurement Operations and Cost Reduction in the Electronics Manufacturing Services Industry ［J］. Journal of Media Management and Entrepreneurship. 2020.

［79］ Sanjeev Bordoloi, James Fitzsimmons etc. Service Management Operations, Strategy, Information Technology ［M］. New York: McGraw-Hill Education. 2019.

［80］ John E. Ettlie. Managing Innovation, Second Edition New Technology, New Products, and New Services in a Global Economy ［M］. Amsterdam: Elsevier Butterworth-Heinemann. 2006.

［81］ Murray Hiebert, Bruce Klatt. The Encyclopedia of Leadership A Practical Guide to Popular Leadership Theories and Techniques ［M］. New York: McGraw-Hill. 2001.

［82］ Peter Gomber, Robert J. Kauffman, Chris Parker & Bruce W. Weber. On the Fintech Revolution: Interpreting the Forces of Innovation, Disruption, and Transformation in Financial Services ［J］. Journal of Management Information Systems. 2018.

［83］ Sherif Barrad, Raul Valverde. The Impact of e-Supply Chain Management Systems on Procurement

Operations and Cost Reduction in the Electronics Manufacturing Services Industry [J]. Journal of Media Management and Entrepreneurship. 2020.

[84] Houda Derbel, Bassem Jarboui, Patrick Siarry. Modeling and Optimization in Green Logistics [M]. Switzerland: Springer Nature Switzerland AG. 2020.

[85] Sheldon Ross, Richard Weber. Introduction to Logistics Systems Planning and Control [M]. Chichester: John Wiley & Sons, Ltd. 2004.

[86] Gianpaolo Ghiani, Gilbert Laporte, Roberto Musmanno. Introduction to Logistics Systems Management [M]. Chichester: John Wiley & Sons, Ltd. 2013.

[87] Zhengbing Hu, Qingying Zhang, Sergey Petoukhov, Matthew He. Advances in Artificial Systems for Logistics Engineering [M]. Switzerland: Springer Nature Switzerland AG. 2022.

[88] Hao Zhang. Reliability Optimization of Urban Logistics Systems [M]. Singapore: Springer Nature Singapore Pte Ltd. 2022.

[89] Gianpaolo Ghiani, Gilbert Laporte, Roberto Musmanno. Introduction to Logistics Systems Planning and Control [M]. Chichester: John Wiley & Sons Ltd. 2004.

[90] Lawrence V. Snyder, Ya-xiang Yuan. Introduction to Logistics Systems Management [M]. Chichester: John Wiley & Sons, Ltd. 2013.

[91] Hao Zhang. Reliability Optimization of Urban Logistics Systems [M]. Singapore: Springer Nature Singapore Pte Ltd. 2022.

[92] Houda Derbel, Bassem Jarboui, Patrick Siarry. Modeling and Optimization in Green Logistics [M]. Switzerland: Springer Nature Switzerland. 2020.

[93] Robert S Bridger. Introduction to Human Factors and Ergonomics, Fourth Edition. [M]. Boca Raton: CRC Press Taylor & Francis Group. 2018.

[94] Jean-Marc Robert, Eric Brangier. What Is Prospective Ergonomics? A Reflection and a Position on the Future of Ergonomics [J]. Ergonomics and Health Aspects. 2009.

[95] Ruipeng Tong, Chunlin Wu, Yang Li, Dongping Fang. An Assessment Model of Owner Safety Management and Its Application to Real Estate Projects [J]. KSCE Journal of Civil Engineering. 2018.

[96] Patrick X W Zou, Riza Yosia Sunindijo. Strategic Safety Management in Construction and Engineering [M]. Chichester: John Wiley & Sons, Ltd. 2015.

[97] Waldemar Karwowski, William S. Marras. Occupational Ergonomics: Design and Management of Work Systems [M]. Boca Raton: CRC Press. 2003.

[98] Patrick X W Zou, Riza Yosia Sunindijo. Strategic Safety Management in Construction and Engineering [M]. Chichester: John Wiley & Sons, Ltd. 2015.

[99] Jean-Marc Robert, Eric Brangier. What Is Prospective Ergonomics? A Reflection and a Position on the Future of Ergonomics [J]. Ergonomics and Health Aspects. 2009.

[100] Ruipeng Tong, Chunlin Wu, Yang Li, Dongping Fang. An Assessment Model of Owner Safety Management and Its Application to Real Estate Projects [J]. KSCE Journal of Civil Engineering. 2018.

[101] Javaherdashti, Reza. Corrosion Policy Decision Making: Science, Engineering, Management, and Economy [M]. Hoboken: John Wiley and Sons, Inc. 2022.

[102] Gregory S Parnell, Patrick J Driscoll, Dale L Henderson. Decision Making in Systems Engineering and Management [M]. Hoboken: John Wiley & Sons, Inc. 2011.

[103] Jeffrey W. Herrmann. Engineering Decision Making and Risk Management [M]. Hoboken: John Wiley & Sons, Inc. 2015.

[104] Charles Yoe. Principles of Risk Analysis Decision Making Under Uncertainty [M]. Boca Raton: Taylor &

Francis Group, LLC. CRC Press. 2019.

[105] Vlasta Molak. Fundamentals of Risk Analysis and Risk Management [M]. Boca Raton: CRC Press, Inc. 1997.

[106] Thomas Pyzdek, Paul A Keller. Quality Engineering Handbook (Quality and Reliability) [M]. New York: Marcel Dekker, Inc. 2003.

[107] K S Krishnamoorthi, V Ram Krishnamoorthi, Arunkumar Pennathur. A First Course in Quality Engineering [M]. Boca Raton: CPC Press, Taylor & Francis Group, LLC, 2019.

[108] Donald W Benbow, Hugh W Broome. The Certified Reliability Engineer Handbook [M]. Milwaukee: ASQ Quality Press, 2008.

[109] Avigdor Zonnenshain, Ron S Kenett. Quality 4. 0—the challenging future of quality Engineering [J]. Quality Engineering, 2020.

[110] Enid Mumford. Effective Systems Design and Requirements Analysis The ETHICS Approach [M]. London: Macmillan Press ltd. 1995.

[111] Leszek A. Maciaszek. Requirements Analysis and System Design (3rd edn.) [M]. Harlow: Pearson Education Limited. 2007.

[112] Jeffrey O Grady. System Requirements Analysis (2nd edn.) [M]. Waltham: Elsevier Inc. 2014.

[113] Gopal Chaudhary, Manju Khari, Mohamed Elhoseny. Digital Twin Technology [M]. Boca Raton: Taylor & Francis Group, LLC. CRC Press. 2022.

[114] Fei Tao (editor), Ang Liu (editor) , Tianliang Hu and A Y C Nee. Digital Twin Driven Smart Design [M]. Cambridge: Academic Press. 2020.

[115] JoAnne Yates, Craig N. MurphyEngineering Rules: Global Standard Setting since 1880 [M]. Baltimore: Johns Hopkins University Press. 2019.

[116] Indeed Editorial Team. What Is a Business Decision? Definition and Types [EB/OL]. https://www. indeed. com/career-advice/career-development/business-decision.

[117] Indeed Editorial Team. Methodologies for Decision-Making (With Definitions and Examples) [EB/OL]. https://www. indeed. com/career-advice/career-development/decision--making

[118] Eugene A Avallone, Theodore Baumeister III, Ali M. Sadegh. Marks′ Standard Handbook for Mechanical Engineers [M]. Chicago: RR Donnelley. 2007.

[119] Colin H Simmons, Dennis E Maguire. Manual of Engineering Drawing [M]. Oxford: Elsevier Newnes publications. 2004.

[120] Ramesh Singh. Applied Welding Engineering: Processes, Codes, and Standards [M]. Waltham: Elsevier Inc. 2020.

[121] Larry W Lake. Petroleum Engineering Handbook [J]. Richardson: Indexes and Standards. 2007.

[122] Owen R Greulich, Maan H Jawad. Primer on Engineering Standards [M]. Chichester: ASME Press and John Wiley & Sons, Ltd. 2018.

[123] Rajwinder Kaur Panesar-Walawege, Mehrdad Sabetzadeh, Lionel Briand. Supporting the verification of compliance to safety standards via model-driven engineering: Approach, tool-support and empirical validation [J]. Information and Software Technology. 2012.

[124] Ayokunle Olubunmi Olanipekuna, Temitope Omotayo, Najimu Sakac. Review of the Use of Corporate Social Responsibility (CSR) Tools [J]. Sustainable Production and Consumption. 2020.

[125] Peter Grindley. Standards, Strategy, and Policy: Cases and Stories [M]. Oxford: Oxford Scholarship Online. 2011.

[126] Ron Schneiderman. Modern Standardization: Case Studies at the Crossroads of Technology, Economics,

and Politics [M]. New York: Standards Information Network IEEE Press. 2015.

[127] William C Dunn. Introduction to Instrumentation, Sensors, and Process Control [M]. Norwood: Artech House Publishers. 2005.

[128] Wolfgang Altmann. Practical Process Control for Engineers and Technicians [M]. Oxford: Elsevier, Newnes. 2005.

[129] William C Dunn. Fundamentals of Industrial Instrumentation and Process Control [M]. New York: McGraw-Hill. 2005.

[130] Jeremy Kourdi. Business Strategy A Guide to Effective Decision-Making [M]. London: Profile Books Ltd. 2003.

[131] Simon Kingsnorth. Digital Marketing Strategy An Integrated Approach to Online Marketing [M]. London: Kogan Page Limited. 2016.

[132] Henry W Chesbrough. Open Innovation: The New Imperative for Creating and Profiting from Technology [M]. Boston: Harvard business school press. 2003.

[133] Zongwei Luo. Service Science and Logistics Informatics: Innovative Perspectives [M]. U. S. : Information Science Reference. 2010.

[134] John Manners, Bell Ken Lyon. The Logistics and Supply Chain Innovation Handbook: Disruptive technologies and new business models [M]. United States: Kogan Page Limited. 2019.

[135] Guus Berkhout et al. The cyclic nature of innovation connecting hard sciences with soft values [M]. Elsevier: JAI Press. 2007.

[136] Paul Trott. Innovation Management and New Product Development [M]. Harlow: Pearson Education Limited. 2017.

[137] Joe Tidd, John Bessant. MANAGING INNOVATION: Integrating Technological, Market and Organizational Changey [M]. Chichester: John Wiley & Sons Ltd. 2009.

[138] Pamela Peterson Drake, Frank J Fabozzi. The Basics of Finance An Introduction to Financial Markets, Business Finance, and Portfolio Management [M]. Hoboken: John Wiley & Sons. 2010.

[139] Olivier Mesly. Project Feasibility: Tools for Uncovering Points of Vulnerability [M]. Boca Raton: CRC Press. 2017.

[140] Paul Pignataro. Financial Modeling and Valuation: A Practical Guide to Investment Banking and Private Equity [M]. Hoboken: John Wiley & Sons, Inc. 2013.

[141] Ronald W Melicher, Edgar A Norton. Introduction to Finance: Markets, Investments, and Financial Management [M]. Hoboken: John Wiley & Sons, Inc. 2017.

[142] Julia Fox-Rushby, John Cairns. Economic evaluation [M]. Maidenhead: Open University Press. 2005.

[143] Magnus Johannesson. Theory and Methods of Economic Evaluation of Health Care [M]. Dordrecht: Springer-Science, Business Media, B. V. 1996.

[144] Weisheng Lu, Chi Cheung Lai, Tung Tse. BIM and Big Data for Construction Cost Management [M]. London: Routledge. 2019.

[145] Kenneth. Humphreys. Project and Cost Engineers' Handbook [M]. New York: Marcel Dekker. 2005.

[146] Gregory S Parnell, Patrick J Driscoll, Dale L Henderson. Decision Making in Systems Engineering and Management, 2nd Edition [M]. Hobokon: John Wiley & Sons, Inc. 2011.

[147] Jeffrey W. Herrmann. Engineering Decision Making and Risk Management [M]. Hobokon: John Wiley & Sons, Inc. 2015.

[148] Reza Javaherdashti. Corrosion Policy Decision Making Science, Engineering, Management, and Economy [M]. Hobokon: John Wiley and Sons, Inc. 2022.